Minds, Brains, and Law

Minds, Brains, and Law

The Conceptual Foundations of Law and Neuroscience

Michael S. Pardo
&
Dennis Patterson

OXFORD
UNIVERSITY PRESS

OXFORD
UNIVERSITY PRESS

Oxford University Press is a department of the University of Oxford. It furthers the University's objective of excellence in research, scholarship, and education by publishing worldwide.

Oxford   New York
Auckland   Cape Town   Dar es Salaam   Hong Kong   Karachi   Kuala Lumpur   Madrid
Melbourne   Mexico City   Nairobi   New Delhi   Shanghai   Taipei   Toronto

With offices in
Argentina   Austria   Brazil   Chile   Czech Republic   France   Greece   Guatemala   Hungary
Italy   Japan   Poland   Portugal   Singapore   South Korea   Switzerland   Thailand
Turkey   Ukraine   Vietnam

Oxford is a registered trade mark of Oxford University Press in the
UK and certain other countries.

Published in the United States of America by
Oxford University Press
198 Madison Avenue, New York, NY 10016

First printing in paperback, 2015.
ISBN 978-0-19-025310-3 ((paperback) : alk. paper)

Library of Congress Cataloging-in-Publication Data

Pardo, Michael S.
   Minds, brains, and law : the conceptual foundations of law and neuroscience /
Michael S. Pardo, Dennis Patterson.
      pages cm
   Includes bibliographical references and index.
   ISBN 978-0-19-981213-4 ((hardback) : alk. paper)
1. Practice of law—Psychological aspects. 2. Law—Philosophy. 3. Brain. 4. Jurisprudence.
5. Cognitive neuroscience. I. Patterson, Dennis M. (Dennis Michael), 1955- II. Title.
   K346.P36 2013
   340'.19—dc23

                                                                    2013014184

Note to Readers

This publication is designed to provide accurate and authoritative information in regard to
the subject matter covered. It is based upon sources believed to be accurate and reliable and is
intended to be current as of the time it was written. It is sold with the understanding that the
publisher is not engaged in rendering legal, accounting, or other professional services. If legal
advice or other expert assistance is required, the services of a competent professional person
should be sought. Also, to confirm that the information has not been affected or changed by
recent developments, traditional legal research techniques should be used, including checking
primary sources where appropriate.

*(Based on the Declaration of Principles jointly adopted by a Committee of the
American Bar Association and a Committee of Publishers and Associations.)*

You may order this or any other Oxford University Press publication
by visiting the Oxford University Press website at www.oup.com.

For Meredith and Nathaniel
-MSP
For Barbara, Sarah, and Graham
-DP

Contents

Preface to the Paperback Edition

As we write, it has been a year since the publication of the hardcover edition of *Minds, Brains, and Law*. During that time the topics that occupied us in the book have continued to see increasing attention and discussion. For example, President Barack Obama has announced the "Brain Research through Advancing Innovative Neurotechnologies" (BRAIN) Initiative and has charged the "Presidential Commission for the Study of Bioethical Issues" to address the application of neuroscience to law and other areas.[1] We have been especially fortunate to have attracted the attention of commentators on our book, for whose attention we are most grateful.[2]

One of the central contentions of our book is that the conceptual issues involved in the intersection between law and neuroscience are of paramount importance. This theme resonates with broader discussions of the impact of neuroscience in a variety of fields. For example,

---

[1] *Presidential Charge to the Commission for the Study of Bioethical Issues* (July 1, 2013), *available at*: http://bioethics.gov/sites/default/files/news/Charge%20from%20President%20Obama.pdf. *See also* Owen D. Jones et al., *Law and Neuroscience: Recommendations Submitted to the President's Bioethics Commission*, 12 J. L. & BIOSCIENCES 224 (2014). Another sign of the continuing development of the field of law and neuroscience is the appearance of the first law textbook devoted to the subject. *See* OWEN D. JONES, JEFFREY D. SCHALL & FRANCIS X. SHEN, LAW AND NEUROSCIENCE (2014).

[2] A very careful treatment of our arguments is found in this review by Alexander Guerrero, NOTRE DAME PHILOSOPHICAL REVIEWS: http://ndpr.nd.edu/news/48119-minds-brains-and-law-the-conceptual-foundations-of-law-and-neuroscience/. For an informative review essay discussing recent books in the field of neurolaw, including ours, *see* Gerben Meynen, *Neurolaw: Neuroscience, Ethics, and Law*, 17 ETHICAL THEORY & MORAL PRACTICE 819 (2014).

Colin McGinn's reviews[3] of recent books by Jean-Pierre Changeux[4] and Patricia Churchland[5] illustrate how philosophy is essential to any competent understanding of the role of the brain in explaining human action. We remain steadfast in our contention that conceptual questions about mind and action are necessarily central to any discussion of the wider implications of neuroscientific research.

The last year has provided a number of opportunities for us to discuss our work. We are grateful to Adam Kolber for convening an online discussion of our book on the Neuroethics & Law Blog, to Bebhinn Donnelly-Lazarov for convening a conference on the book at Swansea University School of Law, and to Veronica Rodriguez-Blanco for organizing a symposium on the book in *Jurisprudence*. We thank the participants in each for engaging with our work and for their insightful commentary. Professor Patterson thanks Peterhouse College, Cambridge University, the World Congress for Freedom of Scientific Research, Rome, Italy, and the European Association of Neuroscience and Law for the opportunity to speak further about the issues in this book. Professor Patterson also thanks the European University Institute Research Council for a grant that enables further research on the role of neuroscience in the criminal law. Professor Pardo thanks the University of Maryland, the Petrie-Flom Center at Harvard Law School, and the Massachusetts General Hospital Center for Law, Brain & Behavior for opportunities to further discuss issues at the intersection of law and neuroscience. Professor Pardo also thanks Dean Mark Brandon and the University of Alabama Law School Foundation for generous research support.

The claims we make in this book about the importance of conceptual clarity for law and neuroscience have generated reactions from some commentators who have misunderstood the nature of our arguments. These reactions concern the relationship between the conceptual issues we identify and empirical investigations of the brain. In order to clarify this relationship, we want to emphasize two general points, one theoretical and one practical.

First, on the theoretical side, our discussion of conceptual issues does not rely on a particular philosophical theory about the nature of concepts or the ascription of terms related to those concepts. For example, although we refer at times to the "concept" of knowledge and question

[3] Colin McGinn, *What Can Your Neurons Tell You?*, N.Y. REV. BOOKS (July 11, 2013), *available at*: http://www.nybooks.com/articles/archives/2013/jul/11/what-can-your-neurons-tell-you/?page=2; Colin McGinn, *Storm Over the Brain*, N.Y. REV. BOOKS (April 24, 2014), *available at*: http://www.nybooks.com/articles/archives/2014/apr/24/storm-over-the-brain/.

[4] JEAN-PIERRE CHANGEUX, THE GOOD, THE TRUE, AND THE BEAUTIFUL: A NEURONAL APPROACH (trans. and rev. by Laurence Garey, 2012).

[5] PATRICIA S. CHURCHLAND, TOUCHING A NERVE: THE SELF AS BRAIN (2013).

whether we would "ascribe" knowledge to someone, our concern is with knowledge itself. Our focus on concepts and ascriptions, in other words, is meant to shed light on the phenomena picked out by the concepts and ascriptions. We thus agree with Neil Levy when, in a review of our book, he asserts that various types of behavior help to fix the reference of terms such as "knowing" or "lying."[6] Levy goes on to argue, however, that when we claim that knowledge is not contained in the brain, we are mistakenly trying to infer "metaphysics from semantics."[7] We disagree. Of course, empirical investigation into the neural correlates underlying genuine cases of knowledge (and non-knowledge) may reveal new insights into, and perhaps lead to revisions in how we understand, the nature of knowledge. In any event, we do not take issue with this possibility, or with similar claims about any of the other issues we discuss in the book. Rather, our arguments about knowledge (similar to other arguments in the book) concern neurolaw claims that rely on confused conceptions by presupposing, for example, that knowledge is a brain state and that it does not require truth, epistemic justification, or depend on other conditions external to the brain.[8] Because of these external conditions, however, two

---

[6] Neil Levy, *Is Neurolaw Conceptually Confused?*, 18 J. ETHICS 171 (2014). We discuss knowledge throughout the book. The primary discussions are in Chapters One, Three, Four, and Five. We focus in detail on lying and lie detection in Chapter Four; we also discuss the topic in Chapter Six.

[7] *Id.* at 176. In this context, the metaphysical aspect is what knowledge actually consists in, and the semantic aspect is when and under what circumstances speakers would ascribe knowledge to themselves and others. Levy's point, as we understand it, is that speakers might be mistaken about the nature of knowledge and so their ascriptions might be an unreliable guide to its nature. We do not take issue with this. Our objection is to claims that purport to be measuring knowledge but, because of conceptual confusion, are measuring something else (or nothing at all). As Levy's point about fixing references makes clear, in order to reveal something about knowledge, one first has to pick out knowledge to investigate and not something else. We think Levy would concede, for example, that an experiment purporting to discover that "knowledge" really consists in "false beliefs unsupported by any evidence" would no longer be measuring the same phenomena that we normally refer to as "knowledge" or that which is studied by epistemologists. This would not necessarily be a critique of the experiment, if for example, the experiment was clear about using "knowledge" in a specialized way; but confusion would arise if the experiment purports to illuminate actual cases of knowledge.

[8] In arguing that knowledge is not in the brain, we do not rely on any particular theory of knowledge. Rather, we make use of some of the great (and relatively uncontroversial) insights of modern epistemology: namely, that whether someone has knowledge depends on conditions external to the person (and, *a fortiori*, the person's brain). If two people can have the same true beliefs, the same perceptual experiences, access to the same evidence, and similar underlying brain states—yet one person can have knowledge while the other does not—then knowledge is not in the brain. Differences regarding truth-value, external epistemic justification, and Gettier conditions each demonstrate that knowledge depends on more than the person (and the brain). *See generally* Jonathan Jenkins Ichikawa & Mathhias Steup, *The Analysis of Knowledge, in* STANFORD ENCYCLOPEDIA OF PHILOSOPHY (2012); Edmund Gettier, *Is Justified True Belief Knowledge?*, 23 ANALYSIS 121 (1963).

people may have the same brain states and yet one has knowledge while the other does not.[9] Therefore, knowledge is not a brain state. Interestingly, Levy appears to agree with us on this conclusion. He writes in a footnote: "knowledge cannot be a brain state because knowledge is a relation between a subject and a state of the world."[10] Indeed, this is precisely the point of some of our critique. In our view, Levy is therefore correct to point out that it is potentially misleading to presuppose knowledge is a brain state.[11] Moreover, we do not think that Levy is erroneously attempting to infer metaphysics from semantics when he points this out. Instead, he is illustrating a reason why, because of *conceptual confusion*, an empirical claim that purports to be about knowledge may fail.

This takes us to our second point. Nothing in this book argues, nor do we mean to imply or suggest, that empirical investigation of the brain cannot inform the mental categories and behavior that matter for law. As a field of inquiry, neurolaw is not conceptually confused—but some of the claims and arguments within its domain are confused and fail for that reason. Neuroscientific investigations that are free from conceptual errors may contribute in a variety of ways to improve the law. These investigations may provide strong evidence on a factual issue on which the law depends (and this evidence may be better than conventionally available evidence on the issue); they may provide greater understanding of the processes and sub-personal mechanisms underlying legal categories to perhaps better align legal doctrine with its underlying normative goals and values; or they may reveal that a legal category is hopelessly confused and ought to be abandoned. But the likelihood of each contribution, we contend, is increased when the empirical investigations avoid conceptual confusion. For this reason, we maintain that philosophy can contribute to each of these projects. This book defends and, if we are successful, vindicates that modest claim.

[9] Or the same person on two separate occasions. Consider the following example. Suppose someone is driving along a highway and sees a barn (a real barn) and asserts, "There's a barn." Hours later, the same person sees what he perceives to be a similar looking barn and again asserts, "There's a barn." Unbeknownst to the driver, however, the second time he is in Fake Barn County, where they make barn facades along the highway to trick passing motorists. *See* Alvin I. Goldman, *Discrimination and Perceptual Knowledge*, 73 J. PHIL. 771 (1976). Our driver, let us assume, has similar perceptual experiences both times and forms similar underlying brain states. Yet, in the first scenario he has knowledge, and in the second he does not. Thus, knowledge is not his brain states, which, by hypothesis, were the same. Again, to be clear, this is not to deny that in some cases there may be neurological differences between cases of knowing and non-knowing.

[10] Levy, *supra* note 6, at 176 n.4.

[11] This mistaken presupposition, made by some in the neurolaw literature, is one our analysis reveals.

Preface to the Hardcover Edition

This book was first sketched on a napkin in a Manhattan hotel bar during an annual meeting of the AALS (Association of American Law Schools). In the years that have elapsed since our first discussion of the issues in this book, much has happened. Interest in law and neuroscience has exploded and, with it, the attention of scholars from a variety of disciplines. We have been willing and eager participants in these debates. Although sometimes taken to be "skeptics" about the prospects of neuroscience for law, we think this label is inaccurate. In this book we make our case in a sustained fashion, covering a variety of topics and, as always, maintaining our stance that the conceptual issues involved are an important dimension of the intersection between law and neuroscience.

Our work on this topic began as an article in the *University of Illinois Law Review*.[1] In that article, we took a broad view of the issues in law and neuroscience, identifying questions we knew we wanted to research further. The publication of that article garnered attention for our positions on the issues, and we were invited to discuss our views in a variety of fora. We thank Neil Levy and Walter Sinnott-Armstrong for convening a special symposium issue of the journal *Neuroethics* discussing our work, and we thank the other contributors in that issue (Walter Glannon, Sarah Robins, Carl Craver, and Thomas Nadelhoffer) for their insightful commentary.[2]

[1] Michael S. Pardo & Dennis Patterson, *Philosophical Foundations of Law and Neuroscience*, 2010 UNIV. ILL. L. REV. 1211 (2010).

[2] Our contributions in this issue include: Michael S. Pardo & Dennis Patterson, *Minds, Brains, and Norms*, 4 NEUROETHICS 179 (2011) and Michael S. Pardo & Dennis Patterson, *More on the Conceptual and the Empirical: Misunderstandings, Clarifications, and Replies*, 4 NEUROETHICS 215 (2011).

In the years since the publication of our first article together, we have endeavored to broaden and deepen our position and our arguments. This book is the result of those efforts.[3]

We have many people to thank for their support of our work.

Our institutions have provided outstanding research support. Professor Pardo thanks Dean Ken Randall for his enthusiastic support of this project, his overwhelming support more generally, and his constant willingness to do whatever is necessary to foster a first-rate research environment. Professor Pardo also thanks the University of Alabama Law School Foundation for generous financial support. Professor Patterson's greatest thanks is to Rayman Solomon, Dean of the Rutgers Camden School of Law. The support shown by Dean Solomon is without equal. Thanks to Dean John Linarelli at Swansea University, Wales, UK for his unflinching support of this work. Much of the writing of this book took place in the congenial atmosphere of Tuscany at the European University Institute in Florence. Professor Patterson thanks Marise Cremona and Hans Micklitz, heads of the EUI Law Department, for their support.

We have had the opportunity to share our work on law and neuroscience at a number of venues throughout the world, and we have benefitted greatly from the many generous comments and questions. We both presented at the conference on "Law and Neuroscience: State of the Art," hosted by the Law & Philosophy Institute at Rutgers School of Law (Camden). Professor Pardo presented at conferences on law and neuroscience hosted by the Institute for Law & Philosophy at the University of San Diego Law School and by University College London, a panel on law and neuroscience at the annual meeting of the Southeastern Association of Law Schools, a panel on fMRI lie detection at the AALS Evidence Section Mid-Year Meeting, a junior scholars workshop on law and neuroscience at Stanford Law School, and a workshop hosted by the Northwestern School of Law Legal

---

[3] In addition to the articles mentioned above, the book also expands on our arguments in Michael S. Pardo & Dennis Patterson, *Neuroscience, Normativity, and Retributivism, in* THE FUTURE OF PUNISHMENT 133 (Thomas A. Nadelhoffer ed., 2013) and draws on some of our individual work, including Michael S. Pardo, *Self-Incrimination and the Epistemology of Testimony*, 30 CARDOZO L. REV. 1023 (2008); Michael S. Pardo, *Neuroscience Evidence, Legal Culture, and Criminal Procedure*, 33 AM. J. CRIM. L. 301 (2006); Michael S. Pardo, *Disentangling the Fourth Amendment and the Self-Incrimination Clause*, 90 IOWA L. REV. 1857 (2005); and Dennis Patterson, *On the Conceptual and the Empirical: A Critique of John Mikhail's Cognitivism*, 73 BROOK. L. REV. 1053 (2007–2008) (symposium on A Cross-Disciplinary Look at Scientific Truth).

Philosophy Club. Professor Patterson presented parts of this work at Swansea University, the EUI Law Department, University of Freiburg, and University of Lucerne. We thank the organizers and participants at each of these events.

We have had excellent research assistance. For this, we thank: Michael Stramiello (class of 2013) at the University of Alabama School of Law, Erin Cooper at Goethe University Frankfurt, and Anna Södersten, Dr. Sofia Moratti, and Bosko Tripkovic at the European University Institute in Florence.

Several individuals provided us with helpful comments on our work, written or in conversation, over the past few years. In particular, we wish to thank: Larry Alexander, Ron Allen, Philip Bobbitt, Teneille Brown, Craig Callen, Ed Cheng, Deborah Denno, Bebhinn Donnelly, Kim Ferzan, Daniel Goldberg, Hank Greely, Andrew Halpin, Adam Kolber, Dan Markel, John Mikhail, Jennifer Mnookin, Michael Moore, Stephen Morse, Eddy Nahmias, Thomas Nadelhoffer, Hans Oberdiek, John Oberdiek, Ralf Poscher, Amanda Pustilnik, Michael Risinger, Adina Roskies, Fred Schauer, Anne-Lise Sibony, Walter Sinnott-Armstrong, Carter Snead, Larry Solum, Nicole Vincent, and Jefferson White.

Our deep and abiding gratitude to Peter Hacker for reading the entire manuscript and saving us from countless errors.

We also thank Jennifer Gong, our editor at Oxford University Press, for her invaluable assistance and counsel throughout the entire process.

Finally, we thank our families. Professor Pardo thanks Meredith and Nathaniel for their support, patience, good cheer, and love. Professor Patterson thanks Barbara, Sarah, and Graham for their love and support over the years it took to complete this book.

Introduction

The relationship between the mind and the brain is a topic of immense philosophical, scientific, and popular interest.[1] The diverse but interacting powers, abilities, and capacities that we associate with the mind and mental life both link humans with other animals and constitute what make us uniquely human. These powers, abilities, and capacities include perception, sensation, knowledge, memory, belief, imagination, emotion, mood, appetite, intention, and action. The brain, in interaction with other aspects of the nervous system and the rest of the human body, makes these possible. The relationship between the mind and the brain is undeniable, and we do not deny it in this book. We think *substance dualism*—that is, the Cartesian idea that the mind consists of an immaterial substance that is somehow in causal interaction with the physical body (including the brain)—is too implausible to be taken seriously. We are not dualists.[2]

---

[1] Recent, accessible discussions of philosophical issues raised by recent neuroscience include Alva Noë, Out of Our Heads: Why You are Not Your Brain, and Other Lessons From the Biology of Consciousness (2010); Raymond Tallis, Aping Mankind: Neuromania, Darwinitis, and the Misrepresentation of Humanity (2011); Paul Thagard, The Brain and the Meaning of Life (2012); Michael S. Gazzaniga, Who's in Charge? Free Will and the Science of the Brain (2012).

[2] In rejecting substance dualism, we endorse moderate or pragmatic forms of "naturalism"; *see, e.g.*, Philip Kitcher, The Ethical Project (2011). However, for reasons discussed in Chapter Two, we reject more extreme "reductive" or "eliminative" forms of naturalism. Although modern neuroscientists (and legal scholars advocating for neuroscientific applications in law) overwhelmingly purport to reject the substance dualism associated with Descartes, their explanations retain the problematic formal structure of Cartesianism by replacing the immaterial soul with the brain. This ironic development is articulated lucidly and in detail in M.R. Bennett & P.M.S. Hacker, Philosophical Foundations of Neuroscience 233–35 (2003). Moreover, as we explore in Chapter Two, the false dichotomy

Nevertheless, the relationship between the mind and the brain is enormously complicated. It is one thing to say that the mind (or some particular aspect of mental life, for example, pain) depends on the brain and another to say that the mind (or a particular aspect of it) just *is* the brain, or can be "reduced" to the brain (in the sense that it can be explained or explained away fully in terms of brain processes). Whether it can or cannot will depend on a number of empirical and conceptual issues. The empirical issues concern the evidential base and the adequacy of the scientific explanations for the phenomena that we associate with the mind and the sensory, affective, cognitive, and cogitative categories that comprise our mental lives. The empirical issues on the relationship of mind and brain have been aided by an explosion of work in cognitive neuroscience over the past couple of decades, itself aided by an explosion of technology providing detailed information about brain structure and process (most important, types of brain imaging).

The conceptual issues are sometimes more difficult to appreciate, but they are there.[3] This is true both with regard to the general relationship between mind and brain and issues involving particular mental categories. On the general relationship, consider the claim: "the mind *is* the brain."[4] When presented with the choice—is the mind one substance (the brain) or another substance (an *immaterial* substance)— then the choice may seem obvious. But notice what is presupposed by the choice when presented this way—that the mind is a *substance*. If it *is* a substance, then the choice should depend on the empirical success of the available rival hypotheses in explaining the nature of the substance. If it is *not* a substance, however, then this way of framing the issue is based on a type of error or confusion. We call this a *conceptual* confusion because the *conception* of mind that is being deployed by each of the rival claims is confused or mistaken (i.e., by presupposing that the mind is a substance).

---

between Cartesianism and reductionism as conceptions of the mind sets the stage for conceptual confusion throughout the neurolaw literature.

[3] Indeed, as we will argue throughout this book, the fact that the conceptual issues are sometimes difficult to recognize helps to generate some of the conceptual problems that we discuss.

[4] *See* PATRICIA SMITH CHURCHLAND, NEUROPHILOSOPHY: TOWARD A UNIFIED SCIENCE OF THE MIND/BRAIN ix (1986) ("Since I was a materialist and hence believed that the mind is the brain...").

What is true of the general question is also true of specific ones. Consider the following example drawn from clinical psychology. In discussing the relationship between depression and brain chemistry, psychologist Gregory Miller explains:

The phenomenon that a particular usage of the term *depression* refers to does not change if we redeploy the term to refer to something else, such as the biochemistry associated with depression. If by consensus the term *depression* refers today to sadness as a psychological state and in 10 years to a brain chemistry state, we have not altered the phenomenon of sadness, nor have we explained it in terms of brain chemistry.[5]

Notice two things about this quotation. First, there is an underlying phenomenon referred to by "depression," and the term expresses a concept. Second, concepts can change, and when they do the meaning of the terms used to express those concepts will change as well. We take no issue with changing concepts (or using terms to mean different things)—doing so may be fruitful and illuminating, particularly in light of scientific developments.[6] But changing the concept does not change the underlying phenomenon previously referred to by the term. Therefore, claims employing the new concept do not necessarily explain the phenomenon referred to previously. In our parlance, a conceptual error or confusion may arise when an empirical claim purports to rely on a current concept (e.g., the concept expressed by the term "depression") but the claim presupposes a changed concept or a mistaken view about the current one.

Understanding the complex relationship between the mind and mental life and the brain thus requires not only increased empirical knowledge about the brain but also conceptual clarity regarding the various issues and claims being made. The brain sciences have contributed much to the former, and philosophy (primarily those working in the philosophy of mind and related areas) to the latter. But a great deal of work remains to be done in both domains and the interactions between them.

---

[5] Gregory A. Miller, *Mistreating Psychology in the Decades of the Brain*, 5 PERSPECTIVES PSYCHOL. SCI. 716, 718 (2010).

[6] For an illuminating discussion of conceptual change in science, see MARK WILSON, WANDERING SIGNIFICANCE: AN ESSAY ON CONCEPTUAL BEHAVIOR (2006). For another example of conceptual change, see SUSANNE FREIDBERG, FRESH: A PERISHABLE HISTORY (2009), discussing changes in the concept of "freshness" as it relates to food.

It is against this intricate backdrop that issues of law and public pol-icy enter the picture.[7] The complex issues regarding the mind and the brain become, like three-body problems in physics, increasingly more complicated by the introduction of this third variable: law. The pro-posed uses of neuroscience to inform issues of law and public policy raise the same types of empirical and conceptual questions discussed above, but they introduce further complications for these issues and they raise new challenges. On the empirical side, the issues are further complicated by the fact that law often employs its own standards for the empirical adequacy of claims, and these standards deviate from those employed by scientists or others.[8] On the conceptual side, the issues are further complicated by the fact that legal doctrine and legal theory make use of our "ordinary" concepts of mind and mental life on some occasions and do not on others. Therefore, further conceptual difficulties are introduced by the concepts employed by legal doctrine and legal theory.[9] Together with increased empirical and conceptual issues, the law also introduces a host of additional practical and ethical issues.

I. Clarifications and Caveats about the Scope of This Project

In exploring the relationships among these three variables (the mind, the brain, and the law), we think it helpful to introduce the following general taxonomy of methodological issues: empirical, practical, ethi-cal, and conceptual. We believe that maintaining clarity among these

---

[7] The MacArthur Foundation's "Research Network on Law and Neuroscience" provides and collects resources on the intersection of law and neuroscience. *See* http://www.law-neuro.org/. The Research Network provides a useful starting point for exploring the grow-ing interdisciplinary field of neurolaw. For overviews of neurolaw scholarship, see Oliver R. Goodenough & Micaela Tucker, *Law and Cognitive Neuroscience*, 6 ANN. REV. L & SOC. SCI. 28.1 (2010); INTERNATIONAL NEUROLAW: A COMPARATIVE ANALYSIS (Tade Matthias Spranger ed., 2012); Francis X. Shen, *The Law and Neuroscience Bibliography: Navigating the Emerging Field of Neurolaw*, 38 INT. J. LEGAL INFO. 352 (2010).

[8] Fred Schauer has emphasized this theme and elucidated the several ways in which the standards diverge. *See* Frederick Schauer, *Can Bad Science Be Good Evidence? Neuroscience, Lie Detection, and Beyond*, 95 CORNELL L. REV. 1191 (2010).

[9] For example, even if neuroscience can tell us something about knowledge in general or a particular type of knowledge, it may or may not tell us anything about knowledge for purposes of *mens rea* in criminal law.

categories is crucial for making progress on issues at the intersection of law and neuroscience. We explain and illustrate the categories with the example of brain-based lie detection. First, some issues are *empirical*—they concern various issues pertaining to neuroscientific data. With the example of brain-based lie detection, these issues will include, for example, the strength of the correlations between particular brain activity and behavior associated with lies and truthful responses, respectively, and whether (and the extent to which) these correlations vary among individuals, different groups, and different types of lies, and a host of other relevant variables. Second, some issues are *practical*—they concern practical challenges regarding the integration of neuroscience into issues of law and public policy. With the example of lie detection, the practical issues involve, for example, determining when and how such evidence should be introduced into legal proceedings, as well as determining what legal standards and instructions will govern the inferences that may or not be drawn from that evidence. Third, some of these issues are *ethical*—they concern various questions regarding privacy, safety, dignity, autonomy, and other values implicated by proposed uses of neuroscience in law. With the example of lie detection, these issues concern, for example, how the compelled uses of lie detection would fit or clash with these values and the rights of parties.

Finally, some issues are *conceptual*. This category of issues is our primary focus throughout this book, and it is one that has garnered considerably less attention in the scholarly literature. The conceptual issues concern the presuppositions and applications of concepts associated with the mind and mental life in claims about neuroscience and law. These concepts include knowledge, belief, memory, intention, voluntary action, and free will, among several others, as well as the concept of mind itself. The primary utility of philosophical work on these issues is *corrective*, by which we mean correcting mistaken inferences and conceptual errors that result from presupposing and deploying problematic or mismatched concepts. We have said that our focus will be on *conceptual* issues and the value of the inquiry will be *corrective*. In order to forestall confusion, we clarify in more detail at the outset what we mean by each of these terms. Once again, we will use the example of lie detection to illustrate.

Conceptual issues concern the application of concepts involving the mind and the diverse array of psychological powers, capacities, and abilities that we associate with having a mind. The conceptual issues focus on the scope and contours of the concepts being employed in claims involving law and neuroscience. One such ability possessed by people with minds is the ability to lie to those around them. It is an *empirical* question whether a particular person is lying on a particular occasion, and it is an *empirical* question whether particular brain activity is correlated with lying behavior. But what constitutes a "lie" is a *conceptual* question. It concerns the scope and contours of what it means to "lie." Notice also that any answer to the two examples of empirical questions noted above (i.e., whether a person is lying and whether brain activity is correlated with lying) will presuppose some conception of what constitutes "lying."

To say that what constitutes a "lie" is a conceptual question is not to deny that there are empirical aspects to this issue, including how the term has been used in the past or how it is currently used by most people. Moreover, "concepts" and "conceptual analysis" are philosophically loaded terms, with a number of different ideas and theories sometimes attaching to each.[10] Therefore, a few additional caveats are necessary to further clarify what we mean by "concepts" and "conceptual analysis." We think of concepts simply as abstractions from the use of words. Concepts are not the same as words because different words may express the same concept,[11] and the same words may express different concepts. But we take ordinary usage as a starting point when the claims at issue involve our everyday "folk psychological"[12] mental concepts, and we take current legal usage as a starting point when the claims at issue involve doctrinal or theoretical concepts in law. We do not presuppose that these concepts necessarily have (1) fixed boundaries (rather, concepts can and do change); (2) sharp boundaries (rather, there may be borderline cases); or (3) essences or necessary

---

[10] For a useful overview of the philosophical literature, see Eric Margolis & Stephen Laurence, *Concepts*, in STANFORD ENCYCLOPEDIA OF PHILOSOPHY (2011), *available at* http://plato.stanford.edu/entries/concepts/. For more detailed discussions of the differing roles played by conceptual analysis, see FRANK JACKSON, FROM METAPHYSICS TO ETHICS: A DEFENCE OF CONCEPTUAL ANALYSIS (2000); CONCEPTUAL ANALYSIS AND PHILOSOPHICAL NATURALISM (David Braddon-Mitchell & Robert Nola eds., 2008).

[11] For example, the words "snow," "Schnee," and "neve" are all expressions of the same concept.

[12] The expression "folk psychology" refers to our common psychological/mental concepts and our ordinary use of words expressing these concepts. The notion of "folk psychology" or "folk psychological concept" is philosophical and controversial. We use the expression without endorsing the many uses to which it is put in the philosophical literature. However, the concept is a staple of the philosophical literature and, for that reason, we employ it. Nothing in our arguments depends upon a rejection of the idea of folk psychology. Thus, we prescind from direct controversy over the viability and explanatory perspicacity of this notion.

and sufficient conditions (rather, criteria for their application may be defeasible). Nevertheless, there are various criteria for applying the relevant concepts (or terms expressing the concepts), and our analysis often focuses on drawing attention to these criteria. The criteria at issue serve a normative role: they partly constitute the meaning of the relevant terms and they regulate applications. To continue with the example of lie detection, the criteria serve as the *measure* of what constitutes a lie and not just a *measurement* of whether someone is lying on a particular occasion.[13]

Beyond these relatively modest methodological commitments, we do not tie our analysis to any particular theory of concepts or conceptual analysis. Nor is our concern merely with words and the use of words. Words such as "lie" pick out certain phenomena in the world. Our—and the law's—concern is with the underlying phenomena. Conceptual clarity will improve our understanding of the phenomena; conceptual confusion will obscure what we are trying to understand.

This is what we mean by *conceptual* issues. In what sense, then, is the primary value of the analysis *corrective*? Empirical claims in the neuro-law literature will rely on concepts (e.g., to lie), and the presupposed criteria for applying terms expressing the concepts may be confused or erroneous (e.g., presupposing a lie necessarily requires an intent to deceive[14]). There is nothing wrong with using a term in a novel way, but it *is* a mistake to use it in a new way *and* think that it has the same meaning or plays the same inferential roles it did previously. A conceptual inquiry will serve a useful corrective function when it identifies conceptual errors or mistaken inferences made in arguments and claims about law and neuroscience. These inferential errors can arise in a variety of ways. For example, consider a claim that certain neural activity is correlated with lying. If the behavior being correlated with the neural activity is not in fact lying, then the claim may be relying on an erroneous conception of what it is to lie. Similarly, it would be mistaken to presuppose that brain activity *constitutes* lying when there is none of the behavior that we typically associate with lying (e.g., saying something believed to be false). Moreover, even when a claim relies on appropriate conceptions, given the ordinary meanings of the terms

---

[13] We discuss the criteria for lying in depth in Chapter Four.

[14] As we discuss in Chapter Four, one can lie without an intent to deceive. For example, a threatened witness may lie on the witness stand in court not intending to deceive the judge and hoping the judge "sees through" the lie (and does not rely on the witness's statement).

employed, a similar error may arise when the claim relies on a mistaken conception of how a term is employed in legal doctrine. Errors may also arise when two premises of an argument rely on different conceptions and draw mistaken inferences based on this mismatch.

In the chapters that follow, we illustrate how a variety of these types of conceptual errors and mistaken inferences arise within the neurolaw literature. It is not surprising that these types of conceptual issues would arise frequently for law and neuroscience. The relationships between neuroscience and the various mental and psychological concepts are themselves enormously complex, and this complexity is further increased by adding a new variable—law—which brings with it a host of issues regarding legal proof, legal doctrine, and legal theory. The conceptual issues we will discuss focus on all three of these levels: proof, doctrine, and theory. The issues of proof concern the use of neuroscientific evidence (for example, brain-based lie detection) in court. The doctrinal issues are drawn primarily from the areas of criminal law and constitutional criminal procedure. The issues in legal theory are drawn from the areas of general jurisprudence, economics, morality, and criminal punishment.

Although the primary thrust of our conceptual inquiry is corrective, we wish to dispel one other potential confusion at the outset. Our aim is ultimately not a negative or skeptical one about the positive role the brain sciences may play in informing and, in some cases, transforming legal issues. We maintain that increased sensitivity to these conceptual matters can only improve our understanding of the relevant issues. Progress on matters that lie at the intersection of law and neuroscience depends not only on increased empirical investigation but also on conceptual clarity regarding these investigations and, more important, the inferences and conclusions drawn from them. Empirical investigations free of conceptual confusions tell us so much more about what we need to know than investigations that proceed from problematic conceptual assumptions; empirical investigations based on conceptual confusions may lead us astray.

Two other caveats about our project must be noted in this Introduction. First, because our focus is on conceptual issues, we will largely take the neuroscientific data presented in the scientific literature or relied upon in legal literature as a given. This is not because we necessarily endorse these empirical claims, and we will point out a number of empirical issues along the way, but rather because it frees us methodologically to pursue the conceptual and legal issues at the heart of our inquiry. More important, we are not neuroscientists, and nothing in our analysis is offered as a critique of neuroscience qua science. Let us be clear about this. Our primary concern is with conceptual claims about how current neuroscientific data relates to our mental concepts as those concepts matter for law, legal theory, and public policy. These concerns must be informed by neuroscience, but the issues they raise exist outside the domain of neuroscientific expertise.

The second caveat concerns our focus on the law. The vast majority of our examples and the bulk of the doctrine we discuss involve law within the United States, and our discussions will predominately focus on doctrine pertaining to criminal law. In part, this is because this is where our particular expertise lies. Additionally, a number of important recent developments involving cases in the United States and criminal law have dominated the discussions. Although the doctrinal analysis will relate primarily to criminal law within the United States, we believe the examples are of more general interest in illustrating how problematic conceptual issues arise at the level of legal doctrine.[15] Moreover, a number of the theoretical issues we discuss are of general relevance for law.

II. A Brief Overview of the Science and Technology

As we explained above, our conceptual investigations in this book will largely take the neuroscientific data produced by various experiments as a given for purposes of discussion. We provide the relevant empirical details when discussing specific issues in the chapters that follow; however, some basic general understanding of the field and the relevant technology may be useful to readers not otherwise familiar with them. In this section, we provide some basic background details that

---

[15] Recent discussions of neuroscience and other doctrinal areas include Jean Macchiaroli Eggen & Eric J. Laury, *Toward a Neuroscience Model of Tort Law: How Functional Neuroimaging Will Transform Tort Doctrine*, 13 COLUM. SCI. & TECH. L. REV. 235 (2012); Jeffrey Evans Stake, *The Property "Instinct,"* in LAW & THE BRAIN 185 (Semir Zeki & Oliver Goodenough eds., 2006); Edwin S. Fruehwald, *Reciprocal Altruism as the Basis for Contract*, 47 LOUISVILLE L. REV. 489 (2009); Richard Birke, *Neuroscience and Settlement: An Examination of Scientific Innovations and Practical Applications*, 25 OHIO ST. J. DISPUTE RES. 477 (2011); Steven Goldberg, *Neuroscience and the Free Exercise of Religion, in* LAW & NEUROSCIENCE: CURRENT LEGAL ISSUES (Michael Freeman ed., 2010); Collin R. Bockman, Note, *Cybernetic-Enhancement Technology and the Future of Disability Law*, 95 IOWA L. REV. 1315 (2010).

some readers may find useful. (Readers already familiar with the field of neuroscience and techniques such as EEG and fMRI can skip ahead.)

Neuroscience investigates the brain and nervous system more generally, focusing on structures, functions, and processes within this system and its interactions with other bodily systems. Within this field, *cognitive neuroscience* investigates the relationship between the nervous system and *mental* attributes, often looking for links between the brain and the various powers, abilities, and capacities that we associate with the mind and mental life such as decision making, knowledge, memory, and consciousness.[16] Many of the issues at the intersection of law and neuroscience concern *cognitive* neuroscience because the law is typically interested in these mental attributes and their roles in human behavior. In addition to neural investigations of mental processes generally, the law also has a great need for knowledge from *clinical* neuroscience, which investigates the neural links to mental disorders that may be relevant to a host of legal issues (e.g., competence to draft a will or criminal defenses), and from *developmental* neuroscience, which investigates brain development and may be relevant to a host of legal issues involving children, young adults, and the elderly.[17]

---

[16] For general discussions, see MICHAEL S. GAZZANIGA, RICHARD B. IVRY & GEORGE R. MANGUN, COGNITIVE NEUROSCIENCE: THE BIOLOGY OF THE MIND (3d ed. 2008); M.R. BENNETT & P.M.S. HACKER, HISTORY OF COGNITIVE NEUROSCIENCE (2008). For a clear, accessible introduction, see A JUDGE'S GUIDE TO NEUROSCIENCE: A CONCISE INTRODUCTION (Michael S. Gazzaniga & Jed S. Rakoff eds., 2010).

[17] Our discussion in this book will focus primarily on claims about cognitive neuroscience and law; clinical issues, however, arise in the discussion of the insanity defense (Chapter Five). A number of important diagnostic issues at the intersection of law and neuroscience—including those involving pain, determination of brain death, and patients in vegetative states—are generally outside the scope of our discussion, but are mentioned occasionally where relevant. On pain, see Amanda C. Pustilnik, *Pain as Fact and Heuristic: How Pain Neuroimaging Illuminates Moral Dimensions of Law*, 97 CORNELL L. REV. 801 (2012); Adam Kolber, *The Experiential Future of Law*, 60 EMORY L.J. 585 (2011). On brain death, see Laurence R. Tancredi, *Neuroscience Developments and the Law*, in NEUROSCIENCE & THE LAW: BRAIN, MIND, AND THE SCALES OF JUSTICE (Brent Garland ed., 2004). On vegetative states, see Adrian M. Owen & Martin R. Coleman, *Functional Neuroimaging of the Vegetative State*, 9 NATURE REV. NEURO. 235 (2008); Rémy Lehembre et al., *Electrophysiological Investigations of Brain Function in Coma, Vegetative and Minimally Conscious Patients*, 150 ARCH. ITAL. BIOL. 122 (2012). On aging and memory, see Rémy Schmitz, Hedwige Dehon & Philippe Peigneux, *Lateralized Processing of False Memories and Pseudoneglect in Aging*, CORTEX (forthcoming, published online June 29, 2012). Developmental neuroscience and law is also outside the scope of our discussion. *See* Terry A. Maroney, *The False Promise of Adolescent Brain Science in Juvenile Justice*, 85 NOTRE DAME L. REV. 89 (2009); Terry A. Maroney, *Adolescent Brain Science after Graham v. Florida*, 86 NOTRE DAME L. REV. 765 (2011). The U.S. Supreme Court has relied upon developmental neuroscience in its recent jurisprudence limiting criminal sentencing. *See* Miller v. Alabama, 567 U.S. (2012); Graham v. Florida, 130 S. Ct. 2011 (2010); Roper v. Simmons, 543 U.S. 551 (2005).

Neuroscience has been aided significantly by technological advances over the past couple of decades. The most significant development has been "neuroimaging" in general and functional magnetic resonance imaging (fMRI) in particular.[18] Neuroimaging techniques allow for safe and noninvasive methods to learn ultrafine details about brain structure and function. Many of the proposals and experiments that we discuss in this book depend on data gathered through fMRI. Both MRI (magnetic resonance imaging) and fMRI work by having people lie down inside a scanner that contains a large and powerful magnet. The key distinction between MRI and fMRI is that MRI investigates structure and fMRI, as its name suggests, investigates function. MRI measures the magnetic properties of water molecules in the body.[19] The scanner creates a magnetic field that aligns the hydrogen nuclei of water molecules, and a radiofrequency pulse is then briefly applied to rotate the hydrogen nuclei into a high-energy state. When the pulse ends, the hydrogen nuclei spin back into alignment, releasing differing amounts of energy. An electromagnetic field then detects energy released by protons in the nuclei. The protons in different types of matter (such as the cerebral cortex, nerve tracks, and cerebrospinal fluid) "resonate" at different frequencies. The differences are translated to an image and appear in different shades, which can be enhanced further through a variety of techniques. The results are "images" of the brain that can even be "sliced" and examined from different angles. MRI is an amazing diagnostic tool.

In measuring brain process, fMRI focuses on the magnetic properties in blood.[20] Magnetic properties in blood are used as a proxy for brain activity because blood flow correlates with brain activity. When hemoglobin in blood delivers oxygen to areas of the brain it becomes "paramagnetic" and disrupts a magnetic field created by the scanner. When brain activity increases in a particular area, "blood flow increases more than needed to supply the increase in oxygen consumption."[21] When there is increased blood flow to an area of the

[18] For general overviews of neuroimaging, see Owen D. Jones et al., *Brain Imaging for Legal Thinkers: A Guide for the Perplexed*, 5 STAN. TECH. L. REV. (2009); Teneille Brown & Emily Murphy, *Through a Scanner Darkly: Functional Neuroimaging as Evidence of a Criminal Defendant's Past Mental States*, 62 STAN. L. REV. 1119 (2012); Henry T. Greely & Judy Illes, *Neuroscience-Based Lie Detection: The Urgent Need for Regulation*, 33 AM. J. L. & MED. 377 (2007); Marcus Raichle, *What Is an fMRI?*, in A JUDGE'S GUIDE TO NEUROSCIENCE, *supra* note 16, at 5–12.
[19] Raichle, *supra* note 18.
[20] *Id.*
[21] *Id.* at 6.

brain, the hemoglobin contains more oxygen, and the MRI signal increases. The increased signal suggests that area of the brain is more "active" or is otherwise involved in whatever activity the person is currently engaged in while in the scanner. This signal is the "blood oxygen level dependent" (BOLD) and it is the foundational principle for fMRI.[22] In the claims and experiments we will discuss, the activities being correlated with the BOLD signal typically include tasks such as answering questions, making decisions, perceiving images, thinking of things, or playing games. Statistical data from the measurements are then processed and translated through one of a variety of statistical techniques into a brain scan "image." In linking brain function and mental processes, claims based on fMRI sometimes rely on inferences from mental processes to "active" brain activity to arrive at conclusions about which brain areas are responsible for producing or enabling the mental process, or on inferences from brain activity to mental process (i.e., because a subject has X brain activity he or she is likely engaged in Y mental process). The latter are more controversial.[23]

In addition to fMRI (and MRI), another technique that features in the neuroscientific claims we will discuss is electroencephalography (EEG). EEG measures electrical activity in the brain, typically through electrodes on the scalp. Based on the presence of particular electrical activity, researchers draw inferences about the brains and minds of subjects. For example, in Chapter Four we will examine a controversial technique that uses EEG as a type of "lie detector," more specifically, as a measure of whether a person has "guilty knowledge" or knows details about a crime. Other neuroscientific techniques for gathering information about the brain include "positron emission tomography" (PET) and "single photon emission computed tomography" (SPECT), along with newer technologies such as "transcranial magnetic stimulation" (TMS) and "near-infrared spectroscopy" (NIRS).[24] We mention these other techniques when relevant to the discussion, but most of the

[22] *See* William G. Gibson, Les Farnell & Max. R. Bennett, *A Computational Model Relating Changes in Cerebral Blood Volume to Synaptic Activity in Neurons*, 70 NEUROCOMPUTING 1674 (2007).
[23] *See* Russell A. Poldrack, *Can Cognitive Processes Be Inferred from Neuroimaging Data?*, 10 TRENDS IN COG. SCI. 79 (2006) (discussing problems with drawing "reverse inferences" about mental processes from brain data).
[24] For a concise general overview, see Amanda C. Pustilnik, *Neurotechnologies at the Intersection of Criminal Procedure and Constitutional Law*, *in* THE CONSTITUTION AND THE FUTURE OF THE CRIMINAL LAW (John Parry & L. Song Richardson eds., forthcoming 2013), *available at* http://ssrn.com/abstract=2143187.

claims and arguments that we evaluate are based primarily on fMRI data (and to a lesser extent on EEG).

III. A Summary of the Chapters

Chapters One and Two discuss general philosophical topics and explain the methodological approach that we employ throughout the book. Chapters Three through Seven employ the methodological framework and philosophical issues presented in the first two chapters to a variety of issues in law, legal theory, and public policy.

Chapter One discusses several philosophical issues at the heart of claims about the ways that neuroscience will or ought to inform (and in some cases, transform) law. In this chapter, we introduce the primary methodological position on which our discussion and arguments depend: the distinction between conceptual and empirical issues. Conceptual issues concern whether a claim "makes sense," by which we mean that the claim employs correct conceptions of the relevant concepts (or presupposes the correct meaning for the terms expressing these concepts). For example, if a claim is about lying, does the claim employ a correct conception of lying? In other words, does "lying" in the claim mean lying or something else (does it express the concept of lying, or a different concept, or no concept at all)? We refer to claims lacking this feature as "nonsensical."

Empirical issues, by contrast, concern whether propositions are true or false, whether certain conditions obtain:[25] for example, "is Jones lying when he asserts that he was not at the crime scene?" In explicating this distinction, we explain two other subsidiary issues: (1) a distinction between criterial and inductive evidence, and (2) the "mereological fallacy."[26] We illustrate these methodological considerations with

---

[25] Of course, for this reason there will be empirical aspects to conceptual claims (e.g., we can ask whether propositions about concepts are true or false). But a key difference between a conceptual and an empirical claim is the role that each plays; conceptual claims primarily involve a normative, regulative role and empirical claims primarily involve a descriptive role. Another way to think about this distinction is that conceptual claims are about the *measure* constituted by the concept, and empirical claims are about particular *measurements made with the concept.* A conceptual claim about lying is about what constitutes a lie; empirical claims about lying are whether someone is lying on a particular occasion or whether particular brain activity is correlated with lying.

[26] BENNETT & HACKER, *supra* note 2.

discussions of competing conceptions of rule following, interpretation, and knowledge.

Turning from the general philosophical considerations underlying many law-and-neuroscience claims, Chapter Two focuses in more detail on the concept of mind itself. Many claims in the neurolaw literature rely upon a "reductionist" conception of the mind, according to which the mind can be "reduced" in the sense of being explained fully (or explained away in some "eliminative" proposals) in terms of brain functions and processes. We discuss the controversial presuppositions underlying this conception of mind. We also outline three general conceptions of mind: Cartesian Dualism, the reductionist conception of mind-as-brain, and an Aristotelian conception of mind as an array of powers, abilities, and capacities.

With these philosophical considerations in place, we then turn in the next several chapters to specific claims made in the neurolaw literature. We sometimes use the term "neurolegalist"[27] as shorthand to denote scholars making strong and enthusiastic claims about how scientific data about the brain can illuminate or transform law and legal issues. Chapter Three discusses several issues at the intersection of neuroscience and legal theory. We first discuss claims about how neuroscience may illuminate issues in general jurisprudence. We next discuss the relationship between the brain and morality, focusing both on work by Joshua Greene and colleagues on emotion and moral decision making and by John Mikhail on "moral grammar." Finally, we examine recent work on neuroeconomics.

Chapter Four discusses brain-based lie detection. We examine two types of brain-based technology that are currently being studied in laboratory settings and marketed for real-world use. Parties in both civil and criminal litigation have attempted to introduce the results of such testing as probative evidence in court. The first type uses fMRI to examine whether someone is exhibiting neural activity correlated with deceptive lies or with sincere responses. The second type uses EEG to examine whether someone possesses "guilty knowledge" (e.g., incriminating details about a crime scene). We outline the various empirical and practical issues facing the use of this type of evidence in litigation settings, but we focus the bulk of our discussion on several

---

[27] We do not mean to refer to everyone writing in the field of law and neuroscience by this term. The field is immense and diverse, with a wide range of views expressing optimism, pessimism, caution, frustration, and concern.

problematic *conceptual* presuppositions underlying arguments about this evidence and the inferences that may legitimately be drawn from it in litigation settings.

Chapters Five and Six focus on legal doctrine in criminal cases. Chapter Five discusses substantive legal doctrine, and examines arguments about the use of neuroscience to inform three primary doctrinal categories for adjudicating guilt: *actus reus*, *mens rea*, and the insanity defense. Chapter Six focuses on criminal procedure, and examines the three primary constitutional provisions that limit the gathering and use of neuroscientific evidence by the government: the Fourth Amendment, the Fifth Amendment privilege against self-incrimination, and Due Process. Throughout these chapters, the discussion will, like the rest of the book, focus primarily on conceptual issues.[28] In addition to our specific analyses of the various provisions, our general aim in these chapters is to illustrate that the arguments for how neuroscience fits (or ought to fit) with legal doctrine depend on these conceptual issues, and the practical consequences that follow.

Chapter Seven turns from doctrine back to theory and examines arguments about the relationship between neuroscience and theories of criminal punishment. We evaluate two different challenges neuroscience purports to present for retribution-based theories of criminal punishment. The first challenge focuses on information about the brains of those engaged in punishment decisions, and seeks to undermine retributivism because of the relationship between emotion and retributive punishment decisions. The second challenge focuses on information about the brains of criminals (and people generally)

---

[28] Two related issues involving neuroscience and criminal law that are outside the scope of our discussion are predicting violence and the unique roles played by neuroscientific evidence in death penalty cases after guilt has been determined. On predicting violence, see Thomas Nadelhoffer et al., *Neuroprediction, Violence, and the Law: Setting the Stage*, 5 NEUROETHICS 67 (2012); Amanda C. Pustilnik, *Violence on the Brain: A Critique of Neuroscience in Criminal Law*, 44 WAKE FOREST L. REV. 183 (2009). On death penalty cases, see O. Carter Snead, *Neuroimaging and the "Complexity" of Capital Punishment*, 82 N.Y.U. L. REV. 1265 (2007). To the extent the relevance of neuroscientific evidence at sentencing in capital cases is to raise doubts about culpability (because of doubts regarding *mens rea*, insanity, or *actus reus*), our analysis in Chapter Five applies here as well. We do not address potential mitigating uses of neuroscience at sentencing that do not track the doctrinal issues. In our discussion of constitutional criminal procedure, we take the constitutional provisions and their surrounding doctrine as a given and we do not address whether new rights should be created in light of developments in neuroscience. For an argument advocating a right to "cognitive liberty," see Richard G. Boire, *Searching the Brain: The Fourth Amendment Implications of Brain-Based Deception Devices*, 5 AM. J. BIOETHICS 62 (2005).

and predicts that this will undermine retributivism by showing that no defendants ever deserve punishment. We illustrate how both challenges depend on a number of problematic conceptual presuppositions. Exposing these problems undermines the challenges and reveals why their conclusions ought to be resisted.

We conclude our book with some thoughts on what we believe our arguments demonstrate and why we believe our approach to the issues has much to recommend it. As we have stated, our position is that the conceptual issues raised by the literature on law and neuroscience are significant and largely neglected. Our purpose in writing this book is to draw attention to these issues, demonstrate their importance, and propose concrete solutions to the problems we identify.

1

Philosophical Issues

A staple of any good argument, whether it is a philosophical argument, a public-policy position, or even a debate about the relative merits of daily exercise, is clarity. What clarity accomplishes is both good and bad for arguments. A clear argument draws its power, in part, from the compelling nature of the connections made in the course of the argument. Likewise, clarity can reveal the flaws in an argument, leaving the proponent of the position to either concede defeat or reformulate the argument in better terms.

One of the principal virtues of philosophy (as method) is the relentless search for flaws—clear or hidden—in argument. As every college student knows, there are multiple fallacies. Fallacies such as the fallacy of composition, appeal to authority, and begging the question are quotidian features of daily newspapers and faculty lounges. In addition to these relatively well-known, common forms of fallacious argument, there are more sophisticated and more difficult argumentative errors. It is on these latter forms of argument that we concentrate in this chapter. The fallacies we focus on are logical or philosophical in nature.

One might rightly ask what is a "philosophical fallacy"? There are errors in computation, and mistakes in reasoning, but what is a "philosophical error"? Throughout this book, we answer this question by carefully scrutinizing the claims made by a broad spectrum of authors who take the view that matters of mind are best understood or explained as neurological events. The mantra for this group is "your mind is your brain." Adopting this view leads to the philosophical errors we highlight. These errors are logical or philosophical in the sense that the claims made take language beyond "the bounds of sense." Claims transgress the bounds of sense when they apply terms expressing concepts to contexts in which they do not apply—without stipulating or presupposing a new meaning for the term. So, for example, we take issue with the idea that a rule or norm can be followed "unconsciously." The very idea of "following" a rule means that one is cognizant of it and ready to invoke it in any context that implicates the rule. Through example and exegesis, we show why the idea of "unconscious rule following" makes no sense.

Before advancing our arguments, we wish to dispel a potential confusion at the outset. Our discussion of problematic conceptions of mind and other mental attributes may suggest to some readers that we are setting up a classic dualist versus materialist discussion, with the neuroscience proponents falling on the materialist side.[1] This is not so. Indeed, as we will discuss, the putative dichotomy is a principal source of the problems we survey. Cartesian dualism—with its picture of mind as an immaterial substance, independent of but in causal relation with the body[2]—is typically set up as the foil in many neuroscience discussions. For example, in introducing the journal *Neuroethics*, Neil Levy writes that "Cartesian (substance) dualism is no longer taken seriously; the relation between the brain and the mind is too intimate for it to be at all plausible.... [N]euroscientific discoveries promise...to reveal the structure and functioning of our minds and, therefore, of our souls."[3] Likewise, in discussing the implications of neuroscience for jurisprudence, Oliver Goodenough writes that the "Cartesian model...supposes a separation of mind from the brain," whereas models of mind for "a nondualist like myself" are "what the brain does for a living."[4] The dichotomy between dualism and mind-as-brain is a false one. Moreover, as we will discuss in Chapter Two, materialists such as Goodenough are *too* Cartesian—he, like many neuroscientists and

---

[1] According to the renowned neuroscientist Michael Gazzaniga, "98 or 99 percent" of cognitive neuroscientists subscribe to the reduction of mind to the brain in their attempts to explain mental phenomena. *See* Richard Monastersky, *Religion on the Brain*, CHRON. HIGHER ED. A15 (May 26, 2006).

[2] For an overview of this position, see Howard Robinson, *Dualism, in* STANFORD ENCYCLOPEDIA OF PHILOSOPHY (2009), *available at* http://plato.stanford.edu/entries/dualism/. We discuss Cartesian dualism in more detail in Chapter Two.

[3] Neil Levy, *Introducing Neuroethics*, 1 NEUROETHICS 1, 2 (2008) (emphasis omitted). We note that Levy does not subscribe to the neuro-reductionism that we critique in this book. *See* NEIL LEVY, NEUROETHICS: CHALLENGES FOR THE 21ST CENTURY (2007).

[4] Oliver R. Goodenough, *Mapping Cortical Areas Associated with Legal Reasoning and Moral Intuition*, 41 JURIMETRICS 429, 431–32 (2000–2001).

neurolaw scholars, keeps the problematic Cartesian structure in place by simply replacing the Cartesian soul with the brain.[5]

Rather than arguing about where the mind is located (e.g., in the brain or elsewhere), we need to step back and contemplate whether this is the right question to ask. First, notice that the question of the mind's location presupposes that the mind is a kind of "thing" or "substance" that is located "somewhere" (e.g., in the body). Why must this be so? Our answer is that it need not be, and is not. An alternative conception of mind—the one that we contend is more plausible—is as an array of powers, capacities, and abilities possessed by a human being.[6] These abilities implicate a wide range of psychological categories including sensations, perceptions, cognition (i.e., knowledge, memory), cogitation (i.e., beliefs, thought, imagination, mental imagery), emotions and other affective states (i.e., moods and appetites), and volition (i.e., intentions, voluntary action).[7]

To be clear, we do not deny that a properly working brain is required for a person to use the diverse array of powers, capacities, and abilities that we collectively identify as mental life. Although neural activity is required for a human being to exercise these powers, capacities, and abilities, neural activity alone is not sufficient. The criteria for their successful employment are not a matter of what is or is not in the brain. These criteria—which are normative in nature—are the basis for our attribution of mental attributes.[8] To outline briefly one of the

---

[5] See M.R. BENNETT & P.M.S. HACKER, PHILOSOPHICAL FOUNDATIONS OF NEUROSCIENCE 233–35 (2003) (tracing the *explicit* Cartesian structure of mind in early neuroscience through its transformation to an *implicit* Cartesian structure around the late nineteenth and early twentieth centuries).

[6] See *id.* at 62–63 ("The mind, as we have already intimated, is not a substance of any kind....We say of a creature (primarily of a human being) that it *has a mind* if it has a certain range of active and passive powers of intellect and will—in particular, conceptual powers of a language-user that make self-awareness and self-reflection possible.").

[7] We do not mean to imply that all of the categories we enumerate are to be understood as being on a par with one another or classifiable under one scheme. For example, what is distinctive about the abilities of creatures with a mind is that they can and do act for reasons. Thus, abilities of intellect and will are to be distinguished from those of sensation and perception. Each category requires its own detailed analysis.

[8] See Donald Davidson, *Three Varieties of Knowledge*, in A.J. AYER: MEMORIAL ESSAYS 153 (A. Phillips Griffiths ed., 1991), reprinted in DONALD DAVIDSON, SUBJECTIVE, INTERSUBJECTIVE, OBJECTIVE 205, 207 (2001) ("No doubt it is true that it is part of the concept of a mental state or event that behavior is evidence for it."). To avoid another potential confusion, note that we are not behaviorists either. Although psychological capacities are manifested in behavior (and thus the behavior provides evidence of them) we are not suggesting, as a behaviorist would, that the capacities are identical with or can be reduced to behavior. Unlike behaviorists, we acknowledge that psychological events may sometimes take place in the absence of behavior and that behavior may take place in the absence of psychological events.

examples that we will explore below, consider what it means to "have knowledge." We believe that "knowing" is not (just) having a brain in a particular physical state. Rather, it is having the ability to do certain things (e.g., to answer questions, correct mistakes, act correctly on the basis of information, and so on). Thus, if behavior of various sorts, and not brain states, constitutes the criteria for "knowing," then it will make no sense[9] to say that knowledge is "located" in the brain. The same is true for other psychological predicates—and for the mind itself. So, to the question "what is the mind: an immaterial substance (Descartes) or the brain?," we answer "neither." To the question "where is the mind located: in the brain or in a nonspatially extended realm (Descartes)?," we answer "neither." Human beings have minds, but minds are not substances located somewhere within their bodies.[10]

We recognize that our claims may initially strike those operating within the dualist versus mind-as-brain dichotomy as unorthodox. Thus, to undermine what we see as entrenched but problematic presuppositions underlying many neurolaw claims, we proceed deliberately and carefully. We begin our argument by introducing an important methodological distinction between conceptual and empirical questions. In the context of neuroscience research, empirical claims are those that are amenable to confirmation or falsification on the basis of experiments or data. By contrast, conceptual questions concern the logical relations between concepts. We explain why the questions of what the mind is and what the various psychological categories under discussion are (e.g., knowledge, memory, belief, intention, decision making) are conceptual rather than empirical questions.

Given that these are conceptual issues, we next discuss the distinction between criterial and inductive evidence. This issue concerns the inferences that may be drawn from a body of evidence (neuroscience research) regarding various capacities and their exercise. We then turn our attention to philosophical problems that arise with claims regarding norms. Again, the critique we offer is philosophical in nature. The topics of unconscious rule following and interpretation are staples of the philosophical literature. We show why the approaches of several neurolegalists to these issues engender conceptual confusions.

---

[9] For a discussion of "sense," see *infra* note 16.

[10] Unless we are speaking metaphorically. Compare: "does he have it in him to win the game?"

We then take up the question of knowledge. Knowledge is a central concept in law, having a wide range of applications from tort law to criminal law and beyond. We make the case that knowing something to be so is best understood as an array of abilities or capacities and not as a particular state of the brain. We finish with one of the most important and controversial aspects of our overall philosophical position, the mereological fallacy. The question raised by the mereological fallacy is whether it makes sense to ascribe psychological predicates to the brain, rather than to the person as a whole.[11] We think not, and we explain why we think this is so.

I. The Conceptual and the Empirical

The important issue of the relationship between conceptual and empirical claims has, unfortunately, received little direct attention in the current debate over the present and future role of neuroscience in law. Empirical neuroscientific claims, and the inferences and implications for law drawn from them, depend on conceptual presuppositions regarding the mind. As we see it, many of the proponents of an increased role for neuroscience in law rest their case on a controversial and ultimately untenable account of the nature of mind. Although we recognize the need for greater emphasis on and interrogation of the empirical claims regarding neuroscience applications in law, we believe that the fundamental conceptual issues regarding the mind are of equal, if not greater, importance.

Devoted as they are to understanding the physiology of the brain, neuroscientists are principally interested in physical processes.[12] Of greatest interest to neuroscientists are questions regarding neural structures, the functioning of the brain, and the physiological bases for a wide range of mental attributes, including consciousness, memory, vision, and emotion. Scientific explanations, including those of neuroscience, are framed in a language of explanation most readily identified as "empirical." Grounded in theories and hypotheses, scientific

---

[11] These include the wide range of capacities noted above regarding sensation, perception, cognition, cogitation, emotion, and volition.

[12] *See* M.R. BENNETT & P.M.S. HACKER, HISTORY OF COGNITIVE NEUROSCIENCE I (2008) ("Neuroscience is concerned with understanding the workings of the nervous system....").

claims are tested by means of experiment. Experimental confirmation or disconfirmation of hypotheses forms the basis of the scientific method.

Empirical and conceptual questions are distinct. We would go so far as to say that they are logically distinct.[13] In addition to their distinct characters, the conceptual relates to the empirical in a certain way: the very success of empirical inquiry depends upon conceptual clarity and coherence. An experiment grounded in confused or dubious conceptual claims can prove nothing.[14]

Conceptual questions concern the logical relations between concepts. Concepts such as mind, consciousness, knowledge, and memory are exemplary instances of the sorts of concepts implicated in neuroscience discussions. To be well-founded, and thus to ground successful empirical claims, conceptual claims must make sense.[15] But what does it mean to say that conceptual claims must make "sense"?[16] The concept

---

[13] As we explain in the Introduction, there are of course empirical aspects to conceptual issues (e.g., it may be an empirical fact whether someone has learned a concept or whether someone is using a concept correctly). By "logically distinct" we mean that one is not reducible to the other or explicable in its terms. The relationship between empirical and conceptual claims is itself a matter of philosophical controversy. A recent philosophical trend—"experimental philosophy"—blends empirical methods and conceptual investigations. A representative collection of papers may be found in EXPERIMENTAL PHILOSOPHY (Joshua Knobe & Shaun Nichols eds., 2008).

[14] For example, imagine an experiment trying to determine whether Dworkinian legal principles weigh more than elephants. Of course, an experiment based on faulty conceptual presuppositions can sometimes produce fruitful results that do not depend on the faulty conceptual presuppositions, but discovering true propositions generally requires understanding the relevant concepts expressed in the propositions. Winnie-the-Pooh's "Expotition" to discover the East Pole was bound to fail not because he didn't look hard enough or because he looked in the wrong places. See A.A. MILNE, WINNIE-THE-POOH (2009). The example is from BENNETT & HACKER, supra note 5, at 71 ("One cannot look for the poles of the Earth until one knows what a pole is—that is, what the expression 'pole' means, and also what counts as finding a pole of the Earth.").

[15] BENNETT & HACKER, supra note 5, at 148 ("A prerequisite for fruitful and illuminating empirical research on the neural foundations of our psychological capacities is clarity concerning the concepts involved.").

[16] Bennett and Hacker explain the relationship of sense to truth thus:

Cognitive neuroscience is an experimental investigation that aims to discover empirical truths concerning the neural foundations of human faculties and the neural processes that accompany their exercise. A precondition of truth is sense. If a form of words makes no sense, then it won't express a truth. If it does not express a truth, then it can't explain anything. Philosophical investigation into the conceptual foundations of neuroscience aims to disclose and clarify conceptual truths that are presupposed by, and are conditions of the sense of, cogent descriptions of cognitive neuroscientific discoveries and theories. If conducted correctly, it will illuminate neuroscientific experiments and their description as well as the inferences that can be drawn from them. In *Philosophical Foundations of Neuroscience* we delineated the conceptual network formed by families of psychological concepts. These concepts are presupposed by cognitive neuroscientific research into the neural basis of human cognitive, cogitative, affective, and volitional powers. If the logical relations of implication,

of sense is bound up with the forms of expression for the use of words in a language. Therefore, to say that a particular claim lacks sense (literally, is nonsense) is not to say that the claim is frivolous or stupid (although the claim may be). It is to say that the claim fails to express something meaningful, and as such cannot be evaluated for its truth or falsity. Often mistakes or ambiguities in use can generate "nonsensical" claims—for example, what is meant by one's claim that a Dworkinian legal principle "weighs" more than an elephant? We suppose no one would endorse the truth of this claim, but we also suppose no one would endorse that it is false either. Or consider a judge's claim that, having heard the arguments from both sides, she will decide the case "in her brain"? It is neither clear what this means (other than that she will decide) nor what evidence would confirm or falsify it. Sometimes mistakes in usage can take the form of simple grammatical errors—compare "he has almost finished his breakfast" with "he has not already finished his breakfast." More important, however, they sometimes ramify in more problematic and significant ways.

One such mistake occurs when we think that the mind must be a substance.[17] This error underlies the fundamental reductionist move in many positive arguments for neuroscience in law.[18] The "reduction" is the reduction of the mind to the brain, and it typically takes one of two forms: an identity form (the mind *is* the brain) or an explanatory form (mental attributes can be explained fully in terms of information about the brain).[19] By making this move, many proponents

exclusion, compatibility, and presupposition that characterize the use of these concepts are not respected, invalid inferences are likely to be drawn, valid inferences are likely to be overlooked, and nonsensical combinations of words are likely to be treated as making sense.

M.R. Bennett & P.M.S. Hacker, *The Conceptual Presuppositions of Cognitive Neuroscience: A Reply to Critics, in* NEUROSCIENCE AND PHILOSOPHY: BRAIN, MIND AND LANGUAGE 127, 128 (Maxwell Bennett, Daniel Dennett, Peter Hacker & John Searle eds., with an introduction and conclusion by Daniel Robinson, 2007) (footnote omitted).

[17] Bennett and Hacker trace the genealogy of this mistake in BENNETT & HACKER, *supra* note 5, at 324–28.

[18] As noted above, Michael Gazzaniga claims that "98 or 99 percent" of cognitive neuroscientists subscribe to the reduction of mind to the brain in their attempts to explain mental phenomena. *See supra* note 1.

[19] Another way to characterize this second form is that statements about the mind can be translated without loss into statements about the brain. The neuroscience literature provides many examples of mind–brain reduction. For example, in his classic book, *The Astonishing Hypothesis*, Francis Crick defends what he refers to as "the scientific belief...that our minds—the behavior of our brains—can be explained by the interactions of nerve cells (and other cells) and the molecules associated with them." FRANCIS CRICK, THE ASTONISHING HYPOTHESIS 3 (1994). Similarly, Colin Blakemore argues that "All our actions are products

of an increased role for neuroscience set the stage for their enterprise, which is the explanation of human behavior in causal, mechanical, and non-volitional terms.[20] As we will show, the reductive impulse is driven by a conceptually problematic account of the relationship between mind and brain. Once this account is undermined, many of the aspirations of the neurolegalists diminish significantly. We expose the problematic foundations of these accounts by focusing on a variety of conceptual issues: the distinction between criterial and inductive evidence, unconscious rule following, interpretation, knowledge, and the mereological fallacy.

II. Criterial and Inductive Evidence

Suppose we were asked to look for evidence of various kinds of psychological faculties or attributes such as perception and belief. Some evidence would provide criterial support—that is, it would provide constitutive evidence for the faculty or attribute.[21] Another class of evidence would provide inductive support—that is, although not constitutive of the faculty or attribute, it might be empirically correlated with the faculty or attribute so that we could say with some degree of confidence that

---

of our brains ...." COLIN BLAKEMORE, THE MIND MACHINE 270 (1988). Again, reductionism is motivated by the belief that a successful explanation of human action need not go beyond the realm of the physical: the brain is the locus of explanation for all accounts of knowledge, intention, understanding, and emotion. We discuss neuro-reductionism and consider more examples of it in Chapter Two. Bennett and Hacker provide a damning counterexample to this reductionism, showing that context can never be eliminated when explaining human action:

> [N]o amount of neural knowledge would suffice to discriminate between writing one's name, copying one's name, practicing one's signature, forging a name, writing an autograph, signing a cheque, witnessing a will, signing a death warrant, and so forth. For the differences between these are circumstances-dependent, functions not only of the individual's intentions, but also of the social and legal conventions that must obtain to make the having of such intentions and the performance of such actions possible.

BENNETT & HACKER, *supra* note 5, at 360. *See also* Gilbert Garza & Amy Fisher Smith, *Beyond Neurobiological Reductionism: Recovering the Intentional and Expressive Body*, 19 THEORY & PSYCHOL. 519–44 (2009) for similar arguments in the context of psychology.

[20] *See supra* note 1.

[21] For discussion of the concept of "criteria," see LUDWIG WITTGENSTEIN, THE BLUE AND BROWN BOOKS 24–25 (1958). For general explication of Wittgenstein on criteria, see JOACHIM SCHULTE, WITTGENSTEIN: AN INTRODUCTION 130–32 (William H. Brenner & John F. Holley trans., 1992).

the presence of this evidence increases (or decreases) the likelihood of the phenomena with which it is correlated.[22]

Criterial evidence for the ascription of psychological predicates, such as "to perceive" or "to believe," consists in various types of behavior.[23] Behaving in certain ways is logically good evidence and, thus, partly constitutive of these concepts. For visual perception, this includes, for example, that one's eyes track the phenomena one perceives, that one's reports match what one observed, and so on.[24] For belief, this includes, for example, that one asserts or endorses what one believes, that one acts in ways consistent with one's beliefs, that one does not believe directly contradictory propositions, and so on.[25] This behavior is not only a way to determine whether someone perceives or believes something in particular. The behavior also helps to determine (indeed, it partly constitutes) what it means to engage in these activities. In other words, it helps to provide the measure for whether someone is in fact engaged in this activity

---

[22] *See* BENNETT & HACKER, *supra* note 5, at 68–70; *see also* James Hawthorne, *Inductive Logic*, *in* STANFORD ENCYCLOPEDIA OF PHILOSOPHY (2012), *available at* http://plato.stanford.edu/entries/logic-inductive/.

[23] Although we endorse the view that behavior plays a central (but not determinative) role in the formation of criteria, we do not ascribe to the behaviorist account of human action. Roughly speaking, behaviorists reduce psychological states to behavior in explaining human action. We think the better explanatory course is to show how behavior is woven together with the language of the mental in the formation of criteria for the ascription of psychological states such as belief, desire, and intention. In this regard, we follow the philosophical approach of Gilbert Ryle and Ludwig Wittgenstein. Ryle and Wittgenstein undermined the Cartesian picture of mind by attacking the fundamental assumption underlying that picture, to wit, the notion that "the mind" is an inner theater that is properly the object of research. The inner/outer dichotomy lies at the heart of Cartesianism and its manifold confusions. For a discussion of Cartesianism and Behaviorism, see Wes Sharrock & Jeff Coulter, *ToM: A Critical Commentary*, 14 THEORY & PSYCHOL. 579, 582–87 (2004).

[24] Of course, people may sometimes be mistaken in particular instances or even systematically mistaken (e.g., one who is color-blind). But if the reports did not appear to have any connection with what was happening around a person, we would not say that the person was *perceiving* anything. *See* BENNETT & HACKER, *supra* note 5, at 127 ("[T]he forms of behaviour that manifest possession of a given perceptual faculty consist in relative efficiency in discrimination, recognition, discernment, pursuit of goals and exploration of the environment, and, in the case of human beings, in corresponding utterances. These kinds of behaviour in response to visibilia, for example, are logical criteria for a creature's seeing things.").

[25] Again, particular instances may create exceptions, but wholesale failures would cause us to question whether the person actually held the beliefs purportedly attributed to him. This is also why assertions such as "P, but I don't believe P" (Moore's paradox) generally are considered to be contradictory. *See* Roy Sorensen, *Epistemic Paradoxes 5.3*, *in* STANFORD ENCYCLOPEDIA OF PHILOSOPHY (2011), *available at* http://plato.stanford.edu/entries/epistemic-paradoxes/#MooPro.

(not just a measurement in a particular instance).[26] If these forms of behavior were not in principle possible for a creature, then it would not make sense to ascribe the predicate to it truly or falsely.[27] Note, however, that this criterial evidence is defeasible; people can assert propositions they do not believe, or say they perceived things they did not, and people can perceive or believe without ever describing what they perceived or asserting or acting on what they believe. The primary point is that the behavior not only provides evidence of whether someone on a given occasion is perceiving something or has a belief, but it also partially determines what it means to perceive or believe.[28]

By contrast, some evidence provides only inductive support for whether one is perceiving or believing. This would be the case if there were, as an empirical matter, a correlation between some evidence and perceiving or believing. For example, there may be a relatively strong inductive correlation between wearing glasses and perception, but the behavior of wearing glasses does not constitute (or partly constitute) what it means to perceive. Neural activity, as demonstrated by neuroscience research, may fill this role; searching for these correlations is precisely the goal of much current research.[29] But note that this inductive correlation only works once we know what to correlate the neural activity with.[30] Physical states of the brain are not criterial evidence

---

[26] See BENNETT & HACKER, *supra* note 16, at 130 ("[T]o characterize a sentence as expressing a conceptual truth is to single out its distinctive function as a statement of a measure, rather than of a measurement." (emphasis omitted)).

[27] Again, the criteria are defeasible in particular instances. See *infra* note 53. Alternatively, such uses may be intended to change the meaning of "perceiving" or "believing." We should note that there is nothing problematic about scientists, philosophers, law professors, or anyone else coining new terms or putting existing terms to new purposes. The conceptual problems we are discussing with regard to neuroscience and neurolaw claims occur because the claims purport to tell us about our extant, ordinary psychological faculties and attributes (such as believing, perceiving, and knowing)—not because the authors are coining new terms or extending existing ones.

[28] See Richard Rorty, *The Brain as Hardware, Culture as Software*, 47 INQUIRY 219, 231 (2004) ("[B]eliefs cannot be individuated in such a way as to correlate with neural states.").

[29] See, e.g., Maxwell Bennett, *Epilogue* to NEUROSCIENCE AND PHILOSOPHY, *supra* note 16, at 163 (discussing the neuroscience of perception).

[30] An analogy may be helpful here. A bounty hunter chasing a fugitive is no doubt interested in catching the fugitive and not the fugitive's picture on the "wanted" poster. But the bounty hunter ought to pay attention to the details on the poster in order to identify the fugitive: to know whom to look for. Likewise, even though neuroscientists and legal scholars may be interested in our psychological capacities rather than our concepts for those capacities, they ought to pay attention to the details of these concepts in order to search for and identify these capacities. This analogy is taken from FRANK JACKSON, FROM METAPHYSICS TO ETHICS: A DEFENCE OF CONCEPTUAL ANALYSIS 30–31 (2000).

for—because they are not partly constitutive of—psychological faculties and attributes such as perception or belief.[31] To refer back to the
metaphor in the above paragraph, neural activity may help to provide
a measurement—but not the measure—of whether one has perceived
or believes something on a particular occasion.[32]

To know whether a brain state is correlated with a particular psychological faculty or attribute, we must first have criteria for identifying the faculty or attribute. Physical states of the brain cannot fulfill
this role. To illustrate this, consider a claim that a certain brain state,
or pattern of neural activity, constitutes perceiving X or thinking that
P is true,[33] but that a person whose brain was in either of these states
engaged in none of the behavior that we associate with thinking or
perceiving.[34] Suppose we ask the person and she sincerely denies that
she had perceived or thought anything. In this example, the claim
that the particular brain states constitute thinking or perceiving would
be false, based in part on the constitutive evidence to the contrary
(her experiences and her sincere denial).[35] Any purported inductive

[31] If neural activity did provide criterial evidence, then having particular brain states
would constitute exercising the ability (perceiving) or having the attribute (believing). *Cf.*
BENNETT & HACKER, *supra* note 5, at 173–74 ("There are sceptical and gullible people, but no
sceptical and gullible brains. We all know what it is for a person to believe or not to believe
in God, to believe in the Conservative Party or in fairies, to believe a person or his story or
to doubt a person's word and be sceptical about his story. But we do not know what a reli-
gious, agnostic or atheist *brain* might be. No sense has been given to such a form of words.").

[32] The same proposition may serve as a *measure* in one context and a *measurement* in
another context. The difference depends on whether it is being used in a normative, constitutive role or a purely descriptive one.

[33] Our favorite example of this, which we discuss in Chapter Two, is the claim that love
is identical with a neural state.

[34] Certain neural activity may be necessary to engage in (and play a causal role in) the
behavior that constitutes the ability to think or perceive, and neuroscientists may discover
this relationship by examining correlations between brain states and neural activity. But,
again, this would show only that such activity was a *necessary* condition, not a *sufficient* condition, for abilities such as perceiving or believing. The behavior with which the activity was
correlated would still be what provided the criterial evidence.

[35] An additional example regarding the criterial–inductive distinction involves mental
imagery. The (defeasible) criterial evidence for whether one has a particular mental image
is the person's say-so and how that person visualizes the image. Neural evidence accompanying such mental imagery may be inductively correlated with such imagery, but having the
neural events is not the criteria for having the images. *See* BENNETT & HACKER, *supra* note 5,
at 187–98 for a discussion of this issue. The issue of mental imagery may have legal relevance
to the issue of eyewitness identification. *See* Jeffrey Rosen, *The Brain on the Stand*, N.Y. TIMES
MAG., Mar. 11, 2007, at 50–51 (citing Professor Owen Jones on the potential relevance of
neuroscience to facial recognition).

correlation between the particular brain states and thinking or perceiving would have to be reexamined.

III. Unconscious Rule Following

One of the most basic questions of ethics and law concerns norms
and conformity with them (or lack thereof). Interest in this question
stems from the desire to learn more about the nature of moral cognition: how it is that we decide what norms there are, and what is
required by those norms. This is the issue of norm application or, in
the language of some philosophers, what it means to follow a rule.

Many scholars take the view that moral knowledge is "encoded" or
"embedded" in the brain.[36] This view of the nature of moral knowledge assumes that the capacity for moral judgment is "hardwired" in
the brain. In other words, moral knowledge is "innate." To explain
moral knowledge is to explain how the brain exercises choice in making moral judgments. Under this explanation, making a moral judgment is a matter of actuating "the machinery to deliver moral verdicts
based on unconscious and inaccessible principles."[37] These principles,
so the argument goes, are brought to bear on an ethical problem in
a manner described as "unconscious."[38] The idea of unconscious rule
following, grounded in the notion that moral knowledge is "encoded"
or "embedded" in the brain, is a fundamental feature of the neurological explanation of human ethical judgment. As a form of explanation
for human judgment, this approach is conceptually problematic. To
be clear, we are not contesting the empirical correctness of the view;

---

[36]   See, e.g., JOHN MIKHAIL, ELEMENTS OF MORAL COGNITION: RAWLS' LINGUISTIC ANALOGY
AND THE COGNITIVE SCIENCE OF MORAL AND LEGAL JUDGMENT 319–60 (2011); John Mikhail,
Moral Grammar and Intuitive Jurisprudence: A Formal Model of Unconscious Moral and Legal
Knowledge, 50 PSYCHOL. LEARNING & MOTIVATION 5, 29 (2009) ("The moral grammar hypothesis holds that ordinary individuals are intuitive lawyers, who possess tacit or unconscious
knowledge of a rich variety of legal rules, concepts, and principles, along with a natural
readiness to compute mental representations of human acts and omissions in legally cog-
nizable terms"). Mikhail takes his cue from some remarks by John Rawls in A THEORY OF
JUSTICE (1971).

[37]   MARC D. HAUSER, MORAL MINDS 42 (2006).

[38]   See John Mikhail, Universal Moral Grammar: Theory, Evidence, and the Future, 11 TRENDS
COGNITIVE SCI. 143, 148 (2007) (arguing that moral knowledge is "tacit" and based on principles that are "unconsciously" applied); Mikhail, Moral Grammar and Intuitive Jurisprudence,
supra note 36, at 27 ("[T]he human moral sense is an unconscious computational mechanism
of some sort.").

we are saying that the view makes no sense, as such, as an explanation. Why does the idea of unconscious rule following make no sense? There are two reasons.

First, the idea of "tacit knowledge" has to be separated from that of "correct performance."[39] It is not enough to say that one's brain "possesses" tacit knowledge because one performs correctly (i.e., in accordance with an ethical standard).[40] Invoking tacit knowledge to explain behavior requires something more than the mere invocation to show exactly *how* tacit knowledge is doing the work claimed for it. If tacit knowledge is to be more than a question-begging explanation, there must be independent criteria for it. Lacking such criteria, the explanation is empty.[41]

Second, we question the intelligibility of the very idea of "unconscious" rule following. What does it mean to say that a person or a brain "follows rules unconsciously"? Of course, a person can "follow" a rule without being "conscious" of it (in the sense of having it in mind or reflecting on it) while acting, but one must still be cognizant of the rule (i.e., be informed of it and its requirements) in order to follow it. A person cannot follow a rule if he is unconscious. (Accordingly, unconscious bodily movements are not considered acts for purposes of criminal law doctrine, as we discuss in Chapter Five.) Brains are neither conscious nor unconscious and so cannot follow rules consciously or unconsciously. Rules are not causal mechanisms in the sense that they do not "act at a distance."[42] Rule following is something human beings do, not alone with their brains, but in concert with others.

This last point can be detailed further. Consider that in many contexts in daily life where rules come into play, the following things seem to be implicated. We may (1) justify our behavior by reference to a rule, (2) consult a rule in deciding on a course of conduct, (3) correct our behavior and that of others by reference to a rule, and (4) interpret a rule when we fail to understand what it requires. Rule following occurs in a wide variety of contexts, each of which has its own unique

[39] *See* G.P. BAKER & P.M.S. HACKER, WITTGENSTEIN: UNDERSTANDING AND MEANING 185 (1 AN ANALYTICAL COMMENTARY ON THE *PHILOSOPHICAL INVESTIGATIONS*, 2d ed. 2005) ("There must be identifiable conditions that will differentiate between possession of tacit knowledge and total ignorance, conditions distinct from correct performance.").

[40] We discuss in Section V what it means to "possess" knowledge in more detail.

[41] One is here reminded of the explanation that opium puts people to sleep because it has "dormative powers."

[42] BAKER & HACKER, *supra* note 39, at 186.

features. These contexts are not "in the brain" but in the world. They are referred to in the course of any explanation of what a subject thinks is required by a norm and what, on the subject's view, that norm requires. When disputes break out about what norms require, appeal to what is in one's head is irrelevant, for the very presence of a different point of view on what a norm requires signals that such appeals would be question-begging.[43] Reason giving in defense of a challenge about what a norm requires cannot be done "unconsciously."

Moreover, there is a fundamental difference between *following* a rule and *acting in accordance* with a rule. Consider a simple example. In the entrance to a club in central London, the following sign appears on the wall: "Gentlemen are required to wear a jacket in the dining room." Mr. Smith is a dapper man, who happens to be the guest of a club member. If Mr. Smith has his jacket on as he enters the dining room, we can safely say that he is "acting in conformity with the rule." But is he "following" the rule? For that, more is required.

To actually "follow" the rule, Smith would have to be cognizant of it.[44] If Smith had no knowledge of the rule prior to his entrance into the club, it is difficult to say how he was "following" the rule. How would he have conformed his conduct to the rule through a course of behavior (e.g., being told the dress code by his friend, the club member)? If Smith had his jacket on his arm and did not see the rule posted on the wall, he would not be acting in accordance with the rule and would, presumably, conform his conduct to the rule once he was apprised of it.

The point here is that there is an epistemic component to rule following: one has to be cognizant of the rules. Making one's conduct conform to the rules is an essential feature of "rule following." Without this epistemic component, one is merely acting in accordance with what a rule requires. This is not rule following in any meaningful sense.

[43] The same difficulty besets Moral Realism. For discussion, see Dennis Patterson, *Dworkin on the Semantics of Legal and Political Concepts*, 26 OXFORD J. LEGAL STUDIES 545–57 (2006).

[44] *See* Bennett & Hacker, *supra* note 16, at 151 ("But for something to constitute following a rule, the mere production of a regularity in accordance with a rule is not sufficient. A being can be said to be following a rule only in the context of a complex practice involving actual and potential activities of justifying, noticing mistakes, and correcting them by reference to the rule, criticizing deviations from the rule, and, if called upon, explaining an action in accordance with the rule and teaching others what counts as following the rule.").

IV. Interpretation

In the view of many neuroscientists and their enthusiasts, the brain does all manner of things. It describes, understands, computes, interprets, and makes decisions. In this section, we will focus our attention on one of these claims, to wit, that the brain achieves knowledge through a process of "interpretation." Although they are not alone in this regard, many scholars writing about neuroscience are enthusiastic in their belief that the brain grasps norms through an internal process of "interpretation." Here is Oliver Goodenough singing the praises of Michael Gazzaniga's "interpreter module" in the legal context:

[Gazzaniga] has postulated the existence of an interpreter module, whose workings are also in the word-based arena. A similar word-based reasoner could work with the word-based rules of law. In experiments on split-brain patients, whose central corpus callosum had been cut as a cure for severe epileptic problems, the interpreter supplied completely erroneous explanations for behavior originating in some nonword-based thinking module.[45]

Our problem with this account of mental life is that it fails to appreciate the fact that interpretation is a "parasitic activity," one that is secondary in moral practice. Like Dworkin in legal theory,[46] neuroethicists want to make the case for interpretation as a fundamental feature of moral judgment. Although we agree that interpretation is certainly an important element of both ethics and law, it is an activity that depends upon existing and widespread agreement in judgment. In short, interpretation cannot "get off the ground" without widespread agreement in judgment already being in place.

As Wittgenstein pointed out, practice and settled regularity are the grounds of normativity and the distinction between understanding and interpretation ("Im Anfang war die Tat"). The point of Wittgenstein's example of the signpost[47] is that only practice and settled regularity can

---

[45] Goodenough, *supra* note 4, at 436.

[46] For discussion of this aspect of Dworkin's jurisprudence and the dilemma posed for his theory of law, see DENNIS PATTERSON, LAW AND TRUTH 71–98 (1996).

[47] "A rule stands there like a signpost. Does the signpost leave no doubt open about the way I have to go? Does it show which direction I am to take when I have passed it; whether along the road or footpath or crosscountry? But where is it said which way I am to follow it; whether in the direction of its finger or (e.g.) in the opposite one?—And if there were, not a single signpost, but a chain of adjacent ones or of chalk marks on the ground—is there only one way of interpreting them?—So I can say, the signpost does after all leave no room

provide the ground for correct and incorrect judgment.[48] Without a practice of following it—a way of acting—the signpost by itself provides us
no clue as to its proper use. In theory, there are as many potential ways of
"following" the signpost as there are possible conventions for determining
how it is to be used and what counts as following it. But once a convention for following signposts takes hold, a background of understanding
evolves. It is against this background that the need for interpretation
arises.[49] Interpretation is a reflective practice we engage in when understanding breaks down. Understanding is exhibited in action. For example,
we show that we understand the request "Please shut the door" by closing
the door. The need for interpretation arises from a firmament of praxis.

As an account of correct and incorrect action in a practice (whether
in ethics, law, arithmetic, or measurement), interpretation is a non-
starter because interpretation draws our attention away from the techniques that make understanding possible. Correct and incorrect forms
of action are immanent in practices. Correct forms of action cannot
be imposed on a practice, by interpretation or otherwise. It is only
when we master the techniques employed by participants in a practice
that we can grasp the distinction between correct and incorrect action
(e.g., in ethics or law). Claims about what morality and law require are
adjudicated through employment of intersubjectively shared standards
of appraisal. As Wittgenstein says, "It is not the interpretation which
builds the bridge between the sign and what is signified/ /meant/ /.
Only the practice does that."[50]

for doubt. Or rather: it sometimes leaves room for doubt and sometimes not. And now
this is no longer a philosophical proposition, but an empirical one." LUDWIG WITTGENSTEIN,
PHILOSOPHICAL INVESTIGATIONS §85 at 39–40 (G.E.M. Anscombe trans., 1953).

[48] All interpretation presupposes understanding. No one could interpret the following: Nog drik legi xfom. The terms first have to be translated or deciphered before interpretation takes place. Contra Quine, translation is not interpretation. W.V.O. QUINE, ONTOLOGICAL
RELATIVITY AND OTHER ESSAYS 51–55 (1969). We interpret an utterance when we choose
between different ways of understanding it. Legal interpretation is the activity of deciding
which of several ways of understanding a rule-given provision is the correct or preferable
way of understanding. This is precisely the sort of activity Wittgenstein has in mind when he
writes: "we ought to restrict the term 'interpretation' to the substitution of one expression
of the rule for another." See WITTGENSTEIN, supra note 47, §201 at 81.

[49] See G.P. BAKER & P.M.S. HACKER, WITTGENSTEIN: UNDERSTANDING AND MEANING 667
(2 AN ANALYTICAL COMMENTARY ON THE PHILOSOPHICAL INVESTIGATIONS, 1980) ("[G]iving a
correct explanation is a criterion of understanding, while the explanation given is a standard for the correct use of the expression explained. Correspondingly, using an expression in
accordance with correct explanations of it is a criterion of understanding, while understanding an expression presupposes the ability to explain it.").

[50] Cited in G.P. BAKER & P.M.S. HACKER, WITTGENSTEIN: RULES, GRAMMAR AND NECESSITY
136 (2 AN ANALYTICAL COMMENTARY ON THE PHILOSOPHICAL INVESTIGATIONS, 1985).

V. Knowledge

In the previous sections, we examined two issues that relate to particular kinds of knowledge: namely, what it means for a person to know how to follow a rule, and what it means for a person to know (and to interpret) what is required by a norm. In this section, we turn to the concept of knowledge more generally. We first articulate a general conception of knowledge as a kind of ability, and we then apply this conception to legal examples that scholars have claimed neuroscience may inform.

The concept of knowledge has been a topic of intense philosophical interest for thousands of years, and understanding its contours is the main agenda for many epistemologists. Aside from theoretical issues in epistemology, knowledge also relates to important ethical and practical issues. Ethical and legal judgments about whether to ascribe moral blame and/or criminal responsibility to someone's actions often depend on what that person did or did not *know* when she acted, as well as what she was capable of knowing. Similarly, someone's knowledge of where he was and what he was doing on a particular occasion will virtually always be highly probative evidence of, for example, whether he is the perpetrator of a crime and ought to be held criminally liable. The promise that neuroscience might help us to determine conclusively what someone knows, or what he or she is or was capable of knowing, is a seductive one.

We outline a number of conceptual points regarding knowledge as a general matter. As with rule following and interpretation, our fundamental methodological point is this: in order to assess the role that neuroscience may play in contributing to these issues, we must be clear about what knowledge is and what would count as someone having knowledge. More specifically, before we can determine whether someone knows something on a particular occasion, or is capable of knowing something more generally, we need some sense of the appropriate criteria for ascriptions of knowledge.[51]

Ascriptions of knowledge generally take one of two forms: that someone knows *how* to do something (e.g., ride a bicycle, juggle, find one's way home, or recite the state capitals while juggling and riding

---

[51] In other words, we are not concerned with the empirical question of whether someone knows (or fits the criteria) on a particular occasion, but rather with the general criteria for ascriptions of knowledge.

a bicycle home), and that someone knows *that* things are so (e.g., "that Springfield is the capital of Illinois," "that he lives on Sherwood Drive").[52] There is considerable overlap between these two types of knowledge ascriptions. Both *knowing-how* and *knowing-that*, in other words, manifest themselves in the ability to display the relevant knowledge. These manifestations—that is, expressions of knowledge—may take a variety of forms depending on the particular circumstances. One may manifest one's knowledge of *how* to do something, for example, by doing it or by saying how it is to be done.[53] One may manifest one's knowledge *that* something is so, for example, by asserting that things are so, by answering questions about it correctly, by correcting others who are mistaken about it, or by acting appropriately based on that knowledge. It is also possible that one may do nothing at all with one's knowledge (how or that). The primary point is that knowledge is a kind of cognitive achievement or success—it consists in a kind of power, ability, or potentiality possessed by a knowing agent.[54]

To be sure, this is not to suggest that knowledge just *is* the relevant behavior. On the one hand, it is possible to have knowledge without expressing it. On the other, it is possible to engage in the relevant behavior without having knowledge. A lucky guess, for example, that something is true or how to do something is not knowledge.

Although knowledge is typically (but not always) manifested in behavior, one might object that certain types of syndromes or injuries pose a fundamental challenge to the conception of knowledge as an ability. Consider the tragic case of "locked-in syndrome," in which victims, due to injury to their brain stems, remain fully conscious— with their memories and knowledge intact—but are unable to move or talk.[55] Plainly, they have knowledge—but they lack the ability to

---

[52] On the distinction between knowing-how and knowing-that, see GILBERT RYLE, THE CONCEPT OF MIND 25–61 (1949). The exact relationship between knowing-how and knowing-that is a matter of philosophical controversy, but this debate is outside the scope of our discussion. On the relationship between knowing-how and knowing-that, see JASON STANLEY, KNOW HOW (2011); KNOWING HOW: ESSAY ON KNOWLEDGE, MIND, AND ACTION (John Bengson & Jeff A. Moffett eds., 2012); Stephen Hetherington, *How to Know (that Knowledge-That is Knowledge-How)*, in EPISTEMOLOGY FUTURES 71–94 (Stephen Hetherington ed., 2006).

[53] The latter might be the case for someone no longer physically capable of performing a task but who still knows how to do something (perform a dance or play a sport, for example).

[54] BENNETT & HACKER, *supra* note 12, at 96 ("To know something to be thus-and-so is ability-like, hence more akin to a power of potentiality than to a state or actuality.").

[55] *See* JEAN-DOMINIQUE BAUBY, THE DIVING BELL AND THE BUTTERFLY (1997). For a discussion of this syndrome and the questions it poses for neuroscience, see ALVA NOË, OUT OF

manifest their knowledge in the typical ways. Does this mean that knowledge is not, in fact, an ability, but rather is something else (a brain state)? We think not. First, those with locked-in syndrome can, quite remarkably, learn to communicate their knowledge through a series of complex eye movements.[56] These communications do manifest knowledge consistent with an ability conception of knowledge. And before a locked-in sufferer learns to communicate in this way—or in cases of "total locked-in syndrome" in which no movements of the eye or any other body parts are possible—he is still able to reflect on his knowledge, to reason from what he knows to be so, and to feel emotions grounded in what he knows. These, too, are abilities or capacities and, indeed, these are reasons we ascribe knowledge to patients in this situation. If such patients were not conscious of their knowledge *in any way,* and could not manifest it in any way, on what basis would we ascribe knowledge to them? We would not. Thus rather than posing a challenge to the claim that the criteria for knowledge ascriptions includes an ability or capacity to manifest that knowledge, this example is consistent and reinforces that conception.

A second potentially challenging example is someone in a vegetative state. This example raises several issues. Does someone in a vegetative state possess knowledge? It depends. If she is in a vegetative state, then there may be no reason to suppose that she knows anything at all. If she recovers, then we would say that she retained whatever knowledge she continues to possess post-recovery.

Moreover, patients in persistent vegetative states are reported to sometimes engage in behaviors that, under other circumstances, might be consistent with manifestations of knowledge. For example, although patients in this condition are thought to be unconscious, they are reported to "respond to sounds, to sit up and move their eyes, to shout out, to grimace, to laugh, smile, or cry."[57] When this occurs, does the patient have knowledge? If they do not, but they have an ability to manifest responses to their environment, does this mean that knowledge is not an ability (to manifest such responses)? We think not. First, as noted above, one may engage in behavior that is consistent with knowing (how to do something or that something is so) without in

---

OUR HEADS: WHY YOU ARE NOT YOUR BRAIN, AND OTHER LESSONS FROM THE BIOLOGY OF CONSCIOUSNESS 14–17 (2010).

[56] *Id.*

[57] NOË, *supra* note 55, at 17.

fact possessing that knowledge (e.g., someone who answers a question correctly by guessing). The behavior, in other words, is not sufficient for knowledge.[58] Second, although knowledge implies an ability to do something, the reverse is not true: being able to do something does not imply knowledge.[59] The ability to do something may apply to many circumstances in which an ascription of knowledge is inappropriate. The ability of a metal to conduct electricity, for example, does not mean the metal *knows* how to conduct electricity. The ability of a thermometer to display the correct temperature does not mean the thermometer *knows*, for example, that it is currently 70 degrees. Knowledge involves a kind of "two-way ability": agents may typically choose to or refrain from exercising it at will.[60] With knowledge, as with rule following, it makes sense to say that an agent knows how to do something correctly, as well as what it means to do it incorrectly, to make a mistake, or to do it wrongly.

VI. The Mereological Fallacy

If anything unites the various problems and projects of neurolegalists, it is the belief that the mind and the brain are one. This belief is a pervasive feature of much of the current research in neuroscience and the neurolaw literature as well as more popular writing. But does it make sense to attribute to the brain psychological attributes normally attributed to persons? Can we intelligibly say that the brain thinks, perceives, feels pain, and decides? If we cannot, what are the implications for neuroscience and law?

Our argument that many neurolegalists commit the "mereological fallacy" begins with the conceptual–empirical distinction. As discussed earlier, two distinct sorts of questions permeate discussions of mental life. Empirical questions are the focus of scientific research, specifically research into the biology and physiology of brain function.[61] By contrast, conceptual questions address how the relevant concepts are articulated and

---

[58] As noted above, the behavior is not necessary either—someone may have knowledge and choose not to express or manifest it in any way.

[59] Likewise, one may know how to do something but not be able to do so. On the distinction between "being able to" and "knowing how to," see BENNETT & HACKER, *supra* note 12, at 97–99.

[60] On "two-way abilities," see *id.* at 97–98.

[61] *See* BENNETT & HACKER, *supra* note 5.

related. The point of the philosophical enterprise is to assess the degree to which articulations regarding the brain make sense.[62]

The mereological fallacy consists in attributing an ability or function to a part that is only properly attributable to the whole of which it is a part.[63] In this case, the mereological principle is that mental attributes apply to human beings, not a part of their bodies (i.e., the brain).[64] But why is it an error—indeed a "conceptual" error—to ascribe a mental attribute to a part of a human being? Consider, once again, "knowledge." Does the claim that knowledge is located in the brain transgress the bounds of sense so that we can say that it "makes no sense" to say that "the brain stores knowledge"? Can knowledge be stored in a brain just as information is stored in books or hard drives?

In their critique of Daniel Dennett's work, Maxwell Bennett and Peter Hacker argue that "[i]n the sense in which a human being possesses information, the brain possesses none."[65] Imagine the schedule for the New York Philharmonic is "encoded" in your brain. Can we say of you that you know when the next Mahler symphony is to be performed by the orchestra? If the question "when is the next Mahler symphony to be performed by the New York Philharmonic?" is put to you and you utter the wrong date, we would conclude—correctly— that you did not know the answer to the question. Knowing is not being in a particular state.[66] Knowing is an ability—the ability, for example, to answer the question correctly. The measure of the truth of your answer is not found in a neural state of your brain. Whether you know the answer to the question is shown, among other ways, by what you sincerely say in response to the question.[67]

---

[62] *Id.*

[63] *See* Achille Varzi, *Mereology, in* STANFORD ENCYCLOPEDIA OF PHILOSOPHY (2009), *available at* http://plato.stanford.edu/entries/mereology/.

[64] *See* Bennett & Hacker, *supra* note 16, at 133–34.

[65] *Id.* at 137 ("In the sense in which a book contains information, the brain contains none. In the sense in which a human being possesses information, the brain possesses none.").

[66] *See* ANTHONY KENNY, THE LEGACY OF WITTGENSTEIN 129 (1984) ("To contain information is to be in a certain state, while to know something is to possess a certain capacity."). Indeed, several classic arguments in contemporary epistemology involve cases in which hypothetical agents possess correct information but do not have knowledge. *See, e.g.,* Edmund Gettier, *Is Justified True Belief Knowledge?*, 23 ANALYSIS 121 (1963); Alvin I. Goldman, *Discrimination and Perceptual Knowledge*, 73 J. PHIL. 771 (1976); KEITH LEHRER, THEORY OF KNOWLEDGE (2d ed. 2000).

[67] Or it may be manifested in other behavior, for example, by showing up on time for the symphony. Although knowledge is typically manifested in behavior, this is not to deny

The upshot of this and countless other examples is that psycho-logical attributes are essentially manifested in the behavior, reactions, and responses of the living human being in the stream of life, not in whatever concomitant neural activity of his brain is to be found. This is the key to the mereological fallacy and the undoing of the reductive impulses of neurolegalists. Behavior is something only a human being (or other animal) can engage in. Brain functions and activities are not behaviors (and persons are not their brains). Yes, one needs a brain in order to engage in behavior.[68] But the reduction of a psychological attribute to a cortical attribute is a fallacious move from whole to part.

If the error of ascribing attributes of a whole to one of its parts is indeed a central error, what are the implications for neurolaw? We suggest the implications are manifold. Most importantly, the neurolegalist reduction of psychological attributes to brain states must be rejected as fallacious. Thus, voluntary action, intentionality, knowledge, and decision making cannot be attributes of brains, but only of human beings. The next chapter discusses the concept of mind in more detail.

---

that someone may lose the ability to manifest his or her knowledge in some ways (e.g., one who knows how to play tennis but is no longer physically able) or perhaps in all ways (e.g., someone with total "locked-in syndrome"). *See* Noë, *supra* note 55; BAUBY, *supra* note 55.

[68] Although having a brain is required, it is a mistake to suppose that having particular brain states is *sufficient*. This criticism is an across-the-board assault on the explanatory power of neuro-reductionism, which we discuss in Chapter Two. Raymond Tallis explains what lies at the heart of the impulse and why it fails as an explanation of behavior:

> The appeal to brain science as an explain-all has at its heart a myth that results from con-fusing necessary with sufficient conditions. Experimental and naturally occurring brain lesions have shown how exquisitely holes in the brain are correlated with holes in the mind. Everything, from the faintest twinge of sensation to the most elaborately constructed sense of self, requires a brain; but it does not follow from this that neural activity is a sufficient con-dition of human consciousness, even less that it is identical with it.

Raymond Tallis, *License My Roving Hands*, TIMES LITERARY SUPPLEMENT, Apr. 11, 2008, at 13.

2

The Concept of Mind

In this chapter, we consider a number of issues that illustrate the central importance of conceptions of "mind" in the debates over how to think about the role of neuroscience in law. The general conceptual issues that we explore in this chapter are important for understanding (and evaluating) the specific applications of neuroscience to law that we discuss later in this book. This is so because, as we will see, presuppositions about these conceptual issues do a lot of the argumentative work in claims about how neuroscience can inform issues in law and public policy.

We begin with a discussion of the explanatory strategy of "reductionism," of which neuro-reductionism is one particular form. The neuro-reductionism at issue aspires to explain the mind and mental life by "reducing" them to the brain and states of the brain. We illustrate the neuro-reductionist conception of mind that underlies much neuroscientific research and the proposals for its increased use in law[1] with an example of a prominent neuro-reductive approach: "eliminative materialism." We then discuss two examples of how this reductionist conception is employed in claims about the relationship between neuroscience and law. Finally, we contrast this conception of mind with two other alternatives: Cartesian and Aristotelian. In the course of our discussion, we consider the implications of these conceptions for issues such as "folk psychology," determinism, free will, naturalism, and normativity. The discussion, along with Chapter One, sets the stage for

[1] This conception also underlies discussions of theoretical problems and challenges facing neurolaw. An illustrative example is the problem of "free will" and its role in assessments of criminal responsibility. We discuss this issue below, and we return to it in more detail in Chapter Seven, in which we discuss the relationship between neuroscience and theories of criminal punishment.

the array of practical and theoretical neurolaw issues that we explore in subsequent chapters.

I. Neuro-Reductionism

The reductive impulse runs deep in philosophy. In fact, it runs so deep that one might be tempted to say that reductionism is at the very heart of many philosophical and scientific projects.[2] Although we acknowledge that a reductive explanatory strategy may sometimes prove to be successful,[3] we resist the urge to reductionism in this context. The most prominent attempt at neuro-reductionism, and the one to which we devote the most attention in this chapter, is "eliminative materialism."[4] We will discuss the claims of eliminative materialism through the work of one of

[2] There are many types of reductionist strategies. The primary types of reduction are (1) logical reduction, in which the true claims about one domain are equivalent to true claims in another domain and can be translated into the latter; (2) explanatory reduction, in which the phenomena described in one domain can be explained fully in the terms of another domain; and (3) nomic reduction, in which the laws of one domain can be derived from the laws in another domain. The first two types—logical and explanatory—are the ones typically employed in the neurolaw literature and on which we focus our discussion. Under these forms of reductionism, true claims about the mind and mental attributes are either identical with claims about the brain or can be explained fully in terms of brain states and brain processes. For an excellent dicussion of types of reductionist strategies, see Shahotra Sarkar, *Models of Reduction and Categories of Reductionism*, 91 SYNTHESE 167 (1991). For an excellent overview of reductionism in biology, see Ingo Brigandt & Alan Love, *Reductionism in Biology*, STANFORD ENCYCLOPEDIA OF PHILOSOPHY (2012), *available at* http://plato.stanford. edu/entries/reduction-biology/. Reductive explanations also appear to be a key feature of reasoning generally; *see* PHILIP JOHNSON LAIRD, HOW WE REASON 177 (2008) ("An explanation accounts for what we do not understand in terms of what we do understand: we cannot construct an explanatory model if the key concepts are not available to us.").

[3] *See, e.g.,* Brigandt & Love, *supra* note 2 (discussing ontological reductionism and the rejection of "vitalism" in biology).

[4] It is debatable whether "eliminative materialism" should even be considered a form of "reductionism" at all because, as its name suggests, it seeks to eliminate and not just reduce some mental attributes. We consider it a form of "reductionism" for our purposes, however, for two reasons. First, although the version we discuss seeks to eliminate our folk psychological vocabulary (and some mental entities presupposed by that vocabulary), it does not seek to eliminate the mind (or other mental attributes that fit with the best neuroscientific account of the mind). Second, like other forms of reductionism, it seeks to explain the mind (and any mental attributes relevant to law) in terms of the brain. It is this similarily that is most important for purposes of our discussion of reductionism and law. We acknowledge, however, that the differences between eliminative materialism and less radical forms of reductionism (which seek to explain but not eliminate) may also have important policy implications. For an excellent overview of eliminative materialism and its relationship to reductionism, see William Ramsey, *Eliminative Materialism*, STANFORD ENCYCLOPEDIA OF PHILOSOPHY (2007), *available at* http://plato.stanford.edu/entries/materialism-eliminative/.

its most prominent proponents, Patricia Churchland. In discussing the work of Professor Churchland, we will be making wider points about the reductionist impulse generally.

Eliminative materialism is an extreme form of naturalism, which itself is a reductionist approach to philosophical questions.[5] A precise formulation of naturalism is difficult to articulate, and no definition is canonical.[6] However, in its most general (and least controversial) form, naturalists reject "super-natural" entities and explanations that posit such entities, and they endorse the view that scientific investigation is the best (although not the only) route to discovering truths about the world.[7] We certainly do not reject all forms of naturalism.[8] To do so would be antiscience, and that is itself a problematic form of reductionism. We caution against the more specific idea that the mind and human behavior can be reduced to naturalistic, physical processes in the brain, at least not without loss of explanatory insight. We argue generally in this book against this type of reductionism, but we will say a few things in this chapter about naturalism in general.

One auspicious goal of proponents of the benefits of neuroscience is to "reduce affective states to brain states."[9] Affective states are at the core

---

[5] For an excellent introduction to the topic, see David Papineau, *Naturalism*, *in* STANFORD ENCYCLOPEDIA OF PHILOSOPHY (2007), *available at* http://plato.stanford.edu/entries/naturalism/.

[6] Here is Hilary Putnam's recent account of the role played by "naturalism":

> Today the most common use of the term "naturalism" might be described as follows: philosophers—perhaps even a majority of all the philosophers writing about issues in metaphysics, epistemology, philosophy of mind, and philosophy of language—announce in one or another conspicuous place in their essays and books that they are "naturalists" or that the view or account being defended is a "naturalist" one. This announcement, in its placing and emphasis, resembles the placing of the announcement in articles written in Stalin's Soviet Union that a view was in agreement with Comrade Stalin's; as in the case of the latter announcement, it is supposed to be clear that any view that is not "naturalist" (not in agreement with Comrade Stalin's view) is anathema and could not possibly be correct. A further common feature is that, as a rule, "naturalism" is not *defined*.

HILARY PUTNAM, *The Content and Appeal of "Naturalism"*, *in* PHILOSOPHY IN AN AGE OF SCIENCE: PHYSICS, MATHEMATICS, AND SKEPTICISM 109–10 (Mario De Caro & David Macarthur eds., 2012).

[7] *See* Papineau, *supra* note 5.

[8] For example, we endorse naturalist projects such as Alvin Goldman's work in epistemology; *see* ALVIN I. GOLDMAN, KNOWLEDGE IN A SOCIAL WORLD (1999); ALVIN I. GOLDMAN, EPISTEMOLOGY & COGNITION (1986), and Philip Kitcher's work in ethics; *see* PHILIP KITCHER, THE ETHICAL PROJECT (2011). Broadly speaking, we endorse the approach to the explanation of social phenomena found in CHARLES TAYLOR, *Interpretation and the Sciences of Man*, *in* PHILOSOPHY AND THE HUMAN SCIENCES: PHILOSOPHICAL PAPERS 2 (1985).

[9] *See* JOSEPH LEDOUX, THE EMOTIONAL BRAIN: THE MYSTERIOUS UNDERPINNINGS OF EMOTIONAL LIFE 302 (1998) ("The brain states and bodily responses are the fundamental facts

of human personhood: they make us what we are. Emotions, attitudes, and moods are all examples of affective states. Not satisfied with mere *correlation* of affective states with brain states, some neuroscientists want to *identify* an affective state with a brain state. Through this identification, they want to explain affective states solely in terms of brain states.

The motivation for such neuro-reductionism is not difficult to understand. If psychological states can be reduced to brain states, then an fMRI can quite literally "read another person's mind." In the legal context, such a powerful technology would have limitless potential. Eyewitness testimony could be immediately evaluated without error, lying would be eliminated, and "memory" of all kinds would be flawlessly evaluated for its efficacy and reliability.

There are both conceptual and empirical limitations to the aspirations of this kind of neuro-reductionism. Although we appreciate the technical limitations of fMRI,[10] we believe there are also deep conceptual problems. Consistent with the overall approach of this book, we concentrate on those aspects of neuro-reductionism that fall within the province of philosophy. We believe the conceptual problems facing neuro-reductionism are substantial and, in some instances, insurmountable. We do not mean to suggest, however, that none of the conceptual or empirical problems we identify can be solved. Rather, our point is that some of the presuppositions of the inquiries are so fraught with difficulty that they are best abandoned.

We discuss several legal examples in subsequent chapters, but to help set the stage for those discussions, consider a non-legal example that well illustrates these general points: love.[11] In an academic paper that received great attention, two researchers sought to identify the "neural basis" of love.[12] They described their project as an attempt "to explore the neural correlates of personal relationships."[13] The experiment

---

of an emotion, and the conscious feelings are the frills"); ANTONIO R. DAMASIO, DESCARTES' ERROR: EMOTION, REASON, AND THE HUMAN BRAIN (1996).

[10] Owen D. Jones et al., *Brain Imaging for Legal Thinkers: A Guide for the Perplexed*, 5 STAN. TECH. L. REV. (2009); Teneille Brown & Emily Murphy, *Through a Scanner Darkly: Functional Neuroimaging as Evidence of a Criminal Defendant's Past Mental States*, 62 STAN. L. REV. 1119 (2012); Henry T. Greely & Judy Illes, *Neuroscience-Based Lie Detection: The Urgent Need for Regulation*, 33 AM. J. L. & MED. 377 (2007).

[11] We are particularly enamored of this example for its ability to illustrate the important differences between conceptual and empirical questions.

[12] Andreas Bartels & Semir Zeki, *The Neural Basis of Romantic Love*, 11 NEUROREPORT 3829 (2000).

[13] *Id.* at 3832.

was elegantly simple. Each subject was shown four photographs, one of a person the subject deeply loved and the other three of friends. When the brain activity of the subject was recorded for the loved one and then the three friends, the differences between the cortical activity generated by the photograph of the loved one far exceeded that of the subject when shown photographs of three friends. On the basis of this evidence, the researchers concluded that romantic love could indeed be isolated in the brain, specifically "in the medial insula and the anterior cingulate cortex and, subcortically, in the caudate nucleus and the putamen, all bilaterally."[14]

We can put to one side the question of the efficacy of fMRI technology. As we discuss elsewhere, there are serious questions not about the technical functioning of fMRI but over exactly what it is that an fMRI shows us about the brain.[15] No one disputes that, at best, fMRI measures the flow of oxygenated blood.[16] There is no "direct access" to cognition through fMRI, let alone isolation of "the one place" where one cognitive function or another "occurs" in the brain.[17] The brain is a far more complicated organ than such characterizations would imply.

Raymond Tallis, who has commented often on the growing claims of neuro-reductionists, has an interesting critique of the claim that the neural basis of love has been identified.[18] As a good scientist, Tallis focuses on weaknesses in the experimental design of the study.[19] He finds three principal faults. His first objection is the oft-seen claim that the BOLD response[20] to stimuli fails to take account of the fact that a response to stimuli in any area of the brain is *in addition to* other areas of the brain already in an active state. The nub of this criticism is that the BOLD response is, at best, a *partial* measure of

[14] *Id.* at 3833. *See also* Andreas Bartels & Semir Zeki, *The Neural Correlates of Maternal and Romantic Love*, 21 NEUROIMAGE 1155 (2004).

[15] *See* WILLIAM R. UTTAL, THE NEW PHRENOLOGY: THE LIMITS OF LOCALIZING COGNITIVE PROCESSES IN THE BRAIN (2003); Russell A. Poldrack, *Can Cognitive Processes be Inferred from Neuroimaging Data?*, 10 TRENDS IN COG. SCI. 79 (2006).

[16] William G. Gibson, Les Farnell & Max. R. Bennett, *A Computational Model Relating Changes in Cerebral Blood Volume to Synaptic Activity in Neurons*, 70 NEUROCOMPUTING 1674 (2007); Marcus Raichle, *What Is an fMRI?*, *in* A JUDGE'S GUIDE TO NEUROSCIENCE: A CONCISE INTRODUCTION (Michael S. Gazzaniga & Jed S. Rakoff eds., 2010).

[17] *See* UTTAL, *supra* note 15; Poldrack, *supra* note 15; Russell A. Poldrack, *The Role of fMRI in Cognitive Neuroscience: Where Do We Stand?*, 18 CURR. OPINION NEUROBIOLOGY 223 (2008).

[18] RAYMOND TALLIS, APING MANKIND: NEUROMANIA, DARWINITIS, AND THE MISREPRESENTATION OF HUMANITY 76–77 (2011).

[19] *Id.* at 77.

[20] We provide in the Introduction a brief description of the BOLD [blood oxygen level dependent] response. *See also* Raichle, *supra* note 16.

brain activity. Thus, the experiment fails to capture (and thus explain) a great deal of activity in other areas of the brain.

Tallis' second objection, also technical, cuts deeper. Relying on data from other scientists,[21] Tallis makes the point that the additional activity measured by the BOLD response is only an average based on raw data that shows wide variations in response to *the same stimulus*. The point is that what is presented as an "average measurement" is not a steady reading but the averaging of widely divergent readings. It is the fact of wide divergence that suggests whatever is being measured cannot be well-correlated. In other words, if the same subject produces widely divergent responses to the same stimulus, it is not at all clear that *any particular thing* is being measured.

The third and final objection Tallis advances is, to our mind, the most important and the most telling. Moreover, the point is completely conceptual. Tallis asks the basic question thus: "Is love the sort of thing that can be measured like a response to a single picture?"[22] The simple fact of the matter is that love is not "a single enduring state"[23] (which it would need to be in order to be measured in the way the experimenters presuppose). Love includes many dispositions, including being anxious, frustrated, jealous, guilty, outraged, or excited. Again, Tallis's claim is conceptual: he is talking about the very idea of love. As we argued in Chapter One, the conceptual and the empirical are such that conceptual matters must be settled prior to any empirical claims.[24] To claim one has found the neural basis of love presupposes that one has gotten the concept of "love" right. We suspect Tallis is right: love is not the sort of thing that is apt for single stimulus measurement.

II. Eliminative Materialism and the "Theory" of Folk Psychology

Like neuro-reductionsts generally, neurolegalists aspire to reduce the explanation of all human behavior to the level of brain processes.

---

[21] TALLIS, *supra* note 18, at 77. As Tallis points out, even very simple actions (such as finger tapping) produce highly variable responses. *Id.* (*citing* J. Kong et al., *Test–Retest Study of fMRI Signal Change Evoked by Electro-Acupuncture Stimulation*, 34 NEUROIMAGE 1171 (2007)).

[22] *Id.* at 77.

[23] *Id.*

[24] We discuss this distinction in Chapter One.

Believing as they do that "the mind is the brain," neurolegalists have attempted to account for mental capacities, abilities, and processes solely at the level of cortical function. As an explanatory account of the nature of human agency, this reductionism aspires to nothing less than the replacement of our talk of beliefs, desires, and intentions with the language of neuroscience. Because all movement is "caused," no non-causal account of human action is permitted. In fact, the aspirations of some reductionists are greater still.

For what are called "eliminativists" or "eliminative materialists,"[25] all of our ordinary talk about mental life is just another "theory"—one that competes with scientific theories in an effort to accurately capture and characterize mental life.[26] Eliminativists, for example, see our verbal descriptions of pain, anger, memory, and recognition as theories (and bad ones at that) of these aspects of human behavior. True to its name, eliminative materialism seeks to eliminate our everyday language for explaining mental life—the language of "folk psychology."[27] The reason folk psychology will be eliminated, they contend, is that it is a bad explanatory theory. Paul Churchland describes the relationship between eliminative materialism and our ordinary conception of mental life this way:

Eliminative materialism is the thesis that our common-sense conception of psychological phenomena constitutes a *radically false theory*, a theory so fundamentally defective that both the principles and the ontology of that theory will eventually be displaced, rather than smoothly reduced, by completed neuroscience.[28]

Eliminative materialism is an extreme expression of a wider movement in philosophy: that is, philosophical naturalism.[29] Inspired by the work of the American philosopher W.V.O. Quine, philosophical

[25] For an introduction to eliminative materialism, see Ramsey, *supra* note 4.

[26] *See* Paul M. Churchland, *Eliminative Materialism and the Propositional Attitudes*, 78 J. PHIL. 67 (1981).

[27] *See* PATRICIA SMITH CHURCHLAND, NEUROPHILOSOPHY: TOWARD A UNIFIED SCIENCE OF THE MIND/BRAIN 299 (1986) ("By folk psychology, I mean that rough-hewn set of concepts, generalizations, and rules of thumb we all standardly use in explaining and predicting human behavior. Folk psychology is common-sense psychology—the psychological lore in virtue of which we explain behavior as the outcome of beliefs, desires, perceptions, expectations, goals, sensations, and so forth.").

[28] Churchland, *supra* note 26 (emphasis added).

[29] Patricia Churchland sees things this way. *See* Patricia Smith Churchland, *Moral Decision-Making and the Brain, in* NEUROETHICS: DEFINING THE ISSUES IN THEORY, PRACTICE, AND

naturalism has come to be the dominant paradigm in analytic philosophy.[30] Although "naturalism" can be understood in more than one way,[31] Quine elevated science to the ultimate tribunal of truth.[32] Quine deflated philosophy from an enterprise devoted to "conceptual analysis" to one that was "co-extensive with science."[33] The Quinean critique of "analyticity," which is at the heart of a more general attack on conceptual analysis, is important to the development of naturalism.[34] Although a complete treatment of the matter is beyond the scope of this discussion, it is fair to say that eliminative materialists hold the views that science is the ultimate arbiter of truth and that scientific inquiry can supplant philosophical inquiry. Quine himself, however, did not include the kind of neuro-reductionism under discussion within his naturalist program and, indeed, he explicitly rejected the reducibility or elimination of everyday mental concepts:

I acquiesce in what Davidson calls anomalous monism, also known as token physicalism: there is no mental substance, but there are irreducibly mental ways of grouping physical states and events....the mental predicates, for all their vagueness, have long interacted with one another, engendering age-old strategies for predicting and explaining human action. They complement natural science in their incommensurable way, and are indispensable both to the social sciences and to our everyday dealings.[35]

POLICY 3-16 (Judy Illes ed., 2006). We hasten to point out that there are naturalist-informed projects in philosophy that prescind from the hyper-reductionism evinced by Churchland. In epistemology, see, for example, GOLDMAN, *supra* note 8; in ethics, see, for example, KITCHER, *supra* note 8.

[30]   See W.V.O. QUINE, *Epistemology Naturalized, in* ONTOLOGICAL RELATIVITY AND OTHER ESSAYS (1969); PUTNAM, *supra* note 6; Papineau, *supra* note 5.

[31]   *See* Papineau, *supra* note 5.

[32]   The particular version of naturalism associated with Quine is so-called "replacement" naturalism and refers to the replacement of traditional philosophical inquiry with scientific inquiry. In Quine's original essay, the "replacement" was epistemology with psychology. *See* QUINE, *supra* note 30 ("Epistemology, or something like it, simply falls into place as a chapter of psychology and hence of natural science.").

[33]   *Id.* For discussions of this aspect of Quine's work, see HILARY KORNBLITH, *What Is Naturalistic Epistemology?, in* NATURALIZING EPISTEMOLOGY (Hilary Kornblith ed., 2d ed. 1997); Richard Feldman, *Naturalized Epistemology, in* STANFORD ENCYCLOPEDIA OF PHILOSOPHY (2001), *available at* http://plato.stanford.edu/entries/epistemology-naturalized/. For a discussion of naturalism in the context of legal theory, see BRIAN LEITER, NATURALIZING JURISPRUDENCE: ESSAYS ON AMERICAN LEGAL REALISM AND NATURALISM IN LEGAL PHILOSOPHY (2007).

[34]   *See* W.V.O. QUINE, *Two Dogmas of Empiricism, in* FROM A LOGICAL POINT OF VIEW (1980).

[35]   W.V.O. QUINE, PURSUIT OF TRUTH (2d ed. 1992). *See also* DONALD DAVIDSON, *Mental Events, in* ESSAYS ON ACTIONS AND EVENTS 207 (2d ed. 2001).

It is against this philosophical background that we now come to one of the most interesting and controversial claims of eliminative materialism, at least as advanced by Patricia Churchland. Over the course of several decades, Churchland has championed the notion that our mental vocabulary can be eliminated in favor of the physical. In true naturalist spirit, this reduction will allow the brain sciences to answer philosophical questions about the mind. Although the spirit of Churchland's undertaking is surely reductionist, it would be an understatement to describe her approach as anything less than full-scale elimination of folk psychology and its replacement by the physical. In her book *Neurophilosophy*,[36] she puts the matter this way:

By "eliminative materialism" I mean the view that holds:

1. that folk psychology is a theory;
2. that it is a theory whose inadequacies entail that it must eventually be substantially revised or replaced outright (hence "eliminative"); and
3. that what will ultimately replace folk psychology will be the conceptual framework of a matured neuroscience (hence "materialism").[37]

Before the question of elimination can arise, we must consider whether folk psychology even constitutes a "theory" (Churchland's first tenet). Why might eliminativists be tempted to think so? Theories involve the application of concepts. Folk psychology contains concepts such as "intention," "belief," and "desire," which people apply to themselves and others. Moreover, folk psychology is used to explain and predict behavior (based on common-sense generalizations that employ these concepts). Therefore, so the argument goes, it qualifies as a theory.[38]

How plausible is the claim that our everyday language of psychological concepts is a theory? We believe this claim is mistaken. Our workaday concepts of belief, desire, perception, sensation, and intention are not theories or theoretical terms. A network of concepts is not "a speculative assumption or theory."[39] The vocabulary with which we make sense of our mental and social life is just that: a vocabulary.

[36] CHURCHLAND, *supra* note 27.

[37] *Id.* at 396. *See also* Churchland, *supra* note 28 and accompanying text (referring to folk psychology as a "radically false theory").

[38] The notion that folk psychology is a theory is defended in detail by Paul Churchland in Churchland, *supra* note 26 ("the semantics of the terms in our familiar mentalistic vocabulary is to be understood in the same manner as the semantics of theoretical terms generally: the meaning of any theoretical terms is fixed or constituted by the network of laws in which it figures.").

[39] M.R. BENNETT & P.M.S. HACKER, PHILOSOPHICAL FOUNDATIONS OF NEUROSCIENCE 369 (2003) (distinguishing networks of concepts from theories).

Our use of this vocabulary is not generally a theoretical exercise. It is behavior. When someone stubs a toe and utters "Ouch!," he is not making a theoretical claim about what is going on in his brain. We see another's joy in his face, anger when his fist hits the table, and fear as he cringes in horror. These actions are all behaviors. As we see it, the fundamental error of the eliminativist proposal is the attempt to reduce behavior to "theory" and then to argue that the theory is defective because it cannot "explain" the inner workings of persons. Our everyday vocabulary was never intended to operate as such a theory, does not function as such, and, thus, cannot be tested as such.

Nevertheless, according to eliminative materialism, the belief that we control our actions through our intentions is one that will be consigned to the dustbin of history in much the same way as our belief that the earth is at the center of the solar system or that the earth is flat.[40] Behavior is not driven by intentions, desires, and beliefs: rather, behavior is the product of causal forces. The promise of neuroscience is to ultimately reveal "the mechanical processes" that cause behavior.[41]

Bennett and Hacker look at the context of children learning psychological concepts as a counter to the claim of eliminative materialists that folk psychology is a theory.[42] When a child acquires language, he or she is able to go from screams in response to pain to being able to express distress at being in pain (e.g., "my toe hurts") to later reporting that he or she was in pain (e.g., "I hurt my toe yesterday"). The conclusion that Bennett and Hacker draw seems quite plausible to us: that is, in learning how to use psychological terms in expressive and reporting contexts, a child is learning language-games. These activities are not "theoretical" but behavioral. What is being learned is how psychological terms are woven into the fabric of behavior. In this way, psychological "concepts" are not like scientific concepts. As they say, "[o]ne needs no theory, folkish or otherwise, to hear or read the expressed thoughts of another."[43] We think this is right.

---

[40] *See* P.M.S. Hacker, *Eliminative Materialism, in* WITTGENSTEIN AND CONTEMPORARY PHILOSOPHY OF MIND 83–84 (Severin Schroeder ed., 2001) ("Eliminative materialism is not a serious option, since it is not a serious possibility for the study of human nature and behaviour to jettison the concepts that define its subject matter and the use of which in discourse is partly constitutive of its subjects. Not only could students of human nature not abandon these concepts and continue to study psychology, but further, it would thereby be shown that that creature was not a person, nor even a human being.").

[41] *See* Joshua Greene & Jonathan Cohen, *For Law, Neuroscience Changes Nothing and Everything, in* LAW & THE BRAIN (Semir Zeki & Oliver Goodenough eds., 2006).

[42] BENNETT & HACKER, *supra* note 39, at 369.

[43] *Id.* at 370.

III. Two Examples of Neuro-Reductionism and Its Implications for Law

We now look at two examples of what neuro-reductionism might imply for the law. The first example continues our discussion of Patricia Churchland's work, examining how she has applied her approach to a substantive area of philosophy: that of ethics (and its relation to law).[44] The second example discusses an influential article by Joshua Greene and Jonathan Cohen.[45] Both examples share the same reductive starting point—"the mind is the brain"—but they reach very different conclusions about what this means for free will, criminal punishment, and law. This disagreement by itself suggests that there are complex normative issues surrounding the relationship between neuroscience and law (even when there is a shared, highly reductive conception of mind in place).[46]

Consistent with her views as outlined above, Churchland takes the position that ethics and law need to be rethought from the ground up in the light of developments in neuroscience. Her thesis is simply stated: "Developments in the biological sciences give rise to difficult but important issues concerning the possible revision and improvement of particular legal practices, especially in the criminal law."[47]

In her recent book *Braintrust*,[48] Churchland takes up the question of the source and evolution of values in more detail. She asks the question "What is it to be fair?"[49] Given the way she poses the question, one might think the inquiry would be a search for the meaning or content of the concept of "fairness." She explains that during most of her career as a philosopher, she shied away from such questions—that is, questions of "value." Her reasons were simple: ethical theory was just a matter of "opinion" with "no strong connection to evolution or to the brain."[50] Although not denying the importance of the social in answering the question "Where do values come from?," Churchland believes that the

---

[44] *See* Churchland, *supra* note 29.

[45] *See* Greene & Cohen, *supra* note 41.

[46] We return to, and discuss in more detail, the relationships among neuroscience, free will, and criminal punishment in Chapter Seven.

[47] *See* Churchland, *supra* note 29, at 15.

[48] Patricia S. Churchland, Braintrust: What Neuroscience Tells Us about Morality (2011).

[49] *Id.* at 2.

[50] *Id.*

main part of the story needs to be told from the point of view of "the neural platform for moral behavior."[51] In other words, if we really want to know about morality, we need to look inside the brain.

In an article[52] written a few years before her recent book, Churchland details just how she thinks one should go about the task of clearly thinking about the relationship of law and morality to the brain. In the opening sentences, Churchland boldly asserts that "it is increasingly evident that moral standards, practices, and policies reside in our neurobiology."[53] What is obviously of interest in Churchland's formulation is that it raises the question of how we decide which moral standards are "correct." Standard approaches to the subject are seemingly rejected, as Churchland is of the view that "traditional assumptions concerning the roots of moral knowledge have been exposed as untenable."[54] Morality is not a matter of debate but is, as Churchland argues, rooted in our "nature and biology."[55] In short, the source of moral standards is biology (specifically neurophysiology).

Churchland believes that ethicists have simply been "looking in the wrong place" when it comes to ethical standards. She maintains that "it is increasingly evident that moral standards, practices and policies reside in our neurobiology."[56] Churchland is quite literal when she writes that neural networks and processes are "the basis for moral standards and practices."[57]

In terms of the theme of reductionism, Churchland is clear that the line between morality and other enquiries is to be elided. "Brains make decisions,"[58] she argues. The brain is "a causal machine."[59] As the brain processes decisions over time, it adapts itself to its environment. As the evidence from evolutionary biology and related fields continues to confirm, "there is *only* the physical brain and its body; there is no non-physical soul, spooky stuff, or ectoplasmic mind-whiffle."[60]

---

[51] *Id.* at 3.

[52] Churchland, *supra* note 29.

[53] *Id.* at 3.

[54] *Id.*

[55] *Id.* We note that one can view morality as rooted in our nature and biology and still be essentially a matter of debate and philosophical argument. *See* KITCHER, *supra* note 8.

[56] Churchland, *supra* note 29, at 3.

[57] *Id.*

[58] *Id.* at 4.

[59] *Id.* at 5.

[60] *Id.* Once again, rejecting "spooky stuff" does not entail Churchland's reductive picture. In addition to KITCHER, *supra* note 8, the work of John Mikhail, which we discuss in Chapter Three, is another example of a naturalist project that rejects "spooky" stuff as well

"Cause" is an important concept in the explanation of human action. It is central to debates about free will, and no explanation of human action is complete without an account of the role of cause in behavior.[61] Churchland wastes no time attacking what she perceives as the completely false dichotomy between causally determined "choice" and unfettered choice (the paradigm of "free will"). What is the relationship between free choice and causal effects? For Churchland, it is all a matter of brain events. The problem, she argues, is that we simply do not understand what "free choice" means.

Free choice is not uncaused. Invoking Hume, Churchland claims that free choice "is caused by certain appropriate conditions that are different from the set of conditions that result in involuntary behavior."[62] The problem with our conception of "choice" is that we think nothing can be a "real" choice unless it "came about through pure randomness."[63] But this is an illusion, she contends.

But if choice is a matter of causes, then when are we ever responsible for our choices? Here Churchland turns to the law, specifically civil and criminal law. Interestingly, she characterizes the question of responsibility as "empirical." Again citing Hume, she writes: "Hume can be construed as proposing a hypothesis: there are discoverable empirical differences between the causes of accountable behavior and excusable behavior."[64] The trick, one might say, is articulating just what those differences are and how they make a difference to assessments of responsibility for action. Churchland's argument is well-developed and worthy of careful articulation.

as Churchland's reductionism. Churchland argues against the idea of innate moral rules and principles in CHURCHLAND, *supra* note 48, at 103–11. In short, there are many ways to be a naturalist about morality. For a clear overview of the main possibilities, see BRIAN LEITER, NIETZSCHE ON MORALITY 3–6 (2002) (distinguishing methodological and substantive naturalist commitments).

[61] Among philosophers who otherwise reject a reductive, eliminative picture, there is substantial disagreement about whether and how best to characterize the causal relationships between mental events and behavior. Prominent non-reduction causal accounts include DAVIDSON, *supra* note 35; FRED DRETSKE, EXPLAINING BEHAVIOR: REASONS IN A WORLD OF CAUSES (1988). By contrast, for a recent argument that explanations of behavior in terms of reasons, etc. are rational/teleological, not causal, explanations, see P.M.S. HACKER, HUMAN NATURE: THE CATEGORICAL FRAMEWORK 199–232 (2007). These philosophical controversies are outside our scope—however one comes down on them, the conclusion regarding neuro-reductionism is the same. For recent discussions of the relevant philosophical issues, see ERIC MARCUS, RATIONAL CAUSATION (2012); ROBERT J. MATTHEWS, THE MEASURE OF MIND: PROPOSITIONAL ATTITUDES AND THEIR ATTRIBUTION (2010).

[62] Churchland, *supra* note 29, at 8.
[63] *Id.*
[64] *Id.*

Starting with Aristotle, Churchland notes that the law's "default condition" toward responsibility is that we are responsible for the effects
of our actions. We are excused from responsibility only under "unusual
circumstances."[65] The paradigm case of "unusual circumstance" is
insanity, where the actor "fail[s] to understand the nature of what he is
doing."[66] Churchland fully appreciates the law's *mens rea* requirements,
specifically the gradations of responsibility expressed as an action that
is purposeful (intentional), knowing, reckless, or negligent.[67] Citing
M'Naghten,[68] Churchland notes that for a successful invocation of the
defense of insanity, the law requires that the defendant prove that "the
cognitive impairment rendered him unable to appreciate the criminal
nature of the act."[69]

How do we make judgments of responsibility? Rejecting anything
like "some abstract relationship between a Platonic conception of justice and contra-causal willing,"[70] Churchland maintains that responsibility is rooted in "the fundamental social need for civil behavior."[71]
She further maintains that it falls to the criminal justice system "to
enforce laws regarded as necessary to maintain and protect civil society."[72] This is true, of course, but the key question in the criminal law
is the criteria for "responsibility," because we punish bad acts for which
we are responsible. Thus, it is critical that neuroscientific developments
contribute to this foundational undertaking. Churchland recognizes
the challenge: "Until the second half of the twentieth century, it was
not really possible to explore systematically the neurobiological differences between a voluntary and an involuntary action. However, developments in neuroscience in the last 50 years have made it possible
to begin to probe the neurobiological basis for decision-making and
impulse control."[73]

Churchland focuses on control. Her question is simple: when is a
brain in control?[74] When lack of control reaches an extreme point, it

[65] *Id.* at 9. We discuss criminal law doctrine, including *mens rea* requirements and the
insanity defense, in detail in Chapter Five.
[66] *Id.*
[67] *See* MODEL PENAL CODE § 2.02.
[68] Regina v. M'Naghten, 9 Eng. Rep. 718 (1843).
[69] Churchland, *supra* note 29, at 10.
[70] *Id.*
[71] *Id.*
[72] *Id.*
[73] *Id.*
[74] *Id.* at 10–12.

may be that the person in question is "insane." Insanity is measured both by "being in control" and in appreciating that one's actions are, in fact, one's own.[75] In terms of the physiology of the brain, a wide variety of cortical structures are in play: "structures that appear to have a pre-eminent role are the anterior and medial."[76] But the situation is, as Churchland sees it, far from clear. She writes: "On the surface...data from lesion studies, anatomy, neuropharmacology and so forth do not seem to coalesce into an orderly hypothesis concerning the neural basis for control."[77] Nevertheless, "it may be possible to sketch a framework for such a hypothesis."[78]

Churchland does, indeed, sketch such a hypothesis. Simply put, she calculates a variety of "N parameters" for various regions of the brain, which, when those parameters are met, the brain can be said to be "in control."[79] She puts the matter thus:

The hypothesis on offer is that within the described n-dimensional parameter space, there is a volume such that when a brain's values for those parameters are within that volume, the brain is "in control", in the sense in which I am using that term, i.e. the person's behavior exhibits those features implying that the person is in control. I suspect that the in-control volume of the control-space is rather large relative to the not-in-control space, suggesting that different brains may be in control by virtue of somewhat different values of the parameters. To put it simply, there may be many ways of being in control.[80]

How does a brain "being in control" connect with choice and, ultimately, responsibility? Churchland maintains that "[t]he important core of the idea of free will consists not in the notion of uncaused choice, whatever that might be, but in choices that are made deliberately, knowingly, and intentionally; where the agent is in control."[81] A brain must be "in control" for a human being to make choices. That cannot be disputed. We agree with Churchland that "'in control' can be characterized neurobiologically [vis-à-vis n parameters]."[82] This is fine, as far as it goes: but does it go far enough? We think it does not.

[75] *Id.* at 11.
[76] *Id.* at 12.
[77] *Id.* at 13.
[78] *Id.*
[79] *Id.* at 13–14.
[80] *Id.* at 14.
[81] *Id.* at 15.
[82] *Id.*

Churchland recognizes the problem. She claims that developments in cognitive neuroscience will "give rise to difficult but important issues concerning the possible revision and improvement of particular legal practices, especially in the criminal law."[83] Solving these problems will be the remit of more than one group of interested parties, for "[n]o single professional or social group is adequately equipped to solve these problems."[84] Again, we agree. What is missing from Churchland's reductionist account of control and responsibility is any mention of the normative side of the equation. Let us explain.

We have no doubt that there is a biological basis to the control/ out-of-control distinction. Just as it is not possible to have beliefs without a well-functioning brain, it is not possible for one to be "in control" of one's actions without a well-functioning brain. As we see it, there are at least three difficulties with Churchland's position as it relates to law, all of which devolve to the conclusion that reductionism of the type favored by Churchland fails to reach the problems that ethics and the law (both civil and criminal) face.

The first response to Churchland is a demurrer: so what? Suppose Churchland is right (surely she is) about certain parts of the brain enabling human beings to control their actions. What does that fact tell us about setting normative standards? For example, suppose someone is "in control" of his actions but fails to close the gate to his backyard, thereby allowing his Rottweiler to escape and bite a neighbor's child? What does being "in control" really tell us about this situation, one that is fundamental to tort law and the notion of responsibility? Our answer is "nothing." As we argued earlier, both in this chapter and others,[85] there are empirical and conceptual questions. The empirical question, "What sort of brain must a human being have to be able to form intentions?" is no answer to the question of whether one is or should be held responsible for intentional acts.

A second problem. Imagine a person with a brain that is "in control." He forms the intention to take the life of another person, a lifelong enemy. He rationally calculates the risks of the action, takes the life of the other person with minimal risk, and has no regrets. Surely this person is "responsible" for his actions. But why? Does the vocabulary of "in control" tell us anything about responsibility? Does

---

[83]   *Id.* (citation omitted).
[84]   *Id.*
[85]   *See* the Introduction and Chapter One.

this person bear more responsibility for his action than one who accidentally takes the life of another through an act of negligence? Again, Churchland has no answers to these questions. Neuro-reductionism has the effect of "flattening" these normative differences—differences that must be taken into account in any sufficiently adequate explanation of "responsibility."

Finally, let us consider a difficult case. It is possible to identify persons who engage in all manner of socially undesirable conduct, everything from pedophilia to alcoholism. We have no doubt that, on average, the brains of such persons are different from "normal" brains, and that these differences may be clearly visible in fMRI studies. But having a proclivity does not give one a "free pass" when it comes to the law.[86] If one has a proclivity to drink alcohol in excess, then one is obliged (out of self-interest, if nothing else) to see that one is not in situations where this proclivity will be actuated or, if it is, it will not harm others. What does reductionism tell us about this state of affairs? Again, nothing.

These cases put the lie to Churchland's central theme: that is, that "it is increasingly evident that moral standards, practices, and policies reside in our neurobiology."[87] This is simply false. One can infer almost nothing from the state of our brains when it comes to the difficult normative questions underlying legal standards. Increased knowledge of brain chemistry will not answer normative questions about responsibility.

Our second example focuses on Greene and Cohen's treatment of voluntary conduct and the problem of free will.[88] According to Greene and Cohen, the attribution of free will to ourselves is an ongoing act of self-deception about our volitional powers. The promise of neuroscience is to talk us out of our illusions of self-control.

With a nod to the work of Daniel Wegner, Greene and Cohen state the problem of free will this way:

We feel as if we are uncaused causers, and therefore granted a degree of independence from the deterministic flow of the universe, because we are unaware of the deterministic processes that operate in our own heads. Our

---

[86] We discuss this issue in more detail from a doctrinal perspective in Chapter Five and from a theoretical perspective in Chapter Seven.

[87] Churchland, *supra* note 29, at 3.

[88] Greene & Cohen, *supra* note 41.

actions appear to be caused by our mental states, but not by physical states of our brains, and so we imagine that we are metaphysically special, that we are non-physical causes of physical events.[89]

If we are not metaphysically special, how and why does it matter? If we are not the uncaused causers of our behavior, and "choice" is an illusion, then there can be no such thing as "responsibility." We are no more responsible for our actions than the apple that falls from the tree. Both the apple and we are simply material objects beholden to the physical laws of the universe. We are not special. Our minds do not animate physical objects (i.e., our bodies). Like other folk psychological notions, "mind" is an illusion. Based on these considerations, Greene and Cohen go on to argue that neuroscience will undermine desert-based justifications for criminal punishment by showing that no one is truly in control of his or her actions and deserving of punishment.[90]

The central notion in this reductionist critique of our ordinary talk of mental life is "cause." In explaining human action, all reductionists (including eliminative materialists) assert that human action can be accounted for in strictly physical terms.[91] When we say that one thing caused another, we usually mean that one action or event brought about another. For example, when a bowling ball hits the pins, we say that the pins fell over because they were hit by the ball. The reason the pins fell over is because they were hit by a bowling ball. One event—the pins falling over—was caused by another: the bowling ball hitting the pins. The explanation of the action of the pins falling over is completely physical and causal. Can all events be explained thus?

Consider an event as simple as a person stopping her car at a red traffic light. Two events together comprise the event "stopping at a red traffic light": the illumination of the red lamp and the pressure of the driver's foot on the brake. Do the light waves from the lamp "cause" the pressure on the brake pedal? Surely not in the way the bowling ball causes the pins to fall over. It is true that the traffic light "causes" us to stop the car. But the "cause" for stopping the car cannot be explained solely by a physical process. By itself, the red light does not "cause" us to stop (i.e., it is not in

---

[89] *Id.* at 218–19.

[90] *Id.* at 213–21. We critique this aspect of their argument in Chapter Seven.

[91] The technical way of putting the matter is to say that behavior (the *explanandum*) can be accounted for in strictly physicalist terms (the *explanans*).

virtue of the power of the light waves that emanate from it); rather, we stop because of the status of the light in an important social convention (i.e., the red light is a reason for stopping). The light functions as a signal because we have conferred this status upon it. Apart from that status, the traffic light is nothing more than an illuminated bulb inside a housing (notice that qua physical object, nothing establishes the lamp's status as a traffic light).

The reductionist wants to eliminate the intentional element (i.e., reasons for action) in the explanation of behavior. In other words, the reductionist wants all explanation to be in terms of causes and not rules or reasons. When we ask the question "Why did you stop at the red traffic light?" the answer will appeal to a traffic rule. Although the rule accounts for your stopping (i.e., the rule is the reason for stopping), a causal account of the event cannot, without more, explain what has happened.

Reasons for action are not causes like the bowling ball is a cause.[92] The reason we stop our car at a red light cannot be explained in the manner of a bowling ball striking a set of pins. The latter event is solely a matter of physical cause whereas the former is one of reasons for action. Unlike the pins, we choose whether to stop at the red light. If we fail to stop, we run the risk of sanction. The pins in a bowling alley have no such choice: they are "compelled" to fall over by force of the impact of the bowling ball. We are neither bowling balls nor pins. We have a choice. It is this choice that is the ground of responsibility, which cannot be accounted for in eliminativist terms.

Finally, notice how far away the conclusion of Greene and Cohen is from Churchland's. For Churchland, recognizing "the mind is the brain" is the basis for delineating a normative distinction between legal responsibility and excusable behavior. For Greene and Cohen, by contrast, recognizing the "mind is the brain" is the basis for eliminating any coherent notion of legal responsibility. Both attempts to flatten the inherent normativity in legal responsibility end up producing oddly shaped, but opposing, pictures. For Churchland, the mind is the brain and so normativity must be in the brain. For Greene and Cohen, the mind is the brain and, so, if normativity is anywhere it must be in the brain—but because they do not see it there, they conclude it

---

[92] Strictly speaking, reasons are not efficient (i.e., mechanical) causes. On the role of causation in non-reductive accounts, see *supra* note 61. For further discussion of causal and normative explanations of behavior, see JEFF COULTER & WES SHARROCK, BRAIN, MIND, AND HUMAN BEHAVIOUR IN CONTEMPORARY COGNITIVE SCIENCE 68–81 (2007).

is nowhere. We reject both pictures.[93] But their diametric opposition provides a nice reminder that nothing necessarily follows from information about the brain in answering the complex normative questions at the heart of law and public policy, not even for those who readily and heartily endorse the reductive view that "the mind is the brain." It is to *that* problematic picture to which we now turn.

IV. Conceptions of Mind and the Role of Neuroscience in Law

What neuroscience can tell us about the mind, and about the mind's relationship to law, will depend on our conception of mind. Put more simply, before neuroscience can tell us about something in particular, we must have some idea about what exactly it is that neuroscience is meant to illuminate (otherwise, how else can we know what to look for?). Empirical claims about neuroscience and its relationship to the mind will presuppose some conception of the mind (and the phenomena picked out by the concept of mind). Whether this conception makes sense will affect the cogency of the claims. Hilary Putnam expresses the point clearly in a recent book:

The idea that there is a scientific problem of "the nature of the mind" presupposes the picture of the mind and its thoughts, or "contents," as *objects* (so that investigating the nature of thought is just like investigating the nature of water or heat). I want to suggest that philosophy can expose this presupposition as a confusion.[94]

Consider an analogy. Suppose an empirical claim about lying presupposes that lying includes nondeceptive, truthful utterances. Although

---

[93] But, for the reasons we explore in Chapter Seven, our sympathies are with Churchland on this divide, as we too think that neuroscience does not undermine criminal responsibility. Like Churchland, we think that a distinction between legal responsibility and excuse is coherent and tenable; however, unlike her, we think the basis for this distinction is located outside the brain.

[94] HILARY PUTNAM, *Aristotle's Mind and the Contemporary Mind, in* PHILOSOPHY IN AN AGE OF SCIENCE, *supra* note 6, at 599. He adds: "There are, to be sure, empirical facts about thought, as about everything else, and science can reasonably hope to discover new—and even some very surprising—empirical facts. But the idea that these facts (or some of them) must add up to something called 'an account of the nature of mind' is an illusion—one of the dominant illusions of a certain part of contemporary science." *Id.*

the claim may use the word "lying," it would not be telling us about actual lying because the conception being presupposed is mistaken.[95] The claim involves a conceptual error. In order to illuminate the actual phenomena picked out by our concepts, empirical claims must employ correct criteria in applying the concepts.[96] As with lying, this is the case with regard to a host of other concepts that we discuss in this book (for example, knowledge, memory, belief, perception, and intent). It is also true with regard to the concept of mind itself.

Two conceptions dominate neurolaw discussions: Cartesian dualism and the neuro-reductionism we discussed above. The former typically serves as a foil for proposals that endorse the latter. But this is a false dichotomy. We present a third possibility below, one that we contend is more plausible.

The first conception is the classic one articulated by Descartes in the *Meditations*.[97] The Cartesian view relies upon a notion of *substance dualism*. Under this conception, the mind is thought to be some type of non-material (i.e., nonphysical) entity or thing that is a part of the human being and is somehow in causal interaction with the person's body.[98] The non-material substance that constitutes the mind is the source and location of the person's mental life—her thoughts, beliefs, sensations, and conscious experiences.[99] Early neuroscientists were avowed Cartesian dualists and set themselves the task of figuring out how the non-material substance known as the mind causally interacted with the physical brain and body of a person.[100]

This conception was later repudiated by neuroscientists[101] and is typically disavowed by neurolegalists. The second conception of mind

[95] We discuss the concept of lying in more detail in Chapter Four.

[96] In referring to "criteria" for applying concepts, we acknowledge that the criteria may be defeasible. We do not presuppose that the concepts necessarily have (1) sharp or fixed boundaries, (2) essences, or (3) necessary and sufficient conditions.

[97] RENÉ DESCARTES, *Meditation VI, in* MEDITATION ON FIRST PHILOSOPHY (John Cottingham trans., 1996).

[98] For an overview of this conception, see Howard Robinson, *Dualism, in* STANFORD ENCYCLOPEDIA OF PHILOSOPHY (2011), *available at* http://plato.stanford.edu/entries/dualism/.

[99] The classic philosophical critique of this conception is GILBERT RYLE, THE CONCEPT OF MIND (1949).

[100] Bennett and Hacker provide a detailed discussion of Descartes' influence on early neuroscientists and the Cartesian conception of mind they adopted. *See* BENNETT & HACKER, *supra* note 39, at 23–67.

[101] Michael Gazzaniga asserts that "98 or 99 percent" of contemporary cognitive neuroscientists subscribe to the reduction of mind to brain in explaining mental phenomena. *See* Richard Monastersky, *Religion on the Brain*, CHRON. HIGHER ED. A15 (May 26, 2006).

is that the mind is identical with the brain. This is the conception endorsed by Churchland, Greene, Cohen, and other neurolegalists. Under this conception, the mind is a material (i.e., physical) part of the human being—the brain—that is distinct from, but is in causal interaction with, the rest of the body. The brain is the *subject* of the person's mental properties (the brain thinks, feels, intends, and knows) and is the *location* of the person's conscious experiences. This conception is deeply problematic. It fails to recognize the proper criteria for the attribution of many of our mental concepts, and it incoherently ascribes psychological attributes to the brain (rather than the person). Notice that this second conception, although repudiating substance dualism, keeps intact the same logical, formal structure. The mind is a kind of entity that interacts with the body (one inner agent is replaced by another: the Cartesian soul by the brain).[102] Conceptual problems arise for neuro-reductionism because the mind-is-the-brain conception is still operating with a formal Cartesian structure.

We reject both of these conceptions and suggest a third. The mind is not an entity or *substance* at all (whether nonphysical (Cartesian) or physical (the brain)). To have a mind is to possess an array of rational and emotional powers, capacities, and abilities exhibited in thought, feeling, and action.[103] The roots of this conception are in Aristotle.[104] Under this conception, the mind is not a separate part of the person that causally interacts with the person's body. It is simply the mental powers, abilities, and capacities possessed by humans. Likewise, the ability to see is not a part of the eye that interacts with other parts of the physical eye, the ability to fly is not a separate part of an airplane, and a car's horsepower is not a separate part of the car in causal interaction with its engine.[105] Under this conception, the question of the mind's location in the body makes no sense just as the location of eyesight within the eye makes no sense.[106]

---

[102] For further discussion of the Cartesianism presupposed by neuro-reductionism, see BENNETT & HACKER, *supra* note 39, at 231–35.

[103] *See id.* at 62–63 ("The mind...is not a substance of any kind.")

[104] *See id.* at 12–23; PUTNAM, *supra* note 94; Hilary Putnam & Martha Nussbaum, *Changing Aristotle's Mind, in* ESSAYS ON ARISTOTLE'S "DE ANIMA" 27 (M.C. Nussbaum & A.O. Rorty eds., 1992).

[105] *See* BENNETT & HACKER, *supra* note 39, at 15.

[106] *Id.* at 46 ("the question of how the mind interacts with the body is not a question that can arise for Aristotle. Within the framework of Aristotelian thought...the very question is as senseless as the question 'How can the shape of the table interact with the wood of the table.'").

As with the second conception, this Aristotelian conception is also materialist/physicalist in an important sense: if we took away or changed the physical structures in the brain, the mind would go away or change as well. Under this conception, a properly working brain is necessary for having a mind, but the mind is not identical with the brain. The criteria for the ascription of mental attributes to human beings are constituted by their manifold behaviors; it is people who think, feel, intend, and know (not parts of their brains).[107]

What does accepting this third conception mean for law? As we will discuss in subsequent chapters, this conception in no way implies that neuroscience cannot make valuable contributions to law. Because certain structures may be necessary to exercise various capacities or to engage in certain behavior, neuroscience may contribute greatly by identifying these necessary conditions as well as by showing that, because of injury or deformity, a person lacks them.[108] Neuroscience may also provide inductive evidence of various mental activities. For example, if certain neurological events could be shown to be empirically well-correlated with lying, then neuroscientific evidence may be probative in determining whether a witness is lying.[109]

Importantly, however, this third conception implies important limitations on how neuroscience can contribute to law. We delineate these conceptual limitations in evaluating claims made on behalf of

[107] Although neurolaw discussions typically invoke or presuppose the first two conceptions discussed above (substance dualism and neuro-reductionism), this third conception is more in line with the conceptions of mind shared by many influential modern philosophers, despite otherwise significant differences among their views. On this list we would include Quine (see *supra* note 35 and accompanying text), as well as Wittgenstein, Davidson, Ryle, Sellars, Rorty, Putnam, Dennett, Searle, Fodor, Brandom, McDowell, and countless others. For recent discussions of Wittgenstein, mind, and mental attributes, see WITTGENSTEIN AND THE PHILOSOPHY OF MIND (Jonathan Ellis & Daniel Guevara eds., 2012). Another prominent idea in contemporary philosophy of mind is the so-called "extended mind" thesis, in which the mind is thought to extend not only outside the head but outside the body as well (and to include other objects in the world—for example, a notebook). *See* Andy Clark & David J. Chalmers, *The Extended Mind*, 58 ANALYSIS 7 (1998); ANDY CLARK, SUPERSIZING THE MIND: EMBODIMENT, ACTION, AND COGNITIVE EXTENSION (2008). We put aside this possibility for purposes of our discussions in this book, but notice that it also implies that neuro-reductionism (that the mind is in the head) is false. For recent discussions of the "extended mind" thesis in the context of ethics and public policy, see NEIL LEVY, NEUROETHICS: CHALLENGES FOR THE 21ST CENTURY (2007); Walter Glannon, *Our Brains Are Not Us*, 23 BIOETHICS 321 (2009).

[108] *See* Chapter Five.

[109] *See* Chapter Four.

neuroscience for law. In order to illuminate our mental concepts, claims made on behalf of neuroscience for law must presuppose correct criteria in applying these concepts. For example, neuroscience cannot tell us where the brain thinks, believes, knows, intends, or makes decisions. People (not brains) think, believe, know, intend, and make decisions. Moreover, the presence of neurological activity is not *sufficient* for the attribution of these concepts to persons; it is not the measure of thinking, knowing, intending, or deciding.

The conceptual issues we have raised in this chapter, and in the previous one, allow for greater clarity and understanding of the tremendous empirical discoveries of contemporary neuroscience. These fundamental conceptual issues are of critical importance because they inform and underlie every important question and debate about the ways in which the law can and cannot, ought and ought not, make use of these neurological discoveries.

3

Neuroscience and Legal Theory: Jurisprudence, Morality, and Economics

This chapter evaluates a number of claims about how developments in neuroscience can inform issues in legal theory. We focus in particular on three areas in which, scholars argue, information about the brain contributes important insights for highly abstract theoretical issues involving law. We begin with a discussion of issues in general analytic jurisprudence about the nature of law and legal reasoning and then discuss moral and economic decision making. After discussing these theoretical issues, the next three chapters will turn to a number of practical issues involving neuroscience and law, including lie detection, criminal law doctrine, and criminal procedure.

I. Jurisprudence

Along with specific legal issues and theoretical approaches, neuroscience advocates include general jurisprudential theories of law[1] among the array of subjects that can benefit from an increased role for neuroscience. Oliver Goodenough, in particular, is supremely confident in the power of neuroscience to revamp our view of law. In an

---

[1] By "general jurisprudence" we mean claims about the nature of law. Classic approaches such as natural law (e.g., Aquinas and Finnis), legal positivism (e.g., Kelsen and Hart), and interpretivism (e.g., Dworkin) are examples. The example we discuss below purports to illuminate the divide between natural law and positivism.

award-winning article,[2] Professor Goodenough argues that neuroscience will dispel our Cartesian presuppositions about the nature of law and turn our attention to the role of the brain in legal reasoning. From our point of view, Goodenough's claims—and the arguments he makes in the service of them—well illustrate the overblown and tendentious presuppositions of neurolegalists.[3]

Goodenough develops his argument against the background of the intellectual history of legal theory. In the nineteenth century, Langdell aspired to a "science" of law—a "top down" approach to the explication of legal doctrine that, in essence, evinced "a form of systematic textual analysis."[4] This emphasis gave way in the era of Legal Realism, when focus shifted from doctrine to sociology. The Realist emphasis on the social scientific study of law is now poised to make a great leap forward with the advent of neuroscientific investigation of "how law actually works in human heads."[5]

Law, Goodenough tells us, "is a mental activity": "We do it in our heads, with our brains."[6] Therefore, we will know more about law by going "inside our heads" to see "how the human brain works."[7] It is the theory of mind (conceptualized as the mind-as-brain) that must be brought into law to supplant the dominant view, that being the Cartesian "dualism between the physical aspects of the brain and the nonphysical, mental world of awareness and feelings."[8]

---

[2] Oliver R. Goodenough, *Mapping Cortical Areas Associated with Legal Reasoning and Moral Intuition*, 41 JURIMETRICS J. 429 (2001). The article received the "Jurimetrics Research Award for proposals for research on the scientific study of law," and was selected by "a committee of lawyers and scientists." *See id.* at 429 n. a1.

[3] However, we believe there is an argument Goodenough could make that is immune from our criticisms of his general jurisprudential claims. We outline this argument below.

[4] Goodenough, *supra* note 2, at 430.

[5] *Id.* at 431.

[6] *Id.*

[7] *Id.*

[8] *Id.* at 432. Goodenough quotes Descartes as representative of the current mind-set in academic law:

> I must begin by observing the great difference between mind and body. Body is of its nature always double. When I consider the mind—that is, myself, insofar as I am merely a conscious being—I can distinguish no parts within myself; I understand myself to be a single and complete thing. Although the whole mind seems to be united to the whole body, yet when a foot or an arm or any other part to the body is cut off I am not aware that any subtraction has been made from the mind. Nor can the faculties of will, feeling, understanding and so on be called its parts; for it is one and the same mind that wills, feels and understands.

> This approach underlies much legal scholarship. A unified intelligence guides both day-to-day behavior and the ability to judge the behavior of others. The job of the law is to supply this intelligence with clear, word-based rules, based in sound policy.

Contemporary neuroscience, Goodenough claims, "offers better tools for understanding human thought"[9] and "some theory of how humans think underlies any coherent argument about the law."[10] To really make progress in our understanding of human thought, Goodenough argues, we need to look no further than the modular theory of the brain, which Michael Gazzaniga describes thus:

The modular organization of the human brain is now fairly well accepted. The functioning modules do have some physical instantiation, but the brain sciences are not yet able to specify the nature of the actual neural networks involved for most of them. It is clear that they operate largely outside the realm of awareness and announce their computational products to various executive systems that produce behavior or cognitive states.[11]

In explaining different types of decision making, Goodenough points to different brain locations. The central insight of the modular theory of mind is that "mental processes" occur in different parts of the brain. In fact, "a separation exists in the brain"[12] such that different cortical areas of the brain perform different functions. If we embrace the thesis of the

---

Id. (quoting Descartes *quoted in* RICHARD M. RESTACK, THE MODULAR BRAIN 11 (1994)). Goodenough's argument makes use of the false dichotomy between Cartesianism and neuro-reductionism (which we discussed in Chapter Two) to bolster his claims. The persuasiveness of his case is presented as following from a rejection of Cartesianism. However rhetorically useful this may be in the neurolaw literature, nothing of significance actually follows for Goodenough's positive claims from rejecting Cartesianism. For arguments positing Cartesianism in legal doctrine, see SUSAN EASTON, THE CASE FOR THE RIGHT TO SILENCE 217 (2d ed. 1998) (arguing that limiting the privilege against self-incrimination to testimonial evidence, and not extending it to physical evidence, reflects a commitment to dualism); Dov Fox, *The Right to Silence as Protecting Mental Control: Forensic Neuroscience and "the Spirit and History of the Fifth Amendment"*, 42 AKRON L. REV. 763 (2009) (positing, likewise, that the testimonial–physical evidence distinction under the Fifth Amendment depends on mind–body Cartesian dualism); Karen Shapira-Ettinger, *The Conundrum of Mental States: Substantive Rules and Evidence Combined*, 28 CARDOZO L. REV. 2577, 2580–83 (2007) (arguing that criminal law doctrine regarding states of mind "is based on the premises of Cartesian dualism"). We discuss these views in more detail in Chapters Five and Six.

[9] Goodenough, *supra* note 2, at 434.

[10] *Id.* at 432.

[11] *Id.* at 434 (quoting MICHAEL S. GAZZANIGA, NATURE'S MIND: THE BIOLOGICAL ROOTS OF THINKING, EMOTIONS, SEXUALITY, LANGUAGE, AND INTELLIGENCE 124 (1992)).

[12] Goodenough, *supra* note 2, at 435.

modularity of mind, what *jurisprudential* insights[13] will we gain? Locating the functions for law and moral reasoning, Goodenough believes, will be the key to greater insight into law and our thinking in law.[14] He cites a variety of authorities for the proposition that our thinking about justice occurs in one cortical area and rule-based application of law is located in another.[15] Accordingly, Goodenough concludes that "[s]cience has developed tools that can be used to test the theory that justice-based thinking occurs separately from rule-based reasoning."[16] How do they work?

In thinking about justice we are aided by "a nonverbal algorithm that is programmed by some mixture of genetic blueprint, cultural heritage, and personal experience."[17] By contrast, word-based systems of thought, such as law, actuate "an interpreter module."[18] In legal activities such as the drafting of contracts, statutes, and regulations, the interpreter module serves to process legal materials through "a word-based formula, [employing] the implicit structural logic of the unarticulated system in which the [legal] norm is generated."[19] Goodenough proposes to test his module theory of law with a series of experiments in which lawyers, nonlawyers, and law students are scanned while answering questions about hypothetical situations, to locate the brain areas associated with what Goodenough characterizes as justice-based answers and the brain areas associated with rules-based answers.[20]

---

[13] We emphasize that Goodenough's argument is that neuroscience gives greater purchase than other theories about the nature of law. *See, e.g., id.* at 439 ("Using the new neuroscience, we can entangle some of Kelsen's apparent contradictions.") and *id.* at 429 (claiming that a "series of brain-scanning experiments" can "help[] us understand the neurological basis of the distinction between natural and positive law.") As we detail, we think neuroscience tells us nothing about the nature of law, but it may have something to say about the nature of persons, which will have implications for law.

[14] Similarly, neuroeconomics advocates argue that understanding how different brain regions "make decisions" will help us understand economic reasoning and decision making. We discuss neuroeconomics in Section IV. In the next section, we discuss a similar argument regarding "emotional" and "rational" areas of the brain in the context of moral decision making.

[15] Goodenough, *supra* note 2, at 439–41.

[16] *Id.* at 439. The jurisprudential payoff, Goodenough argues, is that "justice-based thinking" will tell us about natural law, and "rule-based reasoning" will tell us about positive law. *Id.* In fusing these two issues, Goodenough conflates theories of law and theories of adjudication. Legal positivism is consistent with judges engaging in justice-based reasoning, and natural law is consistent with rule-based reasoning.

[17] *Id.*

[18] *Id.* at 435.

[19] *Id.* at 436.

[20] *Id.* at 439–42. He refers to a pilot study. *Id.* at 442 n.64. It is not at all clear that this would "test" his theory. At best it might show which parts of the brain are using more oxygen than others while the agent is engaged in some activity. It would show nothing about algorithms, genetic blueprints, or cultural heritage.

Even if we accept Goodenough's claims regarding cortical separation between justice and rule-based decision making, what follows? Suppose we could locate the precise areas in the brain where, as Goodenough would have it, these two functions occur: what could we infer from such a discovery? There is no denying that one must have a brain to think, just as one must have a brain to walk. The important question is whether "legal thinking" is explicable solely in terms of brain function. To the extent he considers this issue, Goodenough begs the question. We shall explain.

Recall Goodenough's contrast between Langdellian legal science and the Realist critique of it. Goodenough claims that neuroscience could tell us far more about the law than either of these theories. And yet, his neurological account tells us nothing about the central element of the formalist/realist divide: the nature of law. Langdellian formalism posited a conceptual space of law that reason could grasp through reflection on the necessary conditions for a given doctrinal department of law.[21] The Realist critique denied the central formalist tenet of the logical structure of law. In essence, the Realist critique was that the person making a legal decision was as important as the rule in question. Goodenough's account of law—that justice-based thinking occurs in one area of the brain and rule-based thinking occurs in another area of the brain—contributes nothing to this debate.[22] Under any conception of "law," simply locating where "in the brain" legal thinking occurs is not a jurisprudential contribution to disagreements between formalists and realists or between natural lawyers and positivists.[23]

Moreover, in arguing for the notion that moral and legal thinking are the product of "embedded algorithms," Goodenough claims that this "hypothesis" can be empirically tested. This is impossible, however,

[21] For discussion of Langdell's project in the context of a "scientific" approach to law, see Dennis Patterson, *Langdell's Legacy*, 90 Nw. U. L. Rev. 196 (1995).

[22] *See* Brian Leiter, *Legal Formalism and Legal Realism: What Is the Issue?*, 16 Legal Theory 111 (2010). In addition to our critique of Goodenough from the perspective of jurisprudence, a different challenge to Goodenough's proposal comes from the work of John Mikhail, who posits that the justice-based decisions that Goodenough discusses are also rule based. *See* John Mikhail, Elements of Moral Cognition: Rawls' Linguistic Analogy and the Cognitive Science of Moral and Legal Judgments (2011). We discuss Mikhail's approach to morality in Section III.

[23] Goodenough claims to the contrary: "Advances in neurosciences and other branches of behavioral biology provide new tools and the opportunity to revisit classic questions at the foundation of legal thinking." Goodenough, *supra* note 2, at 429.

because the hypothesis is question-begging. First, if legal thinking is grounded in or actuated by a hardwired algorithm, what explains legal disagreement?[24] Second, the existence of such an algorithm could never be confirmed by experiment because it has no features detectable by scientific experiment.[25] These limitations are ironic because the entire point of Goodenough's claims for neuroscience is that the science of the brain will advance our understanding of law and legal reasoning, but his proposal would neither resolve important jurisprudential questions nor provide falsifiable empirical claims. In trying to solve jurisprudential problems with science, the proposal serves neither.

Despite these problems, Goodenough raises an issue that does connect with legal theory. Recall the American Legal Realist claim that, at least in the realm of appellate decisions,[26] the law is indeterminate. By "indeterminate," we mean that controversies at the appellate level cannot be settled by existing law, thereby forcing judges to choose between plausible alternative interpretations of the law and to be creative in fashioning legally defensible solutions to hard cases.

Now, assume that Goodenough is correct in the claims he makes about law and the brain. Suppose neuroscience can really tell us something about which areas of the brain are active when legal decisions are made.[27] If this is so, then the implications for legal theory are clear. If some appellate cases really are indeterminate (the Realist claim), then information about the judge or judges deciding the case is of great importance.[28] In other words, perhaps

---

[24] This dilemma plagues metaphysical realist accounts of law as well. *See* Dennis Patterson, *Dworkin on the Semantics of Legal and Political Concepts*, 26 OXFORD J. LEG. STUD. 545–57 (2006).

[25] Given the manifold appeals to science by neurolegalists, it is ironic that several of their central claims are not amenable to empirical verification or falsification. The idea that we are "hard-wired" or otherwise have an "innate" moral code in our brains is a familiar feature of neurolegalist arguments. But, as Richard Rorty argued, this claim is not provable. *See* Richard Rorty, *Born to Be Good*," N.Y. TIMES, August 27, 2006 (reviewing MARC. D. HAUSER, MORAL MINDS (2006)).

[26] Many scholars caricature the Realists as thoroughgoing indeterminists (i.e., that they believed law was indeterminate "all the way down"). This is false. When it came to most legal questions, the Realists provided an account of law that was consistent with the tenets of legal positivism (e.g., the Rule of Recognition, primary and secondary rules, etc.). It was only in the realm of appellate decision making that the Realists believed the law was indeterminate. For an excellent discussion, see BRIAN LEITER, *Legal Realism and Legal Positivism Reconsidered*, *in* NATURALIZING JURISPRUDENCE 59, 73–79 (2007).

[27] Our thanks to Kim Ferzan for suggesting this point.

[28] Of course, this information would have to be far more detailed than what is available now, which is the measure of oxygenated blood flow in the brain.

neuroscience really can tell us something about how judges decide hard cases, and the information it provides can be used to predict future decisions better than other variables. The information would surely be useful, and it would be far more perspicuous than the usual claims one hears about "politics" or "personal values" doing the real work in the appellate realm.[29]

Goodenough does not discuss this use of neuroscience.[30] But we think if (and we mean *if*) it turned out that neuroscience provided insight into the mind of a jurist in the discretion-laden context of appellate decision making, a real contribution would be made. As we have indicated, however, we reject specious claims about "hard-wired algorithms" and other speculative explanations of legal reasoning.

II. Emotion and Moral Judgments

The relationship between law and morality is incredibly complex. The two intersect in numerous ways, and these intersections have been the subject of extensive debate in legal theory. One area of intersection concerns how and the extent to which moral decision making does and should affect legal decision making. In answering these questions, legal scholars have been turning to neuroscience for insights into moral decision making, focusing in particular on a number of studies by Joshua

---

[29] This line of inquiry would thus be a neuroscientific approach similar to the "attitudinal model," which seeks to predict judicial decision making based on judges' perceived political "attitudes and values." *See* JEFFREY A. SEGAL & HAROLD J. SPAETH, THE SUPREME COURT AND THE ATTITUDINAL MODEL REVISITED (2002). Noting the "epistemically feeble condition" of current "predictive-explanatory" models of legal decision making, Brian Leiter outlines a number of ways in which a more robust predictive model may fit with jurisprudential issues. *See* BRIAN LEITER, *Postscript to Part II: Science and Methodology in Legal Theory*, *in* NATURALIZING JURISPRUDENCE, *supra* note 26, at 183–99 (discussing the attitudinal model and its relevance to "naturalized" jurisprudence). Whether neuroscience can deliver a better predictive-explanatory model of decision making is an open empirical question, but this avenue would have greater relevance to jurisprudential issues than the avenues Goodenough discusses. Such a move would parallel developments in neuroeconomics, in which scholars are looking to improve upon the psychological explanations of behavioral economics by providing neuroscientific explanations.

[30] In a subsequent article, Goodenough discusses other possible legal applications of his neuroscientific approach to law; he proposes studies on emotional reactions by jurors and attitudes about intellectual property. *See* Oliver R. Goodenough & Kristin Prehn, *A Neuroscientific Approach to Normative Judgment in Law and Justice*, *in* LAW & THE BRAIN 77 (Semir Zeki & Oliver Goodenough eds., 2006).

Greene and colleagues.[31] In the discussion to follow, we first describe the neuroscientific studies and their claimed implications for moral decision making; we next describe some of the ways in which legal scholars have relied on these studies; finally, we explain the limitations on inferences about law that may be drawn from the studies.

The neuroscientific studies are "scenario studies" in which test subjects are presented with a number of short vignettes and then asked whether particular actions are "appropriate" or not.[32] Greene et al.'s initial study—and the one principally relied on by legal scholars making use of this work—presented subjects with over forty scenarios involving moral "dilemmas" (as well as several involving "non-moral dilemmas").[33] Two of those scenarios, however, have garnered much of the discussion because of the divergent results they produced. The scenarios involve variations on the so-called "Trolley Problem."[34] One scenario tested (called "Standard Trolley" in the Supplemental Materials to the study) is as follows:

You are at the wheel of a runaway trolley quickly approaching a fork in the tracks. On the tracks extending to the left is a group of five railway workmen. On the tracks extending to the right is a single railway workman.

If you do nothing the trolley will proceed to the left, causing the deaths of the five workmen. The only way to avoid the deaths of these workmen is to hit a switch on your dashboard that will cause the trolley to proceed to the right, causing the death of the single workman.

---

[31] Joshua D. Greene et al., *An fMRI Investigation of Emotional Engagement in Moral Judgment*, 293 SCI. 2105 (2001); Joshua D. Greene et al., *The Neural Bases of Cognitive Conflict and Control in Moral Judgment*, 44 NEURON 389 (2004); Joshua D. Greene et al., *Pushing Moral Buttons: The Interaction between Personal Force and Intention in Moral Judgment*, 111 COGNITION 364 (2009). A Westlaw search on December 17, 2012 of "Greene w/p fMRI" in the "Journals and Law Reviews" database produced fifty-nine legal academic articles citing one or more of the studies.

[32] For a general methodological discussion of such studies, see John M. Darley, *Citizens' Assignments of Punishments for Moral Transgressions: A Case Study in the Psychology of Punishment*, 8 OHIO ST. J. CRIM. L. 101 (2010). In recent articles, Gabriel Abend has cautioned against reliance on both the types of judgments in such studies and the "thin" moral concepts at issue (e.g., "appropriate or not," or "permissible or not") in order to draw conclusions about morality. *See* Gabriel Abend, *What the Science of Morality Doesn't Say about Morality*, PHIL. SOCIAL SCI. (forthcoming, published online July 20, 2012); Gabriel Abend, *Thick Concepts and the Moral Brain*, 52 EURO. J. SOCIOLOGY 143 (2011).

[33] Greene et al., *An fMRI Investigation*, *supra* note 31.

[34] *See* Philippa Foot, *The Problem of Abortion and the Doctrine of Double Effect*, *in* VIRTUES AND VICES (2002) (originally published in 5 OXFORD REV. (1967)) (introducing the trolley problem); Judith Jarvis Thomson, *The Trolley Problem*, 94 YALE L.J. 1395 (1985) (introducing the "bystander" version of the problem).

Is it appropriate for you to hit the switch in order to avoid the deaths of the five workmen?[35]

Most test subjects said, yes, that it is appropriate.[36]

The second scenario ("Footbridge") is as follows:

A runaway trolley is heading down the tracks toward five workmen who will be killed if the trolley proceeds on its present course. You are on a footbridge over the tracks, in between the approaching trolley and the five workmen. Next to you on this footbridge is a stranger who happens to be very large.

The only way to save the lives of the five workmen is to push this stranger off the bridge and onto the tracks below where his large body will stop the trolley. The stranger will die if you do this, but the five workmen will be saved.

Is it appropriate for you to push the stranger on to the tracks in order to save the five workmen?[37]

Most test subjects said, no, that it is not appropriate.[38]

The divergent responses for the two scenarios are thought by some to create a puzzle because each case involves a decision of whether to kill one person in order to save five, thus suggesting that the results should be similar. In the study and in subsequent papers, Greene and colleagues seek to explain the difference by linking three separate issues: (1) whether the decision is consistent with deontological or utilitarian moral considerations; (2) whether the decision is a "personal" or "impersonal" one; (3) and whether the decision is correlated with areas of the brain associated with "emotion."

The proffered explanation begins with the role of emotion. In the Footbridge scenario, areas of the brain associated with emotion were "significantly more active" than in the Standard Trolley scenario.[39] Decision making in the Standard Trolley scenario, by contrast, involved increased activation in areas of the brain associated with "cognitive" processing.[40] They next note that the decisions that involved more emotional responses were those they labeled as "personal" (such as Footbridge) and

---

[35] See Greene et al., An fMRI Investigation, supra note 31, Supplemental Data, available at http://www.sciencemag.org/content/293/5537/2105.abstract.

[36] Id. at 2105.

[37] Supplemental Data, supra note 35.

[38] Greene et al., An fMRI Investigation, supra note 31, at 2105.

[39] Id. at 2107. The areas include the medial frontal gyrus, posterior cingulated gyrus, and angular gyrus. Id.

[40] Id. The areas include the middle frontal gyrus and the parietal lobe. Id.

that those they labeled as "impersonal" (such as Standard Trolley) produced less emotional and more cognitive processes.[41] After linking the personal–impersonal distinction to the emotional–cognitive distinction, the next move is to map both distinctions onto the utilitarian–deontology distinction. Because the "impersonal," less "emotional" decisions were generally consistent with utilitarian outcomes and the "personal," more "emotional" decisions were generally consistent with deontological outcomes, they posit that different brain areas (emotional and cognitive) may control different types of moral reasoning (deontological and utilitarian).[42] Subsequent studies have built on these initial results and explored a variety of related issues involving emotions and moral reasoning.[43]

The initial study and follow-up papers had explicitly descriptive aims and were cautious about normative conclusions.[44] Nevertheless, Greene has since drawn more bold and wide-ranging normative conclusions about moral judgments based on the distinction he draws between emotional and cognitive processes.[45] He argues that the distinction undermines deontological judgments and vindicates utilitarian judgments. Deontological judgments, he argues, are produced by the "emotional" psychological process rather than the "cognitive" process, and utilitarian judgments are produced by the cognitive process.[46] The

---

[41] The study characterizes "personal" dilemmas as those that involve actions that "(a) could reasonably be expected to lead to serious bodily harm, (b) to a particular person or a member or members of a particular group of people, (c) where this harm is not the result of deflecting an existing threat onto a different party." Id; Joshua Greene & Jonathan Haidt, How (and Where) Does Moral Judgment Work?, 6 TRENDS IN COG. SCI. 517, 519 (2002). Greene later acknowledged that this distinction does not explain some of the data; see Joshua D. Greene, The Secret Joke of Kant's Soul, in MORAL PSYCHOLOGY, VOL. 3: THE NEUROSCIENCE OF MORALITY: EMOTION, DISEASE, AND DEVELOPMENT (Walter Sinnott-Armstrong ed., 2007), but whether the judgment is "personal" (or involves physical contact) continues to be a key variable in subsequent research; see Greene et al., Pushing Moral Buttons, supra note 31.

[42] See Greene et al., Neural Bases, supra note 31, at 398. See also Greene & Haidt, supra note 41, at 523 ("the ordinary concept of moral judgment refers to a variety of more fine grained and disparate processes.").

[43] See Greene et al., Neural Bases, supra note 31; Greene et al., Pushing Moral Buttons, supra note 31. In a recent article, Selim Berker notes that, as an empirical matter, all three distinctions (personal–impersonal, emotion–cognitive, and deontological–utilitarian) come apart when considering other variations on the trolley problem. Selim Berker, The Normative Insignificance of Neuroscience, 37 PHIL. & PUB. AFFAIRS 293, 312 (2009).

[44] See Greene et al., An fMRI Investigation, supra note 31, at 2107 ("We do not claim to have shown any actions or judgments to be morally right or wrong."); Greene & Haidt, supra note 41; Joshua D. Greene, From Neural "Is" to Moral "Ought": What Are the Moral Implications of Neuroscientific Moral Psychology?, 4 NATURE REV. NEUROSCIENCE 847 (2003).

[45] Greene, Secret Joke, supra note 41.

[46] Id. at 50–55. Cf. Berker, supra note 43, at 311 ("sorting personal from impersonal moral dilemmas [is] an inadequate way of tracking the [deontological–utilitarian] distinction. To

cognitive process is more likely to involve "genuine moral reasoning," as opposed to the "quick," "automatic," and "alarm-like" deontological judgments produced by emotional responses.[47] This, Greene argues, undermines deontology as "a rationally coherent moral theory"; an "attempt to reach moral conclusions on the basis of moral reasoning"; "a school of normative moral thought"; and as reflecting any "deep, rationally discoverable moral truths."[48] Rather, deontology is characterized as merely an attempt to rationalize our emotional responses, which are based on, and may have developed evolutionarily because of, nonmoral factors. By contrast, he contends that utilitarian principles "while not true, provide the best available standard for public decision making."[49]

Legal scholars have followed Greene down this path, drawing normative implications for aspects of the law from Greene's studies. Many of the references to the Greene studies in the legal literature cite them for the (unobjectionable) proposition that emotions play some role in moral judgments.[50] Most troubling from our perspective, however, is the inference that the studies show that the "emotional," deontological judgments are incorrect or unreliable. Consider two examples. In a recent article discussing international criminal law, Andrew Woods relies on the studies and contends that "[h]ow moral heuristic failure occurs has been shown using fMRI scans of the brain."[51] According to Woods, when subjects "felt an emotional surge" in Footbridge, they relied on moral heuristics (for example, "Do no harm"), and when they did not feel this surge they engaged in utilitarian reasoning.[52] Woods maintains this is relevant to international criminal law because "strong emotional intuitions may guide decision makers to outcomes

claim that characteristically deontological judgments only concern bodily harms is nothing short of preposterous.").

[47] Greene, *Secret Joke*, *supra* note 41, at 65.

[48] *Id.* at 70–72.

[49] *Id.* at 77. Greene also relies on these arguments to attack retributivist theories of criminal punishment. We discuss this aspect of his argument in Chapter Seven. For a critique of Greene's normative conclusions, see Richard Dean, *Does Neuroscience Undermine Deontological Theory?*, 3 NEUROETHICS 43 (2010).

[50] *See, e.g.*, Janice Nadler, *Blaming as a Social Process: The Influence of Character and Moral Emotion on Blame*, 75 LAW & CONTEMP. PROBS. 1 (2012); R. George Wright, *Electoral Lies and the Broader Problems of Strict Scrutiny*, 64 FLA. L. REV. 759, 783 n.155 (2012); Thomas W. Merrill & Henry E. Smith, *The Morality of Property*, 48 WM. & MARY L. REV. 1849 (2007).

[51] Andrew K. Woods, *Moral Judgments & International Crimes: The Disutility of Desert*, 52 VA. J. INT. L. 633, 667 (2012).

[52] *Id.* at 668.

that do not maximize utility."[53] Similarly, Terrence Chorvat and Kevin McCabe contend that the studies are relevant to jury decision making at trial because juries will tend to make more "rational" decisions and "socially optimal choices when they keep the subject of the decision at a distance."[54] Therefore, the law has an interest in "depersonalizing" jury decision making.[55] They suggest that evidentiary rules ought to be designed with this consideration in mind.[56]

We resist the normative conclusions that legal scholars have drawn from the Greene studies. Before turning to the major conceptual problems that undermine these conclusions, we shall first clarify three limitations on using the results of the studies to draw conclusions about legal issues.

First, even if subjects experience strong emotional reactions to Footbridge and less so to Standard Trolley, this does not support a two-process model (emotional and cognitive) of decision making. Rather than causing the decisions, the emotional reactions may instead have simply *accompanied* decisions made for moral, deontological reasons. Indeed, as John Mikhail has pointed out, virtually all of the "personal" scenarios presented to subjects involved violent crimes and torts.[57] Thus, it should not be surprising (indeed, it should be expected) that subjects had (1) emotional responses, and (2) reactions to the effect that the conduct was impermissible. This does not show that subjects were not engaged in genuine moral reasoning (and instead engaged in an emotion-driven moral failure). In short, the presence of emotion neither rules out moral reasoning, nor does it specify a particular causal role for the emotions.[58]

[53]   *Id.* at 669. Woods ties this point to arguments about theories of criminal punishment in the international context.

[54]   Terrence Chorvat & Kevin McCabe, *Neuroeconomics and Rationality*, 80 CHI-KENT L. REV. 1235, 1252 (2005).

[55]   *Id.*

[56]   Terrence Chorvat, Kevin McCabe & Vernon Smith, *Law and Neuroeconomics*, 13 SUP. CT. ECON. REV. 35, 61 (2005).

[57]   John Mikhail, *Emotion, Neuroscience, and Law: A Comment on Darwin and Greene*, 3 EMOTION REV. 293 (2011), *available at* http://ssrn.com/abstract=1761295.

[58]   *See* Gilbert Harman, Kelby Mason & Walter Sinnott-Armstrong, *Moral Reasoning, in* THE MORAL PSYCHOLOGY HANDBOOK 206–42 (John M. Doris ed., 2010) (outlining several possible types of moral reasoning compatible with emotional reactions); Jesse J. Prinz & Shaun Nichols, *Moral Emotions, in* THE MORAL PSYCHOLOGY HANDBOOK 111–41 (discussing the role of emotions in moral cognition). The inference from particular brain activity to particular mental functions or processes faces a number of empirical limitations. *See* Russell A. Poldrack, *Can Cognitive Processes Be Inferred from Neuroimaging Data?*, 10 TRENDS IN COG. SCI. 79 (2006) (discussing limitations on drawing such "reverse inferences"). In arguing for a

Second, the relationship between emotion and the law is incredibly complex.[59] Therefore, *even if* the deontological judgments were caused by emotional reactions, it begs the question to assume that the law should try to depersonalize decisions and eliminate these types of judgments. This is obvious in the context of jury decision making. The very judgments that Chorvat and McCabe contend are problematic because they may lead to suboptimal decisions are ones the U.S. Supreme Court has found to be integral to jury decision making. In criminal cases, for example, the Supreme Court has explained that evidence may serve a legitimate role at trial by implicating "law's moral underpinnings and a juror's obligation to sit in judgment" and that the prosecution may need such evidence to show that a conviction would be "morally reasonable."[60] In civil cases, the Court has also explained that punitive damages ought to depend, in part, on judgments of reprehensibility, blame, and moral outrage by jurors toward the actions of defendants.[61] This is not to suggest that emotional reactions are never a problem, both for jury decision making in particular and law in general.[62] Our point is merely that the Greene studies are too blunt of an instrument to read off any clear policy results for the proper role of emotion in law.

Third, we note one other mismatch between the neuroscientific studies and the uses to which they are put by some legal scholars. Greene and colleagues tested a scenario involving the driver of the trolley and a scenario involving pushing someone on the track from a footbridge. It is important to clarify that in the Standard Trolley scenario the subject is *the driver* of the trolley, not a bystander. The legal scholarship citing the studies typically does not mention this fact

---

two-process model of moral judgments (emotional–deontological and cognitive–utilitarian), the Greene studies point to a number of differences in the time subjects take to make judgments (for example, subjects take longer if they must engage in more reasoning or override an initial inclination). According to a recent study, however, the timing differences depend not on the difference between deontological and utilitarian judgments, but rather whether the judgments were "intuitive" or not. *See* Guy Kahane et al., *The Neural Basis of Intuitive and Counterintuitive Moral Judgment*, 10 SOC. COGNITIVE & AFFECTIVE NEUROSCIENCE (2011).

[59] For an illuminating discussion of this complexity, see Terry A Maroney, *The Persistent Cultural Script of Judicial Dispassion*, 99 CAL. L. REV. 629 (2011).

[60] *See* Old Chief v. United States, 519 U.S. 172, 187–88 (1997).

[61] *See* Cooper Indus., Inc. v. Leatherman Tool Group, Inc., 532 U.S. 424 (2001). *See also* Todd E. Pettys, *The Emotional Juror*, 76 FORDHAM L. REV. 1609 (2007) (discussing ways in which emotions may aid and detract from accuracy at trial).

[62] *See* FED. R. EVID. 403.

(describing the choice as simply whether to push a button or flip a switch, leaving it ambiguous whether it is driver or bystander).[63] Recall, the driver scenario was the example of an *impersonal* dilemma, and the footbridge scenario was the example of a *personal* dilemma. Exactly what it would mean for the law to further "depersonalize" decisions as characterized by the studies is not entirely clear. For example, any decision by a jury is surely more "impersonal" than deciding to drive a trolley into and killing one or several people. This is true even for decisions to send someone to prison or voting to impose the death penalty. We can imagine some decisions by legal actors that straddle the impersonal–personal line as it is drawn by the studies (for example, police interactions with citizens), but that distinction is inapposite to most legal decision making.

If we turn now to the more serious conceptual problems, it begs the question to presuppose that the utilitarian judgments are correct and the deontological judgments are mistaken. This is true both as a general matter and with the particular judgments at issue in the trolley problems. As a general matter, there are intense philosophical debates between deontologists and utilitarians; to the extent legal issues depend on a choice between conflicting moral judgments, the legal issues also depend on these philosophical debates. The Greene studies do not resolve any of the contentious normative issues; indeed, as Selim Berker argues, the empirical results are irrelevant to those debates.[64] Any attempt to derive a normative conclusion from the neuroscientific results depends on an "appeal to substantive normative intuitions (usually about what sorts of features are or are not morally relevant)," and it is this appeal, not the neuroscience, that drives the

[63]   *See, e.g.*, Woods, *supra* note 51, at 667 (describing Standard Trolley as "a train is heading down a track where five people are chatting, and the only way to save them is to switch the train's path to another track where only one man is in the way."); Chorvat & McCabe, *supra* note 54, at 1250 (describing Standard Trolley as "a train is coming down a track, and, if they do nothing, the train will hit a car on the track and five people will be killed, but, alternatively, if they press a button, the train will be diverted to a side track and only one person will be killed."). Some of this ambiguity may arise from Greene's own descriptions, which also do not mention whether the person deciding whether to flip the switch is the driver or a bystander. Although the Supplemental Data, *supra* note 35, makes clear that subjects were told they are the driver, the 2001 article, by contrast, describes the problem as "A runaway trolley is headed for five people who will be killed if it proceeds on its present course. The only way to save them is to hit a switch that will turn the trolley onto an alternate set of tracks where it will kill one person instead of five." Greene et al., *An fMRI Investigation, supra* note 31.

[64]   *See* Berker, *supra* note 43. Also problematic is the assumption that utilitarian and deontological principles exhaust the basis of moral judgments.

normative inferences.[65] Berker illustrates this by outlining what he calls "the best-case scenario" for a normative role for neuroscience in moral judgment—suppose "a portion of the brain which lights up whenever we make a certain sort of obvious, egregious error in mathematical or logical reasoning also lights up whenever we have a certain moral intuition."[66] He asks whether we should abandon moral judgments based on these intuitions, concluding that it likely will depend on further details. If there is no connection between the two, then there does not appear to be any reason to abandon the moral intuitions. (For example, we would not suddenly conclude that murder is not wrong because of such a link.) By contrast, if the moral judgments depend on the same sort of error or mistake present in the mathematical or logical reasoning, then we should also come to see the moral judgments as mistaken or erroneous. But, if so, then it will be the common error or mistake that undermines the judgments, not the neuroscientific results. In sum, whether the law should foster or limit particular deontological or utilitarian judgments requires a normative argument, not appeal to the areas of the brain that are active during those judgments. Areas of the brain do not provide the right criteria for resolving philosophical debates about moral judgments and the legal issues that build upon them.

With regard to the specifics of the trolley problems, it also begs the question to assume that particular judgments about the scenarios are correct or incorrect. We acknowledge the possibility that the judgments of most people could be mistaken about the right thing to do in one or more of the scenarios, but we disagree that the Footbridge results are incorrect or exhibit a "moral heuristic" gone awry.[67] To the contrary, there is a plausible principled explanation for reconciling the judgments in the two cases. Recall again that in the Standard Trolley

---

[65] *Id.* at 294. Francis Kamm makes a similar point in F.M. Kamm, *Neuroscience and Moral Reasoning: A Note on Recent Research*, 37 PHIL. & PUB. AFFAIRS 331 (2009). For example, Greene and the legal scholars relying on the studies assume that the presence of emotion makes moral judgments irrational. Not only is this substantive assumption highly questionable—there are often good reasons to feel certain emotions, and to not feel emotions in some contexts is itself wrong (e.g., anger at injustice, compassion for those suffering, and joy at the good fortune of loved ones). Moreover, some moral standards involve emotional dispositions (e.g., to feel guilty when ignoring one's duties and obligations).

[66] Berker, *supra* note 43, at 329.

[67] To conclude that Footbridge is an example of a "moral heuristic" failure requires some prior, non–question-begging argument about what the correct result ought to be. We are aware of no such arguments demonstrating that the correct judgment in each case is the

scenario the subject is *the driver* of the trolley, not a bystander. Thus, in one scenario the subject is already involved and can either continue driving straight, killing five, or turn the trolley and kill one (most people turned). In the other scenario, the subject is a third party faced with a choice of intervening in the situation by pushing a large man to his death (most did not push) or letting the train proceed. Judith Jarvis Thomson argues for a principled moral distinction between the driver (permissible to turn the trolley), on the one hand, and the footbridge and bystander cases (both not permissible), on the other.[68] According to Thomson, the "killing versus letting die" principle justifies the difference.[69] The driver must kill one rather than kill five, but a bystander who could push a large man or pull a lever to turn the train must let the five people die rather than kill one person. Thus, it is at least plausible that the results from the two scenarios Greene et al. tested do not reveal any problems that the law must be concerned with resolving.

If Thomson's argument is sound, this may suggest other potential problems. Most significantly, subjects in the bystander case do often judge that pulling the lever is permissible,[70] and they may be mistaken to do so.[71] But notice that if this is so (and whether it is so is beyond the scope of our discussion[72]), then the mistake subjects are making is that they are being too utilitarian and not deontological enough—exactly the opposite normative conclusion that some legal scholars draw from

utilitarian one. As a general matter, we do not think an appeal to intuitions, or the brain areas correlated with intuitions, is the way to evaluate normative conclusions regarding any of these issues. *See* HERMAN CAPPELEN, PHILOSOPHY WITHOUT INTUITIONS 158–63 (2012) (explaining why the primary philosophical arguments about the trolley problems do not appeal to intuitions).

[68] Judith Jarvis Thomson, *Turning the Trolley*, 36 PHIL. & PUB. AFFAIRS 359 (2008). As an empirical matter, however, most test subjects also pull the lever in the bystander case. For the results of several experiments and variations of the trolley problem, see MIKHAIL, *supra* note 22, at 319–60.

[69] Thomson, *supra* note 68, at 367.

[70] *See* MIKHAIL, *supra* note 22, at 319–60.

[71] Thomson argues that turning the trolley is impermissible in the bystander cases because the subject is choosing to make the one person killed pay a cost the bystander would likely not himself be willing to pay. Thomson, *supra* note 68, at 366. She concludes it is thus no more permissible than stealing from someone else in order to give the money to charity. Unlike the bystander, who may permissibly decline to do a good deed (throwing himself or the large man in front of the train), the driver must not kill five people if she can kill one instead. Thomson speculates that the drastic means undertaken by the bystander may explain the distinction between the lever and footbridge cases.

[72] Our point is not to take sides on this particular issue, but rather to endorse the more general methodological point that the normative issues raised by the trolley problems are matters to be resolved by (empirically informed) philosophical arguments, not appeals to

the Greene studies. This again raises our fundamental point: how the law ought to respond to conflicting moral judgments depends on philosophical arguments, not on empirical information about the brain. Whether the reasoning in these arguments is valid or justified depends on the relations of propositions, not the firing of neurons. Evidence about the brain may sometimes be relevant to moral issues, but it is a conceptual mistake to presuppose that the moral questions that face the law can be answered by looking in the brain.

III. Mind, Moral Grammar, and Knowledge

John Mikhail has developed a detailed and wide-ranging account of the cognitive basis of moral and legal decision making.[73] Mikhail argues that much of our capacity for decision making in the realms of morality and law are "hard-wired." Drawing inspiration from the work of Noam Chomsky and John Rawls, Mikhail argues that moral knowledge is tacit, grounded in a moral grammar contained in the brain.[74] Mikhail's work is relevant both on its own merits and because it is a fine illustration of how questionable philosophical presuppositions can undermine aspects of even the most elegantly formulated theories of cognition.[75]

---

brain activity underlying intuitions and judgments. As with the general neuro-reductionist approach we discuss in Chapter Two, neuro-reductionist approaches to morality also sometimes rely on a false dichotomy to support their cases. *See, e.g.*, Goodenough & Prehn, *supra* note 30, at 83:

> [T]his assertion begs a question [*sic*]: if ought is something more than the conclusion of a particular kind of natural mental process, where does that something more come from? Even the Kantian move to duty, rationalism and universals merely shifts the exercise from one mental process to another. In all of its forms, this train of argument attributes to moral standards an independence from physical causation in the discoverable processes of the brain. And the question remains: if not physical processes, then what? At heart, the romantic approach rests on an often unacknowledged spiritualism.

Just as neuro-reductionism and Cartesianism is a false dichotomy with regard to the mind in general, so too neuro-reduction and spiritualism is a false dichotomy with regard to morality. For a non-spiritual, naturalist, non-neuro-reductionist account of morality, see PHILIP KITCHER, THE ETHICAL PROJECT (2011).

[73] *See* MIKHAIL, *supra* note 22; John Mikhail, *Moral Grammar and Intuitive Jurisprudence: A Formal Model of Unconscious Moral and Legal Knowledge*, 50 PSYCHOL. LEARNING & MOTIVATION 5 (2009); John Mikhail, *Universal Moral Grammar: Theory, Evidence, and the Future*, 11 TRENDS IN COG. SCI. 143 (2007).

[74] MIKHAIL, *supra* note 22, at 17 ("the best explanation of the properties of moral judgment is the assumption the mind/brain contains a moral grammar.").

[75] Mikhail is not, strictly speaking, a neurolegalist: his theory is not grounded in neuroscientific details about the brain, and he does not propose ways for neuroscience to transform law.

We start with what Mikhail identifies as the core questions for a theory of moral cognition. These questions frame Mikhail's inquiry into the nature of mind and delineate the central focus of his research into the relationship between mind and moral knowledge. He asks:

1. What constitutes moral knowledge?
2. How is moral knowledge acquired?
3. How is moral knowledge put to use?
4. How is moral knowledge physically realized in the brain?
5. How did moral knowledge evolve in the species?[76]

In describing the main features of what he takes to be our innate moral capacity, Mikhail makes a number of key claims about the nature of mind and moral grammar. These are:

1. "[T]he mind/brain contains a moral grammar."[77]
2. "[T]he manner in which this grammar is acquired implies that at least some of its core attributes are innate, where 'innate' is used in a dispositional sense to refer to cognitive systems whose essential properties are largely pre-determined by the inherent structure of the mind."[78]
3. Moral intuitions "are best explained by assuming [that individuals] possess tacit knowledge of specific rules, concepts or principles."[79]

Our discussion focuses on two philosophically suspect claims that Mikhail makes about the relationship among mind, moral grammar,

Nevertheless, his claims proceed from a cognitive perspective and overlap with several of the philosophical issues we discuss in this book. He analogizes his work to that of Noam Chomsky and, as we detail, his accounts of "moral knowledge" are philosophically controversial and, we maintain, subject to some of the same critique that we make of the work of neurolegalists.

[76] *Id.* at 27.

[77] *See supra* note 74.

[78] Mikhail, *Universal Moral Grammar, supra* note 73, at 144. The idea of innate moral knowledge is controversial even among naturalists about morality. Patricia Churchland, whose neuro-reductionism we discuss in Chapter Two, rejects the idea on evidential grounds. PATRICIA S. CHURCHLAND, BRAINTRUST: WHAT NEUROSCIENCE TELLS US ABOUT MORALITY 103–11 (2011) (noting that much of the evidence cited in favor of innateness is consistent with other hypotheses, including learned behavior and simply finding reasonable solutions to common problems); KITCHER, *supra* note 72, at 10 (rejecting the innateness hypothesis because, among other reasons, it underplays the social environment of ethical practices). *See also* Joshua D. Greene, *Reply to Mikhail and Timmons, in* MORAL PSYCHOLOGY, VOL. 3: THE NEUROSCIENCE OF MORALITY: EMOTION, DISEASE, AND DEVELOPMENT (Walter Sinnott-Armstrong ed., 2007) (arguing that in some trolley experiments only about half the participants decided as Mikhail's theory predicts and that massive disagreement is inconsistent with innate knowledge).

[79] Mikhail, *Universal Moral Grammar, supra* note 73, at 144.

and moral knowledge. These are the two claims: first, moral reasoning is a matter of unconscious application of rules, principles, and "domain specific algorithms."[80] Second, moral knowledge is in the brain.[81]

The first claim asserts that the mind's methodology for tackling ethical problems involves a combination of "unconscious" rule following and "interpretation."[82] The second claim asserts that the outputs of this interpretive process constitute knowledge and that this knowledge is located in the brain. We discuss each in turn.

The first claim (i.e., that we can explain moral cognition by positing that the mind follows rules by unconsciously interpreting whether particular cases fall within their ambit) faces two distinct problems. The first problem concerns the idea that to understand what a rule requires in a particular circumstance we need to interpret it. The second problem concerns the idea that "following a rule" is something a person does "unconsciously." As we discuss in Chapter One, these claims rely on problematic notions of interpretation and rule following.

Mikhail's claim that we apply rules to scenarios through interpretation is one made in a wide variety of humanistic and social-scientific

---

[80] *Id.* at 148. Knowledge of these moral rules is "tacit." *Id.* at 145. In solving ethical problems, "a pattern of organization…is imposed on the stimulus by the mind itself." *Id.* The process of computation is "unconscious." *Id.*

[81] *See supra* note 74. This grammar is "innate" in that its "essential properties are largely pre-determined by the inherent structure of the mind." Mikhail, *Universal Moral Grammar, supra* note 73, at 144.

[82] In a recent review of Patricia Churchland's book, BRAINTRUST, Mikhail clarifies the significance of "unconscious" rule following for computational theories of mind such as his: "The particular computations…can be conceived on the model of rules or rule-following, but care must be taken to dissociate any such conception from claims about the *conscious* possession or application of rules. Rather, the dominant trend in the cognitive sciences is to assume that these mental rules are known and operate unconsciously…In short, unconscious computation, not conscious application of rules, is the more significant rule-based proposal to evaluate in this context." John Mikhail, *Review of Patricia S. Churchland,* Braintrust: What Neuroscience Tells Us about Morality, 123 ETHICS 354 (2013). The interpretive aspect of Mikhail's theory involves the fit between factual scenarios and rules. Mikhail puts it this way: "[H]ow the mind goes about interpreting these novel fact patterns, and assigning a deontic status to the acts they depict, is not revealed in any obvious way by the scenarios themselves." Mikhail, *Universal Moral Grammar, supra* note 73, at 144. Our discussion of interpretation and rules also applies to the process of interpreting the factual scenarios and their fit with the rules. If understanding a factual scenario requires an act of interpretation, then understanding that interpretation also requires an interpretation, and so on.

disciplines.[83] The problem with the claim is conceptual. If understanding a rule (or the particulars of a context to which the rule may apply) first requires interpretation of it, then there is no reason the interpretation itself does not similarly stand in need of interpretation. This process of interpretive regression can go on infinitely.[84] Hence, the term "infinite regress" has been used to describe the argument against the idea that to be understood, rules must first be "interpreted."[85] This argument, however, is compressed: we shall spell it out in more detail, using Wittgenstein's arguments regarding understanding and interpretation.[86]

Wittgenstein's basic claim is that "understanding" is primary, and "interpretation" is a second-order or "parasitic" activity.[87] Interpretation is parasitic in the sense that interpretation only arises where understanding is already in place. Understanding, according to Wittgenstein, is unreflective; when we follow rules, we ordinarily do so without second-guessing ourselves and without reflection on what the rule requires.

---

[83] For detailed discussion, see generally Dennis Patterson, *The Poverty of Interpretive Universalism: Toward the Reconstruction of Legal Theory*, 72 TEX. L. REV. 1 (1993).

[84] Wittgenstein made the point this way:

> But how can a rule show me what I have to do at this point? Whatever I do is, on some interpretation, in accord with the rule.—That is not what we ought to say, but rather: any interpretation still hangs in the air along with what it interprets, and cannot give it any support. Interpretations by themselves do not determine meaning.

LUDWIG WITTGENSTEIN, PHILOSOPHICAL INVESTIGATIONS § 198 (G.E.M. Anscombe trans., 1958). *See also* ROBERT B. BRANDOM, MAKING IT EXPLICIT: REASONING, REPRESENTING, AND DISCURSIVE COMMITMENT 508–09 (1994) ("Linguistic understanding depends on interpretation…only in extraordinary situations—where different languages are involved, or where ordinary communication has broken down."); Jeff Coulter, *Is Contextualising Necessarily Interpretive?*, 21 J. PRAGMATICS 689, 692 (1994) ("Understanding is not an activity: it is akin to an ability. To understand is to have achieved knowledge of some kind, whilst interpreting is an activity which is akin to hypothesis formation or, in a different sense, to the assignment of significance (explanatory or otherwise) broader than the determination of intelligibility." (footnote omitted)).

[85] Peter Hacker explains:

> [I]t is a grievous error to think that in understanding an utterance one always or even usually engages in interpretation. To interpret an utterance is to explain it, typically to paraphrase it in the same language or to translate it into a different language…. Obscurities, ambiguities or complexities may call out for an interpretation, but it would be wholly incoherent to think that all understanding is interpreting. For then the interpretation given, i.e. the paraphrase, would itself stand in need of an interpretation in order to be understood; and a vicious regress would be generated. This misconception has manifold roots. One is the bizarre idea that what we hear or utter are mere sounds which have to be correlated with or mapped on to meanings in order to be understood. But we no more hear or utter mere sounds than we see or paint patches of colour. We hear and utter meaningful words and sentences …

P.M.S. Hacker, *Language, Rules and Pseudo-Rules*, 8 LANGUAGE & COMMC'N 159, 168 (1988).

[86] For detailed discussion of the understanding/interpretation distinction and its relevance for law, see DENNIS PATTERSON, LAW AND TRUTH 86–88 (1996).

[87] WITTGENSTEIN, *supra* note 84, §§ 139–242.

Wittgenstein begins his argument for the primacy of understanding by presenting us with a paradox. He writes:

This was our paradox: no course of action could be determined by a rule, because every course of action can be made out to accord with the rule. The answer was: if everything can be made out to accord with the rule, then it can also be made out to conflict with it. And so there would be neither accord nor conflict here.[88]

Why does Wittgenstein question the importance of interpretation as an explanation of the meaning of a rule or what the rule requires? His point is that if understanding an utterance or sign were a matter of interpretation (which is just another utterance or sign), then the interpretation itself would require its own interpretation, and so on, infinitely. This argument—the infinite regress argument—is meant to question the idea of understanding as interpretation. Wittgenstein urges us to rethink the notion that before we can understand an utterance we must first interpret it. Understanding a rule and what it requires is fundamental to participating in a practice. Interpretation, by contrast, is an activity we engage in when our understanding breaks down (e.g., there is more than one way of understanding a rule in a given circumstance).

Wittgenstein's insight is that rule following is not solely a mental phenomenon. Succinctly stated, Wittgenstein relocates normativity (i.e., the distinction between being correct and incorrect) in action, specifically social action. The normativity of rule following—the ground of correctness and incorrectness—is not to be found in the agreement of others as such. Rather, the agreement of rule followers over time is the basis of understanding. Agreement is a necessary feature of the normativity of our practices, but the agreement must be a regularity in reaction to circumstances (i.e., unreflective action in context). In short, when we say there must be "agreement in actions" what we are really saying is that there must be harmony in application over time.[89] This harmony in reaction and application is constitutive of all practices, including legal practice. It is the basis of our moral and legal judgments.

---

[88] *Id.* at § 201.

[89] For an illuminating discussion, see MEREDITH WILLIAMS, WITTGENSTEIN, MIND AND MEANING: TOWARDS A SOCIAL CONCEPTION OF MIND 176 (1999):

It is in this sense that community agreement is constitutive of practices, and that agreement must be displayed in action. There are two important features about this account that need to be highlighted. First, it is the social practice that provides the structure within

The distinction between correct and incorrect rule following is a matter of community agreement in judgments over time.[90] As we discuss in Chapter One, the idea of unconscious rule following does not make sense. Following a rule, making judgments about what a rule requires, and distinguishing between correct and incorrect action all require a role for others in the intersubjective constitution of norms of correctness. The Mikhail view of unconscious rule following never gains traction because it never moves beyond the ground of what he sees as some version of the internal constitution of mind.

Like Chomsky's rules of generative linguistic grammar,[91] Mikhail's moral rules are postulated to be innate. This claim makes no sense. How can a child be said to "know" how to follow moral norms without being cognizant of them? In other words, before a child even learns a syllable of language, how can she be said to possess moral knowledge? The problem posed by these questions cannot be avoided by asserting that we "follow" rules "unconsciously." Again, the problem is conceptual.[92] Following a rule includes a panoply of normative activities. When we follow rules we may do the following things:

1. Justify our behavior by reference to the rule;
2. Consult the rule in deciding on a course of conduct;
3. Correct our behavior and that of others by reference to the rule; and
4. Interpret the rule when we fail to understand what it requires.

which individual understanding can obtain or individual judgment be made. Central to Wittgenstein's thought is the claim, repeatedly argued for, that no isolated event or behavior can correctly be described as naming or obeying or understanding. The rule as formula, the standard as chart, or the paradigm as an instance have no normative or representational status in their own right. They have this status only in virtue of the way the formula or the chart or the instance is used. It is the use that creates the structured context within which sign-posts point, series can be continued, orders be obeyed and paradigms be exemplary. Only then can we see a particular action as embodying or instancing a grammatical structure. In short, the mandatory stage setting is social practice.

Second, community agreement does not constitute a justification for particular judgments. What is indispensable for correct, or appropriate, judgment and action is that there is concord, not that each individual justifies his (or anyone else's) judgement and action by appeal to its harmony with the judgement of others. (footnote omitted).

[90]   See id. at 169.

[91]   Generative grammar is a theory of syntax. The grammar takes the form of a system of formalized rules that mechanically generate all and only the grammatical sentences of a language. See generally NOAM CHOMSKY, ASPECTS OF THE THEORY OF SYNTAX 3–10 (1965).

[92]   In the opinion of one careful reader, Chomsky—the inspiration for Professor Mikhail's model of unconscious rule following—has abandoned the idea. See John Searle, End of the Revolution, N.Y. REV. BOOKS, Feb. 28, 2002, at 36 (reviewing NOAM CHOMSKY, NEW HORIZONS IN THE STUDY OF LANGUAGE AND MIND (2000)) ("Chomsky has now given up on the idea

It is difficult to see how these normative activities are possible when we are not cognizant of the existence of a rule. Of course, we may act in a manner consistent with a rule, but that is not *following* the rule.

We turn now to Mikhail's second, and more fundamental, claim: that "the mind/brain contains a moral grammar"[93] and thus that moral knowledge is located in the brain.[94] Mikhail presupposes that the object of explanation (in this case, "moral knowledge") is located in a place. In Mikhail's view, moral knowledge is in the brain.

As we discuss in Chapter One, however, knowledge is not a thing, located in the brain (or anywhere). Knowing something ("how to" or "how that") is an ability. "To know" is a success verb.[95] To "know" something is neither to be in a certain state nor is it to be in possession of a particular structure of mind or brain.[96] Like other abilities, knowledge of moral rules is exhibited in behavior. Criteria for the ascription of knowledge consist of correct performances. "Knowledge" includes, among other things, being able to spot error, explain the error, and correct it. In doing these things, one demonstrates that one knows the rules—not that one's mind or brain "contains" the rules.[97]

Consider: when we say "Jones knows the train schedule from Warsaw to Krakow," we are not saying that Jones has the schedule hardwired into his mind or brain. Even if he did, that would still not be sufficient to say that he "knows" the schedule because to know the schedule means knowing how to read the schedule correctly. To do this, Jones needs to be able to do things with the schedule. It is that doing that is the ground of the ascription "Jones knows."

In addition to confusing an ability with a thing (or being in a particular state), there is a second, related problem. This problem arises from the presupposition that moral knowledge has a location. Mikhail locates "moral grammar" in the brain. But knowing does not have a

---

that Universal Grammar is a matter of unconscious rule-following. But he also dismisses the idea that real human languages are governed by rules. That, I believe, cannot be right.").

[93] MIKHAIL, *supra* note 22, at 17.

[94] *Id.* at 24.

[95] *See* ALVIN I. GOLDMAN, KNOWLEDGE IN A SOCIAL WORLD 60 (1999).

[96] ANTHONY KENNY, THE LEGACY OF WITTGENSTEIN 129 (1984) ("To contain information is to be in a certain state, while to know something is to possess a certain capacity."). Indeed, it is a tenet of classical and modern epistemology that someone can have true information (true beliefs) and not have knowledge. *See* PLATO, THEAETETUS (Robin H. Waterfield trans., 1987); ALVIN I. GOLDMAN, EPISTEMOLOGY AND COGNITION 42 (1986); Edmund Gettier, *Is Justified True Belief Knowledge?*, 23 ANALYSIS 121 (1963).

[97] *See* P.M.S. Hacker, *Chomsky's Problems*, 10 LANGUAGE & COMMC'N. 127, 128–29 (1990).

bodily location.[98] Yes, we need a brain to know, but this does not mean that knowledge is something located in the brain, any more than that there is a thing called "walking" that is located in the legs.[99]

Finally, there is a third problem with the claim that moral knowledge is contained in the brain. This problem arises from the relationship between knowledge and truth.[100] Having moral knowledge means that the things "known" are true (i.e., that what is known is indeed so). Thus, *even if* the brain contains a moral grammar and uses it to interpret and classify fact patterns, the rules, principles, and judgments produced would qualify as moral knowledge (as opposed to moral beliefs) only if they are true.[101] Mikhail does not provide arguments for the normative adequacy of the results produced as a result of the posited moral grammar.[102]

It is on this last problem that his work connects with our discussion of Greene and colleagues in the previous section. Although Mikhail's

---

[98] John Searle recently compared thinking with digestion. He postulated that just as digestion occurs in the stomach, so does thinking occur in the brain. *See* John Searle, *Putting Consciousness Back in the Brain: Reply to* BENNETT AND HACKER, PHILOSOPHICAL FOUNDATIONS OF NEUROSCIENCE, *in* NEUROSCIENCE AND PHILOSOPHY: BRAIN, MIND, AND LANGUAGE 97, 108–09 (2007). But the analogy does not hold. If we open someone's stomach, we can see the process of digestion occurring. But if we open someone's brain, we do not find anything we might call "thinking." Of course, an fMRI scanner will show that certain areas of the brain are actuated when a person is thinking. Although the brain is necessary for one to have thoughts, the thoughts are not "located" in the brain. Maxwell Bennett & P.M.S. Hacker, *The Conceptual Presuppositions of Cognitive Neuroscience: A Reply to Critics, in* NEUROSCIENCE AND PHILOSOPHY: BRAIN, MIND, AND LANGUAGE 143.

[99] *See* Hacker, *supra* note 97, at 134.

> Neurophysiologists may discover that certain neural configurations are causally necessary conditions for having the ability to speak a language. But they will never find any knowledge in the brain. Neither what one knows, namely truths, facts, or propositions, nor abilities to say, show or tell what one knows (i.e. abilities constitutive of knowing) can (logically) be found in the brain. For truths, facts, and propositions, although they can be recorded on paper or on a computer disc, cannot be recorded on or in the brain. For whereas we record facts by means of a symbolism, a language, and write the information down in a notebook or store it on a computer disc, there is no such thing as the brain's employing a language, understanding or speaking a language, nor is there any such thing as human beings employing brains as repositories for written records, let alone as computer discs. To say that truths, facts, or propositions are stored, filed away, or retained in one's mind is just to say that they are known and not forgotten.

[100] *See* GOLDMAN, *supra* note 96, at 42 ("To know a proposition is to know that it is true. But you cannot know that p is true unless it *is* true.").

[101] Things are even more complicated epistemically. Even if true, the results produced by a moral grammar may fail to qualify as knowledge for other reasons. For example, they may be true but not epistemically justified (*see id.*), or true and justified but subject to Gettier conditions (*see* Gettier, *supra* note 96).

[102] Mikhail recognizes this issue but places it outside the scope of his discussion. MIKHAIL, *supra* note 22, at 31–33. These conceptual issues, however, are fundamental if the framework is intended to illuminate moral *knowledge*.

work is different (and much more sophisticated) in many ways than Greene's emotional–rational framework, the problem we see with each is the attempt to locate moral knowledge (or lack thereof) in the brain. This is also a problem with Goodenough's account of legal reasoning, as well as the accounts of legal responsibility by Churchland and by Greene and Cohen that we discuss in Chapter Two. As we will see, it is also a fundamental problem with recent work on neuroeconomics, to which we now turn.

IV. Neuroeconomics

Similar to moral decision making, a neuroscientific literature focuses on economic decision making,[103] and scholars have likewise attempted to apply neuroeconomic insights about the brain to issues in law.[104] The field investigates the neurological activity of people while they are engaged in economic decision making, and is similar to the field of behavioral economics, which studies the extent to which, and attempts to explain why (typically, at the psychological level), people deviate from the conduct predicted by classical economic, rational-actor models.[105] Rather than seeking to illuminate economic behavior with psychological explanations, however, neuroeconomists seek to explain this behavior with explanations of brain activity.[106] Legal scholars then apply these explanations to legal issues, just as behavioral economists do with

---

[103] See Alan G. Sanfey et al., Neuroeconomics: Cross-Currents in Research on Decision-Making, 10 TRENDS IN COG. SCI. 108 (2006); Alan G. Sanfey et al., The Neural Basis of Economic Decision-Making in the Ultimatum Game, 300 SCI. 1755 (2003). See also Ariel Rubinstein, Comment on Neuroeconomics, 24 ECON. & PHIL. 485 (2008) ("Neuroeconomics will remain a hot topic in economics for the coming decade, probably one of the hottest.").

[104] See Jedediah Purdy, The Promise (and Limits) of Neuroeconomics, 58 ALA. L. REV. 1 (2006); Morris B. Hoffman, The Neuroeconomic Path of the Law, in LAW & THE BRAIN (Semir Zeki & Oliver Goodenough eds., 2006); Terrence Chorvat & Kevin McCabe, The Brain and the Law, in LAW & THE BRAIN; Paul Zak, Neuroeconomics, in LAW & THE BRAIN; Terrence Chorvat & Kevin McCabe, Neuroeconomics and Rationality, 80 CHI.-KENT L. REV. 1235 (2005).

[105] See generally Christine Jolls, Cass R. Sunstein & Richard Thaler, A Behavioral Approach to Law and Economics, 50 STAN. L. REV. 1471 (1998).

[106] Sanfey et al., Neuroeconomics, supra note 103, at 108; see also Chorvat & McCabe, Neuroeconomics, supra note 104, at 1242 ("Carried to their logical extreme, for example, these models might reveal that the reason a particular decision was made was a change in the membrane permeability in certain neuronal and glial cells.").

psychological explanations.[107] According to one legal scholar, "the promise of neuroeconomics" is to render "literally visible the activity of other minds. It will let us see reason, fear, and principle at work, let us watch utility accumulate or dissipate."[108]

Current neuroeconomic studies use fMRI to scan the brains of people while they make simple economic decisions. One prominent series of studies, and the example we will discuss, focuses on the "ultimatum game."[109] Here is how this game is played. Two participants are told that a particular sum of money is to be divided between them; player 1 proposes a division and then player 2 will choose to accept or reject it.[110] In a one-shot game, the players keep the proposed division if player 2 accepts; if player 2 rejects the offer, they both walk away with nothing.[111] According to the classic rational-actor model of economic decision making, the rational thing for player 1 to do is to propose that player 2 should take the smallest unit above 0, and that player 1 should therefore then keep the rest for himself. This is the "rational" thing for player 1 to do because (1) this maximizes player 1's share (and maximization is the ultimate goal according to the model), and (2) it is rational for player 2 to accept any amount offered greater than 0 because any amount will be higher than 0, and 0 is player 2's only other option).[112] Not surprisingly, as in many other areas, people deviate routinely from the outcomes predicted by the rational-actor model. For example, in most studies about half of the player 2s who perceived an offer as unfair rejected it.[113]

The neuroscience research of Alan Sanfey and colleagues purports to tell us why some people engaged in the "irrational" behavior of rejecting offers they perceived as unfair.[114] The studies used fMRI scans to examine the brains of players presented with "unfair offers"; the researchers noticed increased activity in several brain regions.[115]

[107] Chorvat & McCabe, *Neuroeconomics, supra* note 104; Zak, *supra* note 104; Purdy, *supra* note 104.

[108] Purdy, *supra* note 104, at 39–40.

[109] Sanfey et al., *Ultimatum, supra* note 103, at 1775. The ultimatum game is just one of several examples in the neuroeconomics decision-making literature. For an overview of others, see Purdy, *supra* note 103.

[110] Sanfey et al., *Ultimatum, supra* note 103, at 1775.

[111] *Id.*

[112] *Id.*

[113] *Id.*

[114] *Id.*

[115] *Id.* at 1756.

Three areas in particular that showed increased activity when presented with unfair offers were the "bilateral interior insula" (which has been associated with "negative emotional states"), the "dorsolateral prefrontal cortex" (which has been "linked to cognitive processes such as goal maintenance and executive control"), and the "anterior cingulated cortex" (which has been "implicated in detection of cognitive conflict" such as between "cognitive and emotional motivations").[116] Moreover, subjects with greater increases in these three areas were more likely to reject the unfair offers. By contrast, subjects whose brains showed increased activity in the more "rational" areas of the brain were more likely to accept the offers.[117]

According to Terrence Chorvat and Kevin McCabe, the results support a particular conception of economic (and, more generally, human) decision making as the product of different brain processes in competition with one another: emotional and rational.[118] This is the same distinction drawn by Greene and colleagues with regard to moral decision making. The "key questions," Chorvat and McCabe explain, are "how does the brain decide which problems it will address?" and "what neural mechanisms are used to solve the problem?"[119] With regard to the ultimatum game, different brain regions (the emotional and rational) "seem to embody different thought processes."[120] Moreover, they contend, because the "anterior cingulate cortex" (ACC) (which is "clearly involved in cognitive conflict resolution"[121]) was "significantly active" for both subjects who accepted and rejected the offers,[122] the ACC therefore "seems to moderate between these different regions."[123] We can summarize the neuroeconomic explanation of what occurred for each subject as follows: the subject is faced with an unfair offer, the subject's brain faces a decision of what to do, and so the subject's brain decides which process to use to decide this question. The two brain processes—the emotional and the rational—begin to analyze the offer.

---

[116] Id. at 1756–57.

[117] Id. at 1757–58.

[118] Chorvat & McCabe, Neuroeconomics, supra note 104. The neuroeconomics literature provides an interesting example of how the vocabulary of one discipline gets transposed into another (e.g., talk of "competition" among brain locations).

[119] Id. at 1248.

[120] Id. at 1253.

[121] Id. at 1249.

[122] Id. at 1253.

[123] Id.

If the processes reach contradictory conclusions, then a third part of the brain adjudicates between them, deciding whether to accept or reject the offer. The researchers define the issues for future research as "under what circumstances do these various systems [in the brain] cooperate or compete? When there is competition, how and where is it adjudicated?"[124]

What implications do these studies have for law? Consider two examples. Chorvat and McCabe argue that the findings may help to construct legal regulations that assure greater compliance by citizens as well as greater social pressures to conform to legal norms.[125] According to this line of argument, greater compliance would presumably follow from regulations less likely to trigger the same kinds of emotional responses that caused people to reject offers in the ultimatum game. (And these same kinds of emotional responses would presumably also generate social pressure regarding conformity to legal norms; deviations would produce the same types of emotional reactions as unfair offers in the ultimatum game.) One example concerns settlement negotiations and "tort reform."[126] McCabe and Laura Inglis argue that the neuroeconomic research is relevant to, and supports, encouraging parties to accept "rational" settlements,[127] rather than allowing emotions to cause parties to reject what they perceive to be "unfair" offers and irrationally "leave money on the table" (like the person in an ultimatum game who refuses a $1 offer and walks away with nothing).[128] A second proposed example concerns property rights. Paul Zak suggests that neuroscience may provide "neural clues" about irrational behavior toward property, such as why "people pay more to protect property than the expected loss associated with its expropriation."[129] In sum, one major policy concern underlying neuroeconomic discussions is that "emotional" areas in the brain cause people to make decisions

---

[124] Sanfey et al., *Neuroeconomics, supra* note 103, at 114.

[125] Chorvat & McCabe, *The Brain, supra* note 104, at 127.

[126] Kevin McCabe & Laura Inglis, *Using Neuroeconomics Experiments to Study Tort Reform,* Mercatus Policy Series (2007), *available at* http://mercatus.org/sites/default/files/20080104_Tort_Final.pdf.

[127] In conventional law-and-economics analysis, a "rational" settlement is one that for plaintiffs exceeds the expected outcome at trial (plus costs), and that for defendants is one that is less than this expected amount (plus costs).

[128] *Id.*

[129] Zak, *supra* note 104. *See also* Goodenough & Prehn, *supra* note 30, at 98–100 (suggesting that neuroscience research may illuminate normative attitudes about intellectual property).

that deviate from the calculated decisions implied by rational-actor models of behavior.

As with moral decision making, we resist drawing any normative conclusions from these studies for law. The characterizations of what the studies purport to show run into a number of conceptual problems. Some of these problems are similar to those discussed above regarding moral decision making.

First, the fact that unfair offers produced negative emotional reactions in subjects does not mean that the emotions, or the brain areas associated with emotions, caused the subjects to reject the offers. In the ultimatum-game studies, the data show what the subjects' brains were doing while they (the subjects) were deciding whether to accept or reject the offer. Consider the following analogy. Suppose a person's face turned red whenever he was angry. Now, suppose when faced with an unfair offer in the ultimatum game, his face turned red and he rejected the offer. Surely we would not say this is evidence that the person's face rejected the offer; similarly, why then conclude that a subject's insula cortex rejected the offer because there was activity in that area on a brain scan?[130] The emotional reactions could have merely accompanied decisions to reject offers otherwise judged to be unfair by subjects. In other words, the emotions could have been effects, not causes.[131]

Second, even if the emotional reactions caused subjects to reject the offers, the emotions could be based on prior judgments about the offers themselves.[132] People may react emotionally to what they perceive or judge to be just and unjust, fair and unfair, and these reactions are affected by a person's background beliefs and knowledge about what constitutes fair and unfair conduct, of how people ought to treat and be treated by one another. If so, then even if subjects rejected unfair offers because of their emotional reactions, the reactions may

---

[130] Similarly, if an increased heart rate occurs when someone is lying, we would not (for good reason) say his heart is causing him to lie.

[131] See Poldrack, *supra* note 58 (discussing limitations of drawing "reverse inferences").

[132] Emotions have objects and causes. These may, but need not, be the same thing. For example, a loud noise may be the *cause* of one's fear, but the *object* of that fear may be the possibility that there is a burglar in the house. See M.R. BENNETT & P.M.S. HACKER, PHILOSOPHICAL FOUNDATIONS OF NEUROSCIENCE 206 (2003) ("what makes one jealous is not the same as what one is jealous of; your indignant tirade may make me feel ashamed, but what I am ashamed of is my own misbehaviour; a change in the fortunes of war may make one feel hopeful, but what one hopes for is final victory.").

themselves have been caused by judgments about the unfair offers.[133] Having a properly working brain (including a properly working insula cortex) may make it *possible* for one to have this emotional reaction, but the reaction may be a link in a causal chain connecting a moral judgment and behavior.

Third, as with the fMRI studies on moral judgments, it begs the question to assume that the "emotional" judgments are incorrect. It also begs the question to presuppose the law ought to limit such judgments and foster the "rational" judgments associated with "cognitive" brain processes.[134] The complex normative questions underlying legal theory and policy cannot be sidestepped with an appeal to "competition" among brain processes and the need to make more "rational" decisions.

There are deeper conceptual problems with some of the characterizations of the neuroscientific results. The descriptions of two competing brain processes, with a third area "adjudicating" conflicts, are examples of what Max Bennett and Peter Hacker refer to as the "mereological fallacy."[135] The fallacy arises when attributes that are ascribed to a part of a person make sense only when ascribed to the person as a whole.[136] It makes no sense to say that a brain or a brain area "decides," "reasons," or "adjudicates." We know what it means for a *person* to make decisions, to consider reasons, and to adjudicate disputes, and we know that the person needs a brain to do these things. But we do not know what it means for the anterior cingulate cortex to decide, reason, or adjudicate because no sense has been given to such claims.[137] Until sense has been given to what it means for an area of the brain to "adjudicate" a conflict—and this meaning will differ from what we ordinarily mean by "adjudicating" and so license different

---

[133] *Cf. id.* at 216 ("If one is indignant at a perceived injustice, what tells one that the object of one's indignation is an evil is not that one feels flushed. On the contrary, one is indignant at A's action because it is unjust, not because one flushes in anger when one hears it. And one knows it to be unjust because it rides roughshod over someone's rights, not because one flushes in anger.").

[134] This question-begging feature is not unique to neuroeconomics. Reliance on a narrow conception of "rationality" in normative arguments is a common feature of economics-inspired legal scholarship. *See* Michael S. Pardo, *Rationality*, 64 ALA. L. REV. 142 (2012).

[135] *Id.* at 133–34.

[136] *Id.*

[137] Characterizing a brain area as engaging in this behavior leads to conceptual confusion. We know, for example, that a person needs a brain to adjudicate disputes. Does the anterior

inferences—then an empirical investigation of where "competition" in the brain is "adjudicated" is bound to fail.[138] Claims must make sense before they can be true or false. The current neuroeconomic explanation of decision making misguidedly ascribes psychological attributes to the brain (e.g., deciding, reasoning, adjudicating) that only make sense when attributed to the person. This confusion undermines attempts to draw conclusions for law.

In addition to ascribing human behavior to parts of the brain, neuroeconomic explanations also go a step further and ascribe behavior of groups of people to areas in the brain. Consider the following description from Sanfey and colleagues:

There are striking parallels between the brain and a modern corporation. Both can be viewed as complex systems transforming inputs into outputs. Both involve the interaction of multiple, highly similar agents (neurons are similar to one another, just as are people), which, however, are specialized to perform particular functions. Thus, in corporations, units often take the form of departments that perform functions such as research, marketing, and so on. Similarly, the brain has systems specialized for different functions. As in a corporation, these functions may be more or less spatially segregated in the brain, depending upon the processing requirements of the specific functions and their interactions.

Furthermore, there is hierarchical structure in both brains and corporations. Both rely on "executive" systems that make judgments about the relative importance of tasks and decide how to mobilize specialized capabilities to perform those tasks.[139]

For the same reasons that it is a mistake to ascribe human attributes to the brain or its parts, it is a mistake to ascribe the qualities of groups of people to the brain and its parts. Corporations, and other groups of people, act through the intentional behavior of individuals. The analogy of the brain to the modern corporation is more confusing

cingulate cortex also need its own brain to adjudicate (which would have its own ACC, which adjudicates with...ad infinitum)?

[138] Compare an experiment (mentioned earlier) to determine whether a Dworkinian principle "weighs" more than an elephant, or a judge's assertion that she will decide the case "in her brain." Until sense has been given to "weight," "in the brain," "adjudicates," or "competition" in the various claims, we cannot empirically investigate whether what is expressed (or what is trying to be expressed) is true or false.

[139] Sanfey et al., *Neuroeconomics*, *supra* note 103, at 109.

than illuminating—despite the superficial similarities, no part of the brain acts with the type of intentionality that explains the behavior of human actors in a modern corporation. Ascribing human behavior to brain activity brings conceptual confusion rather than empirical elucidation to legal theory.

4

Brain–Based Lie Detection

Perhaps no issue discussed within either popular culture or the legal literature on law and neuroscience has garnered more attention than neuroscience-based lie detection.[1] This attention is no doubt due to the bold claims made by the proponents of such technology[2] coupled with the general, age-old fascination with trying to discover surefire methods of lie detection more generally.[3] The ability to accurately and convincingly distinguish lying from truth telling promises to provide a solution to complex issues at the heart of virtually every litigated legal issue in criminal and civil cases: namely, which witnesses to believe. The appeal to neural data to detect lying purports to cut through this complexity by bypassing the usual behavioral or other evidence of

---

[1] In the press, see Jeffrey Rosen, *The Brain on the Stand*, N.Y. TIMES (Magazine), Mar. 11, 2007; Robert Lee Hotz, *The Brain, Your Honor, Will Take the Witness Stand*, WALL ST. J., Jan. 16, 2009, at A7; Lone Frank, *The Quest to Build the Perfect Lie Detector*, SALON.COM, Jul. 23, 2011, *available at* http://www.salon.com/2011/07/23/lie_detector_excerpt/. In the legal literature, see Daniel D. Langleben & Jane Campbell Moriarty, *Using Brain Imaging for Lie Detection: Where Science, Law and Policy Collide*, PSYCHOL., 19 PUB. POL'Y & L. 222 (2013); Francis X. Shen & Owen D. Jones, *Brain Scans as Legal Evidence: Truth, Proof, Lies, and Lessons*, 62 MERCER L. REV. 861 (2011); Frederick Schauer, *Can Bad Science Be Good Evidence? Neuroscience, Lie Detection, and Beyond*, 95 CORNELL L. REV. 1191 (2010); Joëlle Anne Moreno, *The Future of Neuroimaged Lie Detection and the Law*, 42 AKRON L. REV. 717 (2009); Henry T. Greely & Judy Illes, *Neuroscience-Based Lie Detection: The Urgent Need for Regulation*, 33 AM. J.L. & MED. 377 (2007); Michael S. Pardo, *Neuroscience Evidence, Legal Culture, and Criminal Procedure*, 33 AM. J. CRIM. L. 301 (2006).

[2] In a recent case, for example, an expert witness's report proffered to admit the results of fMRI lie detection stated that "a finding such as this is 100 % accurate in determining truthfulness from a truthful person." United States v. Semrau, 693 F.3d 510, 519 (6th Cir. 2012). We discuss this case in detail below.

[3] For a fascinating discussion of the history of lie detection in the United States, see KEN ALDER, THE LIE DETECTORS: THE HISTORY OF AN AMERICAN OBSESSION (2007).

lying and revealing whether the witness's brain is correlated with lying or truth telling. The probative value of such evidence will depend on the strength of these correlations, which promise to be quite strong.[4] Indeed, authors sometimes go further and assert that the neuroscience will reveal not only correlations with lying or truth-telling behavior but also whether lies and incriminating knowledge are in the brains of subjects.[5]

Along with, and no doubt because of, the strong claims made on behalf of such technology, the legal and scientific literature is filled with growing concern, caution, and warnings about its use. The flipside to promises of highly probative evidence is the potential for such evidence to be highly prejudicial when the evidence has low probative value or is misinterpreted by legal decision makers, or the inferences that are warranted from the data are poorly understood. In addition to these epistemic concerns, a variety of other concerns include possibilities for abuse, for violations of rights, and other practical difficulties.[6]

In this chapter we discuss the current state of brain-based lie detection. We first provide a general overview of the two types of lie detection, the science on which they are based, and the recent court cases in which they have been presented. We next analyze the inferences drawn from, and the claims made on behalf of, such technology in litigation settings. The proposed uses of this evidence in legal settings raise three categories of issues: empirical, conceptual, and practical. Consistent with the general theme running throughout this book, we emphasize the conceptual issues, the important methodological point of clearly

---

[4] The published studies relied on by the defendant in the *Semrau* case report accuracy rates of between 86 and 97 percent. 693 F.3d at 517. By way of comparison, traditional polygraph testing was found to have an accuracy rate of 85–87 percent in certain settings, according to a 2003 report from the National Academy of Sciences. NATIONAL RESEARCH COUNCIL, THE POLYGRAPH AND LIE DETECTION (2003).

[5] *See* Lawrence A. Farwell & Sharon S, Smith, *Using Brain MERMER Testing to Detect Knowledge Despite Efforts to Conceal*, 46 J. FORENSIC SCI. 135 (2001) ("the brain of the criminal is always there, recording the events, in some ways like a video camera"); Paul Root Wolpe, Kenneth Foster & Daniel D. Langleben, *Emerging Neurotechnologies for Lie Detection: Promises and Perils*, 5 AM. J. BIOETHICS 39 (2005) ("using modern neuroscience techniques, a third party can, in principle…gain direct access to the seat of a person's thoughts, feelings, intention, or knowledge" and "peer into an individual's thought processes with our without his or her consent"); Andre A. Moenssens, *Brain Fingerprinting—Can It Be Used to Detect the Innocence of a Person Charged with a Crime?*, 70 UMKC L. REV. 891, 903 (2002) ("Brain fingerprinting, at its best, can only detect whether certain knowledge exists in the subject's brain.").

[6] These issues are discussed in the articles cited in *supra* note 2. *See also* Wolpe et al., *supra* note 5; Richard. G. Boire, *Searching the Brain: The Fourth Amendment Implications of Brain-Based Deception Devices*, 5 AM. J. BIOETHICS 62 (2005).

distinguishing the conceptual from the empirical, and the insights that follow from this clarity. Along the way, however, we also outline the significant empirical and practical issues raised by the proposed use of brain-based lie detection.

To be clear, our aim in discussing the conceptual issues is neither to challenge the scientific project nor to dismiss outright the possibility for such technology to provide probative legal evidence. Far from it. Thus we disagree wholeheartedly with critics of our prior work who have asserted that research in neurolaw "could not even be taken seriously if Pardo and Patterson are right"[7] and that we can "entirely sidestep the method-ological, moral, and legal objections that ordinarily crop up in discussions of neural lie detection."[8] We think there is much to take seriously in neurolaw, given our arguments, and our analysis does not eliminate the need to engage with difficult methodological, moral, and legal issues. The soundness of the theoretical conclusions and practical applications drawn from the experiments depend on clarity regarding the relevant concepts, and our analysis is continuous with, and intended to be a contribution to, these neurolaw projects, not an outright rejection of them.

Current proposals for brain-based lie detection fall into two main types. The first type relies on the results of fMRI brain scans to deter-mine whether subjects who are engaged in lying or deception exhibit neural data that are distinguishable from subjects who are engaged in truth-telling or nondeceptive behavior.[9] The second type relies on the results of EEG scans to determine whether subjects exhibit brain waves correlated with prior recognition or knowledge of a particular fact, image, object, or other item of information.[10] We first provide a brief overview

---

[7] Sarah K. Robins & Carl F. Craver, *No Nonsense Neuro-law*, 4 NEUROETHICS 195 (2011).

[8] Thomas Nadelhoffer, *Neural Lie Detection, Criterial Change, and Ordinary Language*, 4 NEUROETHICS 205 (2011).

[9] It is important to note that lying and deception are distinct phenomena: one can lie without deceiving, and one can deceive without lying. It is also important to distinguish sin-cerity from veracity: lie-detection technologies (polygraph and fMRI) purport to measure whether a person is asserting what that person *believes* to be true or false, not whether what the person is asserting actually is true or false. The latter requires a further inference based on judgments about the speaker's testimonial qualities other than sincerity. The epistemology of testimony, of which sincerity is just one component, is a rich topic in recent philosophy. For an overview of the literature, see Jonathan Adler, *Epistemological Problems of Testimony*, *in* STANFORD ENCYCLOPEDIA OF PHILOSOPHY (2012), *available at* http://plato.stanford.edu/entries/testimony-episprob/, and for a discussion of how this literature relates to legal proof, see Michael S. Pardo, *Testimony*, 82 TULANE L. REV. 119 (2007).

[10] This type of test thus does not measure whether someone is engaging in lies or truth-telling in response to questions, but instead whether the person has prior or "guilty" knowledge of relevant information. This type of testing may work as a "lie detector"

of fMRI lie detection, the studies examining it, and the legal cases in which parties have tried to present it. We then turn to EEG lie detection, likewise providing a general overview of the proposed technique, the studies examining it, and the legal cases in which parties have tried to present it. After providing an overview of the techniques, we then analyze the empirical, conceptual, and practical issues underlying brain-based lie detection.

I. fMRI Lie Detection

In broad outline, proposed fMRI lie detection works as follows.[11] Subjects (or suspects, defendants, witnesses, etc.) lie down in an MRI scanner. Subjects in the scanner are presented with a series of questions[12] that call for a simple, binary answer (yes–no, true–false, heads–tails). Subjects typically answer such questions by pressing one of two handheld buttons. During this process the MRI machine measures the brain activity of subjects indirectly by measuring blood flow to different areas of the subjects' brains. The measurements depend on a number of important scientific principles. Most important, the measurements depend on the BOLD ("blood oxygen level dependent") signal to infer conclusions about brain activity.[13] The relationship between the signal and activity in particular areas of the brain depends on the following two fundamental ideas. First, when hemoglobin in blood delivers oxygen to areas of the brain (or other organs) it becomes "paramagnetic" and thus will disrupt a magnetic field, such as the one created in an MRI scanner; and, second, when brain activity increases in a particular area, "blood flow

by purportedly revealing whether someone's avowals that he does or does not know the incriminating details are sincere. For examples of criminal defendants attempting to use the tests for this purpose, see Slaughter v. State, 105 P.3d 832 (Okla. Crim. App. 2005); Harrington v. State, 659 N.W. 2d 509 (Iowa 2003).

[11] For general overviews, see A JUDGE'S GUIDE TO NEUROSCIENCE: A CONCISE INTRODUCTION (Michael S. Gazzaniga & Jed S. Rakoff eds., 2010); Greely & Illes, *supra* note 1; Owen D. Jones et al., *Brain Imaging for Legal Thinkers: A Guide for the Perplexed*, 5 STAN. TECH. L. REV. (2009); Teneille Brown & Emily Murphy, *Through a Scanner Darkly: Functional Neuroimaging as Evidence of a Criminal Defendant's Past Mental States*, 62 STAN. L. REV. 1119 (2012).

[12] The questions typically are either presented visually on a computer screen or aurally through headphones.

[13] For general discussions, see the sources cited in *supra* note 11. See also William G. Gibson, Les Farnell & Max R. Bennett, *A Computational Model Relating Changes in Cerebral Blood Volume to Synaptic Activity in Neurons*, 70 NEUROCOMPUTING 1674 (2007).

increases more than needed to supply the increase in oxygen consumption."[14] When there is increased blood flow to an area of the brain, the hemoglobin contains more oxygen, and the signal increases. The increased signal is thus thought to imply that the relevant area of the brain is more "active" or is otherwise involved in whatever behavior the subject is currently engaged in while in the scanner—for example, answering questions about an event. Statistical data from these magnetic measurements are then processed and translated through one of a variety of statistical techniques into a brain "image," which is not a picture but is rather a visual representation of the statistical data projected onto a template of a brain.[15]

From this rudimentary summary of the process, we can already see the basic ideas behind fMRI lie detection begin to emerge. What if the fMRI signal for one area increased when subjects were lying and the signal increased for a completely different area when subjects were telling the truth? Moreover, if subjects cannot control the blood flow to areas of their brains, then perhaps this technique would be superior to relying on the traditional measures of polygraphs machines (e.g., heart rate, breathing, and galvanic skin responses)? Indeed, would we then have a surefire lie-detection technique, along with answers to some of the most common—and vexing—questions arising in criminal and civil legal disputes regarding the credibility of witnesses?

These are the types of questions motivating the rise of fMRI lie detection. Before we can begin to understand and answer them, we must first look at the current science. There have been several dozen published studies related to fMRI lie detection.[16] Reviewing the

---

[14] Marcus Raichle, *What Is an fMRI?*, in A JUDGE'S GUIDE TO NEUROSCIENCE, *supra* note 11.

[15] *See* Adina L. Roskies, *Neuroimaging and Inferential Distance*, 1 NEUROETHICS 19 (2008).

[16] Although not intended to be exhaustive, the following two dozen articles (listed in reverse chronological order) provide a representative sample of the scientific literature and include the studies most often discussed in the neurolaw literature: Ayahito Ito et al., *The Dorsolateral Prefrontal Cortex in Deception When Remembering Neutral and Emotional Events*, 69 NEUROSCIENCE RES. 121 (2011); Giorgio Ganis et al., *Lying in the Scanner: Covert Countermeasures Disrupt Deception Detection by Functional Magnetic Resonance Imaging*, 55 NEUROIMAGE 312–19 (2011); Catherine J. Kaylor-Hughes et al., *The Functional Anatomical Distinction between Truth Telling and Deception Is Preserved among People with Schizophrenia*, 21 CRIM. BEHAVIOR & MENTAL HEALTH 8 (2011); Tatia M.C. Lee et al., *Lying about the Valence of Affective Pictures: An fMRI Study*, 5 PLoS ONE (2010); Kamila E. Sip et al., *The Production and Detection of Deception in an Interactive Game*, 48 NEUROPSYCHOLOGIA 3619 (2010); George T. Monteleone et al., *Detection of Deception Using fMRI: Better than Chance, but Well Below Perfection*, 4 SOCIAL NEUROSCIENCE 528–38 (2009); S. Bhatt et al., *Lying about Facial Recognition: An fMRI Study*, 69 BRAIN & COGNITION 382 (2009); Joshua D. Greene & Joseph M. Paxton, *Patterns of Neural Activity Associated with Honest and Dishonest Moral Decisions*, 106 PROC. NAT. ACAD. SCI. 12506–11 (2009); Matthias Gamer et al., *fMRI-Activation Patterns in the Detection of Concealed Information*

literature in 2010, Anthony Wagner, a professor of psychology, concludes that "there are no relevant published studies that unambiguously answer whether fMRI-based neuroscience methods can detect lies at the individual level."[17]

A first wave of studies explored whether differences between truth telling and lying (or deception[18]) could be established by comparing data across groups of subjects.[19] In other words, the studies did not examine whether any particular subject was lying or telling the truth on any particular occasion or in general. Rather, they looked at whether generalities could be inferred about lying and truth telling by combining the fMRI data from groups of subjects. In these studies,

Rely on Memory-Related Effects, SCAN (2009); F. Andrew Kozel et al., Functional MRI Detection of Deception after Committing a Mock Sabotage Crime, 54 J. FORENSIC SCI. 220 (2009); F. Andrew Kozel et al., Replication of Functional MRI Detection of Deception, 2 OPEN FORENSIC SCI. J. 6 (2009); Rachel S. Fullam et al., Psychopathic Traits and Deception: Functional Magnetic Resonance Imaging, 194 BRIT. J. PSYCHIATRY 229–35 (2009); Sean A. Spence et al., Speaking of Secrets and Lies: The Contribution of Ventrolateral Prefrontal Cortex to Vocal Deception, 40 NEUROIMAGE 1411 (2008); Giorgio Ganis & Julian Paul Keenan, The Cognitive Neuroscience of Deception, 4 SOCIAL NEUROSCIENCE 465–72 (2008) (reviewing existing literature); Nobuhito Abe et al., Deceiving Others: Distinct Neural Responses of the Prefrontal Cortex and Amygdala in Simple Fabrication and Deception with Social Interactions, 19 J. COG. NEUROSCIENCE 287 (2007); Feroze B. Mohamed et al., Brain Mapping of Deception and Truth Telling about an Ecologically Valid Situation: Functional MR Imaging and Polygraph Investigation—Initial Experience, 238 RADIOLOGY 679 (2006); F. Andrew Kozel et al., Detecting Deception Using Functional Magnetic Resonance Imaging, BIOL. PSYCHIATRY 58 (2005): Jennifer Maria Nunez et al., Intentional False Responding Shares Neural Substrates with Response Conflict and Cognitive Control, 267 NEUROIMAGE 605–13 (2005); F. Andrew Kozel et al., A Pilot Study of Functional Magnetic Resonance Imaging Brain Correlates of Deception in Healthy Young Men, 16 J. NEUROPSYCHIATRY CLIN. NEUROSCI. 295–305 (2004); Sean A. Spence et al., A Cognitive Neurobiological Account of Deception: Evidence from Functional Neuroimaging, 359 PHIL. TRANS. R. SOC. LOND. 1755–62 (2004); Giorgio Ganis et al., Neural Correlates of Different Types of Deception: An fMRI Investigation, 13 CEREBRAL CORTEX 830–36 (2003); Tatia M.C. Lee et al., Lie Detection by Functional Magnetic Resonance Imaging, 15 HUMAN BRAIN MAPPING 157–64 (2002); Daniel D. Langleben et al., Brain Activity during Simulated Deception: An Event-Related Functional Magnetic Resonance Study, 15 NEUROIMAGE 727–32 (2002); Sean A. Spence et al., Behavioural and Functional Anatomical Correlates of Deception in Humans, 12 NEUROREPORT 2849 (2001).

[17] Anthony Wagner, Can Neuroscience Identify Lies?, in A JUDGE'S GUIDE TO NEUROSCIENCE, supra note 11. As Fred Schauer notes, however, whether Wagner's statement is correct depends on "the evaluative variables 'relevant' and 'unambiguously,'" and the use of neuroscientific evidence for juridical purposes depends ultimately on legal, not scientific, standards. See Frederick Schauer, Lie Detection, Neuroscience, and the Law of Evidence, available at http://ssrn.com/abstract=2165391 (last visited 4-17-13).

[18] See supra note 9.

[19] For a meta-analysis of this wave in the literature, see Shawn E. Christ, The Contributions of Prefrontal Cortex and Executive Control to Deception: Evidence from Activation Likelihood Meta-Analyses, 19 CEREBRAL CORTEX 1557–66 (2009).

subjects were instructed to give true or false answers[20] about a variety of different matters, including biographical information,[21] daily activities,[22] numbers,[23] playing cards,[24] and false past events,[25] and under which object money was hidden.[26]

Although not of immediate practical application in legal settings, these studies serve a useful theoretical purpose—investigating the hypothesis of whether a neurological account for the behavior of lying or deception is plausible and how it might be constructed and further developed, based on the data.[27] The studies found that certain areas of the brain were correlated more with lying than with truth telling[28]: the prefrontal and anterior cingulate cortices,[29] in particular, featured most prominently with "deception" and "lies" (as characterized by the studies). However, many different brain locations turned out to be implicated with deception in these studies, and they varied from study to study.[30] Although some areas showed up more than others, no one area showed up in all the studies.[31] Also, some of the subjects who "lied" did not show activation in any of these areas, and some of

[20] The experiments typically either asked subjects a series of questions or had them practice the protocols beforehand to determine the true and false answers and to ensure the subjects understood the game they were being asked to play.

[21] *See* Lee et al., *Lie Detection, supra* note 16.

[22] Spence et al., *Behavioural and Functional Anatomical Correlates, supra* note 16.

[23] Lee et al., *Lie Detection, supra* note 16.

[24] Langleben et al., *Brain Activity, supra* note 16.

[25] Ganis et al., *Neural Correlates, supra* note 16.

[26] Kozel et al., *Pilot Study, supra* note 16.

[27] *See* Christ, *supra* note 19.

[28] *See* Ganis et al., *Neural Correlates, supra* note 16, at 830 ("fMRI revealed that well-rehearsed lies that fit into a coherent story elicit more activation in right anterior frontal cortices than spontaneous lies that do not fit into a story, whereas the opposite pattern occurs in the anterior cingulate and in posterior visual cortex."); Kozel et al., *Pilot Study, supra* note 16, at 611 ("We have shown that fMRI can be used to detect deception within a cooperative individual."); Langleben et al., *Brain Activity, supra* note 16, at 727 ("Increased activity in the anterior cingulate cortex (ACC), the superior frontal gyrus (SFG), and the left premotor, motor, and anterior parietal cortex was specifically associated with deceptive responses."); Lee et al., *Lie Detection, supra* note 16, at 161 ("Our imaging data revealed four principle regions of brain activation: prefrontal and frontal, parietal, temporal, and sub-cortical."); Spence et al., *Behavioural and Functional Anatomical Correlates, supra* note 16, at 169 ("Attempted deception is associated with activation of executive brain regions (particularly prefrontal and anterior cingulate cortices)").

[29] The prefrontal cortex and the anterior cingulate cortex are thought to be responsible for a variety of cognitive functions. For a basic overview of these brain regions, see MICHAEL S. GAZZANIGA, RICHARD B. IVRY & GEORGE R. MANGUN, COGNITIVE NEUROSCIENCE: THE BIOLOGY OF THE MIND (3d ed. 2008).

[30] *See* Monteleone et al., *Detection of Deception, supra* note 16.

[31] *Id.*

the subjects who "told the truth" showed activation in many of these areas.[32] Moreover, the areas that appeared most often to be correlated with deception are also thought to be related to a variety of other cognitive and emotional tasks.[33]

A second wave of studies has been exploring whether fMRI data about subjects can be used to determine whether a particular subject is lying or telling the truth on a particular occasion. Such determinations are measured in terms of overall accuracy and in terms of false negatives (declaring "truth" when the subject is lying) and false positives (declaring "lying" when the subject is telling the truth). In the relevant literature, the measure of false negatives is often described as the technique's "sensitivity," and the measure of false positives is often described as the technique's "specificity." Some of these studies have reported impressive results in detecting deception. In one study, for example, subjects were instructed to "steal" a watch or a ring from a room, and to answer as if they had stolen neither object when questioned in the scanner.[34] Researchers were able to identify which object was stolen 90 percent of the time. In a subsequent study, some subjects were asked to participate in a mock crime while others were not. Using fMRI testing, researchers were able to identify all nine participants in the mock crime (100 percent sensitivity) but only five of the fifteen no-crime participants (33 percent specificity).[35] Despite these results, however, there are reasons (discussed below) to doubt the external and construct validity of these studies. Moreover, fMRI lie detection may not be as resistant to "countermeasures" (attempts by subjects to defeat the test) as contended by some proponents. According to one recent study, employing simple countermeasures such as imperceptibly moving one's finger or toe reduced the accuracy of fMRI to detect deception to 33 percent (from 100 percent without countermeasures).[36]

Despite these limitations, a market for real-world use of fMRI is beginning to emerge, and in 2010 parties in two legal cases attempted to admit the results of fMRI lie-detection testing.[37] In both cases, one civil and one criminal, the parties seeking to admit the evidence relied on the same company, Cephos Corp., and the same expert witness,

[32]   Id.

[33]   Id. See also Gamer et al., fMRI-Activation Patterns, supra note 16.

[34]   See Kozel et al., Detecting Deception, supra note 16.

[35]   See Kozel et al., Functional MRI Detection, supra note 16.

[36]   Ganis et al., Lying in the Scanner, supra note 16.

[37]   Wilson v. Corestaff Services L.P., 900 N.Y.S.2d 639 (May 14, 2010); United States v. Semrau, 2010 WL 6845092 (W.D. Tenn, June 1, 2010).

Dr. Steven Laken, president and CEO of Cephos. In both cases, the court excluded the evidence.

In *Wilson v. Corestaff Services L.P.*, the plaintiff, Cynette Wilson, sued Corestaff, a temporary employment agency, for allegedly retaliating against her after she complained of sexual harassment while placed at a temporary work assignment.[38] The plaintiff's key evidence was a witness, a Corestaff employee named Ronald Armstrong, who would testify that he was instructed by another Corestaff employee (one of the defendants, Edwin Medina) not to place Wilson in temporary work assignments because she complained of sexual harassment.[39] Wilson also wanted to introduce expert testimony about the results of fMRI lie detection conducted on the witness Armstrong about the alleged incident. Specifically, Wilson wanted to call Cephos CEO Steven Laken to testify that the fMRI results indicate "to a very high probability" that Armstrong "is being truthful when he testifies" that "Edwin Medina told him to not place Cynette Wilson in temporary work assignments because she complained of sexual harassment."[40]

In excluding the expert testimony, the court applied the *Frye* test[41] for the admissibility of scientific expert testimony. Under this test (as applied by New York state courts), parties may introduce relevant scientific expert testimony only if two conditions are met. First, the principles, procedures, or theories on which the testimony is based must "have gained general acceptance in the relevant scientific field," and, second, the testimony must be on a topic "beyond the ken of the average juror."[42] The court excluded the testimony based on this second prong, concluding that the testimony is relevant to a "collateral matter—the credibility of a fact witness" and "credibility is a matter solely for the jury and is clearly within the ken of the jury."[43] The court also noted that "even a cursory review of the scientific literature demonstrates that the plaintiff is unable to establish that the use of the fMRI test to determine truthfulness or deceit is accepted as reliable in the relevant scientific community."[44]

---

[38] 900 N.Y.S.2d 639 (May 14, 2010).

[39] *Id.* at 640.

[40] *Id.*

[41] *See* Frye v. United States, 293 F. 1013 (D.C. Cir. 1923) (articulating "general acceptance" test in excluding an early form of lie-detection technology).

[42] *Wilson*, 900 N.Y.S.2d at 641.

[43] *Id.* at 642.

[44] *Id.* A more recent criminal case applying the *Frye* test also excluded fMRI lie detection on the ground that the technique was not generally accepted in the relevant scientific community. Maryland v. Smith, Case No. 106589C (Maryland Cir. Ct. 2012).

In *United States v. Semrau*, a criminal case in federal court, the court excluded similar fMRI evidence after a detailed discussion of the scientific literature, the testing procedure, and the multifactor *Daubert* test for admissibility in federal court.[45] The defendant, Lorne Allan Semrau, a licensed psychologist, was charged with multiple counts of health care fraud and money laundering.[46] Semrau owned two companies that provided mental-health services to nursing home patients in Tennessee and Mississippi. According to the indictment, the charges stem from an alleged scheme by Semrau to defraud Medicare, Medicaid, and other health care benefits programs by submitting false and fraudulent claims for payment between 1999 and 2005, totaling approximately $3 million.[47] The factual allegations constituting the fraudulent conduct by Semrau included two types of practices: (1) directing billing personnel to bill for more expensive services than those marked by treating psychiatrists, and (2) instructing treating psychiatrists to perform "AIMS" (Abnormal Involuntary Movement Scale) tests every six months and directing billing personnel to bill for these tests separately, even though the tests were not a separately reimbursable test and should have been performed as part of regular services. To convict Semrau of health care fraud, the government needed to prove that he (1) "knowingly devised a scheme...to defraud," (2) "executed or attempted to execute this scheme," and (3) "acted with intent to defraud."[48]

Semrau sought to introduce evidence of his own fMRI results indicating that he was not lying when he claimed that he did not intend to defraud with his billing practices, that mistakes in billing were the result of confusion and unclear billing codes, and that he was following billing instructions provided by CIGNA and CAHABA representatives.[49] Semrau attempted to call Steven Laken to testify about fMRI lie-detection examinations Semrau undertook regarding the allegations in the indictment. One test concerned the practice of billing for services other than those performed, and a second test concerned the billing practices regarding the AIMS test. For both tests, Semrau was asked three types of questions: neutral, control, and "specific incident

---

[45] United States v. Semrau, 2010 WL 6845092 (W.D. Tenn, June 1, 2010). *See* Daubert v. Merrell Dow Pharm., Inc., 509 U.S. 579 (1993) (articulating multifactor test for admissibility of scientific expert testimony under Federal Rule of Evidence 702).

[46] *Semrau*, 2010 WL 6845092, slip op. at 1.

[47] *Id.* at 2.

[48] *Id.*; 18 U.S.C. §§ 1347 and 2; 18 U.S.C. §§ 1956, 1957 and 2.

[49] *Semrau*, 2010 WL 6845092, slip op. at 4–8.

questions [SIQs]." The neutral questions (e.g., "Do you like to swim?" "Are you over age 18" "Do you like to watch TV?") were used to establish a baseline for Semrau. The control questions (e.g., "Do you ever gossip?" "Have you ever cheated on your taxes?") were used to fill empty spaces during the scan; they were not considered as part of the analysis. The SIQs concerned questions about the alleged fraud and the alleged AIMs charges.[50]

While in the scanner, Semrau was visually instructed to "lie" or "tell the truth" when presented with the SIQs and to tell the truth for the neutral and control questions.[51] According to Laken's proposed testimony, Semrau was "not being deceptive" in answering questions about billing for services not performed.[52] Regarding the AIMS test, however, Laken concluded that Semrau was being deceptive after a first test, but Laken ultimately concluded Semrau was not being deceptive after a second test, attempting to explain away the first test as the result of fatigue.[53] During cross-examination, Laken acknowledged that he could not determine whether Semrau was being deceptive or not with regard to each (or any) individual question; rather, his opinion related only to whether he was, in general, being deceptive or truthful with regard to the details of the test.[54]

The court concluded that Laken's testimony should be excluded under Federal Rule of Evidence 702.[55] In analyzing Laken's testimony, the Court found that he was a qualified expert, and analyzed the proposed testimony according to four factors: whether the subject matter and content was (1) tested; and (2) subjected to peer review and publication; (3) whether there were known (and acceptable) error rates

---

[50] *See id.* for a list of the SIQs.

[51] *Id.* at 6 ("In each fMRI scan, Dr. Semrau was visually instructed to 'Lie' or to tell the 'Truth' in response to each SIQ. He was told to respond truthfully to the neutral and control questions. Dr. Semrau practiced answering the questions on a computer prior to the scans. Dr. Laken observed Dr. Semrau practice until Dr. Laken believed that Dr. Semrau showed sufficient compliance with the instructions, responded to questions appropriately, and understood what he was to do in the scanner.").

[52] *Id.*

[53] *See id.* ("According to Dr. Laken, 'testing indicates that a positive test result in a person purporting to tell the truth is accurate only 6% of the time'…Dr. Laken also believed that the second scan may have been affected by Dr. Semrau's fatigue. Based on his findings on the second test, Dr. Laken suggested that Dr. Semrau be administered another fMRI test on the AIMS tests topic, but this time with shorter questions and conducted later in the day to reduce the effects of fatigue.").

[54] *Id.* at 7–8.

[55] *Id.* at 14.

and standards of control; and (4) whether the principles and methods on which the testimony was based were generally accepted in the relevant scientific community.[56] Regarding the first two factors, the court noted that fMRI lie detection had been subjected to testing in a number of studies, including some coauthored by Laken, that were published in peer-reviewed scientific journals.[57]

The court, however, noted several problems regarding the third factor: error rates and standards of control.[58] Although the court acknowledged that the laboratory studies produced error rates, the court noted several limitations in relying on this data in cases such as Semrau's. First, the error rates in controlled laboratory settings may not translate to real-world litigation settings, for which there were no known error rates. Second, there were no industry standards controlling real-world examinations, and Laken appeared to have deviated from his own protocols in retesting Semrau.[59] Third, the details of Semrau's situation varied in several ways from the subjects in the published studies: at age sixty-three he was older than most test subjects (who were eighteen to fifty); he was tested regarding events six to eight years old (whereas most subjects were tested about recent events); the potential for negative consequences for Semrau was significantly greater than for test subjects; and test subjects were instructed to "lie" whereas Semrau had independent reasons for lying beyond compliance with testing protocols.[60] Finally, the studies themselves were based on a small number of nondiverse subjects; they reported inconsistent results; many of the findings had not been replicated; and little was known about the effectiveness of various types of countermeasures.[61] Regarding the fourth factor—general acceptance—the court concluded that fMRI was not generally accepted by neuroscientists, citing several publications asserting the technique was not ready for use in real-world applications.[62]

[56] *Id.* at 10–14.

[57] *Id.*

[58] *Id.*

[59] *Id.* at 13 ("Assuming, *arguendo,* that the standards testified to by Dr. Laken could satisfy *Daubert,* it appears that Dr. Laken violated his own protocols when he re-scanned Dr. Semrau on the AIMS tests SIQs, after Dr. Semrau was found 'deceptive' on the first AIMS tests scan. None of the studies cited by Dr. Laken involved the subject taking a second exam after being found to have been deceptive on the first exam.").

[60] *Id.*

[61] *Id.*

[62] *Id. But see* Schauer, *supra* note 17, arguing that neuroscientists should not have the last word on whether the evidence is appropriate for juridical uses because that question is a legal, not a scientific, one.

In addition to excluding the testimony under FRE 702, the court concluded that FRE 403 provides additional grounds for exclusion. Here, the court found it significant that Semrau obtained the fMRI unilaterally, without first notifying the government and allowing government participation in designing the test questions, and that Laken had deviated from his own testing protocols. The court also noted that the testimony was potentially unfairly prejudicial and not particularly probative because Laken could offer only general conclusions and not answers regarding specific questions.[63]

Although the court ultimately concluded that the testimony ought to be excluded, the court left open the possibility for future admissibility:

[I]n the future, should fMRI-based lie detection undergo further testing, development, and peer review, improve upon standards controlling the technique's operation, and gain acceptance by the scientific community for use in the real world, this methodology may be found to be admissible even if the error rate is not able to be quantified in a real world setting.[64]

Semrau was ultimately convicted at trial of three counts of health care fraud.[65] He appealed the conviction, and challenged the exclusion of the fMRI lie-detection evidence. The federal appellate court affirmed the conviction and the ruling to exclude the evidence. The Court explained that Federal Rules of Evidence 702 and 403 each provide an independent and sufficient ground for excluding the evidence:

After carefully reviewing the scientific and factual evidence, we conclude that the district court did not abuse its discretion in excluding the fMRI evidence under Federal Rule of Evidence 702 because the technology had not been fully examined in "real world" settings and the testing administered to Dr. Semrau was not consistent with tests done in research studies. We also hold that the testimony was independently inadmissible under Rule 403 because the prosecution did not know about the test before it was conducted, constitutional concerns caution against admitting lie detection

---

[63] *Semrau,* slip op. at 16 ("Based on his inability to identify which SIQs Dr. Semrau answered truthfully or deceptively, the court fails to see how his testimony can assist the jury in deciding whether Dr. Semrau's testimony is credible.").

[64] *Id.* at 12 n.18.

[65] *See* United States v. Semrau, 693 F.3d 510 (6th Cir. 2012). He was acquitted of the other charges. *Id.*

tests to bolster witness credibility, and the test results do not purport to indicate whether Dr. Semrau was truthful about any single statement.[66]

II. EEG Lie Detection ("Brain Fingerprinting")

A second type of brain-based lie detection involves measuring the brain waves of subjects through EEG (electroencephalography) when presented with various types of stimuli.[67] After first taking baseline brain-wave measures, subjects are shown various stimuli, for example, images of objects or descriptions of dates, names, or other information. The principle underlying this type of "lie detection" is that a subject's neural activity will be different if the subject recognizes the stimuli than it would be if the subject does not recognize the information.[68] The foundation for this principle, and the technique, is the "P300" brain wave, which is a "particular pattern of neuronal firing that signal[s] an individual's recognition of a unique or meaningful item."[69] Therefore, unlike the fMRI technique discussed above, the EEG technique does not measure whether the subject is lying or telling the truth in response to particular questions: it purports to measure whether the subject has prior knowledge of the stimuli. In others words, the technique purports to show whether a suspect has "guilty knowledge" or "concealed knowledge," and it functions as a "lie detector" by providing information about whether a suspect recognizes information he claims not to recognize, or vice versa.[70]

---

[66]   *Id.* at 516.

[67]   *See* Farwell & Smith, *supra* note 5; Moenssens, *supra* note 5; Lawrence A. Farwell & Emanuel Donchin, *The Truth Will Out: Interrogative Polygraphy ("Lie Detection") with Event-Related Brain Potentials,* 28 PSYCHOPHYSIOLOGY 531, 531–32 (1991); J. Peter Rosenfeld et al., *A Modified, Event-Related Potential-Based Guilty Knowledge Test,* 42 INT'L J. NEUROSCIENCE 157, 157–58 (1988). For a helpful general overview, see John B. Meixner, Comment, *Liar, Liar, Jury's the Trier? The Future of Neuroscience-Based Credibility Assessment in the Court,* 106 Nw. U. L. REV. 1451 (2012).

[68]   The brain activity generated as response to the stimuli is referred to as the "event-related potential." *See* STEVEN J. LUCK, AN INTRODUCTION TO THE EVENT-RELATED POTENTIAL TECHNIQUE (2005).

[69]   Meixner, *supra* note 67, at 1458. Discovery of the "P300" wave (so called because it occurs approximately 300 milliseconds after presentation of the meaningful item) was reported in Samuel Sutton et al., *Evoked-Potential Correlates of Stimulus Uncertainty,* 150 SCI. 1187, 1187 (1965).

[70]   By contrast, the fMRI lie detection discussed above is an example of a "control question" test, which seeks to determine whether particular answers or statements are "deceptive" or "honest" and thus are false or true.

The proposed technique would work in a real-life case by, for example, providing a criminal defendant with information the perpetrator of a crime would know (but that an innocent person would not know) and measuring whether the defendant exhibits brain waves correlated with recognition. Subjects undergoing testing would be presented with the target items ("probes") such as a murder weapon along with other similar but irrelevant items such as other weapons not used in the murder ("irrelevants").[71] When asked questions about the murder, an EEG would measure whether the subject exhibited an increased brain response (the "P300" wave) for the probes but not for the irrelevants, with such an increase indicating prior knowledge and no such increase indicating no prior knowledge.[72]

As with a number of the fMRI lie-detection studies, the EEG-based lie-detection studies report mixed but overall impressive results. Studies report a range of accuracy in detecting "prior knowledge" from 50 percent to 100 percent.[73] In one study, for example, subjects participated in planning a mock terrorist attack and were provided with information relevant to the mock attack (e.g., the city, the date, and the method of attack); other subjects did not participate in the planned attack.[74] When researchers had prior knowledge of the relevant details, they were able to identify twelve of twelve subjects in the participation group, with no false positives for the twelve in the nonparticipation group. When researchers did not have prior knowledge of the relevant details, they were able to identify ten of twelve subjects (with no false positives) and twenty of thirty relevant details. Another study, however, found only a 50 percent detection rate in a mock-crime setting;[75] other studies have shown an 80–95 percent rate in detecting "guilty" participants.[76] As with fMRI, however, these results are based on highly artificial and tightly controlled testing conditions; therefore, the validity and reliability of the technique when applied to more complex, "real world" situations is unknown.[77]

---

[71] *See* John B. Meixner & J. Peter Rosenfeld, *A Mock Terrorism Application of the P300-Based Concealed Information Test*, 48 PSYCHOPHYSIOLOGY 149 (2011).

[72] *Id.*

[73] The error rates of the studies are summarized in Meixner, *supra* note 67, at 1484–87.

[74] Meixner & Rosenfeld, *supra* note 71.

[75] Ralf Mertens & John J.B. Allen, *The Role of Psychophysiology in Forensic Assessments: Deception Detection, ERPs, and Virtual Reality Mock Crime Scenarios*, 45 PSYCHOPHYSIOLOGY 286, 286 (2008).

[76] Meixner, *supra* note 67, at 1485 (summarizing error rates for several studies).

[77] Also largely unknown is the effectiveness of various possible countermeasures. *See* Ganis et al., *Lying in the Scanner*, *supra* note 16.

There is one company currently marketing EEG-based lie-detection services, referring to the technique as "brain fingerprinting."[78] The technique, developed by Dr. Lawrence Farwell, relies not only on measurements of the P300 wave but also on a second brain response referred to under the acronym MERMER.[79] The MERMER response has not been subjected to the same kinds of peer-reviewed testing as the P300 response.[80] Results from "brain fingerprinting" testing by Farwell were proffered by two criminal defendants in state court as part of post-conviction proceedings. In one case, *Harrington v. State*, the court reversed on other grounds without reliance on the "brain fingerprinting" evidence,[81] and in the second case, *Slaughter v. State*, the court refused to grant post-conviction relief based on the evidence because the validity and reliability of Dr. Farwell's technique had not been independently corroborated.[82] No other reported legal cases have considered the admissibility of "brain fingerprinting."

III. Analysis: Empirical, Conceptual, and Practical Issues

The use of brain-based lie-detection technology depends on the inferential relationships between the validity and reliability of the technology and its applications, on the one hand, and the particular legal issues the applications are offered to prove, on the other. In this context, the legal issue is whether someone is speaking sincerely and accurately

[78] *See* http://www.governmentworks.com/bws/. *See* Farwell & Smith, *supra* note 5. For discussions of Farwell's technique, *see* Moenssens, *supra* note 5; Meixner, *supra* note 67.

[79] Farwell & Smith, *supra* note 5.

[80] *See* Meixner, *supra* note 67.

[81] Harrington v. State, 659 N.W.2d 509, 516 (Iowa 2003) ("Because the scientific testing evidence is not necessary to a resolution of this appeal, we give it no further consideration."). The court explained the evidence as follows:

> This testing evidence was introduced through the testimony of Dr. Lawrence Farwell, who specializes in cognitive psychophysiology. Dr. Farwell measures certain patterns of brain activity (the P300 wave) to determine whether the person being tested recognizes or does not recognize offered information. This analysis basically "provide[s] information about what the person has stored in his brain." According to Dr. Farwell, his testing of Harrington established that Harrington's brain did not contain information about Schweer's murder. On the other hand, Dr. Farwell testified, testing did confirm that Harrington's brain contained information consistent with his alibi.

Id. at 516 n.6.

[82] Slaughter v. State, 105 P.3d 832, 834–36 (Okla. Crim. App. 2005) ("[B]eyond Dr. Farwell's affidavit, we have no real evidence that Brain Fingerprinting has been extensively tested").

when she asserts a proposition that is relevant to a legal dispute or when she asserts or denies having prior knowledge of a relevant proposition. A number of important conceptual, empirical, and practical issues under-lie the use of neuroscientific evidence on these legal issues.

It is important to keep the conceptual and empirical issues distinct. As we demonstrate below, the failure to do so leads to confusions, which in turn have important theoretical and practical consequences. As a theoret-ical matter, the conceptual confusions undermine some of the conclu-sions drawn from the data generated by the neuroscientific experiments. As a practical matter, they limit the inferences that may be drawn from applications of the technology in the context of juridical proof.

In discussing the relationship between neuroscience and lie detection, Sarah Robins and Carl Craver assert that "this is an empirical matter, not something that can be derived from the ordinary use of the terms 'lie' and 'deception.'"[83] Although we agree that the relationship between brain activity and lying or deception is an empirical matter, whether or not someone is lying or engaged in deception involves both empirical and conceptual aspects. The conceptual aspects play a normative, regulative role in this context. The conclusion that someone is lying on a particular occasion (a matter of empirical fact)[84] depends, in part, on what that per-son is doing (also a matter of empirical fact) and, in part, on the meaning and use of the terms "lie" and "deception" and the criteria for application of these concepts. The conceptual aspect is not given by empirical data about the brain; rather, it is constituted by the complex behavior that provides criteria for "lying" or "deception." The reduction of mind (or meaning) to the brain does not go through in this context because brain activity does not (indeed, cannot) play this normative, regulative role. To put it another way, the behavioral criteria serve a normative role in pro-viding the *measure* for what constitutes lying or deception, a role not played by brain activity. It is this conceptual aspect that we draw attention to in order to avoid the confusions that can arise when it is neglected.[85]

---

[83] *See supra* note 7.

[84] We agree with Robins and Craver that the judgment that one is lying is a matter of "inference to the best explanation."

[85] For example, one conceptual issue that we discuss below concerns the relationship between a lie and an intent to deceive. The latter is neither necessary nor sufficient for the former, and confusion arises when claims and arguments presuppose otherwise. This is not to suppose that the concept of a "lie" has sharp boundaries or necessary and sufficient condi-tions. There may be gray areas and widespread disagreement, in some cases, about whether something constitutes a lie. For example, if someone utters something he believes to be false, but it turns out (because he also has false beliefs) that what he said is in fact true, has he lied or has he attempted to lie and failed? *See* Amy E. White, *The Lie of fMRI: An Examination of*

Successful theoretical and practical progress depends on clear understanding of the relevant concepts involved and their articulations, not
merely determining which empirical facts obtain—which presuppose
the relevant concepts and their sense.[86] A clear understanding of the
neuroscience research, and its possible legal application, requires a clear
articulation of the psychological concepts presupposed by it and the psychological capacities about which the research seeks to provide empirical
evidence.[87] The research presupposes several behavioral and psychological
capacities—most prominently, "to lie," "to deceive," and "to know"—but
also to "to think," "to believe," "to remember," "to intend," "to perceive,"
"to recognize," and "to infer." In presupposing these concepts, the research
and the inferences drawn from it must not run afoul of the boundaries of
these concepts in order to say something about the underlying behavioral
and psychological capacities.[88] In other words, the concepts provide an
outer boundary for the meaningful empirical claims that may be asserted

---

the *Ethics of a Market in Lie Detection Using Functional Magnetic Resonance Imaging*, HEC FORUM
(2012) ("The most common understanding of lying is that it requires an intent to deceive;
however, even this point can be disputed. For example, Thomas Aquinas claimed that the
transmission of any false information is a lie regardless of if the liar knows the information is
false (*Summa Theologica*, Q 110).").

[86] *See* M.R. BENNETT & P.M.S. HACKER, PHILOSOPHICAL FOUNDATIONS OF NEUROSCIENCE
402–07 (2003). The authors explain:

> Neuroscience research…abuts the psychological and clarity regarding the achievements of
> brain research presupposes clarity regarding the categories of ordinary psychological descrip-
> tion—that is, the categories of sensation and perception, cognition and recollection, cogita-
> tion and imagination, emotion and volition.

Id. at 115. *See also* Dennis M. Patterson, review of PHILOSOPHICAL FOUNDATIONS OF
NEUROSCIENCE, NOTRE DAME PHILOSOPHICAL REVIEWS (2003), *available at* http://ndpr.
nd.edu/review.cfm?id=1335; P.F. STRAWSON, ANALYSIS AND METAPHYSICS 17–28 (1992).

[87] The concern, in other words, is not just with the correct use of words and concepts, but
rather with the complex phenomena picked out by the concepts (as opposed to other, adjacent
phenomena not picked out by the concepts). Here are two analogies for the "modest" type of
conceptual analysis that we have in mind. A bounty hunter searching for a fugitive is target-
ing the fugitive, not his picture on the "wanted" poster, but the failure to attend to the details
of the poster will make it less likely the hunter will find his target. *See* FRANK JACKSON, FROM
METAPHYSICS TO ETHICS: A DEFENCE OF CONCEPTUAL ANALYSIS 30 (1998). Similarly, wearers of
eyeglasses care more about the world they see through the glasses than the glass itself, but they
still care about flaws in the glass nonetheless. To dismiss flaws in the glass because one cares
more about the world than the glass would be absurd. *See* BENNETT & HACKER, *supra* note 86,
at 401. Likewise, it would be absurd to dismiss the focus on our psychological concepts, and
the language we use to express them, because we are interested in the capacities themselves.
See also Timothy Williamson, *Past the Linguistic Turn?*, *in* THE FUTURE FOR PHILOSOPHY 125–26
(Brian Leiter ed., 2004).

[88] The legal issues concern these underlying capacities, and the value of neuroscientific
evidence in legal settings thus depends on whether it can inform our understanding of these
capacities.

in this context. To be sure, the *probative value* of such evidence in legal settings depends on much more than the conceptual issues; it depends on whether manifold empirical claims, which we will outline below, are true or false. But in addition to these empirical issues, further inferential problems arise when claims run afoul of the concepts. These conceptual confusions generate serious theoretical and practical problems.

A. Empirical Issues

Before turning to the conceptual issues, we outline the various empirical issues that also affect the probative value of this evidence in law. Having a clear sense of the scope of the issues will sharpen the discussion of which issues are genuinely empirical and which are conceptual. We do not contend that either category is ultimately more important than the other; they are both of critical importance if this evidence is to play the significant role its proponents contend it ought to play.

The fundamental empirical question in this context is how likely a particular answer provided by neuroscientific technology (or, more accurately, expert testimony informed by such technology) is to be accurate in a particular instance. The question depends on a number of underlying empirical issues. How often does the test declare "lie," "deception," or "prior knowledge" when the person tested is lying, engaged in deception, or has prior knowledge, and how often does it declare these answers when the person is not lying, deceiving, or does not have prior knowledge? How often does the test declare "truth," "no deception," or "no prior knowledge" when the person is telling the truth, not deceiving, or has no prior knowledge, and how often does it declare these answers when the person is lying, deceiving, or has prior knowledge?[89] These ratios will depend on the validity (whether it measures what it purports to measure) and the reliability of the tests. Validity and reliability will depend on a number of additional underlying empirical questions.[90] Problems with any one of these issues will affect the probative value of the evidence in drawing inferences about a particular person's answers in a legal setting.

---

[89] The issues raised in this and the previous sentence are distinguished in the literature on lie detection as a test's "specificity" (i.e., its accuracy in labeling actual lie as lies) and "sensitivity" (i.e., its accuracy in labeling honest statements as not lies).

[90] Two general issues include the base rates for lies and the boundaries of the "reference classes" in which lies are grouped. Both of these issues will affect the probative value of the evidence in individual cases. On the base rates of lies, see P. DePaulo et al., *Lying in Everyday Life*, 70 J. PERSONALITY & SOC. PSYCHOL. 979 (1996). On the "reference class" problem, see Ronald J. Allen & Michael S. Pardo, *The Problematic Value of Mathematical Models of Evidence*, 36 J. LEGAL STUD. 107 (2007).

To be clear, we do contend that any of these issues are in principle fatal to the admissibility of neural lie detection.[91] Indeed, it may be possible for each to be overcome as the technology improves. We point them out now because each will affect the probative value of evidence in individual cases, and to distinguish these issues from the conceptual issues that will be our focus in the next section. The empirical issues include:

1. The specifics of procedures used for scanning and analyzing neural data.[92] The process of converting raw data to a brain "image" requires a number of complex inferences, and these inferential steps may affect the value of the evidence in individual cases. This may turn, for example, on the statistical procedures and thresholds used to construct fMRI brain images.

2. The sample size of the subjects tested.[93] The neuroscience studies on lie detection have involved small groups of test subjects. This limits the inferences that may be drawn for individuals in the population more generally.

3. The diversity of subjects tested. The subjects in the experiments have typically involved healthy young men and (to a lesser extent) women. It is thus not clear how inferences from this relatively homogenous group could be drawn about individuals who differ in age or health; who are taking medications; who are sociopaths; or who are affected by other variables not present in the groups typically tested.[94]

4. Time. The subjects in the experiments are typically tested close in time to the events or to receiving information they are asked about in the scanner. Testing in litigation settings, however, may involve events that took place months, years, or decades earlier.

5. Types of lies or deception. As with differences among subjects, differences among types of lies or deceptive tasks may be correlated with different types of brain activity.[95]

---

[91] Fred Schauer outlines a number of ways these empirical issues *may* be overcome, and he argues persuasively that a number of other similar issues apply (and in some cases have been overcome) in other areas of social science. *See* Schauer, *supra* note 17.

[92] For excellent discussions of these issues, see Brown & Murphy, *supra* note 11; Jones et al., *supra* note 11.

[93] For an excellent discussion of this and related limitations, see Greely & Illes, *supra* note 1.

[94] *See* White, *supra* note 85 ("Research studies have been performed on healthy adult subjects and there is a lack of evidence to support the conclusion that such methods would be effective on other populations."). But current research is beginning to address this issue. *See, e.g.*, Kaylor-Hughes et al., *supra* note 16 (schizophrenia); Fullam et al., *supra* note 16 (psychopathic traits).

[95] *See* Ganis et al., *Neural Correlates, supra* note 16.

6. Stakes. One significant difference between test subjects and individuals in litigation settings involves often an enormous difference in the stakes between those tested.[96]

7. The brain activity correlated with lies, deception, or knowledge (memory) is also correlated with other types of behavior and mental activities.[97]

8. Countermeasures. The value of the evidence will depend on the likelihood that individuals can "beat" or trick the technique.[98]

These empirical issues each take place within a framework of conceptual presuppositions. Additional problems with these presuppositions cause additional potential inferential problems. It is to these conceptual issues that we now turn.

B. Conceptual Issues

1. Location and the Mereological Fallacy

In the context of brain-based lie detection, properties that apply to the activity of persons (as a whole) are sometimes incoherently ascribed to brains or areas of the brain. This occurs when lies, deception, or knowledge are thought to be in the brain or engaged in by areas of the brain, and it is a particular example of what Bennett and Hacker refer to as the "mereological fallacy."[99] The fallacy has important theoretical and practical consequences in the lie-detection context.

Consider, first, fMRI tests to discover lies or deception. Some brain activity is necessary to lie or to engage in deception (as well as to speak sincerely and to act without deception). Although it is possible that some *specific* brain activity may be necessary to lie or to engage in deception—and neuroscience may possibly provide good inductive evidence of that activity—it is a conceptual mistake to *identify* lies or deception with that neural activity. This identification occurs when areas of the brain are characterized as *deciding* when and whether to

---

[96] As Schauer, *supra* note 17, notes, however, this is a common complaint among psychological studies generally, and there is research responding to it by demonstrating correlations between lab conditions and the "real world." *See id.* at n.16 (collecting studies). It is thus possible that something similar may be found in the lie-detection context.

[97] *See* Gamer et al., *fMRI-Activation Patterns*, *supra* note 16; Wagner, *supra* note 17.

[98] *See* Ganis et al., *Lying in the Scanner*, *supra* note 16.

[99] *See* BENNETT & HACKER, *supra* note 86, at 73 ("The neuroscientists' mistake of ascribing to the constituent parts of an animal attributes that logically apply only to the whole animal we shall call 'the mereological fallacy.'"). We discuss the "mereological fallacy," and the conceptual issues that give rise to it, in Chapter Two.

lie and then engaging in the processes to carry out this decision. For example, in summarizing neuroscience studies on deception, one legal scholar asserts that "there was some agreement among all investigations to date that: (1) some form of 'executive' function that deals with conflicting pressures, generally the anterior cingulated gyrus, was used to handle the 'choice' of whether and when to lie, and (2) this often acted with some form of inhibitory mechanism to suppress the truthful response."[100] Two articles by scientists assert that fMRI examines "directly the organ that produces lies, the brain" and allows one to "peer into an individual's thought processes."[101]

The brain activity at issue, however, is not a lie or deception. The criteria for telling a lie or engaging in deception involve behavior, not neurological states.[102] To lie requires, among other things, a false assertion (or one the speaker believes to be false).[103] Roughly, deception involves believing things to be so and saying or implying the opposite, and it involves judgments about the beliefs and knowledge of the audience.[104] At most, neuroscientific evidence might be able to provide well-grounded empirical correlations between this type of behavior and brain states. This will be *inductive* evidence. The neuroscience, in other words, may be able to provide a *measurement* regarding lies or deception, but not the *measure* of it.[105] It is a conceptual mistake to conclude that lies take place in the brain; that a particular area of the brain chooses to lie; that neuroscience can reveal lies being "produced"

---

[100] *See* Charles N.W. Keckler, *Cross-Examining the Brain: A Legal Analysis of Neural Imaging for Credibility Impeachment*, 57 HASTINGS. L.J. 509, 535 (2006).

[101] *See* Ganis et al., *Neural Correlates, supra* note 16, at 830 (claiming that neuroscience can "examine directly the organ that produces lies, the brain"); Wolpe et al., *supra* note 5, at 39–40 (noting the possibility that neuroimaging will allow scientists to "peer into an individual's thought processes").

[102] We explore these criteria in more detail below.

[103] It also involves a context in which a norm not to say something believed to be false is violated.

[104] *See* Robins & Craver, *supra* note 7 ("brains do not lie.") Curiously, these conceptual points about lies are sometimes acknowledged in many of the same studies that also identify lies with brain states. *See, e.g.,* Spence et al., *Behavioural and Functional Anatomical Correlates, supra* note 16, at 1757 ("Deceiving another human subject is likely to involve multiple cognitive processes, including theory of mind concerning the victim's thoughts (their ongoing beliefs)"); Lee et al., *Lie Detection, supra* note 16, at 163 ("[A]n essence of lying is the recognition of, and attempt to manipulate, the mental states of others"); Kozel et al., *Pilot Study, supra* note 16, at 605 ("Lying is a complex process requiring suppression of the truth, communication of a coherent falsehood, and modifications of behaviors to convince the receiver of ones actions.").

[105] *See* Robins & Craver, *supra* note 7 ("brains do not lie.").

in the brain; or that it can "peer into" one's brain and see the thoughts that constitute lies or deception.

Why does this matter? If there is a discrepancy between the types of behavior associated with lies or deception and the brain states thought to be correlated with the behavior, then the behavioral evidence will override the inductive (neuroscience) evidence. What was thought to be a well-grounded correlation will turn out to have been false, and the assumptions underlying it would have to be rethought and reexamined. To illustrate this, suppose the reverse were true. If particular brain states *did* provide the criteria for lies or deception, then by hypothesis having certain neural activity would be a sufficient condition for engaging in an act of deception—even if one did not intend to deceive and one asserted a true proposition.[106] Would we really say this person was lying? Of course not. What constitutes "deception" or a "lie" is a conceptual not an empirical question,[107] and the criteria for the application of these concepts are behavioral not neurological.

Now consider EEG-based lie detection. Here, the conceptual mistake is to assume or presuppose that prior knowledge is "housed," "stored," or "encoded" in the brain and that the technology can reveal its presence. For example, in discussing EEG-based lie detection, Farwell and Smith assert that "the brain of the criminal is always there, recording events, in some ways like a video camera" and the "brain fingerprinting" technique will reveal whether the relevant information is present or absent in the subject's brain's "recording."[108] Also, as we noted above, a variety of legal scholars likewise assert that neuroscience may be used to "accurately distinguish between the presence and absence of" knowledge in a person's brain; EEG lie detection "is based on the principle that the human brain houses information," and EEG lie detection can "detect whether certain knowledge exists in the subject's brain."

This characterization depends on a confused conception of knowledge. Neither knowing something nor what is known—a detail about a crime, for example—is located in the brain. As a conceptual matter,

---

[106] We concede that the criteria for what constitutes a lie may change to refer to brain states rather than behavior, but then the future concept will no longer refer to the same phenomenon as the current concept. The law cares about the behavioral phenomenon picked out by the current concept and brain states only to the extent they provide inductive evidence of the former.

[107] To further illustrate this, imagine trying to construct an experiment to prove whether lies are really brain states *and not* situations in which someone says something false to another.

[108] Farwell & Smith, *supra* note 5, at 135; Moenssens, *supra* note 5 (EEG lie detection "at best, can only detect whether certain knowledge exists in the subject's brain.").

neural states of the brain do not fit the criteria for ascriptions of knowledge. Suppose, for example, a defendant has brain activity that is purported to be knowledge of a particular fact about a crime. But, suppose further, this defendant sincerely could not engage in any behavior that would count as a manifestation of knowledge. On what basis could one claim and prove that the defendant truly had knowledge of this fact? We suggest there is none; rather, as with a discrepancy regarding lies and deception, the defendant's failure to satisfy any criteria for knowing would override claims that depend on the neuroscientific evidence.[109]

The conception of knowledge "stored" or "housed" in the brain rests on two problematic presuppositions. The first presupposition is that whether one remembers something may be identified with particular neurological states of the brain. The second presupposition is that someone's *retaining* an ability (e.g., remembering something) implies the *storage* of that ability in a particular location. Exposing these problematic presuppositions further reveals what is wrong conceptually with these claims regarding brain-based lie detection.

Memory is the retention of knowledge previously acquired or possessed by a person.[110] Like knowledge more generally, memory is an ability, power, or capacity, and it may be manifested in manifold ways. One may say what one remembers, think but not say what one remembers, act on what one remembers, and so on. Memories may be *factual* (e.g., remembering that X), *experiential* (e.g., remembering seeing X), or *objectual* (e.g., remembering the sight of X).[111] In addition, memory may be declarative—that is, expressed in propositional form and possibly true or false—or it may be non-declarative (e.g., remembering how to X). In none of these distinct varieties of memory is the criterion for whether one remembers that one is in any particular neurological state. Rather, memory is the retention of knowledge, and, like knowledge, the criteria for its ascriptions include the various ways that this ability, power, or capacity may be manifested in behavior. To be clear, we are not suggesting that particular brain states and synaptic

---

[109] The behavior provides "criterial" evidence of knowledge, and the neuroscience provides "inductive" evidence of knowledge. If there is a discrepancy between them, the problem is with the inductive correlations; the brain activity, in other words, would not be well-correlated with knowledge.

[110] For further discussion of the conceptual contours of memory, see M.R. BENNETT & P.M.S. HACKER, HISTORY OF COGNITIVE NEUROSCIENCE 99–112 (2008).

[111] *Id.* at 100.

connections are not *necessary* for one to have the capacity to engage in this behavior, and understanding these conditions is, of course, an important avenue of neuroscientific research. But, it is a mistaken leap to move from the fact that brain structures may be *necessary* for memory to the conclusion that memories are *identical* with such neurological states.[112]

Indeed, scientific work on memory and attempts to detect prior knowledge through neuroscience presuppose these very conceptions. For example, in a study of whether fMRI could be used to detect prior knowledge of faces, the researchers presented subjects with a large set of faces and then scanned the subjects.[113] In one experiment, subjects were asked whether they had seen particular faces before or whether they were new to them; in a second experiment, subjects were asked to classify the faces as male or female (to examine whether prior knowledge of the face could be detected indirectly by the researchers). The researchers found a correlation between the *subjective* experience of remembering and the particular neuroscientific data, but not whether the person *actually remembered*.[114] The researchers correctly presupposed that the criterion for memory was *correct* performance, not particular neural data. Subjects who had thought they saw a face previously, but had not, were mistaken, despite their neural data; subjects who had seen a face previously but did not manifest this knowledge, likewise did not remember, despite their neural data.[115]

A similar presupposition underlies psychological research of memory more generally. A great deal of research has been done exploring how and whether knowledge may be "encoded" in the brain,[116] but

---

[112] *See* Walter Glannon, *Our Brains Are Not Us*, 23 BIOETHICS 321, 325 (2009) ("it is misleading to ask questions such as 'Where in the brain is the memory of one's past?'").

[113] Jesse Rissman, Henry T. Greely & Anthony D. Wagner, *Detecting Individual Memories through the Neural Decoding of Memory States and Past Experience*, 107 PNAS 9849 (2012).

[114] *Id.* at 4 ("in contrast to the decoding of subjective memory states, the veridical experiential history associated with a face could not be easily classified when subjective recognition was held constant. For faces the participants claimed to recognize, the classifier achieved only limited success at determining which were actually old vs. novel; for faces the participants claimed to be novel, the classifier was unable to determine which had been previously seen. Finally, a neural signature of past experience could not be reliably decoded during implicit recognition.").

[115] *Id.* Similar conceptual presuppositions apply to other recent work on memory and lie detection. Martin J. Chadwick et al., *Decoding Individual Episodic Memory Traces in the Human Hippocampus*, 20 CURRENT BIOLOGY 544 (2010); Gamer et al., *fMRI-Activation Patterns, supra* note 16.

[116] For a critical discussion of this literature, see BENNETT & HACKER, *supra* note 86, at 154–71.

the evidence for encoding is the manifestation of memory itself in the ways we have described. As psychologist Lila Davachi explains:

Encoding is an interesting concept in memory research because its existence can only be defined in terms of some other event occurring later in time. In other words, successful retrieval or recovery of a stimulus or event is the prima facie evidence that the stimulus or event was encoded. Thus, once retrieved the fact that a memory was encoded becomes a truism. This means that, at present, the only means to measure encoding, whether it is at the cognitive level or a cellular level, is through assessments of what the organism is able to retrieve at some point in the future.[117]

Turning to the second problematic presupposition, *retaining* knowledge in memory does not necessarily imply the knowledge is *stored* or *housed* in the brain (or elsewhere). One may possess an ability, power, or capacity without the ability, power, or capacity being stored anywhere; indeed, it is not clear what it even means to store an ability, power, or capacity—which is our point.

The idea that the brain records, stores, and houses the events a person perceives (like a video camera), and that in memory one "plays" this recording, is not a plausible explanation.[118] First, it itself presupposes memory (and therefore cannot explain it) because to make use of such a neural recording in the way described people would have *to remember how to access the recording and interpret its content.*[119] Second, even if such neural "recordings" existed *in the brain*, they would typically be unavailable for viewing (people typically cannot see their brains). To be clear, we readily acknowledge that knowledge and memory causally depend on neurological states and, likewise, that possessing and retaining knowledge will result in neurological changes. But it does not follow from these facts that the neurological phenomena "store"

---

[117] Lila Davachi, *Encoding: The Proof Is Still Required, in* SCIENCE OF MEMORY: CONCEPTS 138 (H.L. Roediger, Y. Dudai & S.M. Fitzpatrick eds., 2007).

[118] *See* Martin A. Conway, *Ten Things the Law and Others Should Know about Human Memory, in* MEMORY AND LAW 368 (Lynn Nadel & Walter Sinnott-Armstrong eds., 2012) (explaining that remembering is a constructive process and that memories are not similar to the products of recording media); Daniel J. Simons & Christopher F. Chabris, *What People Believe about How Memory Works: A Representative Survey of the U.S. Population,* 6 PLoS ONE 5 (2011) (noting that a majority of those surveyed believed that memory works like a recording and that this belief "contradicts the well-established idea that memory is a constructive process.").

[119] *See* BENNETT & HACKER, *supra* note 110, at 107. Likewise, one can use a video recording to remember past events only if one remembers what the recording is a recording *of.*

or "house" knowledge. Proposed lie detection that relies on such a problematic conception does not provide empirical information that particular claims to this effect are true.

People, not their brains, lie, deceive, know, and remember. It is an instance of the mereological fallacy to suppose otherwise, and the evidential value of neuroscientific evidence is affected by how it is conceived. If lies, knowledge, and intent are mistakenly thought to be identical with particular brain states, then proof of the brain states may (again, mistakenly) appear to provide conclusive or strong proof of the corresponding mental states.[120] Indeed, those in the grip of this fallacy might even suggest that we attach legal consequences directly to people who have brains in particular neurological states.[121] Once it is recognized, however, that such evidence may have some inductive correlation with certain behavior—but does not provide a sufficient condition to establish the categories at issue—then mistaken inferences to the contrary will be avoided.[122]

2. "Direct" and "Indirect" Evidence

A second mistaken presupposition in the literature is that brain-based lie detection is superior to traditional polygraph lie detection because brain-based lie detection measures lies, deception, or knowledge "directly" whereas polygraphs measure these features only "indirectly" by measuring physiological changes. Moreover, brain-based lie detection is also thought to be superior because the neuroscientific information is not subject to manipulation by subjects as are the physiological

---

[120] A conviction in India based on use of brain-scan lie-detection evidence illustrates how mistaken conceptual assumptions have significant practical consequences. *See* Anand Giridharadas, *India's Novel Use of Brain Scans in Courts Is Debated*, N.Y. TIMES, Sept. 14, 2008 ("But it was only in June, in a murder case in Pune, in Maharashtra State, that a judge explicitly cited a scan as proof that the suspect's brain held 'experiential knowledge' about the crime that only the killer could possess, sentencing her to life in prison."). For a detailed discussion of this case, see Dominique J. Church, *Note, Neuroscience in the Courtroom: An International Concern*, 53 WM. & MARY L. REV. 1825 (2012).

[121] Current legal issues depend on the behavior (and indirectly on brain states only to the extent they provide evidence of the behavior).

[122] The evidence may nevertheless be probative in certain cases, but it will not be conclusive. *See* Pardo, *supra* note 1, at 315–17; Schauer, *supra* note 17. Deception may be similar to pain in the sense that although certain behavior provides criterial evidence for pain, strong inductive correlations between cortical activity and being in pain suggest that the cortical activity may provide probative evidence of pain. On the neuroscience of pain, see Amanda C. Pustilnik, *Pain as Fact and Heuristic: How Pain Neuroimaging Illuminates Moral Dimensions of Law*, 97 CORNELL L. REV. 801 (2012); Adam Kolber, *The Experiential Future of Law*, 60 EMORY L.J. 585 (2011).

measures with polygraphs. For example, Paul Root Wolpe et al. write, "for the first time, using modern neuroscience techniques, a third party can, in principle, bypass the peripheral nervous system…and gain direct access to the seat of a person's thoughts, feelings, intention, or knowledge."[123]

It is a conceptual mistake to assume that brain-based lie detection provides direct access to lies, deception, or knowledge.[124] The neuroscience-based lie-detection techniques share the common assumption that lies, deception, or knowledge involve stable and detectable neurological correlates. [125] As with traditional polygraphs, the neuroscience research is looking for a correlation between lies, deceptive behavior, or knowledge, on one hand, and *something else going on with the subject's body*, on the other. With polygraphs it is increased heart rates, breathing, and perspiring;[126] with neuroscience it is increased blood flow to certain regions of the brain or electrical activity.[127] With both brain-based lie detection and polygraph, the techniques involve *indirect* measures of lying based on bodily measures. A direct–indirect distinction simply does not distinguish the two. Moreover, although the types of countermeasures that work for each technique may differ, brain-based lie detection is not countermeasure-proof simply because subjects cannot voluntarily control blood flow or electrical activity. As with polygraphs, subjects may be able to manipulate these measures in a variety of ways—for example, by subtle bodily movements, with drugs, or perhaps by directing their thoughts to various objects or topics.[128]

3. Mental States and Eliminative Materialism

The third conceptual issue is of primarily theoretical interest. In Chapter Two, we discuss the radical position of "eliminative materialism," which purports to "eliminate" folk psychology as explanatorily otiose. According to this position, mental states such as beliefs, intentions, and acts of will are fictitious, causally inert, or otherwise epiphenomenal. In the lie-detection context, an eliminative project may,

[123] Wolpe et al., *supra* note 5, at 39. A number of studies rely on a direct–indirect distinction to tout why brain-based lie detection will be superior to traditional polygraphy. *See, e.g.*, Langleben et al., *Brain Activity, supra* note 16, Ganis et al., *Neural Correlates, supra* note 16; Kozel et al., *Pilot Study, supra* note 16; Farwell & Smith, *supra* note 5.
[124] Indeed, displays of knowledge through correct behavior are more "direct."
[125] *See supra* note 16. If not, there would be no point to the experiments.
[126] *See* NATIONAL RESEARCH COUNCIL, THE POLYGRAPH AND LIE DETECTION 12–21 (2003).
[127] *See* the sources cited in *supra* note 16.
[128] *See* Ganis et al., *Lying in the Scanner, supra* note 16.

for example, seek to replace the mental attributes of lying with brain states.[129] We discuss the general problems with eliminative materialism in Chapter Two—here we simply point out that radical reductionism or eliminative projects would be nonsensical in the lie-detection context.[130] Such a project could never get off the ground because the research into lies, deception, and prior knowledge all presuppose the mental attributes that eliminative materialism seeks to eliminate. The mental attributes are necessary to make sense of, and explain, human actions as lies, deception, or knowledge.[131] The research presupposes that subjects have beliefs (sometimes expressing them and sometimes suppressing them), intentions (for example, to deceive), and recognitions of previously known facts, on which they then choose to act or refrain from acting. Moreover, the research presupposes that subjects also possess these mental states and will ascribe such mental states to their audience.[132] Indeed, in order to deceive another person, a subject must make assumptions about what the other person already knows or believes and is likely to infer from the answers given. Although this point is primarily of theoretical rather than practical significance, it provides another reminder that from a practical standpoint the legal issues concern various types of behavior, and the underlying neurological data is relevant only to the extent it provides probative evidence of such behavior. If someone has the neural states without the behavior, she has not lied or deceived.

[129] See, e.g., Paul Churchland, Eliminative Materialism and the Propositional Attitudes, 78 J. PHIL. 67 (1981). For a general discussion of this position, see William Ramsey, Eliminative Materialism, in STANFORD ENCYCLOPEDIA OF PHILOSOPHY (2003), available at http://plato.stanford.edu/entries/materialism-eliminative/.

[130] We also return to the issue in Chapter Seven in discussing theories of criminal punishment.

[131] Donald Davidson has made this general point in several essays. To interpret human behavior as intentional and as an action requires a description of it employing these presupposed mental concepts. See, e.g., DONALD DAVIDSON, Three Varieties of Knowledge, in SUBJECTIVE, INTERSUBJECTIVE, OBJECTIVE 217 (2001) ("it is part of the concept of an intentional action that it is caused and explained by beliefs and desires; it is part of the concept of a belief or a desire that it tends to cause, and so explain, actions of certain sorts."). The law explains action in terms of mental states. See Stephen J. Morse, Determinism and the Death of Folk Psychology: Two Challenges to Responsibility from Neuroscience, 9 MINN. J.L SCI. & TECH. 1 (2008).

[132] See, e.g., Spence et al., Behavioural and Functional Anatomical Correlates, supra note 16, at 1757 ("Deceiving another human subject is likely to involve multiple cognitive processes, including theory of mind concerning the victim's thoughts (their ongoing beliefs)"); Lee et al., Lie Detection, supra note 16, at 163 ("An essence of lying is the recognition of, and attempt to manipulate, the mental states of others.").

4. Lies and Deception Are Not Identical

A fourth conceptual issue involves a distinction between lies and deception. The fMRI research is often touted as supporting a method for detecting lies. The primary subject of the research, however, appears to be deception or, more specifically, identifying an intent to deceive by subjects.[133] Lies and deception, however, are conceptually distinct. One can lie without deceiving or intending to deceive, and deceive or intend to deceive without lying. The research purports to focus on both by aiming to uncover deceptive lies,[134] but this is potentially problematic as a technique for discovering lies in legal settings because it is under-inclusive.

Deceptive acts involve some attempt to cause an audience to believe something false.[135] Lying with an intent to deceive thus involves a complex ability beyond merely asserting something believed to be false. This behavior typically includes (1) recognizing the truth (or what is believed to be true), (2) choosing not to manifest knowledge (or beliefs), (3) making assumptions about what the listener already believes and is likely to believe, and (4) uttering something false. Suppose the fMRI technique could accurately detect an intent by a witness to deceive. Now consider, under federal law in the United States, both the definitions for perjury and for making false statements. A witness commits perjury if, while testifying under oath, he "willfully" asserts something "he does not believe to be true."[136] Likewise, a potential witness commits a federal crime if he "knowingly and willfully" makes a "false statement" to a government agent on a matter within the jurisdiction of the United States.[137] Notice

---

[133] Although whether they are actually measuring this is a different question, which we turn to next.

[134] *See* the sources cited in *supra* note 16. In the *Semrau* case (discussed above), for example, Dr. Laken testified that "A lie is the intentional act of deceit." *Hearing Tr.* at 159. *See also* Sip et al., *supra* note 16 (arguing that lying requires an "intentional aspect of deception").

[135] Both "deception" and "lie" are complex concepts. *See* Marantz Henig, *Looking for the Lie*, N.Y. TIMES (Magazine), Feb. 5, 2006 ("The English language has 112 words for deception, according to one count, each with a different shade of meaning, collusion, fakery, malingering, self-deception, confabulation, prevarication, exaggeration, denial."); *see also* White, *supra* note 85 (quoting Henig and discussing the complexity of lying).

[136] *See* 18 U.S.C. § 1621(1) ("having taken an oath before a competent tribunal, officer, or person, in any case in which a law of the United States authorizes an oath to be administered, that he will testify, declare, depose, or certify truly, or that any written testimony, declaration, deposition, or certificate by him subscribed, is true, willfully and contrary to such oath states or subscribes any material matter which he does not believe to be true.") "Willfully" in this context means the witness makes the statement with the intent to give false testimony. *See* United States v. Dunnigan, 507 U.S. 87, 94 (1993).

[137] *See* 18 U.S.C. § 1001(a) ("whoever, in any matter within the jurisdiction of the executive, legislative, or judicial branch of the Government of the United States, knowingly and willfully...(2) makes any materially false, fictitious, or fraudulent statement or

that someone may commit either of these crimes without having any intent to deceive. For example, suppose a witness has been threatened by a criminal defendant to provide an alibi for the defendant. A witness may knowingly testify falsely about the alibi, but she may do so hoping the jury will see through her lie, not believe it, and convict the defendant.[138] Thus, if the neuroscience is measuring deception, and not lies, we should not assume that a measure of the former is necessarily a measure of the latter.

5. Are the Participants in the fMRI Experiments Lying?

The most significant conceptual issue raised by the fMRI lie-detection research is whether the studies are measuring lies. As noted above, the fMRI studies may be under-inclusive if they are measuring "intent to deceive" rather than lying because some lies do not involve any intent to deceive. More important, however, the studies may be *over*-inclusive in that they count as "lies" actions by subjects that are not in fact acts of lying. If so, then this undermines attempts to draw inferences from neural data about the test subjects to whether actual witnesses are engaged in acts of actual lying.

Here is the problem. Not every utterance that a speaker believes to be false is a lie. For example, when a speaker is telling a joke or reciting a line in a play, a false assertion is not a lie. As Don Fallis notes in an insightful article, the difference that makes "I am the Prince of Denmark" a lie when told at a dinner party but not a lie when told on stage at a play are the norms of conversation in effect.[139] Fallis explores the conceptual contours of lying through numerous examples and presents the following schematic definition:

You lie to X if and only if:

(1) You state that p to X.
(2) You believe that you make this statement in a context where the following norm of conversation is in effect:
  Do not make statements that you believe to be false.
(3) You believe that p is false.[140]

representation…shall be fined under this title, imprisoned not more than 5 years or, if the offense involves international or domestic terrorism (as defined in section 2331), imprisoned not more than 8 years, or both.").

[138] For an illuminating discussion of lies without an intent to deceive, see Don Fallis, *What Is Lying?*, 106 J. PHIL. 29 (2009).

[139] *Id.* at 33–37.

[140] *Id.* at 34. Astute readers will notice that Fallis's definition does not include that the statement actually be false. Although we accept the definition for purposes of our analysis

This definition "capture[s] the normative component of assertion that is necessary for lying."[141]

The fMRI studies do not fit. The subjects in the studies are instructed to assert false statements on certain occasions, sometimes with an intent to deceive an audience; however, their false statements are not acts of lying.[142] Even when subjects commit or plan mock "crimes," they are not in a situation where the following norm is in effect: do not make statements that you believe to be false. Indeed, they are instructed to do precisely that.[143] Thus, the acts being measured, even when they involve deception, appear to be closer to actions of someone playing a game, joking, or role-playing. If this is so, then the relationship between the neural activity of these subjects and acts of lying is not clear. In the legal context, this norm—do not make statements that you believe to be false—is in place, as the perjury and false-statements crimes make clear. The practical significance of this conceptual issue is obvious: to draw conclusions about whether someone is actually lying based on the fact that her neural activity resembles subjects who are not lying (but mistakenly thought to be) could be a disaster. To draw conclusions about whether someone is actually lying in a legal context, the underlying studies must examine actual lying or at least provide compelling reasons why the results from non-lies should inform judgments about lying.[144]

---

below, we are indifferent to whether an additional falsity requirement should be added. *See supra* note 85. For readers who endorse this additional requirement, statements that fit the definition but turn out (unbeknownst to the speaker) to be true should be characterized as "attempted" or "failed" lies. This issue relates to the sincerity–veracity distinction noted above, *see supra* note 9. Just as a person who is being sincere may be mistaken about the truth value of what she asserts, so too a person who is being insincere may be mistaken about the truth value of his assertion.

[141]   *Id.* at 35.

[142]   This is a different issue than the related issue pointed out by Schauer, *supra* note 17, and Jones & Shen, *supra* note 1, that many of the experiments involve "instructed lies." An instructed lie is still a lie—for example, an employee instructed by an employer to lie in a deposition—when the statement is made in a context where the norm against false statements is in effect. When this norm is not present in a study, then the responses are not instructed lies.

[143]   *See, e.g.,* Kozel et al., *Functional MRI Detection, supra* note 16 ("Both groups were instructed to report that they picked up an envelope, but did not sabotage any video evidence.").

[144]   Within the extant literature, the best attempt to study actual lies appears to be Greene & Paxton, *supra* note 16. *See also* Schauer, *supra* note 17 (noting that the subjects in the Greene and Paxton study "have real incentives to tell real lies"); *accord* Jones & Shen, *supra* note 1. Participants were told that the study was examining paranormal activity to predict the future. Subjects were asked to predict coin flips—they were instructed to hold their predictions in mind and then were asked after the randomized coin tosses whether their predictions were accurate. Subjects were rewarded with small amounts of money for accurate guesses, and lost some of the money for inaccurate guesses. In fact, Greene and Paxton were studying "honest" and "dishonest" responses and looking for the neural correlates of each.

6. Has or Will Neuroscience Change(d) the Criteria?

The conceptual issues discussed in this chapter have explored aspects of the criteria for lies, deception, and knowledge. We conclude this section by considering two possible challenges posed recently by Thomas Nadelhoffer.[145] His challenges are based on: (1) the possibility of changed conceptual criteria based on neuroscientific knowledge, and (2) the views of many people about the current concepts. Although we do not think these issues challenge or undermine our arguments, discussing them will help to further extend and clarify our analysis.

The first issue concerns the possibility of changed criteria for lies, deception, or knowledge. Nadelhoffer contends that developments in neuroscience may cause brain states to replace behavior as the criteria for lies or deception. Nadelhoffer cautions that "yesterday's impossibilities have a way of becoming tomorrow's platitudes."[146] He notes that in areas such as medicine, physics, and chemistry, scientific developments have also brought with them conceptual changes in the criteria for the application of concepts. At one point, the molecular level did not feature in the criteria for "water," but now it does. He also raises the example of the flu. He argues that former criteria—for example, "sore throat, fever, shivering, coughing, and the like"—are now "demoted to the status of mere symptoms."[147] Thus, it may be possible to successfully ascribe the condition to someone even when that person does not suffer from the symptoms. The analogy with neural lie detection is straightforward: the behavior that now constitutes the criteria for lies may be demoted to "mere symptoms," and neural states may become the new criteria (as with molecular facts and water).

We do not take issue as a general matter with extending or changing concepts. Thus we do not embrace the position that Nadelhoffer refers

---

(Those with high prediction rates were labeled "dishonest" and those around 50 percent were labeled "honest.") Although the authors found a correlation between neural activity and the "dishonest" participants, they note a number of limitations on drawing conclusions about lie detection. Greene & Paxton, *supra* note 16, at 12510 ("our task design does not allow us to identify individual lies...our findings highlight the challenge in distinguishing lying from related cognitive processes.") Moreover, the cover story of "paranormal abilities" may have introduced an additional problem: some "dishonest" subjects may have actually convinced themselves they were predicting accurately and thus were not lying to the researchers. *See* R. Wiseman et al., *Belief in the Paranormal and Suggestion in the Séance Room*, 94 BRITISH J. PSYCHOL. 285 (2003).

[145] Thomas Nadelhoffer, *Neural Lie Detection, Criterial Change, and Ordinary Language*, 4 NEUROETHICS 205 (2011).

[146] *Id*. at 206.

[147] *Id*. at 209.

to as "criterial conventionalism."[148] He contends that we must explain how "it is possible for language to change in light of scientific progress even though the criteria that govern how we can meaningfully talk about the world are fixed."[149] This is not our position. We acknowledge that language is fluid and that concepts can change based on scientific progress (and much else); we also do not object to scientists, lawyers, philosophers, or anyone else coining new terms or extending or limiting the uses of existing terms or concepts.[150] Our objections arise in situations in which inferences are drawn from premises that presuppose our current concepts (e.g., of lying, deception, or knowledge) and that betray the criteria for the application of those concepts. We can call certain brain states "lies" (or "lies★") if we want to; the key questions would be why, and what would follow when we did so?

In the context of law, however, the analogy breaks down. The law cares about the behavioral criteria themselves, not as "mere symptoms" of something else. Consider the hypothetical case of Wendy Witness, who saw a crime take place, was questioned by the police, and is called to testify at trial. If the change Nadelhoffer envisions were to go through, then whether she said something she knew to be false to the police or on the witness stand would not be "a lie," it would be "mere symptoms" that may or may not be lies depending on what is going on in her brain. On the flipside, she may have lied to the police or on the witness stand because of her brain, regardless of whether she uttered anything false ("mere symptoms"). We think this example provides a reductio ad absurdum for the analogies. Consider again the crimes of perjury and making false statements.[151] Wendy committed these crimes in the first scenario, even if she did not have the brain states that are correlated with deception; she did not commit these crimes in the second scenario, even if she had brain states correlated with deception. Regardless of whether our concepts "lie" and "deception" change because of neuroscience, *the behavioral and psychological phenomena currently referred to by the terms expressing these concepts—what the law cares about—will still be with us and will not have changed.*

The example provides a useful illustration of how the conceptual issues we are exploring—not just in this chapter but throughout this book—are not just about words and how we use them. They are also

---

[148]   *Id.* at 210.

[149]   *Id.* at 211.

[150]   For several examples of conceptual change in science, see MARK WILSON, WANDERING SIGNIFICANCE: AN ESSAY ON CONCEPTUAL BEHAVIOR (2006).

[151]   *See supra* notes 136 and 137 and accompanying text.

about the underlying phenomena and how clarity regarding concepts can contribute to greater understanding of the phenomena, and how conceptual confusion distorts our understanding. Changing conceptual criteria is fine when it serves a useful purpose. Again, we can call certain brain states "lies" or "lie★" if we want to; the key questions would be why, and what would follow if we did so? Importantly, however, the change in usage would not change the current phenomena referred to by terms expressing our current concepts. Psychologist Gregory Miller makes a similar point regarding psychological terms such as "depression" and "schizophrenia":

The phenomenon that a particular usage of the term *depression* refers to does not change if we redeploy the term to refer to something else, such as the biochemistry associated with depression. If by consensus the term *depression* refers today to sadness as a psychological state and in 10 years to a brain chemistry state, we have not altered the phenomenon of sadness, nor have we explained it in terms of brain chemistry.[152]

And

Whatever *schizophrenia* refers to 100 years from now (one certainly hopes it will evolve to mean something much more precise), the (psychological) phenomena it has long referred to will not have changed, will still exist, and will still have the potential to disrupt millions of lives.[153]

Similarly, the concept of "lie" may change as Nadelhoffer suggests, but this will not change the fact that some people will willfully say things they believe to be false on the witness stand and to government agents, and the law will still have a strong interest in determining when they are doing so and when they are not.

Nadelhoffer poses a second issue. He contends that the current criteria depend on the usage of (most) ordinary speakers, but "if you were to ask people on the street," many would concur that, for example, knowledge *is* stored in the brain. Moreover, with the dissemination of more and more neuroscientific information, many folks on the street might also increasingly concur with the view that lies and deception

---

[152] Gregory A. Miller, *Mistreating Psychology in the Decades of the Brain*, 5 PERSP. PSYCH. SCI. 716, 718 (2010).

[153] *Id.*

are likewise "in the brain." If so, on what basis can we claim that the folk would be mistaken?

The underlying phenomena currently referred to by "lying," "deception," or "knowledge" would not change even if most people think the terms refer to brain phenomena. The underlying phenomena are what the law cares about and on which legal doctrine focuses. If most people think the terms refer to brain phenomena, then either most people would be mistaken (if employing the current concepts)[154] or the concepts would have changed. If the latter is the case, then this just takes us back to the first issue in this section and our response. If the former is the case, then this may not be surprising given the complexity of the concepts involved.[155] Many people who otherwise understand complex concepts may sometimes draw mistaken inferences in using them. For example, even if many people think it is more probable that "Linda is a librarian and a Democrat" than that "Linda is a librarian," this is not necessarily a criterial change in the meaning of "probable."[156] Many who initially make the erroneous inference will, upon reflection, acknowledge the error. "Lies," "deception," and "knowledge" may be similar. Moreover, the criteria for the application of concepts and words will not always be transparent to those who otherwise employ the concepts and words successfully in most instances. Consider, by analogy, the concept of law or the word "law" (as used in the legal context). Although "people on the street" understand the concept and how to use the word, the criteria are opaque to and a matter of dispute among not only people on the street but also lawyers, law professors, and philosophers.[157] Those with legal training develop skills to employ "law" and legal concepts with more sophistication, and much of the methodology of legal argumentation involves demonstrating how certain inferences appear to betray criteria accepted elsewhere within legal practices.[158] Our concepts of lies, deception, and knowledge appear

---

[154] *Cf.* Simons & Chabris, *supra* note 118 (documenting that many people have mistaken beliefs about memory).

[155] *Id.* As we discuss in Chapter Seven, it may also be possible that many people have mistaken beliefs about the relationships among free will, determinism, and the justification of criminal punishment.

[156] *See* Amos Tversky & Daniel Kahneman, *Extensional Versus Intuitive Reasoning: The Conjunction Fallacy in Probability Judgment, in* HEURISTICS AND BIASES: THE PSYCHOLOGY OF INTUITIVE JUDGMENT 19 (Thomas Gilovich et al. eds., 2002).

[157] *See* Jules L. Coleman & Ori Simchen, *"Law"*, 9 LEGAL THEORY 1 (2003).

[158] Timothy Williamson analogizes legal and philosophical training and argues that both improve judgments about the application of the relevant concepts. TIMOTHY WILLIAMSON, THE PHILOSOPHY OF PHILOSOPHY 187–95 (2007).

to be like law in these respects. They involve neither simple, transparent criteria nor do they appear to be "natural kinds" to which we can defer to the relevant scientists to discover their true essence. Rather, they each involve arrays of behavior that both serve a normative, regulative role in providing a standard for the application of the concepts *and* an empirical, evidential role of whether that concept applies in a particular instance. Given this complexity, it is no surprise that mistaken inferences will arise.

C. Practical Issues

In addition to the empirical and conceptual issues affecting the pro-bative value of brain-based lie-detection, the use of such evidence in court will depend on a number of additional practical issues.

To be admissible in court, the evidence must first be relevant. To be relevant it must make a fact of consequence to the determination of the case more or less probable. Witness credibility is always relevant, and so the evidence will be relevant so long as it has some rational bearing on the question of witness credibility. In addition, the evidence and the technique on which it is based must be shown to have sufficient validity and reliability to warrant admission under the applicable expert-testimony rule. In federal courts, this approach requires that the technique employs reliable principles and methods that are applied reliably to the case. Courts employ the *Daubert* factors as a guideline in applying this rule, considering various factors such as controls and standards, error rates, peer review and publication, and general acceptance in the relevant community. Given the empirical and conceptual limitations discussed above, we think that the *Semrau* opinion was a sound application of this test to the current fMRI lit-erature. But it is conceivable that the research may evolve to a point where a court could reasonably find the test to be met.[159]

As the research develops, reliable individualized results may emerge. At this point, the results would be admissible under federal rules of admissibility. To do so, however, it must remain within the bounds of the conceptual issues we outline in the previous section. The tech-nique must actually measure acts of lying, and the research must be clear about the empirical relationship between the neuroscientific data and the complex behavior with which it is correlated. In such a case, the evidence may be based on sufficient data and reliable principles

---

[159] This will depend on the empirical issues that we outline above, and whether the research provides reason to think it provides probative evidence of actual lies.

and methods.[160] In addition, the evidence may satisfy additional guiding factors the Supreme Court identified in *Daubert*: the techniques and underlying principle would be falsifiable, subject to peer review and publication, and have identifiable error rates.[161] Given the wide discretion to trial judges to determine admissibility in the area,[162] there may be an initial divergence in the willingness of courts to admit the evidence. But (perceived) reliable use in some initial cases may lead to an increased willingness of other courts to exercise their discretion and admit it.[163]

When evidence has sufficient probative value to warrant admission under this standard, a number of additional practical issues may potentially raise further grounds for exclusion. We briefly discuss three of them, and we conclude that none necessarily provides a compelling case for exclusion.

The first issue concerns misinterpretation by juries (and judges). Even if neuroscientific lie-detection evidence is relevant and reliable enough to satisfy *Daubert*, it may nevertheless be excluded if its probative value is substantially outweighed by the likelihood that legal fact finders will give it more weight than it deserves. The baseline for assessing this evidence should be that juries in general appear to be quite competent in evaluating complex scientific evidence, including DNA evidence.[164] Assuming expert neuroscientific evidence is sound

---

[160]   *See* FED. R. EVID. 702(1)–(2).

[161]   Daubert v. Merrell Dow Pharmaceuticals, Inc., 509 U.S. 579, 593–94 (1993). The last variable—known error rates—is a serious problem for many types of expert testimony (such as handwriting, voice, bite-mark, ballistics, and fingerprint identifications). *See* NATIONAL RESEARCH COUNCIL, STRENGTHENING FORENSIC SCIENCE IN THE UNITED STATES: A PATH FORWARD (2009).

[162]   In General Electric Co. v. Joiner, 522 U.S. 136 (1997), the Court stated that district-court decisions regarding the admissibility of expert testimony should be reviewed for abuse of discretion. And then in Kuhmo Tire Co., Ltd. v. Carmichael, 526 U.S. 137 (1999), the Court clarified that *Daubert* applies to all expert testimony, and that the abuse-of-discretion standard applies to both conclusions about admissibility and decisions about which factors are important for assessing the reliability of such evidence.

[163]   Therefore, states that adhere to the standard of "general acceptance" articulated in Frye v. United States, 293 F. 1013 (D.C. Cir. 1923), will likely take longer to admit such evidence. Even when evidence meets the admissibility rules for expert testimony, additional evidentiary rules such as those that regulate hearsay may also provide a basis for exclusion in some cases. *See* Jeffrey Bellin, *The Significance (if any) for the Federal Criminal Justice System of Advances in Lie Detection Technology*, 80 TEMP. L. REV. 711 (2007) (arguing that hearsay rules will be a major obstacle to admitting lie-detection evidence that meets expert reliability standards).

[164]   For an overview of the empirical literature on juries, see NEIL VIDMAR & VALERIE P. HANS, AMERICAN JURIES: THE VERDICT (2007).

and presented in a clear and detailed manner, there should be no a priori reason to exclude such evidence on grounds of misinterpretation. Perhaps, however, neuroscience-specific studies may give additional reasons to distrust the jury. Here, again, this does not appear to be the case. Although some studies suggest that lay subjects may give too much weight to neuroscientific evidence (particularly when presented as brain images),[165] other studies focusing on neuroscience in legal settings do not support a general jury-incompetence problem.[166] The burden should be on those seeking exclusion on this ground to provide compelling reasons in a given case.

Even if juries would not generally misinterpret the evidence, a second concern is that it would "usurp" the jury's function of determining witness credibility. This was the ground for excluding the evidence in *Corestaff*. The argument was also expressed by Justice Clarence Thomas in a U.S. Supreme Court case upholding a rule excluding polygraph evidence.[167] The court in *Corestaff* relied upon Justice Thomas's opinion and other polygraph cases for its usurps-the-jury rationale. A proper understanding of the conceptual issues regarding the neuroscientific evidence, however, illustrates why this is a bad argument.

The argument for exclusion applies to expert testimony on any form of lie-detection evidence. The government has a legitimate interest,

---

[165] *See* David P. McCabe & Alan D. Castel, *Seeing Is Believing: The Effect of Brain Images on Judgments of Scientific Reasoning*, 107 COGNITION 343 (2008); Deena Skolnick Weisberg et al., *The Seductive Allure of Neuroscience Explanations*, 20 J. COG. NEUROSCIENCE 470 (2008); David P. McCabe et al., *The Influence of fMRI Lie Detection Evidence on Juror Decision-Making*, 29 BEHAV. SCI. & LAW 566 (2011); Jessica R. Gurley & David K. Marcus, *The Effects of Neuroimaging and Brain Injury on Insanity Defenses*, 26 BEHAV. SCI. & LAW 85 (2008). For discussions of these studies expressing caution regarding the conclusions about jury competence that may be drawn from them, see Schauer, *supra* note 17; Walter Sinnott-Armstrong et al., *Brain Scans as Legal Evidence*, 5 EPISTEME 359 (2008).

[166] *See* N.J. Schweitzer et al., *Neuroimages as Evidence in a Mens Rea Defense: No Impact*, 17 PSYCH., PUB. POLICY & LAW 357 (2011); N.J. Schweitzer et al., *Neuroimage Evidence and the Insanity Defense*, 29 BEHAV. SCI. & LAW 592 (2011). *See also* Martha J. Farah & Cayce J. Hook, *The Seductive Allure of "Seductive Allure,"* 8 PERSPECTIVES PSYCHOL. SCI. 88 (2013) ("we find little empirical support for the claim that brain images are inordinately influential.").

[167] United States v. Scheffer, 523 U.S. 303 (1998). The case upheld a rule excluding polygraph evidence in military tribunals. *Id.* Jurisdictions have taken different approaches to polygraph evidence, with a trend toward either categorical exclusion, see, e.g., State v. Blanck, 955 So.2d 90, 131 (La. 2007), or admissibility in limited circumstances (e.g., when stipulated by the parties or for impeachment purposes), State v. Domicz, 907 A.2d 395 (N.J. 2006); United States v. Piccinonna, 885 F.2d 1529, 1536 (11th Cir. 1989). New Mexico generally allows polygraph evidence. *See* N.M. R. EVID. § 11-707. *See generally* DAVID L. FAIGMAN ET AL., MODERN SCIENTIFIC EVIDENCE: THE LAW AND SCIENCE OF EXPERT TESTIMONY § 40 (2011).

Justice Thomas explained, in preserving the "core function" of "credibility determinations in criminal trials"; a "fundamental premise" of that function is "that 'the *jury* is the lie detector.'"[168] The lie-detection expert, rather than the jury, would be the primary judge of credibility, with the jury deferring to the expert's opinion:

Unlike other expert witnesses who testify about factual matters outside the jurors' knowledge, such as the analysis of fingerprints, ballistics, or DNA found at a crime scene, a [lie-detection] expert can supply the jury only with another opinion, in addition to its own, about whether the witness was telling the truth.[169]

Consequently, jurors may blindly defer to the expert and "abandon their duty to assess credibility and guilt."[170]

But, Justice Thomas's distinction notwithstanding, the problem of deference to expert opinion is a problem for *all* expert testimony.[171] Although it is possible that jurors may be prone to overvalue neuroscientific evidence in particular, this is an open question in need of further testing and one not borne out by current research. There is no a priori reason to believe that jurors will be less able to assess the neuroscientific evidence than they are to assess DNA evidence or other complex scientific evidence. Highly reliable DNA results may be just as likely to cause deference, yet jurors are trusted not to abandon their duties to determine credibility and guilt. Nor does the fact that the neuroscience evidence would be tied more directly to the *credibility* of witness statements render the evidence problematic. Despite some initial resistance, courts have become more receptive to other kinds of expert testimony that may help jurors assess witness statements. Testimony regarding eyewitness identifications[172] and false confession[173] are two prominent examples. Like these

---

[168] United States v. Scheffer, 523 U.S. 303, 312–13 (1998) (quoting United States v. Barnard, 490 U.S. 907, 912 (9th Cir. 1973) (emphasis added)).

[169] *Id.* at 313.

[170] *Id.* at 314.

[171] *See* Ronald J. Allen & Joseph S. Miller, *The Common Law Theory of Experts: Deference or Education?*, 87 Nw. U. L. Rev. 1131 (1993).

[172] *See* Newsome v. McCabe, 319 F.3d 301, 306 (7th Cir. 2003) ("it may be prudent to avoid complicating criminal trials with general scientific evidence about the psychology of identification—though scientific evidence that a given person deviates from the norm (for example, is exceptionally suggestible) may be invaluable.").

[173] *See* United States v. Hall, 93 F.3d 1337, 1345 (7th Cir. 1996) ("It was precisely because juries are unlikely to know that social scientists and psychologists have identified a personality

areas, the neuroscience evidence, when properly explained, may *assist* rather than *usurp* jurors in assessing the credibility of statements—and such assistance is the whole point of expert testimony.[174]

Even a highly reliable neuroscientific test would not establish knowledge or lies directly. Therefore, jurors would still need to play their traditional role in assessing such evidence. (Similarly, highly probative DNA evidence does not usurp jurors of their traditional role.) In the lie-detection contexts, juror assessments should consider, for example, whether other (criterial) evidence regarding credibility should override the test results (rendering the test conclusion unlikely); the possibility of errors in conducting or analyzing the test (with known error rates told to the jury); and the possibility of perjury by the expert. These considerations, as well as other evidence in the case, would all affect the probative value of the evidence—and nothing in the nature of the neuroscience evidence or its complexity would prevent jurors from adequately assessing its probative value in light of the above considerations. If the jury is properly instructed, there is no reason to think that the evidence would usurp jury powers any more than DNA evidence or testimony regarding eyewitness identifications and false confessions would.

Finally, a third practical issue concerns the overall costs and benefits of admitting the evidence. Professor Michael Risinger has raised the general challenge most clearly in the context of any kind of lie detection.[175] According to Risinger, the practical effects of admitting reliable lie-detection evidence may be too "drastic" for the system, as it would potentially apply to all witnesses and parties in every case, and, if reliable enough, criminal defendants may have a constitutional right to present such evidence. There is no way to determine a priori, however, whether drastic effects (should they occur) would be for the better or worse.[176] DNA had drastic effects for the better. Moreover,

---

disorder that will cause individuals to make false confessions that the testimony would have assisted the jury in making its decision. It would have been up to the jury, of course, to decide how much weight to attach to Dr. Ofshe's theory, and to decide whether they believed his explanation of Hall's behavior or the more commonplace explanation that the confession was true.").

[174] *See* FED. R. EVID. 702; Allen & Miller, *supra* note 171.

[175] *See* D. Michael Risinger, *Navigating Expert Reliability: Are Criminal Standards of Certainty Being Left on the Dock?*, 64 ALB. L. REV. 99, 129–30 (2000) (arguing admissibility of lie-detection evidence would have "drastic" practical effects on litigation).

[176] The changes may be for the better if the evidence is more probative than other evidence that is presented instead. *See* Schauer, *supra* note 1; Schauer, *supra* note 17.

more widespread application may, of course, mean more widespread improvement. Should the evidence ever become reliable enough, the key practical issues will involve how to incorporate this evidence effectively into the system while cabining the various potential problems at the heart of Risinger's concern.

The discussion in this chapter has focused on the voluntary use of brain-based lie detection. An additional, significant issue concerns the *compelled* use of such evidence. We discuss this issue in Chapter Six. In the next chapter we focus on several issues concerning neuroscience and doctrinal issues pertaining to criminal law.

5

Criminal Law Doctrine

Neuroscience's potential to transform the criminal law reaches every important doctrinal issue that gives structure and content to criminal litigation. In the previous chapter, we considered one specific evidentiary issue—lie detection—that may have widespread ramifications in criminal and civil litigation, as well as in non-litigation settings. In this chapter, we examine several additional doctrinal issues in criminal law on which, scholars argue, neuroscience may have a transformative effect. In the next two chapters, we discuss a variety of issues involving constitutional criminal procedure (Chapter Six) and challenges to criminal punishment that purport to undermine the philosophical foundations on which criminal law depends (Chapter Seven).

The doctrine regulating criminal liability may be divided into three main issues. These include, first, whether the defendant engaged in voluntary conduct (the "*actus reus*" requirement). Second, liability typically requires that the defendant engaged in the voluntary act with an accompanying mental attribute such as intent, knowledge, or recklessness (the "*mens rea*" requirement). Third, certain conditions may justify or excuse conduct that may otherwise constitute criminal liability under the first two conditions. Scholars have argued that neuroscientific evidence may contribute to each of these three categories. We discuss each in turn. For each category, we first outline the basic doctrinal requirements, we then explain the role of the mind in constituting and underlying this doctrine, and finally we evaluate a variety of claims about how evidence about the brain can inform the doctrinal issues.

I. *Actus Reus*

Criminal liability requires voluntary conduct by defendants. This foundational doctrinal category is referred to as the "*actus reus*" (or "guilty act") requirement. Modern criminal statutes, including the Model Penal Code, exclude from the guilty-act category: bodily movements such as reflexes, convulsions, and sleepwalking; acts performed while under hypnosis; and other movements that are not "a product of the effort or determination of the actor."[1]

The voluntary-act requirement depends on a distinction between bodily movements that are "consciously willed" and those that are not consciously willed.[2] This category depends on the mind in two ways: the bodily movements must be, in some sense, *conscious* and they must be, in some sense, *willed*. Both notions depend on relatively thin conceptions. The type of consciousness necessary to constitute a voluntary act for purposes of the criminal does not require, for example, that the defendant reflected on his actions (or on the objects or goals of his actions) while performing them.[3] Someone switching lanes in traffic is acting voluntarily for purposes of the criminal law even when she is not consciously reflecting on what she is doing or the lanes in which she is moving.[4] Voluntariness

---

[1] MODEL PENAL CODE § 2.01. *See also* People v. Newton, 8 Cal. App. 3d 359 (1970) (defendant's bodily movements in firing a gun held not to be voluntary because not conscious); Gideon Yaffe, *Libet and the Criminal Law's Voluntary Act Requirement, in* CONSCIOUS WILL AND RESPONSIBILITY 192 (Walter Sinnott-Armstrong & Lynn Nadel eds., 2011) ("the law supplies no positive description of the kind of consciousness in question, but merely provides, instead, a list of circumstances in which the relevant sort of consciousness is absent: reflexes, and cases of hypnosis and somnambulism.").

[2] Larry Alexander, *Criminal and Moral Responsibility and the Libet Experiments, in* CONSCIOUS WILL AND RESPONSIBILITY, *supra* note 1, at 204 (referring to "a consciously willed bodily movement" as "the principal unit of criminal and moral assessment").

[3] The mental component that separates a voluntary act from other bodily movements is typically characterized as a "volition." For a comprehensive philosophical account of volitions and their relationship to criminal law, see MICHAEL MOORE, ACT AND CRIME: THE PHILOSOPHY OF ACTION AND ITS IMPLICATIONS FOR CRIMINAL LAW 113–65 (1993). *See also* Yaffe, *supra* note 1, at 190 ("Volition is best thought of as an executory mental state: it performs the role of realizing in bodily motion the plans and purposes set out by other mental states like intention."). For a philosophical critique of some of the conceptual presuppositions underlying "volitional" accounts, see P.M.S. HACKER, HUMAN NATURE: THE CATEGORICAL FRAMEWORK 146–60 (2007).

[4] Part of the confusion that arises in this area stems from the different possible senses of the words "conscious," "consciously," and "unconscious," and the fact that conscious–unconscious do not always form a dichotomy. The fact that one is not conscious

does, however, require a type of awareness or attention that sepa-rates the driver switching lanes from someone sleepwalking, hypno-tized, or in an altered state of consciousness. The "will" requirement depends on a notion of control.[5] A minimal level of control over one's actions will make them voluntary for purposes of the crimi-nal law. The type of control necessary to make an act voluntary in this minimal sense depends on a type of two-way power: the agent not only has the power to act but also the power to refrain from so acting.[6] The various intentions or other mental attributes that may have caused an action are typically irrelevant for this category, so long as the defendant had awareness and control over the fact that he was *moving* his body.[7] Spasms, reflexes, being pushed, or falling are the types of movements that fall outside of the doctrinal category.[8] Defendants in these categories do not have the power to refrain from moving, and the criminal law thus does not hold them respon-sible for these movements.

The examples excluded from the doctrinal category of voluntary action reveal possible ways in which neuroscience may contribute to the issue of *actus reus*. Evidence about the brain may be probative on

---

of one's bodily movements while driving does not mean that one is driving while unconscious. *See* Michael S. Pardo & Dennis Patterson, *More on the Conceptual and the Empirical: Misunderstandings, Clarifications, and Replies*, 4 NEUROETHICS 215 (2011). The key distinction is between a transitive use (conscious *of* something or *that* something is so) and an intransitive use (akin to being awake and alert, on the one hand, or akin to being asleep, anesthetized, or otherwise "knocked out," on the other). Both senses have borderline cases. For a discussion and analysis, see M.R. BENNETT & P.M.S. HACKER, PHILOSOPHICAL FOUNDATIONS OF NEUROSCIENCE 239–60 (2003). Similar considerations apply to "voluntary" and "involuntary." The fact that someone's actions are not voluntary does not necessarily mean that they are moving involuntarily.

[5] The two notions—conscious and willed—are not always clearly separated in discussions of criminal law's act requirement. We separate them because they present different ways the act requirement depends on the mind and thus two different reasons that bodily movements may fail to fit into the doctrinal category. Sometimes a defendant's movements may be "willed" in a minimal doctrinal sense (goal-directed and responsive to the environment) but not rise to the requisite level of "consciousness" (e.g., someone sleepwalking or the defen-dant in *Newton*, 8 Cal. App. 3d 359); likewise, people may have the requisite doctrinal level of conscious awareness of their bodily movements but not have sufficient control to stop or to will different movements (*see, e.g., infra* notes 9 and 11).

[6] For (differing) philosophical analyses of how to further characterize voluntary move-ments, see BENNETT & HACKER, *supra* note 4, at 224–35; MOORE, *supra* note 3; Yaffe, *supra* note 1 (tracing different conceptions in the work of Locke).

[7] *See* MOORE, *supra* note 3, at 173; Yaffe, *supra* note 1.

[8] *See* MODEL PENAL CODE § 2.01(2).

this issue if, as an empirical matter, it contributes along one of the two dimensions discussed above—either by showing that defendants lack the minimal level of consciousness or that they lacked the control required to make their movements voluntary acts for purposes of the criminal law. Here are examples of what we have in mind: A defendant with "alien limb syndrome" may have an arm or hand that moves without sufficient control by the defendant to render the movements voluntary.[9] Even though the defendant may be conscious or aware of the hand's movement, the movements may not be within the defendant's control so as to render them voluntary acts.[10] Similarly, a defendant who suffers from a similar syndrome known as "utilization behavior" may grasp objects within reach and use them in their usual ways, but at "inappropriate" times.[11] For example, someone may pick up and put on a pair of eyeglasses even though he is already wearing glasses or pick up a toothbrush at a store and immediately begin brushing her teeth. The impulses to act in such ways may be beyond the control of defendants.[12] In these exceptional types of cases, neuroscientific evidence may provide probative evidence that a defendant suffers from one of these or similar syndromes. For example, MRI may reveal lesions, or fMRI may reveal patterns of neural activity, correlated with the conditions.[13] Essentially, whenever neuroscience can provide

[9] Petroc Sumner & Masud Husain, *At the Edge of Consciousness: Automatic Motor Activation and Voluntary Control*, 14 NEUROSCIENTIST 476 (2008) ("Patients with the alien limb syndrome demonstrate involuntary actions of a limb. Their hand may grasp nearby objects—even other people—and may have great difficulty releasing them.").

[10] *See id.* at 477 ("When the patient is fully aware of such movements, some authors have preferred to refer to the limb as *anarchic* rather than *alien*.").

[11] *Id.* ("individuals [with 'utilization behavior' syndrome] may experience difficulty resisting their impulse to use an object placed within their reach, even when such an object is not needed.").

[12] *Id.*

[13] Alien limb syndrome is "classically associated with focal lesions involving the medial frontal lobe, most prominently the supplementary motor regions, sometime in association with the corpus callosum"; "it may also occur after posterior vascular legions in the right hemisphere"; and it may also result from neurodegenerative conditions. *Id.* (*citing* I. Biran & A. Chatterjee, *Alien Hand Syndrome*, 61 ARCHIVES NEUROLOGY 292 (2004); E. Coulthard et al., *Alien Limb Following Posterior Cerebral Artery Stroke: Failure to Recognize Internally Generated Movements*, 22 MOVEMENT DISORDERS 1498 (2007); R. Murray et al., *Cognitive and Motor Assessment in Autopsy-Proven Corticobasal Degeneration*, 68 NEUROLOGY 1274 (2007)).

Ulitization behavior syndrome "has been linked to frontal lesions" in the "supplementary motor area (SMA), pre-SMA, cingulated motor areas." Sumner & Husain, *supra* note 9, at 477 (*citing* F. Lhermitte, *Utilization Behaviour and Its Relation to Lesions of the Frontal Lobes*, 106 BRAIN 237 (1983); E. Boccardi, *Utilisation Behaviour Consequent to Bilateral SMA Softening*, 38 CORTEX 289 (2002)).

diagnostic evidence of whether a defendant has a condition that makes his behavior not voluntary (as characterized by criminal law doctrine), the neuroscientific information will be probative evidence.[14]

There are, however, important conceptual limitations on the use of neuroscience to inform *actus reus*. Recognizing these limitations, we thus take issue with stronger claims about the sweeping power of neuroscience to revolutionize the doctrinal issue as a general matter. The clearest and most detailed proposal along these lines comes from Deborah Denno. Professor Denno argues that "neuroscience research on consciousness"[15]—primarily the work of Benjamin Libet[16]— "confirms that there appears to be no sound scientific basis" for the doctrinal distinction between voluntary and involuntary conduct.[17] Her argument consists not only in applying empirical results from the research to the criminal law, but it is also an argument about the *conceptual* relationships among the empirical results, the concepts "voluntary," "non-voluntary," and "involuntary," and the doctrinal categories. When these conceptual relationships are properly understood, it becomes clear that the empirical results do nothing to undermine the existing legal framework.

Professor Denno begins by characterizing voluntary acts as involving three components: "(1) an internal event, or volition; (2) an external, physical demonstration of that volition; and (3) a causal connection between the internal and external elements."[18] These characteristics constitute a conceptual claim about voluntary acts—in other words, Denno presupposes that when we describe movements as "voluntary" for purposes of the criminal law we are picking out movements with these characteristics. She elaborates on this conceptual claim by asserting that "willed" movements "lie at the heart" of voluntary acts, and glosses this characteristic as follows: "[i]n other words, when do people

[14] Having such a condition may not necessarily be exculpatory, however (for example, if a defendant has prior knowledge and ignores the risks created).

[15] Deborah W. Denno, *Crime and Consciousness: Science and Involuntary Acts*, 87 MINN. L. REV. 269, 320 (2002).

[16] *See* BENJAMIN LIBET, MIND TIME (2004); Benjamin Libet, *Are the Mental Experiences of Will and Self-Control Significant for the Performance of a Voluntary Act?*, 10 BEHAV. & BRAIN SCI. 783 (1997); Benjamin Libet, *Unconscious Cerebral Initiative and the Role of Conscious Will in Voluntary Action*, 8 BEHAV. & BRAIN SCI. 529 (1985). The literature on the Libet studies is voluminous. For an excellent collection of commentaries on the nature and the implications of Libet's findings, see CONSCIOUS WILL AND RESPONSIBILITY, *supra* note 1.

[17] Denno, *supra* note 15, at 328.

[18] *Id.* at 275–76.

consciously feel they have engaged in a voluntary act?"[19] The problem, as Denno sees it, is that "[s]ome of the most powerful research in neuroscience" indicates that "unconscious" brain processes "may be in charge of how humans make decisions about willed movements."[20] We may summarize the argument as follows:

(1) voluntariness for criminal liability requires willed movements;
(2) willed movements require internal, conscious decisions;
(3) decisions about willed movements, however, are made by "the unconscious";
(Conclusion) Therefore, willed movements are not really voluntary in a sense that distinguishes them from the movements the criminal law acknowledges are not voluntary.

To support this argument, Professor Denno relies on the innovative and controversial experiments by Benjamin Libet and colleagues.[21] Subjects in the experiments were instructed to watch a light revolving around the periphery of a clock and also to flex a wrist at whatever time they wished. Subjects were also instructed to note the location of the light on the clock when they "first became aware of the wish or intention" to flex their wrist. During the experiments, subjects were monitored by EEG (measuring electrical activity in the brain through the scalp) and by EMG (measuring muscular motion). The key findings, based on averages of multiple flexes per subject and from several subjects, are that (1) electrical activity in the brain—referred to as the "readiness potential"—preceded the beginning of any muscular motion resulting in a flex of the wrist by approximately 550 milliseconds, and (2) the "readiness potential" preceded subjects' reported awareness of their "wish or intention" to act by approximately 350 milliseconds. Thus the causal chain appears to run from readiness potential to wish or intention to flexing.[22] Denno

---

[19] *Id.* at 326.

[20] *Id.*

[21] *See supra* note 16. What follows in the text is a brief summary of the experiments and the findings that are relevant to Denno's argument.

[22] Although this causal possibility is consistent with the data, it is not the only way to interpret the results. The relationship between the readiness potential and intentional action raises a number of conceptual questions, and depends not only on the empirical results but also on how concepts such as "intention," "conscious awareness," "wish," and other mental attributes are conceived and individuated. For illuminating discussions of the underlying conceptual issues linking Libet's empirical findings to the issues of voluntary movement—each rejecting the inference that the readiness potential renders bodily movements involuntary—see MOORE, *supra* note 3; Michael S. Moore, *Libet's*

summarizes the experiments and results on which she relies in the following way:

A typical Libet experiment—much simplified for this discussion—goes as follows: Libet would ask human subjects to make hand movements whenever they felt like it while he measured the electrical activity in their brains. With EEG recordings, this could be done with almost millisecond precision. Libet found that the subjects' brain impulses associated with their movements began about 300 to 350 milliseconds—or about a third of a second—before the subjects reported any conscious awareness of their intention to make the movement. In essence, the motor-planning areas in their brains began to stir a third of a second prior to when the subjects became aware of the desire to act. According to Libet and others, a subject's decision to move a finger or a wrist must have originated unconsciously and only appeared to that person as a conscious wish about a third of a second later.[23]

Denno claims that the "now accepted" view (based on this research) is that "consciousness evolves gradually, starting from the unconscious and moving toward pre-conscious states on the way to becoming a settled state of consciousness," and "[w]hat seems like two modes of processing [conscious and unconscious] is really a whole brain reaction" originating with the readiness potential.[24] Libet's research, she contends, "confirm[s] that there appears to be no sound scientific basis" for the criminal law's distinction between voluntary and involuntary conduct.[25]

Challenge(s) to Responsible Agency, in CONSCIOUS WILL AND RESPONSIBILITY, *supra* note 1; ALFRED R. MELE, EFFECTIVE INTENTIONS: THE POWER OF CONSCIOUS WILL (2009); BENNETT & HACKER, *supra* note 4, at 228–31.

[23] Denno, *supra* note 15, at 326–27 (footnotes omitted). Denno also suggests that the movements in the experiments may be similar to a defendant's movements in firing a gun. *Id.* Stephen Morse demurs:

> Libet's task involved "random" finger movements that involved no deliberation whatsoever and no rational motivation for the specific movements involved. This is a far cry from the behavioral concerns of the criminal law or morality, which address intentional conduct in contexts when there is always good reason to refrain from harming another or to act beneficently. In fact, it is at present an open question whether Libet's paradigm is representative of intentional actions in general because Libet used such trivial behavior.

Stephen J. Morse, *Determinism and the Death of Folk Psychology: Two Challenges to Responsibility from Neuroscience,* 9 MINN. J.L Sci. & TECH I, 30 (2008).

[24] Denno, *supra* note 15, at 328. Denno notes that the conscious mind may still have a "veto" option in the "150 to 200 milliseconds" between when the actor becomes aware of the intention and the act. *Id.* This would reduce voluntary action to something akin to deciding whether to inhibit a sneeze or a cough that you feel is about to occur.

[25] *Id.*

There are two conceptual problems with this argument. Each problem is sufficient on its own to undermine the conclusion; together, they reveal that the presupposed conception of voluntariness is implausible. First, voluntary action does not require an "internal process" or "feeling" of "consciously deciding" to act preceding the bodily movements.[26] If voluntary acts did require an "internal" conscious decision of this sort, then this would lead to an infinite regress: a voluntary act would depend on an internal decision, and this decision would itself depend on a prior internal conscious decision to make the first decision, and so on.[27] The absurdity suggests that this conception of what makes acts voluntary is mistaken. An internal, conscious decision—or the "feeling" of making such a decision (whatever that might be)—preceding movement is neither a necessary nor sufficient condition for the act to be voluntary, both in general and in criminal law doctrine.[28] On the one hand, one may move voluntarily (for example, in answering the telephone when it rings, typing a sentence, or switching lanes in traffic) without "feeling" or consciously experiencing a decision, urge, desire, or intention milliseconds before moving. On the other hand, feeling, experiencing, or having an urge, desire, or intention prior to moving does not render the movements voluntary. For example, one may experience an urge or desire prior to sneezing or coughing without the subsequent sneezing or coughing being voluntary. If voluntary acts do not require an internal conscious decision preceding

---

[26] In tracing the link between conscious awareness and voluntariness to Locke, Gideon Yaffe articulates both a thin and thick concept of "conscious awareness." *See* Yaffe, *supra* note 1, at 196. The thin concept requires only that one's bodily movements are guided by mental events; the thick concept requires knowing not only that your body is moving but also "something about the mental causes of that bodily movement." *Id.* Notice that even this thick concept, which Yaffe argues is manifested in current doctrine, does not require an internal feeling or decision prior to movement. *See also* HACKER, *supra* note 3 (providing a brief historical philosophical overview of the major approaches, including Locke's, to conceptualizing voluntary action).

[27] Gilbert Ryle raised a similar "regress" objection to internal acts of "willing" in THE CONCEPT OF MIND (1949). As Michael Moore has noted, there are possible ways out of Ryle's objection, but the objection still carries weight when actions are explained in terms of prior mental actions. *See* MOORE, *supra* note 3, at 116 ("to define acts like moving one's hand in terms of duplicate mental acts of willing the movement seems an ontologically expensive way of gaining very little ground, for acting is still left unexplained.").

[28] These conclusions are conceptual points (i.e., the criteria for the application of the concept "voluntary" as used in general parlance and in legal doctrine do not include internal feelings or decisions). These conceptual points neither presuppose that there are necessary and sufficient conditions for all voluntary actions, nor that the concept possesses sharp

movement—or the "feeling" of such a decision—then the inference from unconscious brain activity, to internal decisions, to willed movements does not go through. The inference is blocked because it relies on a necessary causal role for internal decisions. This conception of voluntariness is not plausible—the doctrinal voluntariness requirement does not presuppose a necessary causal role for internal conscious decisions to act.

The first conceptual problem concerns the link between voluntariness and conscious decisions to act (or feelings of such decisions). The second conceptual problem concerns the relationship between brain activity and voluntary movements. The problematic inferential leap in this instance moves back a step: from brain activity to a conscious decision to act. Under this conception, voluntary "willed" movements result from "choices" made by the brain ("the unconscious"); the choices result in "decisions" to cause the internal conscious decisions to act (or feelings of such an act), which then cause the "willed" movements, rendering them involuntary.[29]

Ascriptions of "deciding" and "choosing" to the brain are examples of the mereological fallacy.[30] The brain is not an agent inside the person making decisions and choices—decisions and choices that then cause the person to make internal, conscious decisions and choices about what to do. Brain activity prior to bodily movements (which is what the Libet experiments show) does not render the movements involuntary. Because voluntariness does not depend on whether a decision is or is not preceded by a readiness potential, the conclusion does not follow. The Libet experiments do not undermine the distinction between voluntary and involuntary movements in general or as it arises in *actus reus* doctrine. Indeed, it should not be surprising that brain activity accompanies (and perhaps precedes) voluntary movements; this, however, does not undermine agent control.[31] There is a clear difference between the movements

boundaries and avoids borderline cases. For further elaboration of the general concept of voluntary action, see BENNETT & HACKER, *supra* note 4, at 228–31.

[29] *See* Denno, *supra* note 16, at 327 (noting that the Libet results "suggest that people could not regulate their own thoughts" because by the time people are aware "that they want to do something...*that decision has already been made by lower-level brain mechanisms*." (emphasis added)).

[30] We discuss this issue in more depth in Chapter One. For a similar point in the context of the criminal law's act requirement, see MOORE, *supra* note 3, at 132–33 (characterizing volitions as occurring at the personal, rather than the subpersonal, level). Moore notes that it may be useful to speak "metaphorically" of mental states occurring at the subpersonal level, so long as "the pretence is dropped when we can cash out the metaphor with a literal description...that make it possible for *us whole persons* to have states of belief, desire, and intention."

[31] Separating brain activity from mental attributes raises a number of conceptual issues about how to individuate each component. Under any plausible account of mental attributes,

of test subjects in the experiments on the one hand, and those suffering from, for example, alien-limb syndrome, utilization behavior, epilepsy, or sleepwalking, and those pushed or falling, on the other.

We concede Denno's point that there are borderline cases.[32] Perhaps a more just law would recognize such intermediate cases rather than forcing a sharp dichotomy, but this is a general problem for law arising from the need to draw lines.[33] More problematic in our view, however, would be the law trying to somehow operationalize the mistaken belief that the Libet experiments have falsified any "coherent distinction" between voluntary and involuntary conduct. The mistaken belief follows from incoherent *conceptual* presuppositions about the voluntariness requirement, not from the empirical results of Libet's studies.

II. *Mens Rea*

The second major doctrinal category for criminal liability is *mens rea* (or "guilty mind"). Criminal liability typically requires that the defendant's *actus reus* (or voluntary act) be accompanied by a culpable mental attribute. Although the *actus reus* and *mens rea* requirements are sometime loosely characterized as "the body" and "the mind" components of criminal liability,[34] for the reasons discussed above, there is also a

however, they are consistent with brain activity preceding, accompanying, and following the mental activity. *See* Morse, *supra* note 23, at 29 ("Prior electrical activity does not mean that intentionality played no causal role. Electrical activity in the brain is precisely that: electrical activity in the brain and not a mental state such as a decision or an intention. A readiness potential is not a decision."). Larry Alexander makes an interesting point about brain activity and a decision to act:

> One should also note that professional baseball players must make a swing or no swing decision in a time period that is shorter than that described in Libet's experiments. A ninety mile per hour pitch from less than sixty feet away when released must be assessed and reacted to in less than half a second. On the other hand, I suspect one would find an increase in the batter's brain activity shortly before the pitch is released.

See Alexander, *supra* note 2, at 206.

[32] Denno gives a number of illuminating examples where a third doctrinal category for "semi-voluntary" acts may be appropriate.

[33] *See* LEO KATZ, WHY THE LAW IS SO PERVERSE (2011); Adam Kolber, *Smooth and Bumpy Laws*, 102 CAL. L. REV. (forthcoming 2014) *available at* http://ssrn.com/abstract=1992034.

[34] *See* Teneille Brown & Emily Murphy, *Through a Scanner Darkly: Functional Neuroimaging as Evidence of a Criminal Defendant's Past Mental States*, 62 STAN. L. REV. 1119, 1128 (2012) ("The separate requirements for the voluntary act (*actus reus*) and the guilty mind (*mens rea*) endorse a separation between mental state and bodily act that remains the dominant view in American criminal law."); Karen Shapira-Ettinger, *The Conundrum of Mental States: Substantive*

mental aspect to the *actus reus*. The mental aspect relating to *actus reus* refers to whether the defendant had control over his bodily movements, and *mens rea* refers to the mental states that explain *why* the defendant engaged in the bodily movements, if voluntary—with what intent, purpose, plan, knowledge, wishes, or beliefs did he act?[35] The same actions may or may not be criminally culpable depending on the accompanying mental states. For example, a dinner host who engages in the voluntary bodily movements of serving poisoned wine to her guests may not be guilty if she did not intend to poison them and did not know the wine contained poison (and had no other culpable mental states).[36] The same voluntary bodily movements will suffice for criminal liability if the host intended to poison the guests or knew the wine contained poison. Although *actus reus* challenges are relatively rare in criminal law litigation, *mens rea* challenges are commonplace. Therefore, the potential effect of neuroscience on the day-to-day operations of criminal trials may be more dramatic if it can inform or change *mens rea* doctrine.

Criminal law codes typically delineate four general *mens rea* categories: intent (or purpose), knowledge, recklessness, and negligence.[37] In addition, specific criminal statutes specify the categories necessary

---

Rules and Evidence Combined, 28 CARDOZO L. REV. 2577, 2580 (2007) (arguing that criminal law doctrine's separation of acts and mental states presupposes a "vague metaphysical" distinction based on Cartesian dualism).

[35] We follow current doctrine and the scholarly literature in referring to the mental attributes for *mens rea* as "mental states." For discussion of the mental states required for *actus reus*, see Yaffe, *supra* note 1 (discussing "executory mental states"); MOORE, *supra* note 3, at 173 ("But notice that the intention required to act at all—the intention to move one's limbs—is not the same in its object as the intention described in the *mens rea* requirement.").

[36] These potentially culpable mental states would include reckless or negligent behavior by the host.

[37] *See* Francis X. Shen et al., *Sorting Guilty Minds*, 86 N.Y.U. L. REV. 1306, 1307–08 (2011); Paul H. Robinson & Jane A, Grall, *Element Analysis in Defining Criminal Liability: The Model Penal Code and Beyond*, 35 STAN. L. REV. 681 (1983). When determining factual issues about a defendant's state of mind, jurors and judges will sometimes also be making general normative assessments about the defendant's culpability and responsibility. Although this was the traditional role played by *mens rea* ("guilty mind") requirements, the rise of detailed criminal codes and statutes has relegated these determinations to a background role, if at all, in favor of more precise doctrinal categories. For a strong critique of this development, see WILLIAM J. STUNTZ, THE COLLAPSE OF AMERICAN CRIMINAL JUSTICE 260 (2011) ("Traditionally, [*mens rea*] law required proof that the defendant acted with a state of mind that was worthy of blame. Some vestiges of that earlier state of affairs still exist in American law...But for the most part, the concept of wrongful intent...has gone by the boards.") Stuntz argues that the rise of more detailed code-like provisions for *mens rea* helped to "make it possible for prosecutors to prosecute more defendants...and induce a larger share of those defendants to plead guilty." *Id.*

for particular crimes or types of crimes.[38] Although a number of intricate doctrinal complexities make these categories terms of art in some instances,[39] the doctrinal categories in many instances track the more everyday folk psychological concepts of intent, knowledge, belief, and so on.[40] The highly influential Model Penal Code (MPC) follows this four-part taxonomy.[41] Under the MPC, a defendant acts "purposely" (that is, with intent) when it is his "conscious object" to engage in particular conduct or to cause a particular result.[42] "Knowledge" depends on how a crime is defined. When an element of a crime includes whether a defendant's conduct is of a particular nature or whether certain circumstances exist, the defendant acts "knowingly" when "he is aware that his conduct is of that nature or that such circumstances exist."[43] When a crime is defined in terms of a result (e.g., "causing the death of another"), a person acts "knowingly" when "he is aware that it is practically certain that his conduct will cause such a result."[44] Conduct is "reckless" when a defendant "consciously disregards a substantial and unjustifiable risk," and it is "negligent" when the defendant "should be aware of a substantial and unjustifiable risk."[45] Both recklessness and negligence depend on the "circumstances known to" the defendant.

Although liability requires classifying mental states according to these categories,[46] there is substantial overlap of the mental concepts that constitute each category. Knowledge, for example, plays a role in each of the four categories. Even when crimes are not explicitly

---

[38] When a statute is silent about *mens rea*, courts will sometimes read a *mens rea* requirement into the statute. *See* Morissette v. United States, 342 U.S. 246 (1952) (construing criminal intent as a necessary element of a crime).

[39] For an illuminating recent discussion, see Kenneth W. Simons, *Statistical Knowledge Deconstructed*, 92 B.U. L. REV. 1 (2012). We put aside these doctrinal complexities for purposes of our discussion.

[40] *See* Morse, *supra* note 23. Sometimes doctrine and jury instructions depart from common conceptions by modifying terms (e.g., "knowledge"). *See, e.g.*, PATTERN CRIMINAL FEDERAL JURY INSTRUCTIONS FOR THE SEVENTH CIRCUIT § 4.10, at 50 (2013), *available at* http://www.ca7.uscourts.gov/Pattern_Jury_Instr/7th_criminal_jury_instr.pdf (including within the definition of knowingly: "If you find beyond a reasonable doubt that [the defendant] had a strong suspicion that [a fact is true], and that he deliberately avoided the truth.").

[41] MODEL PENAL CODE § 2.02; Robinson & Grall, *supra* note 37. *See also* Kenneth W. Simons, *Rethinking Mental States*, 72 B.U. L. REV. 463 (1992).

[42] MODEL PENAL CODE §§ 2.02(2)(a)–(b).

[43] *Id.* at §2.02(b)(i).

[44] *Id.* at §2.02(b)(ii).

[45] *Id.* at §2.02(c)–(d). Both recklessness and negligence also include a normative component determined by whether the defendant's conduct results in a "gross deviation" from an applicable standard of care. *Id.*

[46] *Id.* § 2.02; Robinson & Grall, *supra* note 37.

defined with "knowledge" as the requisite *mens rea*—but are instead defined in terms of purpose/intent, recklessness, or negligence—the *mens rea* determination may still depend on judgments about the defendant's knowledge. In some cases, a defendant may act with "purpose" or "intent" by knowing that certain things are so. For example, one can commit theft purposely or intentionally when one knows that the property she is taking belongs to another.[47] If a defendant believes he is taking someone else's umbrella but is mistaken (e.g., it is his umbrella) or mistakenly picks up someone else's umbrella believing it to be his own, he has not committed theft. Similarly, a judgment of whether a defendant acted "recklessly" or "negligently" may depend on the "circumstances known to" her at the time of her actions.[48]

Claims about the potentially transformative role of neuroscience for law have focused on the issue of *mens rea* and whether the science can reveal whether defendants acted with the culpable mental attributes necessary for liability.[49] The science may interact with *mens rea* in three different ways.

First, neuroscience-based lie detection may purport to provide evidence of whether a defendant is engaged in deception in answering questions about his previous mental states or whether he possesses "guilty knowledge" or memories of a crime.[50] This is just a specific application

---

[47] MODEL PENAL CODE § 223.6 ("A person commits theft if he receives, retains, or disposes of stolen movable property of another knowing that it has been stolen...").

[48] *Id.* at §2.02(c)–(d). The four categories intertwine in a number of different ways. For a recent argument that considerations of recklessness can also explain the knowledge and purpose elements, see LARRY ALEXANDER & KIMBERLY KESSLER FERZAN (WITH STEPHEN MORSE), CRIME AND CULPABILITY: A THEORY OF CRIMINAL LAW 31–41 (2009). *See also* LEO KATZ, BAD ACTS AND GUILTY MINDS 188 (1987) ("There are important differences between knowing and intentional actions. But in concrete cases, it will be awfully hard to tell—for conceptual, not evidentiary, reasons.") A further complication concerns whether the ways in which jurors apply the categories match or deviate from the doctrinal boundaries. *See* Shen et al., *supra* note 37; Pam Mueller, Lawrence M. Solan & John M. Darley, *When Does Knowledge Become Intent? Perceiving the Minds of Wrongdoers,* 9 J. EMP. LEGAL STUD. 859 (2012).

[49] For discussions noting the potential role of neuroscience to make significant contributions to the issue of *mens rea,* see Denno, *supra* note 16; Brown & Murphy, *supra* note 34; Eyal Aharoni et al., *Can Neurological Evidence Help Courts Assess Criminal Responsibility? Lessons from Law and Neuroscience,* 1124 ANN. N.Y. ACAD. SCI. 145 (2008); Erin Ann O'Hara, *How Neuroscience Might Advance the Law, in* LAW & THE BRAIN (S. Zeki & O. Goodenough eds., 2006); *see also* N.J. Schweitzer et al., *Neuroimages as Evidence in a Mens Rea Defense: No Impact,* 17 PSYCHOL., PUB. POLICY & LAW 357 (2011) (a study of mock jurors finding "no evidence that neuroimagery affected jurors' judgments...over and above verbal neuroscience-based testimony"...[but that] "neuroscientific evidence was more effective than clinical psychological evidence.").

[50] *See* Chapter Four. Professor O'Hara provides the additional example of using neuroscience to separate deception (and thus fraud) from self-deception (and thus no fraud). *See*

of the same issues we explored in the previous chapter applied to the doctrinal issue of *mens rea*. The conceptual limitations we explicated in that chapter thus apply to the use of neuroscientific evidence to prove a defendant's mental state with lie detection.

Second, neuroscience may inform whether a defendant acted with a particular mental state by providing evidence of whether he had the *capacity* to have the requisite mental state. Obviously if a defendant lacks a general capacity to form a type of mental state (and lacked it at the time of the crime), then this negates whether the defendant had a particular mental state of that type. The issue of capacity overlaps to a considerable extent with the defense of insanity. Although *mens rea* and insanity overlap, they are distinct doctrinal issues and neither necessarily entails the other.[51] A defendant who meets a jurisdiction's legal test for insanity may still have the requisite *mens rea* at the time of a crime (e.g., he may have been insane, but still intended to kill the victim); a defendant who fails to meet the tests for insanity or diminished capacity may still not have the requisite *mens rea*. The overlap of these issues raises a number of complicated doctrinal and procedural issues, however, and for clarity's sake we discuss this possible use of neuroscience regarding *mens rea* in more depth in the next section where we also parse the doctrinal issues relating to the defense of insanity.

Finally, if we put aside forms of lie detection and affirmative defenses based on mental disease or defect (or other excusing mental conditions), a third possibility that has been suggested for using neuroscience regarding *mens rea* is more troubling. The suggestion is that evidence about the brain may indicate whether the defendant had a particular mental state at the time of the crime. Here the details are murky, and the proposed relationships between the neuroscientific information and particular mental states are not clear. Nevertheless, defendants have attempted in a number of cases to introduce evidence about their brains on the issue of *mens rea*,[52] experts

O'Hara, *supra* note 49, at 28–29. She posits that neuroscience may inform intent, knowledge, and recklessness because they each require the defendant to be "consciously aware of his actions and/or their harmfulness at the time of acting." *Id.*

[51] For an excellent discussion of how evidence of mental disorder intersects with these and other doctrinal issues, see Stephen J. Morse, *Mental Disorder and Criminal Law*, 101 J. CRIM. & CRIMINOLOGY 885 (2011).

[52] *See, e.g.*, the cases on lie detection that we discuss in Chapter Four. *See also Brain Waves Module 4: Neuroscience and the Law* (Royal Statistical Society, 2011), *available at* http://royalsociety.org/policy/projects/brain-waves/responsibility-law/ (providing a chart of 843 opinions and 722 cases in which neurological evidence has been presented by criminal defendants in the United States); Schweitzer et al., *supra* note 49 (noting possible effectiveness of neuroscientific evidence on issues of *mens rea*).

have offered (and continue to offer) their services,[53] and scholars have likewise noted these possibilities.[54]

There are a number of empirical hurdles that would need to be overcome to connect brain-imaging evidence to a defendant's mental state at the time of a crime.[55] Most obviously, the defendant will not be scanned while committing a crime (except perhaps for crimes of perjury or other crimes based on false statements), so use along these lines will typically require an inference to a past mental state from current neural data. As Helen Mayberg, a professor of neurology and psychiatry, notes: "any data regarding brain structure or function is unlikely sufficiently contemporaneous to the time of the crime to be meaningful."[56] Even if this obstacle were overcome, however, the empirical gap between current information about the brain and particular mental states is too large to infer whether a defendant did or did not have a particular mental state. Surveying the literature, Mayberg asserts that "at our current state of knowledge, it is beyond the data generated from any currently published scanning protocol…to make inferences as to [a] defendant's intent at a specific moment in time."[57] We will grant for the sake of our discussion to follow, however, that these empirical hurdles can be overcome and that we will be able to learn a great deal about the workings of a defendant's brain while he is engaged in criminal acts. We do not underestimate the sophistication of the developing science or the creativity of those working on these problems.

Our contribution here is conceptual. We focus on issues that have caused a great deal of confusion in discussions of *mens rea*. Untangling these issues will help to delineate how neuroscience can contribute to criminal law doctrine on issues of intent and knowledge, the two mental states that feature most prominently in neurolaw discussions of *mens rea*. Even if we learned the details about the neural activity of defendants while acting, it is an error to suppose that we will find the intent

---

[53]   *See* http://www.cephoscorp.com/; http://www.noliemri.com/.

[54]   *See supra* note 49. Professor Denno also argues, as with *actus reus*, that neuroscience may challenge us to rethink how we define the purpose/intent and knowledge requirements. *See* Denno, *supra* note 15.

[55]   For a detailed and illuminating account of the numerous empirical issues, see Brown & Murphy, *supra* note 34.

[56]   *See* Helen Mayberg, *Does Neuroscience Give Us New Insights into Criminal Responsibility?*, *in* A JUDGE'S GUIDE TO NEUROSCIENCE: A CONCISE INTRODUCTION 37, 38 (Michael S. Gazzaniga & Jed S. Rakoff eds., 2010).

[57]   *Id.* at 41.

or knowledge lurking in the neural activity. The conceptual presuppositions that particular intentions and knowledge are identical with, or may be reduced to, states of the brain are examples of the problematic neuro-reductionism that we discussed in Chapter Two. The criteria for ascribing intent and knowledge are not states of the brain. Elucidating these criteria will help to clarify current understanding of the relationship between the brain and these doctrinal issues and to inform future empirical research. We discuss intent first, and then turn to knowledge.

A person acts with a particular intent, or purpose, when he is in control of his movements (the *actus reus*) and is acting for a particular reason or with a particular goal or plan.[58] A few conceptual distinctions help to illuminate the category. The first is a distinction between the *mens rea* of intent and voluntariness. A voluntarily action may or may not be done intentionally or with a particular purpose.[59] There is also a sense in which an intentional action may not be voluntary; for example, someone threatened or coerced to carry out certain actions may be acting with intent or purpose but not doing so voluntarily.[60] Second, we can distinguish between "proximal" and

[58] It is important to distinguish the general property of intentionality from the particular mental state of an intention or intent. The first is a philosophical term of art that refers to mental states in general (beliefs, hopes, desires, fears, and so on) that have propositional content. The belief that it is raining is a mental state (belief) with content (that it is raining). Mental states with content (that are about something or that take an object) are thus sometimes referred to as "intentional states" in the philosophical literature, and any creature with such states is thus taken to display intentionality. Some of these mental states are intentions or one's intent, the contents of which are the conditions in the world the person attempts to bring about with his actions. Someone's intention to buy an umbrella may thus be the reason (or goal toward which) he is acting by walking to the store. In addition to its noun form, this sense of intention or intent can be expressed as a verb ("He intends to hit the target"), an adverb ("He missed intentionally"), or an adjective ("He committed an intentional foul"). For an overview of these different senses of intentionality, and their role in folk psychological explanations, see Michael S. Moore, *Responsible Choices, Desert-Based Legal Institutions, and the Challenges of Contemporary Neuroscience*, 29 SOC. PHIL. & POLICY 233 (2012). In both senses, intentionality is conceptually distinct from states of the brain, although having a properly working brain is necessary to engage in the activities that form the defeasible criteria for general and particular intentionality.

[59] For example, a dinner host who unknowingly places poison in the food may have engaged in voluntary bodily movement in doing so without intending to place poison in the food.

[60] For example, a dinner host may intentionally place poison in the food but not be doing so voluntarily (because the host is being coerced or is acting under duress). The dinner host's action is thus intentional and non-voluntary. As with "intentionality," "voluntariness" also exhibits different senses. For example, one cannot at the same time act intentionally and involuntarily. If a dinner guest's involuntary movements cause him to drop a dish, then he has not dropped the dish intentionally (although one can intend to put oneself in a position

"distal" intentions.[61] A proximal intention refers to someone's intent to act *now* (for example, to flex a wrist in a Libet experiment) or to continue a course of action. A distal intention refers someone's plan to act in the near or distant future. The *mens rea* issue of intent typically depends on proximal intentions of defendants during the *actus reus*, but distal intentions may also be the object of legal inquiry (for example, to show planning in a conspiracy case or premeditation in a murder case), and distal intentions may also provide evidence of proximal intentions. Third, whether proximal or distal, intentions may or may not be formed by previous, explicit deliberation or reasoning—they may simply be manifested in conduct, as when a driver intentionally switches lanes in traffic (proximal) or when I say, "Let's have Indian food for dinner tonight" (distal). Fourth, in ascribing intentions to another person, the person's linguistic and other behavior provide (defeasible) criterial evidence of that person's intentions.[62] We explain behavior, in part, by describing the person's intentions.[63]

Intentions are not brain processes or inner feelings, nor are they the neural activity that precedes an internal process or feeling.[64] It is

to have involuntary movements). For an overview of the complexities with these concepts, see HACKER, *supra* note 3.

[61] For a discussion of distal and proximal intentions, see MELE, *supra* note 22.

[62] One's intentions may be identified by finding the appropriate descriptions that explain why one engaged in the conduct. See G.E.M. ANSCOMBE, INTENTION II (1957). To illustrate this point, consider Anscombe's famous example: the same act may be described as (1) contracting one's muscles, (2) moving one's arm up and down, (3) pumping water, (4) replenishing the house's water supply, and (5) poisoning its inhabitants. See *id.* at 37–45. The descriptions that supply motivational significance for the actor help to locate her intentions. These explanations will often include conditions of which the actor is aware, but not always. For examples of how one can do something intentionally without being aware that one is doing it, see MELE, *supra* note 22, at 39. For additional clarifying discussions of intention, see MICHAEL E. BRATMAN, FACES OF INTENTION (1999); R.A. DUFF, INTENTION, AGENCY, AND CRIMINAL LIABILITY: PHILOSOPHY OF ACTION AND THE CRIMINAL LAW (1990); Kimberly Kessler Ferzan, *Beyond Intention*, 29 CARDOZO L. REV. 1147 (2008).

[63] There is a sense in which intent and knowledge are the flip side of each other. They each involve a connection between the mind and the world but these connections run in opposite directions. To illustrate, consider Anscombe's example of the shopper with a grocery list being followed by a detective who writes down everything the shopper puts in the cart. If there is a discrepancy between the shopper's list and what is in the cart, the error is with what is in the cart (a failure of intent); if there a discrepancy between the detective's list and what is in the cart, the error is with the detective's list (a failure of knowledge). See ANSCOMBE, *supra* note 62.

[64] For characterizations of intentions as internal experiences or feelings, see DANIEL M. WEGNER, THE ILLUSION OF CONSCIOUS WILL (2003) and Denno, *supra* note 15, at 326–27. *Cf.* BENNETT & HACKER, *supra* note 4, at 103 ("How might a parent teach a child [the uses of 'intention']? Again, *not* by getting the child to identify an inner phenomenon of intending, and then naming it. There *is* no such inner phenomenon—there is no phenomenology of

an example of the mereological fallacy to ascribe "intent" to a particular array of neural activity (brains states do not intend to do things—people do), and it is similarly a mistake to try to identify a person's intention with a state of his brain. To illustrate that intentions are not brain states, consider someone's statement "I intend to X, and X is impossible."[65] For example, suppose someone said to us, "I intend to rob the bank tomorrow, and robbing the bank is impossible." It is not clear what this person means. It is nonsensical, if taken literally, to both intend to perform an action and to believe that the action is impossible. In other words, intending to X implies (belief in) the possibility of X-ing. Because of the tension in this statement, we are apt to try to make sense of this statement by not interpreting it literally. Perhaps he is going to *try* to rob the bank, intending on being arrested or otherwise foiled, or perhaps he does not really believe robbing the bank is impossible, but will just be *really difficult*. Suppose, however, that having an intention *just was* having a particular brain state or pattern of neural activity. In other words, his intention to rob the bank just was the fact that his brain was in a particular brain state (BS). Now, the tension would evaporate; it is perfectly coherent to interpret the defendant to be speaking literally if he were to say, "my brain is in BS, and robbing the bank is impossible." Because the combination of brain state and the impossibility of the task makes sense, but the intention and the impossibility do not, the BS and the intention are not identical.

Turning to knowledge, it is an example of the mereological fallacy to ascribe knowledge to brain activity, and it is similarly a mistake to identify whether a person has knowledge with a state of her brain. The criteria for the ascription of knowledge are various kinds of linguistic and other behavior, not the obtaining of brain states.[66] Knowledge is manifested, for example, by asserting true propositions and evidence, identifying and

---

intending, no distinctive experience called 'intending'—and 'I intend' is neither the name of nor a description of any 'inner experience.'").

[65] *Id.*; MAX BENNETT & P.M.S. HACKER, *The Conceptual Presuppositions of Cognitive Neuroscience: A Reply to Critics, in* NEUROSCIENCE AND PHILOSOPHY: BRAIN, MIND, AND LANGUAGE 127 (2007).

[66] This is true both for "knowledge that" (propositional knowledge) and "knowledge how" (to do things). On the distinction see GILBERT RYLE, THE CONCEPT OF MIND (1949). The relationship between knowledge-that and knowledge-how continues to be a matter of philosophical inquiry and controversy. For recent discussions see JASON STANLEY, KNOW HOW (2011); KNOWING HOW: ESSAY ON KNOWLEDGE, MIND, AND ACTION (John Bengson & Mark A. Moffett eds., 2012); Stephen Hetherington, *How to Know (That Knowledge-That Is Knowledge-How), in* EPISTEMOLOGY FUTURES 71 (Stephen Hetherington ed., 2006). We discuss the topic of knowledge in more detail in Chapter One.

correcting errors, and acting on what is known.[67] It is a mistake to suppose that knowledge is "housed" or "located" in the brain.[68] As with lies or deception, neuroscience may provide inductive evidence of whether someone knows something, but it cannot locate that knowledge in the brain or identify brain states that are *sufficient* for the possession of such knowledge.[69]

Let's assume we have overcome the practical limitation that we typically cannot scan the brains of defendants while they are committing crimes[70] and ask: what if we could? Imagine we had an fMRI scan of a defendant's brain while committing an allegedly criminal act. Suppose, for example, we need to determine whether he (1) knew the suitcase he walked off with was not his but belonged to another, (2) knew about the illegal drugs in his suitcase, (3) knows "that it is practically certain that his conduct will cause" a particular result, or (4) knows any other specific thing. Exactly where in his brain would we find this knowledge? Because knowledge is an ability, and not a state of the brain, the answer is: nowhere.

As with intentions, we can illustrate this with a conceptual distinction between knowledge and brain states. Although it makes no sense to say "I know X, and X is false,"[71] it makes perfect sense to say "my

---

[67] For these reasons, "to know" is characterized as a "success" or "achievement" verb in the sense that it implies that some sort of goal or aim has been accomplished. *See* ALVIN I. GOLDMAN, KNOWLEDGE IN A SOCIAL WORLD 60 (1999); Dennis M. Patterson, *Fashionable Nonsense*, 81 TEX. L. REV. 841 885–92 (2003) (review essay).

[68] *See, e.g.*, Denno, *supra* note 15, at 333 ("Brain fingerprinting is based on the principle that the human brain houses information"); Lawrence A. Farwell & Sharon S. Smith, *Using Brain MERMER Testing to Detect Knowledge despite Efforts to Conceal*, 46 J. FORENSIC SCI. 135 (2001) ("recent advances in neuroscience allow scientists to detect information stored in the brain"). The concept of knowledge exists in a web of epistemic concepts along with belief, conviction, suspicion, supposition, conjecture, doubt, certainty, evidence, truth, probability, reasons, justification, and confirmation. Elucidation of the conceptual relationships among these concepts cannot be accomplished by telling us empirical information about the brain. For a discussion, see HACKER, *supra* note 3.

[69] Claims to the contrary ignore the social, normative aspect of knowledge. Attributing knowledge to another (or oneself) involves attributing further commitments and entitlements to them (or oneself). *See* ROBERT BRANDOM, MAKING IT EXPLICIT: REASONING, REPRESENTING & DISCURSIVE COMMITMENT 213–21, 253–62 (1994).

[70] The crime of perjury or other crimes involving false statements might allow for simultaneous scanning.

[71] It makes no sense if taken literally because knowledge implies truth. Therefore, claims to know are also claims that what is known is true. Such a statement is even more problematic than Moore's paradox ("X, but I don't believe X"). *See* Roy Sorensen, *Epistemic Paradoxes*, *in* STANFORD ENCYCLOPEDIA OF PHILOSOPHY (2011), *available at* http://plato.stanford.edu/entries/epistemic-paradoxes/#MooPro.

brain is in state (BS), and X is false." For example, suppose our previous bank robber says, "I know there is money in the safe at the bank, and it is false that there is money in the safe at the bank." Once again, we would not know what he meant. If we wanted to interpret him charitably, we would assume he was not speaking literally. By contrast, there would be no apparent tension in interpreting the following statement literally: "my brain is in state (BS), and it is false that there is money in the safe at the bank." If, however, his knowledge is identical with his brain state, then a similar tension should arise. His knowledge and his brain state are conceptually distinct.

III. Insanity

In addition to the doctrinal issues of *actus reus* and *mens rea*, a third major category of criminal law doctrine concerns affirmative defenses. Of these, the defense of insanity is the one most frequently invoked in neurolaw discussions.[72] Proof of insanity and related issues constitutes, in our opinion, one of the more plausible avenues by which neuroscience may contribute to the law. There are currently a number of empirical hurdles that would need to be overcome to do so, but, in principle, use in this area avoids some of the conceptual problems that plague issues such as lie detection and proof of particular intent or knowledge. We explain the reasons for this distinction below.

As a doctrinal matter, "insanity" is a legal and not a medical or psychological concept, although medical and psychological expertise informs judgments of insanity. The defense of "not guilty by reason of insanity" is a judgment not to hold criminally culpable a defendant, who may otherwise have satisfied the elements of a crime, because some mental disease or defect affected the defendant's cognitive or volitional capabilities at the time of the crime.[73] Jurisdictions vary

[72] Some jurisdictions allow for an affirmative defense of "diminished responsibility" or "diminished capacity," which typically operates as a mitigating factor or partial excuse for mental disorders or conditions that exist but fall short of the insanity standard. However, the defense is rare as a stand-alone defense and often overlaps with *mens rea*. For an argument that this doctrinal option should be recognized more broadly, see Stephen J. Morse, *Diminished Rationality, Diminished Responsibility*, 1 OHIO ST. CRIM. L. 289 (2003).

[73] For overviews of the various theoretical and empirical issues underlying insanity and related defenses, see Morse, *supra* note 51; Michael Corrado, *The Case for a Purely Volitional Insanity Defense*, 42 TEX. TECH. L. REV. 481 (2009); Walter Sinnott-Armstrong & Ken Levy,

in the tests they employ for judging insanity defenses. The two most common types rely on some variant of the common law *M'Naghten* test or the Model Penal Code's (MPC) test.[74] The *M'Naghten* test, which focuses on a defendant's cognitive capacities, depends on whether the defendant "was laboring under such a defect of reason, from disease of the mind, as not to know the nature and quality of the act he was doing; or if he did know it, that he did not know that what he was doing was wrong."[75] Jurisdictions differ as to what they require in order to satisfy either prong of this test—for example, does "wrong" mean "legally wrong" or "morally wrong," and if the latter, what does "moral" mean?[76]—and whether to include both prongs.[77] The MPC test, which focuses on both cognitive and volitional capacities, depends on whether "as a result of mental disease and defect [the defendant] lacks substantial capacity either to appreciate the criminality (wrongfulness) of his conduct or to conform his conduct to the requirements of the law."[78] As with the *M'Naghten* variants, jurisdictions differ in implementing versions of the MPC test. Variations include whether the defendant must appreciate that the act is criminal

---

Insanity Defenses, in THE OXFORD HANDBOOK OF PHILOSOPHY OF CRIMINAL LAW 299 (John Deigh & David Dolinko eds., 2011). For a critical discussion of the role of mental-health expert testimony on insanity and other issues in criminal law, see CHRISTOPHER SLOBOGIN, PROVING THE UNPROVABLE: THE ROLE OF LAW, SCIENCE, AND SPECULATION IN ADJUDICATING CULPABILITY AND DANGEROUSNESS (2007).

[74] Regina v. M'Naghten, 9 Eng. Rep. 718 (1843); MODEL PENAL CODE § 4.01(1). Less prominent doctrinal tests for insanity have included the so-called "product test" (or "Durham rule") in which a defendant "is not criminally responsible if his unlawful conduct was the product of mental disease or defect," Durham v. United States, 214 F.3d 862 (1954), and the "Parsons rule" in which a defendant is not responsible if because of mental disease he has "lost the power to choose between the right and wrong," Parsons v. State, 81 Ala. 577 (1887). Our discussion will focus primarily on the M'Naghten and MPC tests.

[75] Regina v. M'Naghten, 9 Eng. Rep. 718 (1843).

[76] For a clear overview of the possibilities and their implications, see Sinnott-Armstrong & Levy, *supra* note 73.

[77] The U.S. Supreme Court upheld as constitutional a state statute limiting the test to "moral incapacity" and eliminating the "cognitive incapacity" prong. Clark v. Arizona, 548 U.S. 735 (2006). The Court explained that this was not problematic because the moral prong entailed any cases that would meet the cognitive prong (but not vice versa). *Id.* at 753–54. In other words, any defendant who did not know the nature and quality of his act would also a fortiori not know that what he was doing was wrong. On the flip side, however, there may be defendants who do not satisfy the cognitive prong but nevertheless can meet the insanity test by satisfying the moral prong.

[78] Stephen Morse has argued that separate volitional (or "loss of control") tests are unnecessary because the cases that meet the tests can be better explained in cognitive terms. *See* Morse, *supra* note 51.

or morally wrong (and exactly what is required to "appreciate" it is wrong) and whether to include a "conformity" prong.[79] Under both types of tests, jurisdictions also differ substantially in how they structure the burden of proof.[80]

As noted in the previous section, this doctrinal issue overlaps with *mens rea*. It should now be clear why. A defendant with mental incapacities may fail to have the requisite intent or knowledge to constitute a crime in the first place. It is important to recognize, however, that insanity is a distinct doctrinal issue. A defendant who satisfies the doctrinal test for insanity may nevertheless have the intent necessary to satisfy *mens rea*. For example, a defendant may have the necessary intent to kill a victim to constitute murder, but do so for "insane" reasons; as a result of a mental illness, the defendant may not know that what he is doing is wrong or he may not be able to conform to the law's requirements. In such a case, the defendant's criminal act is excused, but it is still a criminal act (in the sense that *actus reus* and *mens rea* are proven).[81] Likewise, a defendant may fail to meet the requirements of an insanity defense but also fail to have the requisite *mens rea* for reasons not relating to insanity. Finally, it is important to note that the same evidence that is relevant to the insanity issue may be probative on the issue of *mens rea*, even when it does not prove insanity. In other words, evidence may negate *mens rea*, even when a defendant fails to prove insanity. This may appear puzzling at first glance, but the puzzle disappears when the burdens of proof are made explicit. A defendant may have the burden of proving insanity (by a "preponderance of the evidence" or by "clear and convincing evidence") whereas the prosecution will have the burden of proving *mens rea* beyond a reasonable doubt. Thus, in particular cases, evidence

---

[79] For example, the test for insanity in U.S. federal courts limits the defense to "severe" mental disease and does not contain a volitional ("loss of control") prong. 18 U.S.C. § 20.

[80] Burdens of proof contain two components: a burden of producing evidence and a burden of persuasion (to an applicable standard). Some states place the burdens of production and persuasion on defendants (to either the "preponderance of the evidence" or "clear and convincing evidence" standards). Other states place the burden of production on defendants, but the burden of persuasion remains on the prosecution. The U.S. Supreme Court has explained that the practice of placing the burden of proof on defendants is constitutional because the constitutional "beyond a reasonable doubt" standard applies only to elements of a crime. For an overview of the different approaches taken by the states, see Clark v. Arizona, 548 U.S. 735 (2006).

[81] In such cases, defendants are typically hospitalized as a matter of course following a successful insanity defense. *See id.* at 752 n.19.

of insanity may fail to be sufficient to prove insanity to the requisite standard, *but it may be sufficient to raise a reasonable doubt on the issue of mens rea.*[82]

Our purpose in this discussion is not to catalog every variant of the insanity defense and the various ways in which neuroscience may be relevant. Rather, consistent with our discussion of conceptual issues, we will focus on the general conceptual relationships among mind, brain, and law that underlie these issues. As with the other matters we discuss in this chapter, there are enormous empirical issues affecting the probative value of neuroscientific evidence regarding issues of insanity, but the proposed uses in this context do not suffer from the same conceptual defects that affect issues of *actus reus* and *mens rea*.

Insanity tests include two general components: source and capacity. The source component requires that a mental illness, disease, or defect caused the defendant's particular incapacities.[83] The capacity component requires a limitation of a defendant's capacities to know or appreciate certain facts during his actions (what he is doing or that it is illegal, immoral, or otherwise wrong) or to act in a way that conforms to the law's requirements. Neuroscience may contribute to both the source and capacity components.

First, with regard to *source*, neuroscientific evidence may serve a *diagnostic* role for particular mental illnesses and defects. Although there are currently significant empirical limitations on it playing this role, this may change. There is nothing conceptually problematic about it serving this role, so long as the diagnoses themselves avoid the conceptual problems. As with the legal categories, the criteria for ascribing mental illnesses also include a variety of behavioral symptoms and psychological constructs, not states of the brain.[84] Just as it is a conceptual mistake to ascribe particular knowledge or

---

[82] In *Clark v. Arizona*, the Court upheld the state's limitation on the use of mental-health expert testimony on the issue of *mens rea*. As a practical matter, this is much more significant and controversial than the aspect of the Court's decision on the cognitive and moral prongs of the doctrine, because there will be defendants who could use expert testimony to negate *mens rea*, but may not be able to prove insanity. *See supra* note 77.

[83] The source component rules out other causes that may produce similar cognitive impairments or lack of control, such as voluntary intoxication. The Model Penal Code also specifies that the "terms 'mental disease or defect' do not include an abnormality manifested only by repeated criminal or otherwise anti-social behavior." MODEL PENAL CODE § 4.01(2).

[84] *See* Gregory Miller, *Mistreating Psychology in the Decades of the Brain*, 5 PERSP. PSYCHOL. SCI. 725 (2010). Miller provides several examples. Here is one involving schizophrenia: "memory

intentions to a location in the brain, it is also a conceptual mistake to ascribe the criteria for the psychological phenomena to locations in the brain. In discussing the relationship among mental illnesses, psychological concepts, and the brain, psychologist Gregory Miller explains, "psychological phenomena do not have a spatial location in the brain and…explanations of brain phenomena are not explanations of psychological phenomena." Moreover:

Decisions, feelings, perceptions, delusions, memories do not have spatial location. We image brain events: electromagnetic, hemodynamic, and optical. We do not image, and cannot localize in space, psychological constructs. We can make inferences about the latter from the former, using bridge principles that connect observable data and hypothetical constructs. But the latter are not the former.… EEG, MEG, fMRI, etc. watch the brain at work. What inferences we want to make about the mind based on such data are our constructions, not our observations.[85]

Thus, as an empirical matter, neuroscientific evidence may provide inductive evidence in diagnosing mental illness and other diseases and defects, whether in medicine, psychology, or law. The quality and strength of such evidence that will be available in the future is an open question. But its strength and quality will depend on whether it proceeds from sound conceptual assumptions. In sum, identifiable states of the brain may be correlated with the source issues underlying insanity defenses and support reliable inferences on these issues.

Second, neuroscience may also contribute to the *capacity* component by providing probative evidence that a defendant lacked (or possessed) the relevant capacities. Of course the possession and exercise of these capacities depend on the brain, and identifiable neurological structures, patterns, or states may be necessary or highly correlated with the possession and exercise of these capacities. Recall that evidence of these capacities may be relevant either to negate *mens rea* or to meet the requirements of an insanity test. Here are three examples that have been proposed about how neuroscience may contribute to the

deficits are well established in schizophrenia. But a memory encoding deficit cannot be located in a specific brain region…Memory deficits are not the sort of thing that are located anywhere in space. Memory deficits are functional impairments that are conceived in cognitive, computational, and overt behavioral terms, not in biological terms." *Id.* Miller makes similar points regarding fear, depression, aggression, and shyness. *Id.* at 722.

[85] *Id.* at 727.

legal issues. If a crime requires a particular type of distal intention (e.g., planning in a case involving conspiracy or fraud), then evidence that a defendant has damage to brain areas necessary for such planning may be evidence that the defendant lacked the particular intention. A distinguished group of scholars speculate, for example, that damage to the pre-supplemental motor area in the brain may provide this evidence.[86] Likewise, if a jurisdiction's insanity test requires a capacity for moral knowledge, then damage to brain areas necessary for moral judgment (perhaps the ventromedial prefrontal cortex) may provide evidence about a particular defendant's lack of capacity.[87] Finally, as Patricia Churchland suggests, similar structures or patterns may also possibly be developed for "control" tests more generally.[88] These uses face a number of empirical and practical limitations, but they are not conceptually problematic in the ways we discuss above.

The current empirical and practical limitations on use in individual cases are significant. These limitations include, first, the wide variability among individual brain activity and behavior. Even when particular brain activity does appear to be correlated with, "associated with," or "implicated in" particular behavior, some people have the brain activity without the behavior, and some people have the behavior without the brain activity.[89] In addition, even if particular brain structures appear to play a causal role in the possession and exercise of particular mental capacities (e.g., complex intentions or moral knowledge) by most people, they may not be *necessary*. Other brain areas may play a causal role and, thus, a person may still possess the capacity even when there is injury or damage to the areas that play a role in most people.[90]

Moreover, inferences about capacities in individual cases face the limitation that brain scans will likely be made some period of time after a crime has been committed, but the legal tests depend on the defendant's capacities at the time of the crime, so the value of the evidence will depend on how well it informs the issue of the capacity at a previous

[86] *See* Aharoni et al., *supra* note 49.

[87] *Id.*

[88] *See* Patricia Smith Churchland, *Moral Decision-Making and the Brain*, in NEUROETHICS: DEFINING THE ISSUES IN THEORY, PRACTICE, AND POLICY 3 (Judy Illes ed., 2006).

[89] *See* Miller, *supra* note 84, at 721 ("There is likely an indefinite set of potential neural implementations of a given psychological phenomenon. Conversely, a given neural circuit may implement different psychological functions at different times or in different individuals.").

[90] *See* Aharoni et al., *supra* note 49, at 154.

point in time. Finally, use in individual cases may face limitations in the testing protocols employed and in determining whether the evidence is reliable enough to meet admissibility standards, whether it will be presented in a manner that legal fact finders can understand, and whether it is worth the time and resources to present it.[91]

The conceptual problems discussed above, however, are avoided when behavioral and other psychological criteria are not ascribed to brain structures or identified with brain processes. Claims about whether brain states are necessary to possess the capacities at issue in legal insanity tests thus avoid the problematic types of neuro-reductionism that we discuss in Chapter Two. Brains are *necessary* to engage in the manifold behavior, experiences, and psychological processes that we identify with mental life. Therefore, *particular* and *identifiable* brain areas, structures, processes, patterns, or states may be *necessary* to engage in the *particular* types of mental activities at issue in criminal law doctrine. As a conceptual matter, we take issue only with the more radical claims that particular brain states are *sufficient for* or *identical with* these activities.[92] Claims that remain within the bounds of the concepts on which legal doctrine depends remain fruitful avenues for future potential use.

We illustrate this point with the example of knowledge and the role that it plays in this doctrine. Many insanity defenses depend upon the issue of knowledge. As noted above, the tests for insanity turn on issues such as whether a defendant failed to "know the nature and quality of the act he was doing,"[93] failed to "know he was doing what was wrong,"[94] failed to "appreciate the wrongfulness of his conduct,"[95] or lacked the capacity to "conform his conduct to the requirements of

---

[91] Regarding admissibility at trial, the two primary hurdles are the standards for admitting expert testimony (*Daubert* and *Frye*, discussed in Chapter Four) and FED. R. EVID. 403, which states that evidence may be excluded if the probative value of the evidence is substantially outweighed by a number of considerations, including misleading or confusing the jury. Brown & Murphy, *supra* note 34, provide an excellent checklist of issues that ought to affect the admissibility of neuroimaging at trial. A recent study of mock jurors involving the insanity defense found no evidence that neuroimaging had an influence beyond neuroscientific evidence generally, but did find that the neuroscientific evidence was more persuasive than psychological and anecdotal evidence. *See* N.J. Schweitzer et al., *Neuroimage Evidence and the Insanity Defense*, 29 BEHAV. SCI & LAW 592 (2011).

[92] *See* Miller, *supra* note 84, making a similar point about psychology.

[93] *See* Clark v. Arizona, 548 U.S. 735, 747 (2006); Regina v. M'Naghten, 9 Eng. Rep. 718 (1843).

[94] *Clark*, 548 U.S. at 747 (*quoting M'Naghten*).

[95] MODEL PENAL CODE § 4.01.

the law."[96] These requirements may depend on either a type of propositional knowledge (knowledge-*that* certain things are so) or a type of practical knowledge (knowledge-*how* to perform certain conduct).[97] Both types of knowledge are kinds of abilities, typically manifested in behavior, and the use of neuroscience to show a lack of capacity to perform either is plausible.[98] A properly working brain is a necessary condition for possessing knowledge. Therefore, particular and identifiable brain structures may be necessary in order to possess certain kinds of knowledge; thus, damages to these structures may result in a lack of capacity to possess some types of knowledge. To the extent that legal categories depend on whether someone possesses the ability to acquire or retain a particular type of knowledge, neuroscience may provide probative (defeasible, non-criterial) evidence on that question.

[96] *Id.*
[97] *See supra* note 66.
[98] We discuss the topic of knowledge in more detail in Chapter One.

6

Criminal Procedure

This chapter focuses on the compelled production and use of neuroscientific evidence against criminal defendants and the constitutional provisions that protect defendants and limit government evidence gathering. As with the doctrinal issues explored in the previous chapter, the procedural issues also require a proper understanding of the conceptual issues underlying the evidence and doctrinal categories. Confusion and mistaken inferences arise when these issues are ignored.

Two constitutional provisions regulate the gathering and use of evidence by the government against criminal defendants. First, the Fourth Amendment prohibition on unreasonable searches and seizures places limits and conditions on government evidence gathering. Second, the Fifth Amendment privilege against self-incrimination prevents the government's use of compelled, incriminating, testimonial evidence from defendants in criminal cases. In addition to these two provisions, general due process requirements place additional limitations on government evidence-gathering practices. The relationship between these provisions and neuroscientific evidence has created a series of doctrinal and theoretical puzzles and confusions. We first discuss the general relationships between these provisions and then focus in detail on each provision.

Within the United States, the Fourth Amendment and the Fifth Amendment's privilege against self-incrimination limit the government's ability to gather and use evidence against criminal defendants. The Fourth Amendment prohibits "unreasonable searches and seizures,"[1]

---

[1] The Fourth Amendment provides that:

> The right of the people to be secure in their persons, houses, papers, and effects, against unreasonable searches and seizures, shall not be violated, and no Warrants shall issue, but on

and the Fifth Amendment maintains that a criminal defendant may not be "compelled to be a witness against himself."[2] The doctrinal relationship between these two Amendments has historically been a source of some confusion, but the relationship is now relatively stable.[3] The Fourth Amendment provides a general—but not an absolute—limitation on government evidence gathering, requiring that searches and seizures be reasonable, and providing detailed doctrinal requirements for what constitutes "search," "seizure," and "reasonable." The limitation is not an absolute one, however, because the government is not prevented from gathering the evidence under any circumstances; rather, the Amendment specifies the procedural steps or standards that must be met for the government to gather and use the evidence legitimately.[4] In addition to this general limitation, the Fifth Amendment privilege provides defendants with a more specific—but absolute—option to prevent the compelled use of a defendant's "testimonial" evidence against him. If the evidence falls within the doctrinal requirements for the privilege, and the defendant invokes the privilege, then the government may not use the evidence against the defendant in a criminal proceeding.[5] The same

probable cause, supported by Oath or affirmation, and particularly describing the place to be searched, and the persons or things to be seized.

U.S. CONST. amend. IV. Ratified in 1791, the Fourth Amendment was held to be applicable to the states (through the Due Process Clause of the Fourteenth Amendment) in Wolf v. Colorado, 338 U.S. 25 (1949), and the "exclusionary rule" (excluding evidence of searches that violate the Fourth Amendment) was held to be applicable to the states in Mapp v. Ohio, 367 U.S. 643 (1961).

[2] The Fifth Amendment provides, in part, that "No person...shall be compelled in any criminal case to be a witness against himself." U.S. CONST. amend. V. The Fifth Amendment was held to be applicable to the states (through the Fourteenth Amendment) in Malloy v. Hogan, 378 U.S. 1 (1964).

[3] The relationship between the Amendments is discussed in Michael S. Pardo, *Disentangling the Fourth Amendment and the Self-Incrimination Clause*, 90 IOWA L. REV. 1857 (2005); H. Richard Uviller, *Foreword: Fisher Goes on Quintessential Fishing Expedition and Hubbell Is Off the Hook*, 91 J. CRIM. & CRIMINOLOGY 311 (2001); Richard A. Nagareda, *Compulsion "to Be a Witness" and the Resurrection of* Boyd, 74 N.Y.U. L. REV. 1575 (1999); Akhil Reed Amar & Renee B. Lettow, *Fifth Amendment First Principles: The Self-Incrimination Clause*, 93 MICH. L. REV. 857 (1995).

[4] The doctrinal starting point is that evidence gathering that constitutes a "search" must be accompanied by a valid warrant supported by probable cause. The warrant requirement is subject to expansive exceptions and may be excused when warrants are not practical (most notably, when "exigent circumstances" are present), and the "probable cause" standard is also subject to exceptions (most notably, for brief stop-and-frisks, which requires "reasonable suspicion" and suspicionless searches in administrative and related contexts). We outline these doctrinal categories in our analysis below.

[5] Defendants may be compelled to furnish the testimonial evidence, however, if they are granted "use and derivative use" immunity. *See* Kastigar v. United States, 406 U.S. 441 (1972); 18 U.S.C. § 6003(a). This type of immunity does not bar prosecution outright but, as its name suggests, it prevents the government from using the evidence, or any evidence derived from that evidence, against a defendant granted immunity.

evidence may fall within the scope of both Amendments, and thus the constitutional protections may overlap to limit government use of the evidence.[6] In addition to the two Amendments, due process requirements place additional limitations on government evidence gathering.[7]

We analyze the compelled gathering and use of neuroscientific evidence in relation to each of these constitutional provisions. As we will see, how the evidence is conceptualized matters a great deal to the amount of constitutional protection it is likely to receive. Uncertainty about how to characterize evidence produced by new technology is an enduring problem in law,[8] and neuroscientific evidence is no exception. As Henry Greely notes, exactly how neuroscientific technology will "play out in light of our current criminal justice system, including the constitutional protections of the Bill of Rights, is not obvious."[9] These legal issues provide additional examples of the important practical consequences that follow from the philosophical issues we raise.

I. Fourth Amendment

When, if at all, may the government, consistent with the Fourth Amendment, compel a criminal suspect to undergo an MRI, fMRI, EEG, or another test to gather evidence about the suspect's brain? As a doctrinal matter, the answer appears to be "sometimes," so long as a number of procedural requirements are met.

The evidence falls within relatively clear and well-developed doctrinal rules that regulate the compelled production of evidence from suspects' bodies.[10] As a general matter, the Fourth Amendment

---

[6] See Pardo, *supra* note 3 (discussing three areas in which the Amendments overlap: "stop and identify" statutes that require detained individuals to reveal their names, subpoenas, and the incriminating use of a defendants' pre-arrest silence).

[7] The Supreme Court has invoked notions of both "procedural" and "substantive" due process in this context. See Chavez v. Martinez, 538 U.S. 760 (2003) (substantive); District Attorney's Office v. Osborne, 557 U.S. 52 (2006) (procedural).

[8] See Jennifer L. Mnookin, *The Image of Truth: Photographic Evidence and the Power of Analogy*, 10 YALE J.L. & HUMAN. 1 (1998) (discussing the history of and anxiety over photographic evidence in court).

[9] Henry T. Greely, *Prediction, Litigation, Privacy, and Property*, in NEUROSCIENCE AND THE LAW: BRAIN, MIND, AND THE SCALES OF JUSTICE 137 (Brent Garland ed., 2004). See also Susan A. Bandes, *The Promise and Pitfalls of Neuroscience for Criminal Law and Procedure*, 8 OHIO ST. J. CRIM. L. 119 (2010).

[10] This is unlike the Fifth Amendment, where there is considerably more doctrinal uncertainty.

prohibits unreasonable searches and seizures. Analysis requires a two-step inquiry: (1) has a "search" or "seizure" occurred; and (2) if so, was it "reasonable"? If a search or seizure has not occurred, then the Fourth Amendment has not been violated. A "search" occurs for purposes of the Amendment when the government's attempt at information gathering physically intrudes on a constitutionally protected area ("persons, houses, papers, or effects"[11]) or implicates a suspect's "reasonable expectation of privacy."[12] Physical trespass is neither a necessary[13] nor a sufficient[14] condition for triggering whether a search has occurred. It is not necessary because government evidence gathering may infringe upon a reasonable expectation of privacy without involving physical trespass. Two examples include the use of a "thermal imaging device" outside of a home to reveal details in the home[15] and the use of a listening device outside of a public phone booth.[16] It is not sufficient because physical trespass in a non-constitutionally protected place may not infringe upon a reasonable expectation of privacy—two examples include search of an open field and a barn.[17] A "seizure" of a person occurs when a government agent either (1) intentionally physically touches a suspect[18] or (2) engages in a show of authority followed by the suspect's submission.[19] A "seizure" of property occurs when there has been some "meaningful interference with an individual's

---

[11] U.S. CONST. amend. IV. "Effects" include a defendant's property; *see* United States v. Jones, 132 S. Ct. 945 (2012) ("It is beyond dispute that a vehicle is an 'effect' as that term is used in the Amendment"); United States v. Chadwick, 433 U.S. 1, 12 (1977) (concluding defendant's footlocker is an "effect" under Fourth Amendment).

[12] *Jones*, 132 S. Ct. 945 (2012); Katz v. United States, 389 U.S. 347 (1967).

[13] *See* Kyllo v. United States, 533 U.S. 27 (2001) (use of a "thermal imaging" device outside a home constitutes a search despite no physical trespass). Although physical trespass is not necessary, the Court's recent foray into the Fourth Amendment, *Jones*, 132 S. Ct. 945 (2012), noted the special role played by physical trespass in the Amendment's history, and that property and trespass are key concepts for delineating the scope of "reasonable expectations of privacy" and help to define its core.

[14] *See, e.g.*, United States v. Dunn, 480 U.S. 294 (1987) (no search when police officers entered a barn because there was no reasonable expectation of privacy).

[15] *Kyllo*, 533 U.S. 27.

[16] *Katz*, 389 U.S. 347.

[17] Oliver v. United States, 466 U.S. 170 (1984) (no reasonable expectation of privacy in an open field); *Dunn*, 480 U.S. 294 (1987) (no reasonable expectation of privacy in a barn located outside the "curtilage" of a home on a ranch).

[18] California v. Hodari D., 499 U.S. 621 (1991). A seizure does not occur when the government's physical contact was not "intentionally applied." *See* Brower v. County of Inyo, 489 U.S. 593 (1989) (no seizure when suspect crashed his car into a police roadblock set up to stop him).

[19] *Hodari D.*, 499 U.S. 621.

possessory interests" in the property.[20] Moreover, evidence gathered during a search has been "seized" even if it is not physical property.[21]

When a search or seizure occurs, the Fourth Amendment requires that it be reasonable. The doctrinal starting point for determining reasonableness is the second clause of the Amendment:[22] namely, searches and seizures are typically reasonable when they are conducted pursuant to a warrant supported by probable cause.[23] "Probable cause" is a vague standard, which the Supreme Court has articulated as a "fair probability that contraband or evidence of a crime will be found in a particular place."[24] The warrant and probable cause requirements, however, are subject to many exceptions, and the exceptions have swallowed the requirements in many contexts. For example, warrants are unnecessary when there are "exigent circumstances,"[25] automobiles are involved,[26] suspects are arrested outside their homes,[27] or searches are conducted incident to arrests.[28] In addition, limited investigatory "stop and frisks" may be conducted without a warrant or probable cause when there is "reasonable suspicion" that a crime has occurred or is about to occur.[29] No suspicion is required when searches are conducted based on "special needs"—two examples include roadblocks

---

[20] United States v. Karo, 468 U.S. 705, 713 (1984).

[21] See Kyllo v. United States, 533 U.S. 27 (2001) (details about the inside of a house revealed through thermal-imaging device were seized); Berger v. New York, 388 U.S. 41, 59 (1967) (conversations revealed through wiretaps were seized); Katz, 389 U.S. at 351 (same).

[22] U.S. CONST. amend. IV:

[Clause 1] The right of the people to be secure in their persons, houses, papers, and effects, against unreasonable searches and seizure, shall not be violated,

[Clause 2] and no Warrants shall issue, but upon probable cause, supported by Oath or affirmation, and particularly describing the place to be searched, and the persons or things to be seized.

Everything after "violated" is seen as modifying "unreasonable." For criticism of this interpretation on original-understanding grounds, see Akhil Reed Amar, Fourth Amendment First Principles, 107 HARV. L. REV. 757 (1994).

[23] See, e.g., United States v. Jeffers, 342 U.S. 48 (1951); Wong Sun v. United States, 371 U.S. 471 (1963). An exception to this rule is Winston v. Lee, 470 U.S. 753 (1985), in which the Court held that it would be unreasonable to force a robbery suspect to undergo surgery under general anaesthesia to remove a bullet lodged in his body when there was uncertainty about the risks to the defendant and the evidence was not critical to the prosecution's case.

[24] United States v. Grubbs, 547 U.S. 90, 95 (2006); United States v. Gates, 462 U.S. 213 (1983). The judgment of a neutral magistrate is meant to resolve some of the problems with the standard's vagueness.

[25] Warden v. Hayden, 387 U.S. 294 (1967).

[26] California v. Acevedo, 500 U.S. 565 (1991).

[27] United States v. Watson, 423 U.S. 411 (1976).

[28] Chimel v. California, 395 U.S. 752 (1969).

[29] Terry v. Ohio, 392 U.S. 1 (1968).

and school drug-testing.[30] In sum, when a search or seizure occurs, the Fourth Amendment provides standards and procedural requirements that must be met for the government to gather incriminating evidence; the evidence and the context of the search or seizure provide the requisite standard and requirements.

Turning now to neuroscience, suppose the government attempts to compel a suspect to undergo some type of neuroimaging to discover relevant evidence about the suspect's brain that may be useful in a criminal investigation or prosecution. It is first necessary to dispel an unnecessary distraction that may cause confusion in this context. It might be thought that the government could not compel such a test in the first place as the results of these tests depend on voluntary compliance by subjects.[31] For example, even slight movements by a suspect who does not wish to comply with an fMRI scan may render the results meaningless. This line of thinking is mistaken, however, because compulsion in this context does not mean only physical compulsion by government agents (for example, immobilizing a suspect in order to take a blood sample). Compulsion may also arise from threats of criminal or civil contempt charges against subjects for noncompliance. Just as a suspect may be compelled to provide voice or handwriting samples (which also require voluntary compliance by suspects) or they will be held in contempt, it is possible for a suspect to likewise be compelled to participate in a brain scan.

First, compelled neuroscientific tests are "searches" and thus subject to Fourth Amendment constraints on evidence gathering. The tests are "searches" under the "reasonable expectation of privacy"[32] standard. Like other information about internal bodily processes, such as the contents of one's blood or urine, subjects have a "reasonable expectation of privacy" in information about their brains and their brain

---

[30] *See, e.g.,* Illinois v. Lidster, 540 U.S. 419 (2004) (roadblocks); Bd. of Educ. v. Earls, 122 S. Ct. 2559 (2002) (school drug testing).

[31] *Cf.* Teneille Brown & Emily Murphy, *Through a Scanner Darkly: Functional Neurimaging as Evidence of a Criminal Defendant's Past Mental States,* 62 STAN. L. REV. 1119, 1133 (2010) ("While prosecutors may one day introduce fMRI as evidence of future dangerousness, presently defense teams appear to be the dominant users of neuroimaging in the courtroom. One practical reason for this is that it would be physically difficult for the state to compel a brain scan of an unwilling person."); Amy White, *The Lie of fMRI: An Examination of the Ethics of a Market in Lie Detection Using Functional Magnetic Resonance Imagining,* 22 HEC FORUM 253 (2010) ("Movements of the head also frequently impact fMRI results. These movements can be lessened by the use of restraints but movements involved in swallowing, fidgeting, or even pressing a button might also impair the results.").

[32] Katz v. United States, 389 U.S. 347, 360 (1967) (Harlan, J. concurring).

activity.[33] Moreover, the fact that the neuroscientific tests may be able to measure brain details from outside the scalp and without physically touching the person does not change this result. By analogy, one also has a reasonable expectation of privacy in the details of one's home (even when measured from outside with a thermal-imaging device and without physical trespass)[34] and in the contents of one's telephone conversations in a public phone booth (even when gathered with an outside listening device).[35] The Supreme Court's recent opinion regarding GPS monitoring is also instructive—although the physical trespass of constitutionally protected places constitutes a search, the Court explained that the scope of "searches" includes more than this and that the same information gathered without physical intrusion constitutes a search when it infringes on a reasonable expectation of privacy.[36] Reasonable expectations of privacy apply to details about brains and brain activity at least as much (if not more) than (other) details about blood, urine, homes, and conversations.[37] Compelling a test would also be a "seizure" whenever it involves a show of authority (for example, requiring the subject to sit for the test or be held in contempt) followed by submission by the subject.[38] Moreover, the information gathered has been "seized," just as the details about homes,

---

[33] Schmerber v. California, 384 U.S. 757 (1966) (blood test); Skinner v. Ry. Labor Exec. Ass'n, 389 U.S. 602 (1989) (urine test). Compelling a neuroscientific test also appears to be a "seizure" because it would involve a show of authority (requiring the subject to sit for the test) followed by submission by the subject. *See* California v. Hodari D., 499 U.S. 621, 625–29 (1991).

[34] Kyllo v. United States, 533 U.S. 27 (2001).

[35] *Katz*, 389 U.S. at 360.

[36] United States v. Jones, 132 S. Ct. 945 (2012).

[37] Indeed, one might argue that the details in one's head are qualitatively *more* private than those regarding blood, urine, homes, and conversations such that to be reasonable, a showing *beyond* probable cause should be required. However, under current doctrine there is no "probable cause plus" standard based on the private nature of the information sought. The one context in which the Supreme Court has required more than probable cause is when a search or seizure poses significant physical risk to a defendant; see Tennessee v. Garner, 471 U.S. 1 (1985) (use of deadly force by police against a fleeing suspect requires more than probable cause that suspect committed a crime; it also requires probable cause that suspect poses a significant threat of death or physical injury to others); Winston v. Lee, 470 U.S. 753 (1985) (compelled surgery under general anaesthesia requires more than probable cause to believe surgery will recover incriminating evidence). Moreover, the Court has rejected a probable cause–plus standard in other contexts. *See* Atwater v. Lago Vista, 532 U.S. 318 (2001) (rejecting such a standard for full custodial arrests based on minor traffic violations). Professor Nita Farahany has suggested such a standard in the neuroscience context. *See* Nita A. Farahany, *Searching Secrets*, 160 U. PA. L. REV. 1239 (2012). We discuss Farahany's arguments below.

[38] *See* California v. Hodari D., 499 U.S. 621, 625–29 (1991).

conversations, and bodily fluids are seized.[39] Because attempts to gather information about the brain are searches and seizures under the Fourth Amendment, neuroscientific tests could be compelled under current doctrine when the government has probable cause and a warrant, or a recognized exception to these requirements obtains.[40]

The Supreme Court's opinion in *Schmerber*, which involved a compelled blood test, provides an illustrative analogy.[41] The defendant was hospitalized after an automobile accident.[42] An officer at the hospital ordered a blood test of the defendant, over the defendant's objection.[43] The test was forcibly conducted, and the blood was analyzed for alcohol content.[44] The Court concluded that the compelled test was a search and seizure under the Fourth Amendment, but that, because the human body is not "inviolate" against all forms of government evidence gathering, such a test would be acceptable if supported by probable cause.[45] Probable cause existed because the officer smelled alcohol on the defendant's breath and observed his bloodshot eyes, and the Court found that a warrant was not required because the time needed to obtain one would allow the evidence to be destroyed.[46] The Court also noted that the test was reasonable because it was conducted in a safe manner with minimal risk, trauma, and pain.[47] Likewise, a compelled fMRI or "brain fingerprinting" test (discussed in the previous chapter) would measure information regarding internal bodily activity—in this case brain states. A suspect, therefore, could be compelled to

---

[39] Kyllo v. United States, 533 U.S. 27 (2001); Katz v. United States, 389 U.S. 347, 360 (1967); Schmerber v. California, 384 U.S. 757 (1966) (blood test); Skinner v. Ry. Labor Exec. Ass'n, 389 U.S. 602 (1989) (urine test).

[40] *See* Wong Sun v. United States, 371 U.S. 471 (1963); Warden v. Hayden, 387 U.S. 294 (1967) ("exigent circumstances" exception to the warrant requirement); Illinois v. Lidster, 540 U.S. 419 (2004) (applying "special needs" exception to the probable cause and warrant requirements for a roadblock); Bd. of Educ. v. Earls, 536 U.S. 822, 828–38 (2002) (applying "special needs" exception to school drug testing). *Cf.* George M. Dery, *Lying Eyes: Constitutional Implications of New Thermal Imaging Lie Detection Technology*, 31 AM. J. CRIM. L. 217, 242–44 (2004) (concluding that the use of thermal-imaging lie detector that measures heat around the eyes may not be a "search" when used on those in public because they voluntarily expose such heat to the public).

[41] Schmerber v. California, 384 U.S. 757 (1966).

[42] *Id.* at 758.

[43] *Id.* at 759.

[44] *Id.*

[45] *Id.* at 767–69.

[46] *Id.* at 768–69. This exigent-circumstances exception to the Fourth Amendment's warrant requirement was established the next year in Warden v. Hayden, 387 U.S. 294, 298 (1967).

[47] 384 U.S. at 771.

take the test when probable cause exists to believe the test will reveal incriminating evidence, and the government obtains a warrant or a warrant exception applies. Moreover, the neuroscientific tests appear in most cases to be less intrusive than blood tests would be. They are safe, relatively painless, and do not involve piercing the skin. Particular conditions, however, may make the tests "unreasonable" (and thus unconstitutional) in certain circumstances. Such conditions would include, for example, fMRI scans of suspects with metallic objects in their bodies, as well as any physical or psychological conditions that would make a compelled scan extraordinarily painful or dangerous.[48]

A more difficult doctrinal question concerns whether the government may compel neuroscientific tests via a grand jury subpoena. If so, under current doctrine, this may perhaps be done without the government first showing probable cause. Consider, for example, a situation in which the government obtains a grand jury subpoena compelling twenty possible suspects to sit for an fMRI lie-detection session. As a doctrinal matter, subpoenas (like searches and seizures generally) must be reasonable, and the evidence they seek to compel must be relevant; they must also not be used to harass or burden subpoena targets.[49] Given the way the Supreme Court has construed subpoena doctrine, however, these formal requirements do not offer much protection in practice. This is because the Court has placed the burden of proof on subpoena targets, not the government, to show that

there is *no reasonable possibility* that the *category* of materials the Government seeks will produce information relevant to the *general subject* of the grand jury's investigation.[50]

It would be virtually impossible for a suspect to show that fMRI lie-detection results or "brain fingerprinting" results would have no reasonable possibility of revealing relevant information about a general subject matter of a grand jury investigation.

---

[48] *See* Winston v. Lee, 470 U.S. 753 (1985) (holding as unreasonable compelled surgery to remove a bullet that may provide incriminating evidence, given the risks involved with surgery and the government's need for the evidence); Rochin v. California, 342 U.S. 165 (1952) (forced stomach pumping at hospital, at direction of sheriff, held to be constitutional). For a general discussion of some of the dangers that may arise with neuroimaging, see White, *supra* note 31.

[49] *See* FED. R. CRIM. P. 17; United States v. Dionisio, 410 U.S. 1 (1973); United States v. R Enterprises, Inc., 498 U.S. 292, 299 (1991) (noting the government cannot "engage in arbitrary fishing expeditions").

[50] *R Enterprises*, 292 U.S. at 301 (emphasis added).

The Court's opinion in *Dionisio* provides an instructive analogy.[51] Twenty suspects were subpoenaed to provide a voice sample to the local U.S. Attorney's office.[52] The Court upheld the subpoena over a Fourth Amendment challenge brought by one of the targets, concluding that, despite any inconvenience or burden to the targets, the government need not make a showing of relevance because the grand jury's powers are necessarily broad, and that a probable-cause showing was not necessary because the subpoena involved less "social stigma" than an arrest.[53] With neuroscientific tests, the government would not need to make relevance or probable-cause showings before rounding up the suspects for a neuroscientific test, which would also involve less "social stigma" than an arrest. Moreover, the tests may be no more burdensome or traumatic than being compelled via subpoena to answer hours of grand jury questioning. For these reasons, Stephen Morse's assertion that "it is clear that the government will not be able to use neuroscience investigative techniques to go on 'mental fishing expeditions'"[54] may not necessarily be true, unless the Fifth Amendment, due process, or statutory protections can limit what the Fourth Amendment may not in this context.[55]

[51]   410 U.S. 1 (1973).

[52]   *Id.* at 3.

[53]   *Id.* at 3–7, 12–13.

[54]   Stephen J. Morse, *New Neuroscience, Old Problems, in* NEUROSCIENCE AND THE LAW: BRAIN, MIND, AND THE SCALES OF JUSTICE 188 (Brent Garland ed., 2004). The Supreme Court has not addressed this issue in the context either of neuroimaging or searches of bodily fluids. There also has not been much doctrinal development among lower courts. *But see In re* Grand Jury Proceedings Involving Vickers, 38 F. Supp. 2d 159 (D.N.H. 1998) (subpoena for saliva sample was reasonable); United States v. Nicolosi, 885 F. Supp. 50 (E.D.N.Y. 1995) (subpoena for saliva sample was unreasonable without probable cause and warrant or warrant exception); *In re* Grand Jury Proceedings (T.S.), 816 F. Supp. 1196 (W.D. K.Y. 1993) (search warrant required for blood sample); Henry v. Ryan, 775 F. Supp. 247, 254 (N.D. Ill. 1991) ("[A] grand jury subpoena for physical evidence must be based on individualized suspicion."). For helpful discussions, see Amanda C. Pustilnik, *Neurotechnologies at the Intersection of Criminal Procedure and Constitutional Law, in* THE CONSTITUTION AND THE FUTURE OF THE CRIMINAL LAW (John Richardson & L. Song Parry eds., forthcoming 2013), *available at* http://ssrn.com/abstract=2143187; Floralynn Einesman, *Vampires among Us—Does a Grand Jury Subpoena for Blood Violate the Fourth Amendment?*, 22 AM. J. CRIM. L. 327 (1995).

[55]   As explained in more detail in Pardo, *supra* note 3, at 1881–90, this gap in Fourth Amendment doctrine best explains the Court's mistaken transposition of a "government knowledge" inquiry into its analysis of whether the privilege against self-incrimination protects subpoena targets from compelled production. The Court's strange requirements in Fisher v. United States, 425 U.S. 391 (1976), and United States v. Hubbell, 530 U.S. 27 (2000), that the relevant information must not be a "foregone conclusion" (*Fisher*) or described with "reasonable particularity" (*Hubbell*) appear to work to prevent the "fishing expeditions" that should be protected by the Fourth Amendment. Nowhere else does the scope

Recent and provocative scholarship by Nita Farahany poses a challenge to a few of the conclusions we reach in this chapter.[56] In exploring the Fourth Amendment, copyright law, and evidence about the brain, Professor Farahany argues that current analysis on these issues "ignores the subtle and nuanced challenges that cognitive neuroscience raises for Fourth Amendment law."[57] The challenges get overlooked, she maintains, in "sweeping claims" that, at one extreme, assert that individuals have a "reasonable expectation of privacy" in information about their brains, and, at the other extreme, maintain that compelled neuroimaging investigations "are not unreasonable searches because they are similar in relevant respects to blood and urine tests."[58] She contends that these challenges may be better appreciated by placing neuroscientific evidence on a spectrum composed of four categories: "identifying," "automatic," "memorialized," and "utterances."[59] Although she concludes that evidence in each of the four categories is entitled to some Fourth Amendment scrutiny and protection, she argues that some evidence falling into the latter two categories is entitled to more Fourth Amendment protection. She characterizes her analysis as a "descriptively robust" analysis of the case law and doctrine, but acknowledges its normative problems.[60]

Before turning to Farahany's proposed spectrum of evidence, we first note that the "extreme" and "sweeping" positions within which she sets up her discussion are not in fact opposed. Indeed, they are not in tension with one another at all; they are perfectly consistent and, we contend, accurate. On the one hand, to recognize that people have a "reasonable expectation of privacy" in their brain activity is merely

---

of the Fifth Amendment privilege turn on what the government knows. Current doctrine aside, a better approach in these situations, and one that better accords with core Fourth Amendment practices and principles, would require the government to make some type of reasonableness showing. Because of a grand jury's need for broad investigatory powers and the less "stigma" involved with a subpoena, the showing need not be one of probable cause. The Fourth Amendment already accommodates such needs for lower standards, for example, by requiring only "reasonable suspicion" for brief investigative stops. A similar standard in this situation could prevent arbitrary "fishing expeditions" as well as the burdening and harassing of innocent targets. *See* Pardo, *supra* note 3. For similar reasons, Erin Murphy argues that Fifth Amendment doctrine should perhaps also be extended to cover DNA evidence; *see* Erin Murphy, *DNA and the Fifth Amendment, in* THE POLITICAL HEART OF CRIMINAL PROCEDURE: ESSAYS ON THEMES OF WILLIAM J. STUNTZ (Michael Klarman et al. eds., 2012).

[56] Nita A. Farahany, *Searching Secrets*, 160 U. PA. L. REV. 1239 (2012).

[57] *Id.* at 1276.

[58] *Id.* at 1275–76.

[59] *Id.* at 1277–1303.

[60] *Id.* at 1308.

to recognize that attempts to gather the evidence are "searches," and, therefore, that these attempts are covered by the Fourth Amendment and its requirements.[61] The requirements allow government evidence gathering when there is probable cause and a warrant, or one of the other doctrinal standards is satisfied in order to make the evidence gathering reasonable. Once one recognizes that compelled tests are in fact "searches," it is perfectly consistent to then recognize that these searches may be "reasonable searches" if they accord with the doctrine's reasonableness requirements, as is the case with compelled blood and urine tests.[62] Thus, the proposed dichotomy of "sweeping claims" is actually an example of scholarly agreement about the relationship between the evidence and Fourth Amendment doctrine.

If we turn now to the spectrum of evidence and Farahany's descriptive claims, the qualitative distinctions she draws between categories of evidence do not track Fourth Amendment doctrine. The spectrum of evidence is arrayed based on the amount of control subjects have over "creation of the evidence."[63] At one end (no control) is "identifying" evidence, which includes a suspect's name, age, blood type, fingerprints, and voice samples.[64] She posits that neuroscientific evidence in this category would include a person's "brainwave signals" recorded through EEG with a "noninvasive helmet," which may provide identifying evidence if "the signals for each individual are unique."[65] Next is evidence that is "automatically generated" in the body.[66] For example, she discusses a PET scan that measures patterns of glucose metabolism in the brain and that may provide incriminating evidence of alcohol

---

[61] *Id.* at 1275. For this position Farahany cites one of us. *See* Michael S. Pardo, *Neuroscience Evidence, Legal Culture, and Criminal Procedure*, 33 AM. J. CRIM. L. 301 (2006) (arguing that neuroimaging would constitute a "search" and be subject to doctrinal requirements for constitutional searches).

[62] For this position Farahany cites Dov Fox, *Brain Imaging and the Bill of Rights: Memory Detection Technologies and American Criminal Justice*, 8 AM. J. BIOETHICS 34, 35 (2008). *See* Farahany, *supra* note 56, at 1275. Like Pardo, *supra* note 61, however, Fox also concludes that neuroimaging constitutes a "search" and is thus subject to other doctrinal requirements that would make the search reasonable and therefore constitutional.

[63] Farahany, *supra* note 56, at 1274 ("Those four categories comprise a spectrum: from the first category to the last, an individual exerts increasingly more control over the creation of evidence.").

[64] *Id.* at 1277–83.

[65] *Id.* at 1281–82 ("Technology has already been developed that can record electroencephalographic (EEG) signals using a noninvasive helmet. Police may one day be able to use this technology for on-the-spot identification by comparing a suspect's brainwave pattern with those in a database of brainwave patterns.").

[66] *Id.* at 1282–88.

intoxication.[67] Next is evidence that is "memorialized," which includes documents, drawings, photographs, electronic records, and "encoded memories in the brain."[68] At the other end (control) are "utterances," which include "thoughts, visual images, words, or statements that are verbalized or recalled to the conscious brain."[69] Utterances may be voluntary or "evoked," the latter of which "arise by compelling a suspect to respond—either silently or aloud—to questions or prompts."[70]

Farahany's descriptive thesis is that for evidence gathering about the brain, the Fourth Amendment provides some protection for identifying or automatic evidence, but greater protection of memorialized evidence and evoked utterances.[71] She argues that when a suspect does not choose to reveal his thoughts, "only extraordinary circumstances should justify an intrusion upon the seclusion of those utterances."[72] The spectrum Farahany articulates is useful for classifying different types of neurological evidence, but the constitutional line she draws does not reflect Fourth Amendment law. First, there is no qualitative distinction between these categories that determines whether it is a "search": they are all searches. Second, there is no qualitative distinction between these categories that tracks the standards for whether the search may be conducted in accord with the Constitution. The probable cause and warrant requirements, and the exceptions to these requirements, apply equally to each category. Moreover, consider the category of "evoked utterances," which purportedly receives the most Fourth Amendment protection under Farahany's analysis. There is no "probable cause plus" standard that applies to evoked utterances.[73] Indeed, in many instances the burden on the government will be lower for evoked utterances than for other types of evidence. Being summoned to testify before a grand jury, for example, is compelling the

----

[67] Id. at 1287 ("The police could one day bypass the use of breathalyzer or blood-alcohol tests by directly measuring the level of alcohol intoxication in the brain.").

[68] Id. at 1288–98. We discuss in Chapter Four conceptual difficulties that arise for reductive conceptions of memory.

[69] Id. at 1298–1303. See also id. at 1303 (referring to "silent utterances in the brain").

[70] Id. at 1298.

[71] Id. at 1307.

[72] Id. at 1303.

[73] The examples in which the Supreme Court has held that the Fourth Amendment requires more than probable cause involve the use of deadly force (see Tennessee v. Garner, 471 U.S. 1 (1985)) or other serious physical risk to a defendant (see Winston v. Lee, 470 U.S. 753 (1985)), not "evoked utterances" by defendants. Cf. Atwater v. Lago Vista, 532 U.S. 318 (2001), in which the Court considered and rejected a higher-than-probable-cause standard for full custodial arrests based on minor traffic violations.

suspect to reveal his or her thoughts thereby evoking utterances. For the reasons discussed above, however, the burden on the government under current subpoena doctrine is a low one.

We share Farahany's concerns about the normative problems that emerge from the interaction of neuroscience technology and current Fourth Amendment doctrine. We are not persuaded, however, that the normative considerations track the distinctions she draws. For example, we assume that many people would expect a greater privacy interest in the content of information about their blood (e.g., HIV status) or their genetic information (each of which fall on the identity-automatic side and would receive less protection under her analysis) than in the content of their memories or evoked utterances on a variety of nonpersonal matters (which would receive more protection under her analysis).

II. Fifth Amendment

The relationship between neurological evidence and the Fifth Amendment privilege against self-incrimination is more complicated than in the Fourth Amendment context. This complication arises for two types of reasons: there are reasons general to the doctrine, and reasons specific to the neuroscience context. The general reasons are that self-incrimination doctrine is itself unclear in certain areas and its complexity appears to defy each of the grand normative theories that have been offered to explain and justify it.[74] The specific reasons are that neuroscience provides examples of evidence that cut across the key doctrinal categories. Most important, the privilege applies to "testimonial" evidence and not to "physical" evidence.[75] But neuroscientific evidence is sometimes both at once. On the one hand, compelled brain scanning is characterized as the government "peer[ing] into an individual's thought process," and "searching and reading someone's mind," and as providing evidence of someone's beliefs, knowledge, intentions, and other mental states.[76] On the other hand, "fMRI scans only detect

---

[74] For a general discussion and examples, see Ronald J. Allen & Kristen Mace, *The Self-Incrimination Clause Explained and Its Future Predicted*, 94 J. CRIM. & CRIMINOLOGY 243 (2004).

[75] Schmerber v. California, 384 U.S. 757 (1966).

[76] Paul Root Wolpe, Kenneth Foster & Daniel D. Langleben, *Emerging Neurotechnologies for Lie-Detection: Promises and Perils*, 5 AM. J. BIOETHICS 39 (2005).

oxygen in the brain...This detection process hardly amounts to read-ing thoughts."[77] As Nita Farahany asserts in a recent article: "[n]either 'physical' nor 'testimonial' accurately describes neurological evidence."[78] Nevertheless, the privilege's current availability to a criminal suspect depends on whether the evidence falls under the doctrinal category of "testimonial evidence," along with the other doctrinal requirements.

The privilege against self-incrimination applies to evidence that meets three formal requirements: (1) compelled, (2) incriminating, and (3) testimonial communications.[79] Our analysis in this section is orga-nized around these elements. For the reasons above, the third element is the most complicated and is our primary focus. We conclude the section by discussing recent Fifth Amendment scholarship, illustrating once again the practical consequences that turn on the conceptual issues we raise.

The first element—compulsion—refers to government conduct that causes a suspect to make incriminating statements or other-wise reveal incriminating testimonial evidence. Whether conduct is "compulsion" for Fifth Amendment purposes turns on the type of government conduct involved, not necessarily the pressure placed on suspects. Clear examples of compulsion include threats of con-tempt for not testifying or threats of violence for not confessing.[80] By contrast, offers of favorable plea agreements or tricking suspects into making statements do not constitute "compulsion."[81] Forcing

---

[77] See White, *supra* note 31.

[78] Nita Farahany, *Incriminating Thoughts*, 64 STAN. L. REV. 351 (2012) ("The neuroscience revolution poses profound challenges to current self-incrimination doctrine and exposes a deep conceptual confusion at its core.").

[79] For clear exposition of the doctrine on each element and the conceptual issues raised by each, see Allen & Mace, *supra* note 74.

[80] See Malloy v. Hogan, 378 U.S. 1 (1964). See also Griffin v. California, 380 U.S. 609 (1965) (prosecution may not refer to defendant's invocation of the privilege); see also Lefkowitz v. Turner, 414 U.S. 70 (1973) (striking down state statute that required state contracts to con-tain a clause that contractors waive their right to invoke the self-incrimination privilege with regard to subject matter relating to the contract). The Supreme Court's decision in Miranda v. Arizona, 384 U.S. 486 (1966) explained that the famous "*Miranda* warnings" were designed to combat the inherently coercive environment of police custodial interrogation.

[81] See, e.g., Illinois v. Perkins, 496 U.S. 292 (1990) (statements made to an undercover officer posing as inmate are not compelled); Oregon v. Mattiason, 429 U.S. 492 (1977) (mis-leading suspect into thinking his fingerprints were found at a crime scene did not constitute compulsion of subsequent statements). In the context of documents, compulsion applies to whether the defendant was compelled to *create* the document, not just produce it. See Fisher v. United States, 425 U.S. 391 (1976). Evidence of a refusal to submit to a blood-alcohol test was held not to be compelled because the state could simply force defendants to submit to the test but instead gave them a choice. See South Dakota v. Neville, 459 U.S. 553 (1983).

a suspect (either through a threat of contempt or through physical force) to sit for an MRI, fMRI, EEG, or other neuroscientific test would constitute compulsion.[82]

The second element—incrimination—refers to the question of whether the compelled information will be used in a criminal prosecution against the subject, either directly or to derive other evidence. "Incrimination" is construed broadly to include any evidence that reasonably "could be used in a criminal prosecution or could lead to other evidence that might be used."[83] "Incrimination," and hence the privilege, does not apply when subjects are granted immunity;[84] when the information would lead to noncriminal sanctions only, such as loss of a job or a license or to disgrace or embarrassment; or when the information is sought to incriminate a third party, including friends and family.[85] Compelled neuroscientific tests fall within the scope of these rules: the incrimination element would be met when the results could lead to evidence used in a criminal prosecution; subjects could not invoke the privilege when they are granted immunity or face noncriminal sanctions only, or the test results are sought to incriminate a third party. This requirement thus means that the Fifth Amendment privilege does not provide a general constitutional right to "mental privacy," "cognitive liberty," or "mental control."[86] Subject to other legal restraints, the government can, consistent with the Fifth Amendment, compel evidence from a suspect's mind or brain whenever that evidence is not self-incriminating.

The third element—testimony—poses greater analytical difficulties than the first two elements. Two principles, however, will help to delineate the scope of this requirement. First, "testimonial" evidence is contrasted with "real" or "physical" evidence. The Supreme Court's opinion in Schmerber drew this distinction explicitly in concluding that

---

[82] A scan of brain activity without a suspect's awareness is a Fourth Amendment search and thus subject to the analysis in the previous section.

[83] Kastigar v. United States, 406 U.S. 441, 445 (1972).

[84] Id.

[85] See Ullmann v. United States, 350 U.S. 422, 430–31 (1956).

[86] See B. Michael Dann, The Fifth Amendment Privilege against Self-Incrimination: Extorting Physical Evidence from a Suspect, 43 S. CAL. L. REV. 597 (1970) (discussing privacy); Richard. G. Boire, Searching the Brain: The Fourth Amendment Implications of Brain-Based Deception Devices, 5 AM. J. BIOETHICS 62 (2005) (discussing "cognitive liberty"); Dov Fox, The Right to Silence Protects Mental Control, in LAW AND NEUROSCIENCE (Michael Freeman ed., 2010); Uviller, supra note 4, at 325 n.50 (privilege protects a person's "sovereignty over the contents of his mind.").

a compelled blood test was outside the scope of the privilege against self-incrimination:

> The distinction which has emerged [from prior case law], often expressed in different ways, is that the privilege is a bar against compelling "communications" or "testimony," but that compulsion which makes a suspect or accused the source of "real or physical evidence" does not violate it.[87]

To this end, in addition to blood tests, the privilege does not apply to other compelled evidence from a suspect's body (such as hair, fingerprints, and breathalyzer tests);[88] to voice[89] and handwriting[90] exemplars (because physical characteristics are what is relevant); and to orders to appear in a lineup[91] or to try on clothing.[92]

As these examples make clear, the category of Fifth Amendment "testimony" is not coextensive with verbal or written utterances. On the one hand, sometimes verbal or written utterances are outside the scope of the privilege—for example, with voice or handwriting samples. On the other hand, however, a verbal or written utterance is not necessary in order to fall within the scope of the privilege. This leads to the second principle for delineating "testimony"—evidence that does not consist of verbal or written assertions may function as testimony and thus fall within the scope of the privilege. The Supreme Court's line of subpoena cases is illustrative of how (nonverbal or nonwritten) physical acts may constitute protected Fifth Amendment "testimony." When the target of a subpoena responds by providing a requested object or document, the Court explained, the target's actions disclose

---

[87] 384 U.S. at 764.

[88] *Id.* at 760–65.

[89] United States v. Dionisio, 410 U.S. 1, 5–7 (1973).

[90] United States v. Mara, 410 U.S. 19, 21–22 (1973).

[91] United States v. Wade, 388 U.S. 218, 221–23 (1967).

[92] Holt v. United States, 218 U.S. 245, 252–53 (1910). In *Schmerber*, the Court explained the "complex of values" the privilege is meant to serve:

> the constitutional foundation underlying the privilege is the respect a government—state or federal—must accord to the dignity and integrity of its citizens. To maintain a "fair state–individual balance," to require the government "to shoulder the entire load"...to respect the inviolability of the human personality, our accusatory system of criminal justice demands that the government seeking to punish an individual produce the evidence against him by its own independent labors, rather than by the cruel, simple expedient of compelling it from his own mouth.

384 U.S. at 762. But the Court then noted that historically the privilege did not extend as far as these values imply and acknowledged that the values may also cover some of the examples of "physical" evidence outside the doctrinal scope of the privilege. *Id.* at 762–63.

the target's (1) knowledge that the object exists, (2) possession of it, and (3) belief that the provided object is the one demanded.[93] In other words, the requested objects or documents are not protected, but the "testimonial"/"acts of production" are protected by the privilege. In *Fisher v. United States*, for example, the Court held that responding to a subpoena for tax documents did not implicate the privilege because the government already knew of the existence and location of the documents; therefore, the government did not use the defendant's testimonial acts of production as evidence against him.[94] By contrast, in *United States v. Hubbell*, the Court found that the privilege did apply to a request for documents that the government could not describe with particularity because the government made use of the "contents of [Hubbell's] mind" and, thus, his testimonial acts of production in gathering and disclosing the requested documents.[95]

From these two principles we can see that the scope of the privilege turns on whether the government is making incriminating use of the *contents* of defendants' *mental states*, whether or not that content is expressed verbally or in writing. When the government relies on non-testimonial physical evidence (including voice and handwriting samples), the evidence does not depend on the defendant's mental states. However, when the government relies on testimonial "acts of production," the evidence does depend on the content of the defendant's mental states, which are implied by his physical actions (for example, in responding to a subpoena). In focusing on the content of mental states, the privilege appears to focus on what philosophers refer to as "propositional attitudes." Propositional attitudes are mental states—such as beliefs, thoughts, doubts, hopes,

---

[93] Fisher v. United States, 425 U.S. 391 (1976).

[94] 425 U.S. 391, 411 (1976). *See also* Doe v. United States, 487 U.S. 201 (1988), where a target of a grand jury subpoena was directed to sign a form releasing details regarding any foreign bank accounts in his name, without admitting their existence. The Court concluded that the privilege did not apply because the act of signing the form did not invoke "testimonial aspects" of production: "By signing the form, Doe makes no statement, explicit or implicit, regarding the existence of a foreign bank account or his control over any such account." *Id.* at 215–16. The Court explained the policies beyond the privilege as follows: "to spare the accused from having to reveal, directly or indirectly, his knowledge of facts relating him to the offense or from having to share his thoughts and beliefs with the Government." *Id.* at 213.

[95] 530 U.S. 27 (2000). *See also* United States v. Doe, 465 U.S. 605, 612–17 (1984), where the Court concluded that a grand jury target's acts of producing business records in response to a subpoena qualified as "testimonial" because they would reveal the existence and authenticity of the documents.

wishes, desires, or knowledge—that reflect a particular attitude toward or about particular propositions;[96] for example, a subject's belief *that so and so* (e.g., "that the victim was out of town during the robbery") or knowledge *that such and such* (e.g., "I robbed the house"). The privilege appears to apply to the *content* of these propositions (in other words, the *"so and so"* and *"such and such"*) and limits the government from making compelled, incriminating use of such evidence.[97] One key difference between evidence that falls within this scope, and evidence outside of it, is its dependence on the defendant as a source of *epistemic* authority. In other words, the privilege prevents the government from using the content of a defendant's mental states as a testimonial source of evidence.

Two examples will help to further flesh out the scope of Fifth Amendment "testimony" and this point about epistemic authority. First, consider a psychiatric examination used during a capital-sentencing proceeding in order to determine future dangerousness. In *Estelle v. Smith*, the Court held that a defendant's statements made during the examination were "testimonial" because "the State used as evidence against respondent the *substance* of his disclosures." (emphasis added).[98] Specifically, the testifying psychiatrist reached the conclusion that the defendant was a "severe sociopath" and "he will commit other similar or same acts," based on the defendant's account of his previous crime during the examination.[99] The expert relied on the content of the defendant's statements; the defendant served as an epistemic source regarding this content. Second, consider a suspect asked whether he knows the date of his sixth birthday in order to determine the extent of his intoxication. In *Pennsylvania v. Muniz*, the Court had to determine whether an answer to this question (in

---

[96] *See* ROBERT J. MATTHEWS, THE MEASURE OF MIND: PROPOSITIONAL ATTITUDES AND THEIR ATTRIBUTION (2010); Thomas McKay & Michael Nelson, *Propositional Attitude Reports*, *in* STANFORD ENCYCLOPEDIA OF PHILOSOPHY (2010), *available at* http://plato.stanford.edu/entries/prop-attitude-reports/; A COMPANION TO THE PHILOSOPHY OF LANGUAGE 679 (Bob Hale & Crispin Wright eds., 1999).

[97] *See* Allen & Mace, *supra* note 74, at 246–47 (arguing that "testimony" for purposes of the privilege applies to "the substantive content of cognition" and "the propositions with truth-value that people hold"). Under the rule articulated above in the main text, the privilege also would apply to a person's false beliefs (e.g., a defendant's false belief that a victim named the defendant as the beneficiary of her will), and to those that are neither true nor false (e.g., if the content were used to identify the person as the culprit of a crime).

[98] Estelle v. Smith, 451 U.S. 454, 459–60, 463–66 (1981). The substance of the defendant's disclosures is the content of what he said. For further analysis of *Estelle*, see Allen & Mace, *supra* note 74.

[99] 451 U.S. at 459–60, 464–65.

this case, "I don't know") qualified as testimonial (along with other compelled evidence such as field-sobriety tests and biographical information elicited during "booking").[100] Although the Court ended up concluding the sixth-birthday question was covered by the privilege against self-incrimination, it technically did not decide whether it was "testimonial." Four justices concluded that it was testimonial,[101] four justices concluded it was not,[102] and Justice Marshall rejected the testimonial/non-testimonial distinction and concluded that the privilege should apply to all the evidence regardless of its testimonial qualities (thus providing the fifth vote of the sixth-birthday question).[103] The question and its answer are not "testimonial" because the *content* of the answer would not be incriminating. The question may test the defendant's mental acuity at the time, which may be incriminating, but it would be incriminating for reasons other than its content.[104] The government would not be relying on the content of the defendant's mental states; the defendant would not be serving as an authority for, or "testifying" to, that content.

These principles provide guidance for determining when compelled neuroscientific tests would and would not be testimonial and, thus, fall within the scope of the privilege. The evidence generated by such tests would be testimonial whenever its relevance depends on the content of the defendant's mental states, in particular the content of her propositional attitudes. When such evidence is also compelled and incriminating, it then falls within the scope of the privilege. Therefore,

---

[100] Pennsylvania v. Muniz, 496 U.S. 582, 586 (1990).

[101] *Id.* at 593–602.

[102] *Id.* at 607–08 (Rehnquist, C.J., concurring in part and dissenting in part).

[103] *Id.* at 616 n.4 (Marshall, J., concurring in part and dissenting in part) ("I believe [the] privilege extends to *any* evidence that a person is compelled to furnish against himself.") Although the "testimonial" requirement appears to be firmly entrenched in current doctrine, Justice Thomas (joined by Justice Scalia) recently has expressed a willingness to consider whether, based on historical grounds, the privilege should be extended to non-testimonial evidence as well. United States v. Hubbell, 530 U.S. 27, 49–56 (2000) (Thomas, J., concurring). Richard Nagareda has argued that this more expansive view of the privilege would better accord with the original understanding of the phrase "to be a witness" in the Fifth Amendment, which he argues meant "to give evidence" not just "testimonial communications." *See* Nagareda, *supra* note 4, at 1587. Akhil Amar and Renee Lettow, by contrast, argue in favor of the "testimonial" limitation on historical, original-understanding grounds. *See* Amar & Lettow, *supra* note 4, at 919 ("Unlike some state constitutions, such as the Massachusetts Constitution of 1780, the Fifth Amendment does not prohibit the government from compelling a defendant to 'furnish evidence against himself.'").

[104] Allen & Mace, *supra* note 74, reach a similar conclusion and provide further analysis of *Muniz*.

even though neurological tests gather physical evidence from the defendants' bodies (such as compelled blood tests), like "testimonial acts of production," the relevance of such evidence may provide evidence of defendants' incriminating beliefs, knowledge, and other mental states. When the government attempts to make evidential use of the content of such states, the privilege applies.

Four examples will help to elucidate this distinction:

Example 1: Winston is a suspect in a bank robbery. Winston denies involvement. The government (with probable cause and a warrant[105]) wants to compel Winston to sit for an fMRI test in order to ask him questions about his involvement in the crime. If the results of the test are consistent with deception,[106] the government plans to use the results at trial as evidence of guilt, or to gather further evidence against Winston.

Example 2: Alex is arrested for criminal fraud. Upon his arrest, his attorney claims that Alex lacked the mental capacities necessary to engage in deception and thus criminal fraud.[107] The government wants to compel Alex to sit for an fMRI test in order to use the results as evidence that, during Alex's answers, his brain activity matched activity correlated with deception, and thus that he can engage in such conduct.

Example 3: Winston, still suspected of bank robbery, is now compelled to sit for the "brain fingerprinting" test.[108] He is shown images of the bank vault (which only employees and the robbers have seen) and presented with details of the crime. The government wants to introduce the test results, which suggest prior knowledge when presented with the images and details, as evidence of Winston's guilt.

Example 4: Alex, still suspected of fraud, claims that he has a short-term memory problem, which explains his conduct, rather than an intent to commit fraud. The government compels Alex to sit for the "brain fingerprinting" test. They first present him with some details and, after a short period of time, test him to see if the results suggest "knowledge" or "memory" when he is presented with the details. The government wants to offer the results

[105]   *See* Section I, *supra.*
[106]   *See* Chapter Four.
[107]   *See* Chapter Five.
[108]   *See* Chapter Four.

as evidence of guilt, arguing that they show that Alex did recognize the details in the test and thus does not have the memory problems he claims.

In these examples, Winston would be able to invoke the privilege whereas Alex would not.[109] In the Winston examples, the compelled tests are relevant in order to generate the incriminating content of Winston's beliefs or knowledge. The evidence of deception is relevant because it provides evidence of Winston's belief that he was involved in the crime; the "brain fingerprinting" evidence is relevant because it provides evidence of Winston's knowledge of the crime scene and details of the crime. By contrast, the Alex examples do not involve attempts to use the incriminating content of Alex's mental states. Both tests provide evidence, rather, of Alex's mental *capacities*: their relevance does not depend on the fact that they reveal incriminating *content*. The tests, therefore, are like other compelled tests where relevance depends on particular physical details—such as blood tests, and handwriting and voice exemplars—and not situations where the defendant is being compelled to serve as a testimonial source (and, thus, an epistemic authority regarding the incriminating content of his mental states). These results are consistent with the Court's dicta in *Schmerber* that a compelled polygraph, although measuring physical details, may still be testimonial:

Some tests seemingly directed to obtain "physical evidence," for example, lie detector tests measuring changes in body function during interrogation, may actually be directed to eliciting responses which are essentially testimonial.[110]

To the extent neuroscientific tests are so directed, the privilege will apply.[111]

---

[109] If the evidence is admissible, the rules of evidence would place limitations on how it could be presented. *See, e.g.*, FED. R. EVID. 704 (limiting expert testimony on the "ultimate issue" of a defendant's mental state during the events in question).

[110] 384 U.S. at 764. *See also* Allen & Mace, *supra* note 74, at 249 ("the universal intuition is that involuntary polygraphs violate the Constitution.").

[111] When it does, the other doctrinal rules for the privilege attach as well. *See, e.g.*, Griffin v. California, 380 U.S. 609 (1965) (prosecution may not make evidentiary use of defendant's invocation of the privilege); Baxter v. Palmigiano, 425 U.S. 308 (1976) (concluding that adverse inferences may be drawn in noncriminal proceedings against parties who invoke the privilege); California v. Byers 402 U.S. 424 (1971) (privilege non-applicable to mandatory automobile-accident disclosures because required to facilitate noncriminal regulatory regime); Baltimore City Dep't of Soc. Servs. v. Bouknight, 493 U.S. 549 (1990) (privilege inapplicable to guardian requirements in order to facilitate noncriminal social-services administration).

We conclude this section by contrasting our analysis with three other scholarly discussions of the relationships between self-incrimination and evidence pertaining to the brain and the mind.

In an insightful recent essay, Dov Fox argues that the right to silence protects all forms of "mental control" generally.[112] According to Fox, the right to silence protects a person's "brainwork from state use" and prohibits "the state from seizing control over [a person's thought] processes, both self-incriminating and non-self-incriminating."[113] Fox's analysis presents a picture of the right to silence that deviates from current doctrine in two crucial respects. First, by extending such a proposed right to "non-self-incriminating" evidence it eliminates the incrimination requirement, which is part of the foundation of current doctrine. Second, in extending the right to all forms of "mental control" it largely eliminates the "testimonial" requirement as it currently exists, which we reconstruct above as applying to compelled incriminating content of a suspect's propositional attitudes. Fox's analysis, for example, implies that the privilege would apply for all four of the examples above (Winston *and* Alex), and it implies that the privilege applies to many areas where it currently does not, such as handwriting and voice exemplars. In short, although we find Fox's discussion to be an interesting proposal for change, our focus is on the relationship between current doctrine and neuroscientific evidence, not whether current constitutional criminal procedure rules ought to undergo wholesale change.[114]

Second, Nita Farahany explores the Fifth Amendment, as well as the Fourth Amendment, in light of the evidentiary spectrum discussed above.[115] Recall, Farahany divides evidence into four categories: (1) identifying, (2) automatic, (3) memorialized, and (4) utterances.[116] Her analysis fuses the analytic categories of her spectrum with a previous theory of the privilege against self-incrimination articulated by William Stuntz.[117] According to Stuntz's "excuse" theory, we generally excuse a defendant's silence in situations where his compelled testimony is likely to result in

---

[112]   Fox, *supra* note 86.

[113]   *Id.* at 265.

[114]   This is also true with regard to other general theoretical accounts of the privilege that deviate from current doctrine. *See, e.g.*, Daniel J. Seidmann & Alex Stein, *The Right to Silence Helps the Innocent: A Game-Theoretic Approach to the Fifth Amendment Privilege*, 114 HARV. L. REV. 430 (2000).

[115]   Farahany, *supra* note 78.

[116]   *See supra* notes 63–70 and accompanying text.

[117]   William J. Stuntz, *Self-Incrimination and Excuse*, 88 COLUM. L. REV. 1227, 1277 (1988).

perjury.[118] In short, the defendant's personal interests in avoiding conviction are great enough to tempt him to act wrongly (committing perjury) in producing evidence. As Farahany explains, the normative appeal of the excuse rationale is enhanced reliability because "[e]xcuse-as-privilege maximizes the reliability of the testimony obtained."[119] Her aim, however, is primarily descriptive. She argues that Stuntz's excuse model provides the best positive account of the privilege, but that it loses its "descriptive force" by failing to appreciate how the excuse rationale maps onto her spectrum.[120] Combining the two, she concludes, "provides the best positive account of how self-incrimination cases are decided."[121]

The categories of memorialized and uttered evidence present the most difficult doctrinal puzzles. This is so because, as Farahany explains, much identifying and automatic evidence will fall on the "physical" side of the physical–testimonial line, and rightly so.[122] The content of memorialized evidence, she argues, will fall outside the scope of the privilege when it was created voluntarily by suspects and not compelled.[123] Analogizing to document cases, Farahany contends, provocatively, that this will also apply to the defendant's memories. In other words, the act of producing memories (e.g., consciously recalling them, uttering them, or writing them down)—but not the *content* of a suspect's memories—will be protected when the government did not compel her to create the memories.[124] Thus, neuroscientific tests that could "extract" memories would fall outside the scope of the privilege and the government could, consistent with the Fifth Amendment, compel suspects to sit for such tests. She explains:

memories are just like commercial papers and other memorialized documentation that the individual created in tangible form. They are stored and recorded evidence of conscious awareness, experience, and inward reflection. This analysis envisions memories as analogous to tangible records that

[118] *Id.*

[119] Farahany, *supra* note 78, at 366.

[120] *Id.* at 365.

[121] *Id.* at 366.

[122] *Id.* at 368–79. Examples in these categories would include physical characteristics, blood type, and voice and handwriting exemplars (identifying) and blinking, heart rate, and sweating (automatic). *Id.* Farahany includes "name" in the category of identifying evidence, *id.* at 368, but revealing one's name could be "testimonial" under certain circumstances, as could disclosing other identifying information (e.g., a birthday). For a discussion, see Pardo, *supra* note 3.

[123] Farahany, *supra* note 78, at 388.

[124] *Id.*

are stored in the brain and can be retrieved without evoking the conscious awareness, expression, or contemplative cooperation of a defendant.
An excuse model of the privilege predicts that the substantive content of
memories falls beyond the scope of the privilege.[125]

Turning to utterances, Farahany draws a distinction between voluntary utterances and "evoked" utterances.[126] Under her analysis, the privilege applies to the latter but not to the former.[127] Utterances—which
include verbal and written acts, things suspects say silently to themselves,
and something she calls "brain utterances"—are evoked when the government causes the person to engage in the utterance (e.g., by asking
questions or presenting the person with images).[128] In other words, a
defendant may remain silent and the government may not make evidentiary use of the defendant's evoked utterances. This may include the
act of *producing* memories, but not the *content* of the memories, because
"[a]ccessing a memory is akin to rifling through a filing cabinet to find
the relevant file."[129]

Farahany's model is both under- and over-inclusive of the privilege's
scope. Before turning to these aspects of the analysis, however, we note
first that the "excuse" theory on which she relies fails by itself to explain
the privilege's scope. As Ronald Allen and Kristen Mace have argued, the
"excuse" theory (like other theories that rely on whether a defendant has
a choice to provide falsified evidence) cannot explain current doctrinal
results on a variety of issues, including handwriting and voice exemplars,
subpoenas to disclose voluntarily created documents, and the hypothetical of a compelled lie-detector test.[130]

On the one hand, Farahany's conclusions regarding memorialized
evidence are under-inclusive. For the reasons explained above, the contents of memories constitute testimonial evidence. Farahany, however,

---

[125] *Id.* at 388.

[126] *Id.* at 389–94.

[127] *Id.*

[128] *Id.* at 390 ("If a [defendant is] compelled to recall his memories of the crime, the
[defendant] will admit to the existence, context, substantive content, temporal encoding
of, and whereabouts of those memories in his brain."). The notion of a "brain utterance"
(which is distinguished in the article from "conscious recall," see *id.* at 407) appears to be an
example of the mereological fallacy; *see* M.R. BENNETT & P.M.S. HACKER, PHILOSOPHICAL
FOUNDATIONS OF NEUROSCIENCE 233–35 (2003), which we discuss in Chapter One.

[129] *Id.* at 391.

[130] Allen & Mace, *supra* note 74, at 266 ("Polygraph tests, exemplars, and document subpoenas all create problems for the current theories of the Fifth Amendment. Privacy- and
choice-based theories fail to properly predict the outcome of cases.").

concludes they are not compelled because they are like voluntarily created documents or photographs. We resist this analogy. Memories are not like photographs or pictures that exist in the brain and that can be extracted like files in a computer or filing cabinet.[131] The content and the production of memories cannot be so easily separated. In compelling a defendant to reveal his memories, the government is forcing the defendant to manifest his retained beliefs or knowledge.[132] The government, in other words, is forcing the defendant to serve as an epistemic authority for his own conviction. This is unlike previously created documents or utterances in which the defendant has already voluntarily expressed his beliefs or knowledge. The privilege applies to the compelled, incriminating content of a defendant's propositional attitudes, including her memories, regardless of how they are obtained. To appreciate the difference between this rule and the one that Farahany proposes, consider the following hypothetical example. Suppose forced hypnosis could compel defendants to reveal what they believe to be true.[133] Under Farahany's

---

[131] *See* Martin A. Conway, *Ten Things the Law and Others Should Know about Human Memory*, *in* MEMORY AND LAW 368 (Lynn Nadel & Walter Sinnott-Armstrong eds., 2012) (explaining that remembering is a constructive process and that memories are not similar to the products of recording media); Daniel J. Simons & Christopher F. Chabris, *What People Believe about How Memory Works: A Representative Survey of the U.S. Population*, 6 PLoS ONE 5 (2011) (noting that a majority of those surveyed believed that memory works like a recording and that this belief "contradicts the well-established idea that memory is a constructive process.").

[132] The two interesting studies that Farahany cites in this portion of her article support rather than contradict our analysis. Martin J. Chadwick et al., *Decoding Individual Episodic Memory Traces in the Human Hippocampus*, 20 CURRENT BIOLOGY 544 (2010); Jesse Rissman, Henry T. Greely & Anthony D. Wagner, *Detecting Individual Memories through the Neural Decoding of Memory States and Past Experience*, 107 PNAS 9849 (2012). (We also discuss these studies in Chapter Four.) In Chadwick et al., researchers predicted which of three scenarios a subject was recalling about half the time, after the subjects had practiced recalling each episode and were scanned while recalling each episode several times. In Rissman et al., researchers tested subjects on whether faces they were seeing were novel or ones they were shown previously; the findings supported some correlation between activity and the *subjective* experience of remembering (i.e., whether the person thought the face was seen previously or not) but not whether the face was actually seen previously or not (i.e., whether a subjective experience of memory was false or whether the person had seen the face even if they did not recall doing so). In other words, neither study supports anything like the notion that memories are previously created documents or records extracted from the subject's brain by a third party. Rather, both provide some modest support for the idea that neural activity may be used to predict the *epistemic states the subject is likely to endorse* and not necessarily epistemic states that are likely to be true or reliable. This is similar to the distinction in the context of lie detection of whether a person *believes* a proposition is true or false (not whether it actually is true or false).

[133] This is a contestable proposition given current understanding about hypnosis, but its feasibility is not necessary for our argument. On the neuroscience of hypnosis, see David A. Oakley & Peter W. Halligan, *Hypnotic Suggestion and Cognitive Neuroscience*, 13 TRENDS IN COG. NEUROSCIENCE 264 (2009).

rule, the government could, consistent with the Fifth Amendment, compel every criminal defendant to undergo hypnosis and reveal his or her memories on the witness stand in court. The privilege would not apply to what he or she had to say. Under this scenario, we have eliminated the act-of-production dangers that place the production of memories within the scope of the privilege (according to the excuse theory and Farahany's analysis); all that is left are the incriminating memories. Farahany may bite the bullet here and conclude that the government could forcibly hypnotize all criminal defendants and make them testify, but we think, to the contrary, that the example provides a reductio ad absurdum for this descriptive picture of the privilege against self-incrimination. Our analysis implies that this forced testimony would fall within the scope of the privilege.

On the other hand, Farahany's conclusions regarding evoked utterances are over-inclusive. Not all evoked utterances fall within the scope of the privilege. Sometimes evoked utterances produce evidence that is "non-testimonial" for purposes of the privilege. Examples include the two Alex hypotheticals above as well as the sixth-birthday question in *Muniz*.[134] Although the government would be evoking utterances for use in a criminal prosecution, the government is not relying on the incriminating content of the defendant's mental states; rather, the incriminating evidence is about general cognitive abilities of the defendant, which doctrinally places it on the "non-testimonial" side along with such examples as voice and handwriting samples and other physical characteristics.[135]

Our final scholarly example takes us back to our general discussion of neuroscientific evidence and the philosophy of mind.[136] Susan Easton criticizes the doctrinal distinction between testimonial and physical evidence on metaphysical grounds. She argues that the distinction follows from a problematic conception of the mind, in particular, a now-defunct version of Cartesian dualism.[137] According to this dualism, she contends, some evidence exists in a spiritual realm of the mind (testimony) and some in the material body (real or physical evidence).[138] She argues that there is "no fundamental difference" between relying on a defendant's words and, for example, relying on

---

[134] See supra note 103.
[135] See supra notes 87–92 and accompanying text.
[136] See Chapter Two.
[137] SUSAN EASTON, THE CASE FOR THE RIGHT TO SILENCE (2d ed. 1998).
[138] Id. at 217.

his blood.[139] To suppose otherwise, she continues, is to fail to grasp that knowledge may be conveyed or "communicated" in many different ways. Similar to Farahany, Easton also posits a continuum of evidence. Easton's continuum includes (1) oral communications; (2) body language intended to communicate (e.g., head nods and pointing); (3) nonverbal communications without an intent to communicate (e.g., reactions that show fear and nervousness); (4) external bodily markings (e.g., scars and tattoos); and (5) bodily samples.[140] She sees no principled reason to draw a distinction along this continuum and, thus, concludes that "the [testimonial-physical] distinction...is artificial and problematic, because both samples and speech are subject to similar considerations and arguments."[141]

This argument resembles (on a doctrinal level) the general arguments about the mind that we considered in Chapter Two. In particular, there is a mistaken presupposition that rejecting the reductionism being offered must go hand in hand with embracing Cartesian dualism. Moreover, because Cartesian dualism is not considered plausible, so the argument goes, anything seen as a consequence of it must also be rejected (and by implication the alternative embraced). As with the general arguments about mind, however, a rejection of the reductive picture does not lead to substance dualism. In this context, Easton's reductive argument seeks to eliminate a principled distinction between testimonial and physical evidence. We resist this reduction, however, because the distinction does not depend on substance dualism. One does not have to presuppose dualism to acknowledge an *epistemic* difference between a defendant's words and his blood.[142] With the defendant's words (and other "testimonial" evidence), the government is relying on the epistemic authority of the defendant; with blood (and other physical evidence), the government is relying on either the perceptions of fact finders to observe the evidence or on the epistemic authority of another person (for example, an expert). The government's proof may

---

[139] *Id.*

[140] *Id.* at 217–18.

[141] *Id.* at 220.

[142] In terms of Easton's continuum (*see supra* note 140 and accompanying text) the line we are drawing is between, on the one hand, oral communications and body language intended to communicate (for example, head nods and pointing) and, on the other hand, nonverbal communications without an intent to communicate (e.g., reactions showing fear and nervousness), external bodily markings (e.g., scars and tattoos) and bodily samples. For a similar line drawing in the context of freedom of speech, see Charles W. Collier, *Speech and Communication in Law and Philosophy*, 12 LEGAL THEORY 1 (2006).

depend on these different epistemic pathways, and the privilege prevents the government from compelling the incriminating content of a
defendant's beliefs and knowledge to function as an epistemic source
against him at trial.[143] An epistemic distinction on these grounds does
not commit one to a Cartesian picture of the relationship between
mind and body. Neuro-reductionists, Cartesians, and Aristotelians alike
can all embrace the distinction.

III. Due Process

In addition to the Fourth and Fifth Amendments, substantive and procedural due process place some restraints on government evidence
gathering.[144] Neither of these doctrines, however, would prevent the
compelled use of reliable neuroscientific evidence under many circumstances. The reason for this is primarily historical. In developing constitutional criminal-procedure doctrine, the Supreme Court
turned to the specific provisions in the Bill of Rights (namely, the
Fourth Amendment and the Fifth Amendment's Self-Incrimination
Clause) as the source for doctrinal rules rather than more general and
open-ended provisions such as the Due Process and Equal Protection
Clauses.[145] Consequently, the rules developed provide complex matri-
ces of rules for the Fourth Amendment and the privilege against
self-incrimination, with due process serving a less prominent role as a
backdrop for generally problematic government conduct that for whatever reason otherwise does not run afoul of the Fourth Amendment or
self-incrimination doctrine.

First, as a matter of substantive due process, government conduct
that does not constitute a violation under the Fourth Amendment
or the Self-Incrimination Clause may still constitute a constitutional

---

[143] For further development of this argument, see Michael S. Pardo, *Self-Incrimination
and the Epistemology of Testimony*, 30 CARDOZO L. REV. 1023 (2008). The argument draws
on a distinction explicated by Sanford C. Goldberg, *Reductionism and the Distinctiveness of
Testimonial Knowledge, in* THE EPISTEMOLOGY OF TESTIMONY 127 (Jennifer Lackey & Ernest
Sosa eds., 2006).

[144] *See* Chavez v. Martinez, 538 U.S. 760 (2003) (substantive); District Attorney's Office
v. Osborne, 557 U.S. 52 (2006) (procedural).

[145] For an illuminating and critical discussion of this history, and a powerful argument
that the Supreme Court chose the wrong path in opting for the specific provisions over the
general ones, see WILLIAM J. STUNTZ, THE COLLAPSE OF AMERICAN CRIMINAL JUSTICE (2011).

violation if it is so outrageous that it "shocks the conscience."[146] For example, the Court explained that this standard might be met when a police officer allegedly denied medical treatment in an ambulance to a suspect, who had been shot, as an attempt to extract a confession.[147] For the reasons explained above, however, neuroscientific testing would not meet this standard so long as it is performed in a manner that is relatively safe and painless. Compelled blood tests do not violate the standard,[148] and neuroscientific testing would generally be safer and less painful. However, the "shocks the conscience" standard would be met in particular circumstances where testing would be dangerous or extremely painful—for example, compelled fMRI lie detection when a defendant has metal in his body.[149]

Finally, compelled neuroscientific tests the government uses as evidence could raise procedural due process considerations if they are unreliable for the purposes for which they are used. Procedural due process, for example, provides some support for excluding involuntary confessions because of their unreliability.[150] If neuroscientific tests reach a sufficient level of evidentiary reliability, however, then this supplementary constitutional protection would be unavailable as well (and indeed defendants may at some point have a right to present such evidence).[151]

---

[146] Chavez v. Martinez, 538 U.S. 760 (2003).

[147] Id. at 763–64, 779.

[148] Schmerber v. California, 384 U.S. 757 (1966). See also Rochin v. California, 342 U.S. 165 (1952) (forced stomach pumping at hospital did not "shock the conscience").

[149] The possibility of compelled testing during discovery in civil cases poses additional challenges (see FED. R. CIV. P. 35), as does the issue of whether the Constitution would place any restrictions on the use of such tests for government purposes outside of criminal prosecutions, such as intelligence gathering or other military purposes. See Sean Kevin Thompson, Note, The Legality of the Use of Psychiatric Neuroimaging in Intelligence Gathering, 90 CORNELL L. REV. 1601 (2005). The use of reliable testing may have some beneficial effects in noncriminal information-gathering contexts: their reliability would lead to better information, they may lead to quicker determinations of who does and does not have information (hence perhaps shortening the detention of innocent suspects who have answered honestly), and the fact that the tests are safe and painless may lessen the need to employ more cruel (possibly abusive, and less reliable) interrogation techniques.

[150] See Mark A. Godsey, Rethinking the Involuntary Confession Rule: Toward a Workable Test for Identifying Compelled Self-Incrimination, 93 CAL. L. REV. 465, 485–99 (2005).

[151] If the tests reached a sufficient level of reliability, defendants may have a constitutional right to be able to present such evidence, regardless of the jurisdiction's evidentiary rules. See United States v. Scheffer, 523 U.S. 303, 314 n.9 (1998) (discussing a defendant's constitutional right to present a defense but concluding that a rule categorically excluding polygraph evidence did not violate this constitutional right because of the technique's questionable

To conclude our survey of the constitutional provisions that may prevent or limit government evidence gathering for criminal prosecutions, we join those who have suggested that specific statutory limitations and guidelines, depending on the details, may be superior to reliance on a patchwork of constitutional doctrine to regulate the use of neuroscience in criminal proceedings.[152] Anything short of this is likely to be ad hoc.

reliability); *see also* District Attorney's Office v. Osborne, 557 U.S. 52 (2006) (discussing defendant's access to reliable evidence at trial and post-conviction).

[152] *See* Henry T. Greely & Judy Illes, *Neuroscience-Based Lie Detection: The Urgent Need for Regulation,* 33 AM. J.L. & MED. 377 (2007). Outside of the criminal context, the Employee Polygraph Protection Act of 1988, 29 U.S.C. §§ 2001–2009, likely limits the use of fMRI lie detection, or should be extended to do so. A number of different statutes regulate aspects of evidence gathering by the government (e.g., wiretaps and electronic communications). For an excellent overview, see Erin Murphy, *The Politics of Privacy in the Criminal Justice System: Information Disclosure, The Fourth Amendment, and Statutory Law Enforcement Exemptions,* 111 MICH. L. REV. 485 (2013).

7

Theories of Criminal Punishment

Theories of criminal punishment provide accounts that purport to legitimate and justify criminal punishment. The theoretical project takes as its impetus that criminal punishment is a form of state-sponsored violence; under the auspices of criminal punishment, states inflict pain and suffering on citizens—depriving them of life, liberty, or property to which they would otherwise be entitled—for their transgressions of the criminal law. What would make such coercive actions by the state legitimate? When is the exercise of this power justified? Finally, how much punishment is justified in particular circumstances? Much ink has been spilled trying to answer these difficult questions. Although a variety of different theories and approaches have been proposed throughout the ages, modern criminal-law theory centers around two groups of punishment theories.[1] Broadly construed, theories in the first group purport to justify punishment on "consequentialist" grounds. Despite important differences among them, theories in this group rely on the beneficial social consequences that are claimed to flow from criminal punishment (primarily, reduced future crime) because of its deterrent, incapacitating, or

---

[1] In an insightful and clarifying recent article, Mitchell Berman observes that despite the

rich diversity of justificatory theories, including deterrence (Bentham and Beccaria), reform (Plato), retribution (Kant), annulment (Hegel), and denunciation (Durkheim), a striking feature of twentieth century punishment theory...has been the steady and generally successful pressure to fold this seeming multiplicity of justifications into a simple dichotomy of justifications that at least appears to mirror the fundamental organizing distinction in moral theory between consequentialism and deontology.

Mitchell Berman, *Two Kinds of Retributivism*, in THE PHILOSOPHICAL FOUNDATIONS OF THE CRIMINAL LAW (R.A. Duff & Stuart P. Green eds., 2011). On political legitimacy generally, see Fabienne Peter, *Political Legitimacy*, in STANFORD ENCYCLOPEDIA OF PHILOSOPHY (2010), *available at* http://plato.stanford.edu/entries/legitimacy/.

rehabilitating effects.[2] Broadly construed, theories in the second group purport to justify punishment on "retributivist" grounds. Theories in this group, despite important differences among them, rely on the notion that criminal offenders somehow *deserve* punishment proportionate to their transgressions of the criminal law.[3]

Although debates rage on within each side and across the consequentialist–retributivist divide, most theorists acknowledge some role for both types of considerations. The U.S. Supreme Court has also explained that, as a matter of constitutional law, the federal and state governments may rely on multiple justifications for punishment.[4] Empirical work suggests that subjects support both rationales for punishment (although particular punishment decisions may be more consistent with retributivist rationales).[5] We do not wish to take sides or offer new arguments in favor of retributivist or consequentialist theories of criminal punishment. Rather, we examine the relationship between neuroscience and this theoretical project, focusing in particular on arguments and inferences regarding criminal punishment drawn from current neuroscientific data.

Our discussion focuses on two separate challenges to retributivist theories of punishment. The first challenge, advanced by Joshua Greene, relies on data about the brains of those making punishment decisions. The second challenge, advanced by Greene and Jonathan

[2] The classic deterrence-based accounts are CESARE BECCARIA, ON CRIMES AND PUNISHMENTS (1764) and JEREMY BENTHAM, AN INTRODUCTION TO THE PRINCIPLES OF MORALS AND LEGISLATION (1789). For an overview of more recent consequentialist rationales, see Anthony Duff, *Legal Punishment, in* STANFORD ENCYCLOPEDIA OF PHILOSOPHY (2008), *available at* http://plato.stanford.edu/entries/legal-punishment/.

[3] The classic retributive account is Kant's. *See* IMMANUEL KANT, THE METAPHYSICS OF MORALS (Mary J. Gregor trans., 1996). *See also* Berman, *supra* note 1, at 6 (referring to the "desert claim" as the "core retributivist contention" that "punishment is justified by the offender's ill-desert."). For overviews, see Duff, *supra* note 2; David Wood, *Punishment: Nonc onsequentialism,* 5 PHILOSOPHY COMPASS 470 (2010).

[4] *See* Harmelin v. Michigan, 501 U.S. 957, 1001 (1991) (Kennedy, J., concurring) ("the Eighth Amendment does not mandate adoption of any one penological theory...The federal and state criminal systems have accorded different weights at different times to penological goals of retribution, deterrence, incapacitation, and rehabilitation."). *See also* Ewing v. California, 538 U.S. 11 (2003).

[5] *See, e.g.,* Kevin M. Carlsmith, John M. Darley & Paul H. Robinson, *Why Do We Punish? Deterrence and Just Deserts as Motives for Punishment,* 83 J. PERSONALITY & SOC. PSYCHOL. 284, 294 (2002) (noting that "[w]hen asked about just deserts and deterrence, participants generally supported both perspectives" and "[p]eople seemed to support these two philosophies and generally to have a positive attitude toward both").

Cohen, focuses on the brains of criminals and takes us back to their discussion of neuroscience, free will, and moral responsibility.[6]

According to the first challenge, "retributive" punishment decisions are correlated with brain activity associated with more "emotional" rather than "cognitive" processes, and this therefore undermines their status as justified, legitimate, or correct.[7] The structure of this argument is similar to the arguments made regarding moral and economic decision making that we critique in Chapter Three[8]: namely, one theoretical "type" of decision is correlated with a "type" of brain activity or process and is thus impugned because of that correlation.[9] In each of these three contexts (morality, economics, and criminal punishment), nonutilitarian judgments are impugned because of their correlations with "emotional" brain activity.[10] Although there are important differences between the criminal-punishment context and the moral and economic contexts—differences we explore below—the argument in the punishment context fails for similar reasons. The success or failure of retributivism does not depend on the success or failure of any particular moral theories, and thus *even if* neuroscience undermined deontological moral theories it would not necessarily also undermine retributivism. Moreover, retributivism does not depend on which areas of the brain are associated with punishment decisions. Brain activity does not provide criteria for whether punishment decisions are correct or just, nor does the fact that retributivist decisions are associated with "emotional" decision making provide evidence that the decisions are incorrect, illegitimate, or unjust.

---

[6] We discuss their reductionist picture of the mind in Chapter Two. In this chapter, we assess the specific conclusions about criminal punishment that they draw from this picture.

[7] *See* Joshua D. Greene, *The Secret Joke of Kant's Soul, in* 3 MORAL PSYCHOLOGY: THE NEUROSCIENCE OF MORALITY: EMOTION, DISEASE, AND DEVELOPMENT 50–55 (Walter Sinnott-Armstrong ed., 2008).

[8] *See* Sections II and IV in Chapter Three.

[9] *See, e.g.,* Joshua D. Greene et al., *The Neural Bases of Cognitive Conflict and Control in Moral Judgment,* 44 NEURON 389 (2004); Joshua D. Greene et al., *An fMRI Investigation of Emotional Engagement in Moral Judgment,* 293 SCI. 2105 (2001); Alan Sanfey et al., *The Neural Basis of Economic Decision-Making in the Ultimatum Game,* 300 SCI. 1755 (2003). For critiques of attempts to draw normative conclusions from such studies, see Richard Dean, *Does Neuroscience Undermine Deontological Theory?,* 3 NEUROETHICS 43 (2010); Michael S. Pardo & Dennis Patterson, *Philosophical Foundations of Law and Neuroscience,* 2010 U. ILL. L. REV. 1211 (2010); Selim Berker, *The Normative Insignificance of Neuroscience,* 37 PHIL. & PUBLIC AFFAIRS 293 (2009); F.M. Kamm, *Neuroscience and Moral Reasoning: A Note on Recent Research,* 37 PHIL. & PUBLIC AFFAIRS 330 (2009).

[10] *See supra* note 8.

According to the second challenge, neuroscientific data will under-mine retributivist intuitions *indirectly* by undermining *directly* the "free will" intuitions, on which, they claim, retributivist theories depend.[11] This argument requires some unpacking before we can evaluate its underlying assumptions. Before we explore the details of this argu-ment, however, it is important to understand more generally how the argument relates to the doctrinal and procedural issues in crimi-nal law that we explore in Chapters Five and Six. The criminal law presupposes "folk psychological" explanations of human action, and neuroscientific data may provide inductive empirical evidence that is relevant for deciding issues within that conceptual framework.[12] We do not take issue with that possibility as a general matter. As we discuss in Chapters Four, Five, and Six, scholars have advanced a variety of dif-ferent proposals suggesting ways in which neuroscience may provide evidence for deciding issues within this conceptual framework. These issues include: *actus reus*, *mens rea*, insanity, competence, voluntariness, lie detection, and several others. We argue, however, that the inferences and conclusions drawn from neuroscientific data on these issues must not run afoul of the contours of the conceptual framework underlying current doctrine in order to contribute meaningfully to these issues.[13]

At the theoretical level of criminal punishment, however, neurosci-ence may offer a deeper and more radical challenge to the entire doc-trinal framework of the criminal law by undermining the conceptual assumptions on which it is based and, with it, theories of punishment that depend on these assumptions. This is the nature of the second challenge to retributivism. The challenge concedes that the current doctrinal edifice of the criminal law remains largely unshaken by neu-roscience. Instead, Greene and Cohen argue that important aspects of the doctrinal edifice depend upon a retributivist foundation—which in turn rests upon a nondeterministic, free-will foundation—and thus, so the argument goes, if neuroscience can bring down the nonde-terministic, free-will foundation, it will also undermine retributivism

---

[11] Joshua Greene & Jonathan Cohen, *For Law, Neuroscience Changes Nothing and Everything*, in LAW & THE BRAIN (Semir Zeki & Oliver Goodenough eds., 2006).

[12] *See* Stephen J. Morse, *Criminal Responsibility and the Disappearing Person*, 28 CARDOZO L. REV. 2545, 2253–54 (2007) ("The law's view of the person is thus the so-called 'folk psy-chological' model: a conscious (and potentially self-conscious) creature capable of practical reason, an agent who forms and acts on intentions that are the product of the person's desires and beliefs. We are the sort of creatures that can act for and respond to reasons.").

[13] *See* Chapters Four to Six.

and the legal doctrine built upon it. We discuss several problems with this argument, and we argue that if neuroscience has the potential to cause the changes Greene and Cohen predict, it will do so by fostering a number of unwarranted and problematic inferences and therefore ought to be resisted.

We proceed by first discussing theories of criminal punishment in more detail and then evaluate each of the two neuroscientific challenges to retributivism.

I. A Brief Taxonomy of Theories of Criminal Punishment

Theories of criminal punishment are primarily normative accounts that purport to answer the question of when the state is justified in subjecting citizens (and noncitizens) to criminal punishment, and derivatively, how much punishment is justified when punishment in general is warranted.[14] In addition to this normative project, theories of punishment may also be directed at answering explanatory questions as to why the state would engage in acts of criminal punishment—whether it is justified or not—and why it would choose particular forms and amounts of punishment.[15] There is also a distinct conceptual project of delineating the scope of what constitutes punishment.[16]

One dominant strategy for answering such questions focuses on the future consequences of punishment. Under this "forward looking" strategy, the perceived beneficial consequences include deterring others not punished from committing similar acts in the future, and preventing (or reducing the likelihood) that those punished will commit future crimes by rehabilitating, incapacitating, or deterring them specifically. Under this consequentialist strategy, punishment is not an end in itself but serves an instrumental value in bringing about the social good of reducing future crime; punishment may be justified to the extent the positive social benefits it brings about exceed the harms it causes.[17] Moreover, specifics about whom should be punished, how, and how much, may be justified under this strategy based on whatever

---

[14] *See* Duff, *supra* note 2; Berman, *supra* note 1.

[15] *See* John Bronsteen, *Retribution's Role*, 84 IND. L.J. 1129 (2009).

[16] *See* H.L.A. HART, PUNISHMENT AND RESPONSIBILITY (2d ed. 2008).

[17] *See* Berman, *supra* note 1.

would bring about the socially optimal or desirable level of benefits to costs. In addition to these normative issues, a consequentialist account may also explain why the state would choose to exercise its right to punish (assuming it is justified in doing so) and would undergo the expenses of doing so (including expenses to those punished and citizens generally).[18]

The second dominant strategy for answering such questions focuses on the acts (together with the mental states and surrounding circumstances) of those subjected to criminal punishment. Under this "backward looking" strategy, actions by those who violate the dictates of the criminal law are such that the actor may deserve punishment and ought to be punished (and, conversely, those who do not violate the criminal law do not deserve punishment and should not be punished), regardless of whether any future beneficial consequences will follow.[19] Under this strategy, it is the fact that the guilty defendant deserves criminal punishment that justifies the state's actions.[20] Retributivists may cash out exactly how desert justifies punishment in a variety of ways. For instance, punishment of those who deserve it may have some innate, intrinsic worth.[21] The desert aspect may also serve a particular type of instrumental value that justifies punishment—for example, it may serve to "cancel out," denounce the criminal acts, or express the community's disapproval of the various acts.[22] Under a more "pure" form of retributivism, the desert aspect may justify punishment regardless of whether punishment itself has any intrinsic worth or serves any other intrinsic value.[23] Turning to the specifics of punishment, the retributivist strategy purports to justify who should be punished, how, and how much by appealing to whether the person is in fact guilty and, if so, the amount of punishment that is proportional to his culpability or ill-desert.[24] In addition to these normative issues, a retributivist account may also explain why the state chooses to punish

[18]   *See* Bronsteen, *supra* note 15.

[19]   *See* Berman, *supra* note 1.

[20]   *Id.*

[21]   *See* MICHAEL MOORE, PLACING BLAME: A GENERAL THEORY OF THE CRIMINAL LAW (1997).

[22]   Berman refers to justifications that depend on intrinsic worth or these other goals as "instrumental retributivism." *See supra* note 1, at 9.

[23]   *Id.* at 16–19.

[24]   Under retributivist theories, "proportionality" may be cashed out in various ways. *See* Alice Ristroph, *Proportionality as a Principle of Limited Government*, 55 DUKE L.J. 263, 279–84 (2005).

and chooses to do so in the ways that it does. Under this explanatory account, such punishment tracks the intuitions of citizens about what is just and may also reduce acts of vengeance and reciprocal violence.[25]

The initial distinction between these two strategies raises a number of further issues. First, the considerations at issue under each strategy may play a variety of theoretical roles. They may each be taken to provide one consideration in whether punishment is justified in a particular context.[26] Under such a view, the criteria of any particular strategy may be neither necessary nor sufficient to justify punishment. Or each strategy may be taken to provide a *necessary* condition for justifying punishment.[27] Or each may be taken to provide a *sufficient* condition for justifying punishment.[28] Second, the strategies may also combine and interact in various ways. For example, each may provide a "constraint" on the other that would defeat otherwise legitimate punishment—punishment that would produce good consequences, all things considered, may be illegitimate if it punishes someone more than that person deserves. Punishing someone as much as he or she deserves may be illegitimate if it would otherwise lead to terrible social consequences.[29] Finally, although the two strategies lend themselves to the familiar distinction in moral theory between utilitarian and deontological theories, they are conceptually distinct.[30] One may believe that deontological considerations ground moral theory or make particular moral judgments right or wrong (true or false)[31] and also think

[25] *See* Paul H. Robinson & John M. Darley, *Intuitions of Justice: Implication for Criminal Law and Justice Policy*, 81 S. CAL. L. REV. 1 (2007).

[26] Under this view, the strategies are consistent with each other.

[27] For example, satisfying the criterion of desert may be required to justify punishment, but it alone may not be sufficient.

[28] For example, deterrence may provide a sufficient condition for punishment under some conceptions, but it may not be necessary.

[29] Under such conceptions, each strategy may provide "defeasible" conditions for justifying punishment. For example, desert might be taken to justify punishment unless it can be shown that the punishment will lead to more crime. For further details on different possible ways to conceptualize retributivism, see Berman, *supra* note 1; LARRY ALEXANDER & KIMBERLY KESSLER FERZAN (with Stephen Morse), CRIME AND CULPABILITY: A THEORY OF CRIMINAL LAW (2009) (distinguishing "mild," "moderate," and "strong retibutivism"); Kenneth W. Simons, *Retributivism Refined—or Run Amok?*, 77 U. CHI. L. REV. 551 (2010) (book review essay); Michael T. Cahill, *Punishment Pluralism, in* RETRIBUTIVISM: ESSAYS ON THEORY AND POLICY (Mark D. White ed., 2011).

[30] Larry Alexander & Michael Moore, *Deontological Ethics, in* STANFORD ENCYCLOPEDIA OF PHILOSOPHY (2007), *available at* http://plato.stanford.edu/entries/ethics-deontological/; Berman, *supra* note 1, at 4–5.

[31] This point holds regardless of whether moral truths are understood in realist or antirealist terms.

(consistently) that the state is not justified in punishing for retributivist reasons.[32] Similarly, one may believe that utilitarian considerations ground moral theory or particular moral judgments and also think (consistently) that the state is justified in engaging in criminal punishment for retributivist reasons.[33]

As our language is meant to suggest, we do not intend to take sides in these debates or to argue that any particular theories in these categories succeed or fail on their own terms. Our aim in this brief section has been simply to explicate the theoretical issues sufficiently in order to properly assess claims about how neuroscience informs the theoretical issues. We now turn to these claims.

II. The First Challenge: Brains and Punishment Decisions

The relationship between the psychology of punishment decisions and the normative project of justifying punishment is a complicated one. Understanding how or why punishment decisions are made does not necessarily tell us how such decisions ought to be made or whether they are justified. A further argument is needed about *how* empirical information is supposed to bear on the normative, theoretical questions. On the one hand, the empirical evidence might be thought to provide positive support for particular punishment decisions or general theories—or at least constrain possibilities—by illustrating the way most people would decide to punish or what most people would judge to be fair or just regarding punishment decisions.[34] Such

---

[32] *See* Alexander & Moore, *supra* note 30 ("Retributivism has two aspects: (1) it requires that the innocent not be punished, and (2) it requires that the guilty be punished. One could be a deontologist generally and yet deny that morality has either of these requirements.").

[33] This may be one normative implication of Paul Robinson's work on "empirical desert." *See* Paul H. Robinson, *Empirical Desert, in* CRIMINAL LAW CONVERSATIONS (Paul Robinson, Stephen Garvey & Kimberly Ferzan eds., 2009). *See also* Alexander & Moore, *supra* note 30 ("a retributivist might alternatively cast these two states of affairs (the guilty getting punished and the innocent not getting punished) as two intrinsic goods, to be traded off both against each other (as in burden of proof allocation) and against other values. Some retributivists urge the latter as a kind of explicitly 'consequentialist retributivism.'"). For a recent defense of a type of consequentialist retributivism, see Dan Markel, *What Might Retributive Justice Be? An Argument for the Confrontational Conception of Retributivism, in* RETRIBUTIVISM: ESSAYS ON THEORY AND POLICY, *supra* note 29.

[34] *See* Robinson, *supra* note 33.

a project might appeal to actual, hypothetical, or idealized punishment situations or conditions. On the other hand, the empirical evidence might be thought to undermine particular decisions or general theories if the evidence shows that the decisions made (or implied by a general theory) are produced by an "unreliable" or otherwise defective process.[35]

The relationship between neuroscience and the normative questions regarding criminal punishment is more complicated still. The theoretical move from neurological processes to normative conclusions about criminal punishment requires an argument not only from what people are doing when they decide to punish to whether they are justified in doing so but also an argument from what their brains are doing, to what they are doing, to whether what they are doing is justified. One way to bridge these conceptual gaps is the one proposed by Joshua Greene and colleagues with regard to moral decision making. Under this framework, decisions are made through one of two psychological processes: a "cognitive" one and an "emotional" one.[36] Each of these processes is associated with different patterns of brain activity or areas in the brain; fMRI data are used to determine which brains areas appear to be more active during particular decisions and, based on this data, inferences are drawn about which psychological process was used to make the decision.[37] An

---

[35] Selim Berker suggests that the "best-case scenario" for undermining certain moral intuitions based on neuroscience would be to show that brain areas correlated with the intuitions are also correlated with "obvious, egregious error[s] in mathematical or logical reasoning," but he concludes that even this claim depends on further assumptions and philosophical argument. *See* Berker, *supra* note 9, at 329.

[36] Greene, *supra* note 7, at 40. The "cognitive" process involves (1) "inherently neutral representations, ones that do not automatically trigger particular behavioral responses or dispositions"; is (2) "important for reasoning, planning, manipulating information in working memory, impulse control"; and is (3) "associated with…the dorsolateral surfaces of the prefrontal cortex and parietal lobes." *Id.* By contrast, the "emotional" process (1) triggers automatic responses and dispositions, or are "behaviorally valenced"; (2) is "quick and automatic"; and (3) is "associated with…the amygdala and the medial surfaces of the frontal and parietal lobes." *Id.* at 40–41.

[37] The data are generated from a number of experiments in which subjects were presented with a series of vignettes involving moral dilemmas (e.g., variations on the "trolley problem") and in which the "consequential" and "deontological" answers appear to diverge. *See supra* note 9. Subjects had their brains scanned while deciding the cases, and the answers to the vignettes were compared with the brain activity of subjects. Greene et al. made two predictions, which were to a large extent borne out by the data: (1) "consequentialist" judgments would be correlated with "cognitive" brain activity and "deontological" judgments would be correlated with "emotional" brain activity, and (2) "consequentialist" judgments would on average take longer to make than "deontological" ones. Our analysis does not take issue with either of these conclusions; we grant them for the sake of our arguments. But for discussion of some potential methodological and empirical issues raised by the studies, see Berker, *supra* note 9; John Mikhail, *Moral Cognition and Computational Theory, in* 3 MORAL

additional argument is then needed to move from the implicated psychological process to normative conclusions about criminal punishment.[38]

As with psychological evidence, neuroscientific evidence regarding
punishment decisions may be used to bolster or to challenge claims or
theories about punishment. Examining a wide swath of both psychological and neuroscientific studies (including his own), Joshua Greene
argues that neuroscience challenges retributivist theories of punishment (and supports consequentialist theories).[39] Greene defines the
two approaches to justifying punishment broadly, with consequential-
ists asserting that punishment is "justified solely by its future beneficial
effects," and retributivists asserting that its "primary justification" is "to
give wrongdoers what they deserve based on what they have done,
regardless of whether such distribution will prevent future wrongdo-
ing."[40] He next examines "the psychology of the criminal punisher,"
and summarizes as follows:

People endorse both consequentialist and retributivist justifications for punishment in the abstract, but in practice, or when faced with more concrete
hypothetical choices, people's motives appear to be emotionally driven.
People punish in proportion to the extent that transgressions make them
angry.[41]

Assuming it is true that people's punishment decisions are "pre-
dominantly emotional," "driven by feelings of anger," proportional
with that feeling, and generally more consistent with retributivism
than consequentalism, what normative conclusions follow from such
facts? As a practical matter, as Paul Robinson has argued, any proposed legal reform would be wise to take account of these facts.[42]
Moreover, punishment decisions that deviated too far from what
most citizens think is fair may face a legitimacy problem. But these
facts by themselves do not yet pose a normative challenge to retributivism per se.

PSYCHOLOGY: THE NEUROSCIENCE OF MORALITY: EMOTION, DISEASE, AND DEVELOPMENT, *supra*
note 7.

[38] Similarly, an additional argument is needed to move from the data and psychological
processes to normative conclusions in morality or economics.

[39] Greene, *supra* note 7.

[40] *Id.* at 50.

[41] *Id.* at 51 ("Several studies speak to this question, and the results are consistent.")

[42] *See* Robinson, *supra* note 33.

The crucial move in the challenge is linking retributivism with deontology. "Deontologists," Greene contends, "argue that the primary justification for punishment is retribution"[43] and that "people's deontological and retributive punitive judgments are primarily emotional."[44] Deontological judgments are produced by the "emotional" psychological process rather than the "cognitive" process, and consequentialist judgments are produced by the cognitive process. The cognitive process is more likely to involve "genuine moral reasoning," as opposed to the "quick," "automatic," and "alarm-like" deontological judgments produced by emotional responses. The supposed normative implications of this empirical information are to undermine deontology as "a rationally coherent moral theory,"[45] an "attempt to reach moral conclusions on the basis of moral reasoning," and "a school of normative moral thought," and as reflecting any "deep, rationally discoverable moral truths."[46] Rather, deontology is portrayed as merely an attempt to rationalize our emotional responses, which are based on, and may have developed evolutionarily because of, nonmoral factors. The same goes for retributivism: "when we feel the pull of retributivist theories of punishment, we are merely gravitating toward our evolved emotional inclinations and not toward some independent moral truth."[47]

This purported neuroscientific challenge to retributivism is based on two conceptual mistakes. The first is to equate retributivism with deontology. To the extent Greene assumes that retributivists about punishment are or must be deontologists about morality—or that retributivism as a theory of punishment necessarily depends on deontology—he is wrong. One may be a retributivist about punishment without being a deontologist about morality, and one may be

---

[43] Greene, *supra* note 7, at 50.

[44] *Id.* at 55.

[45] *Id.* at 72.

[46] *Id.* at 70–72.

[47] *Id.* at 72. Greene provides no arguments that utilitarianism or consequentialist judgments constitute or are the product of "a rationally coherent moral theory" or discover "deep, rationally discoverable moral truths." He does assert that "the only way to reach a distinctively consequentialist judgment…is to actually go through the consequentialist, cost–benefit reasoning using one's 'cognitive' faculties, the ones based in the dorsolateral prefrontal cortex." *Id.* at 65. But the fact that one engages in explicit cost–benefit reasoning does not establish that the reasoning is the product of a coherent moral theory, much less that it discovers "deep" (or even shallow) moral truths. These further conclusions require the very types of philosophical arguments Greene decries when they are offered to support deontology or retributivism.

a deontologist about morality without being a retributivist about criminal punishment.[48] The second mistake is to assume that retributivism entails the view that retributivist principles provide necessary and sufficient conditions for punishment. There are many coherent forms of retributivism that reject this assumption. For example, a retributivist theory may assert that the core retributivist idea of desert (1) provides a defeasible condition for punishment but concede that desert-based principles may be overridden by consequentialist considerations; (2) provides a necessary but not sufficient condition for punishment that would constrain consequentialist punishment decisions; or (3) justifies punishment, but that consequentialist principles do so as well. Because of these two conceptual mistakes, Greene's argument does not go through. The neuroscientific facts to which he points do not undermine retributivism in all its forms.

Even though Greene's argument does not extend to all forms of retributivism, he might perhaps reply that it does provide a plausible challenge to a limited subset of retributivist views. Specifically, his argument may challenge retributivist theories that meet two conditions: (1) the theory depends on a foundation of deontological morality, and (2) the decisions implied by this theory are correlated with neural activity in more "emotional" areas in the brain. But his argument does not effectively undermine even this subset of retributivist views. The argument would succeed only if there were reason to think that punishment decisions implied by this theory were somehow incorrect or unreliable. But this would presuppose some criteria by which we could establish whether particular decisions are correct or whether types of decisions are reliable.[49] Greene provides no such criteria. He attacks deontology (and, by a loose extension, retributivism) for not having access to some "independent [moral] truth," but this is precisely the kind of access he would need to impugn the decisions implied by a retributivist theory. Further, there is no reason to think decisions implied by consequentialist theories of punishment would have better access to an independent moral truth.[50]

---

[48] See the discussion in Section I; Alexander & Moore, *supra* note 30.

[49] Moreover, even if there were some independent criteria by which to measure whether decisions are correct or reliable, it might turn out that engaging in cost–benefit analysis or consequentialist reasoning would lead to more mistakes. These would be open empirical questions that would depend on first having established normative criteria.

[50] See *supra* note 47.

In sum, retributivism does not depend on any particular moral theory, much less on particular brain activity. The success or failure of retributivism does not depend on the success or failure of moral theories and it does not depend on the areas of the brain associated with punishment decisions. Brain activity does not provide criteria for whether punishment decisions are correct or just, nor does the fact that retributivist decisions are associated with emotional decision making provide evidence that the decisions are incorrect or unjust.

III. The Second Challenge: Neuroscience and Intuitions about Punishment

The second challenge focuses on the neural activity of criminals while committing criminal acts, and, indeed, the neural activity underlying all human action. Through this focus, Greene and Cohen argue: "[n]euroscience will challenge and ultimately reshape our intuitive sense(s) of justice" and with it retributivism.[51]

Greene and Cohen begin by outlining familiar[52] philosophical positions regarding free will (or freedom of action) and physical determinism on which their argument relies. "Determinism" is the position that the world in its current state is "completely determined by (1) the laws of physics and (2) past states of the world," and that future states will be likewise so determined.[53] "Free will," as they define it, "requires the ability to do otherwise."[54] "Compatibilism" is the position that determinism, if

---

[51] Greene & Cohen, *supra* note 11, at 208.

[52] Although familiar, these notions and their implications are not always clear.

[53] *Id.* at 210 ("Given a set of prior conditions in the universe and a set of physical laws that completely govern the way the universe evolves, there is only one way that things can actually proceed."). Greene and Cohen acknowledge the existence of a certain amount of indeterminacy or randomness in the universe based on quantum effects, but they point out that this amendment adds little to the debate about how free will can emerge within the physical universe. *Id.* at 211. *See also* Peter van Inwagen, *How to Think about the Problem of Free Will*, 12 ETHICS 327, 330 (2008) ("Determinism is the thesis that the past and the laws of nature together determine, at every moment, a unique future."); David Lewis, *Are We Free to Break the Laws?*, 47 THEORIA 112 (1981).

[54] Greene & Cohen, *supra* note 11, at 210. *See also* van Inwagen, *supra* note 53, at 329 ("The free-will thesis is that we are sometimes in the following position with respect to a contemplated future act: we simultaneously have both the following abilities: the ability to perform the act and the ability to refrain from performing the act (This entails that we *have been* in the following position: for something we did do, we were at some point prior to our doing it able to refrain from doing it, able not to do it.)").

true, is compatible with human free will.[55] "Incompatibilism" is the position that determinism and free will are incompatible and thus both cannot be true. Within incompatibilism, "hard determinism" recognizes the incompatibility and denies free will; by contrast, "libertarianism" recognizes the incompatibility but denies determinism and accepts free will.[56]

The first step in their argument is to link the legitimacy of law with the question of whether it "adequately reflect[s] the moral intuitions and commitments of society."[57] They note that although "current legal doctrine" (including criminal law and sentencing) may be "officially compatibilist," the intuitions on which the doctrine is based are "incompatibilist" and "libertarian."[58] Indeed, they contend that within "modern criminal law" there has been a "long, tense marriage" between "compatibilist legal principles" and "libertarian moral intuitions."[59] Neuroscience will "probably render the marriage unworkable" by undermining the moral intuitions: "if neuroscience can change those intuitions, then neuroscience can change the law."[60]

---

[55] Greene & Cohen, *supra* note 11, at 211. *See also* van Inwagen, *supra* note 53, at 330 ("Compatibilism is the thesis that determinism and the free-will thesis could both be true."). Note that the compatibilist need not take a stand on the empirical question of whether determinism is actually true. Rather, assuming the truth of determinism, the compatibilist is committed to the possibility that some human actions will be consistent with free will. Likewise, an incompatibilist also need not take a stand on the truth of determinism but may instead endorse the conditional position that, if determinism is true, then free will does not exist.

[56] Greene & Cohen, *supra* note 11, at 211–12. Note also that one may reject free will for reasons independent from the issue of determinism. In other words, one could reject hard determinism and also reject free will.

[57] *Id.* at 213.

[58] *Id.* at 208. Given their preference for empirical data over philosophical arguments, it is curious how little empirical support Greene and Cohen provide for the claim that criminal law doctrine is based on libertarian intuitions. They rely on two sources that, for different reasons, raise the possibility that brain damage (one source) or brain development in juveniles (the other source) may be relevant to criminal responsibility. *See id.* at 213–17. As an empirical matter, however, nonlegal actors appear to be "compatibilist" in their moral intuitions about particular cases. *See* Eddy Nahmias et al., *Surveying Freedom: Folk Intuitions About Free Will and Moral Responsibility*, 18 PHIL. PSYCH. 561 (2005). Moreover, legal doctrine in this area does not appear to depend on explicit or tacit libertarian assumptions. *See* Stephen J. Morse, *The Non-Problem of Free Will in Forensic Psychiatry and Psychology*, 25 BEHAV. SCI. & LAW 203 (2007); Peter Westen, *Getting the Fly Out of the Bottle: The False Problem of Free Will and Determinism*, 8 BUFFALO CRIM. L. REV. 599 (2005). If Greene and Cohen are intent on debunking libertarian presuppositions in law, then perhaps a better target would be the doctrine in criminal procedure regarding the voluntariness of confessions and *Miranda* warnings, not criminal responsibility writ large. *See* Ronald J. Allen, Miranda's *Hollow Core*, 100 Nw. U. L. REV. 71 (2006).

[59] Greene & Cohen, *supra* note 11, at 215.

[60] *Id.* at 215, 213.

The tension between legal doctrine and underlying moral intuitions is particularly acute with criminal punishment based upon retributivist principles. Retributivism and the doctrine it supports depend on notions of moral responsibility and "the intuitive idea that we legitimately punish to give people what they deserve based on their past actions."[61] Both "retributivism" and "moral responsibility," they contend, are incompatibilist, libertarian notions that rely on some kind of "magical mental causation"[62] within a "folk psychological system" of explaining human action.[63] The "folk psychological system deals with unseen features of minds: beliefs, desires, intentions, etc."[64] A "crucial, if not the defining feature" of a "mind" and its mental states ("beliefs, desires, intentions, etc.") is "that it is an uncaused causer."[65] They contend that retributivism depends on moral blameworthiness[66] and that moral blameworthiness depends on the "folk psychological system" and its "crucial…defining feature" of minds and mental states as uncaused causers. As Greene and Cohen put it, "folk psychology is the gateway to moral evaluation"[67] and "[s]eeing something as an uncaused causer is a necessary but not sufficient condition for seeing something as a moral agent."[68]

The problem, as they see it, is that "hard determinism is mostly correct," and the "folk psychological system" based on "uncaused causation" is "an illusion."[69] The notions of free will, moral responsibility, blameworthiness, and retributive punishment that depend on the folk psychological system are therefore without a legitimate foundation. Neuroscience will help us to see the light by undermining "people's common sense, libertarian conception of free will and the retributivist thinking that depends on it, both of which have been shielded by the inaccessibility of sophisticated thinking about the mind and its neural basis."[70] Once the folk psychological illusion has been revealed, we can

---

[61] *Id.* at 210.

[62] *Id.* at 217.

[63] They contrast the "folk psychological system" with the "folk physics system," which "deals with chunks of matter that move around without purposes of their own according to the laws of intuitive physics." *Id.* at 220. The two systems are different "cognitive systems" for "making sense of the behavior of objects in the world." *Id.*

[64] *Id.*

[65] *Id.*

[66] *Id.* at 210.

[67] *Id.* at 220. They add: "To see something as morally blameworthy or praiseworthy…one has to first see it as 'someone,' that is, as having a mind." *Id.*

[68] *Id.* at 221.

[69] *Id.* at 221, 209.

[70] *Id.* at 208.

"structure our society accordingly by rejecting retributivist legal principles that derive their intuitive force from this illusion."[71]

How exactly will neuroscience do this? It will do so, they predict, by revealing the "mechanical nature of human action," along with the "when," "where," and "how" of the "mechanical processes that cause behavior."[72] As they acknowledge, this is not a new conclusion: "[s]cientifically minded philosophers have been saying this ad nauseam."[73] But the neuroscience will reveal this mechanical nature in a way that "bypasses complicated [philosophical] arguments," for it is one thing to hold your ground in the face of a "general, philosophical argument" but "quite another to hold your ground when your opponent can make detailed predictions about how these mechanical processes work, complete with images of the brain structures involved and equations that describe their functions."[74]

To illustrate how this might work, they present the following hypothetical. Imagine a group of scientists who create an individual ("Mr. Puppet") who engages in criminal activity. At Mr. Puppet's trial, the lead scientist explains his relationship to Mr. Puppet as follows:

I designed him. I carefully selected every gene in his body and carefully scripted every significant event in his life so that he would become precisely what he is today. I selected his mother knowing that she would let him cry for hours and hours before picking him up. I carefully selected each of his relatives, teachers, friends, enemies, etc. and told them exactly what to say to him and how to treat him.[75]

According to Greene and Cohen, Mr. Puppet is guilty according to the law if he was rational at the time of his actions, which, they assume, he was. However, they conclude that given the circumstances of his creation, "intuitively, this is not fair."[76] It is not fair, they contend, because "his beliefs and desires were rigged by external forces, and that is why, intuitively he deserves our pity more than our moral condemnation."[77] What neuroscience will reveal—without the need

---

[71] Id. at 209.
[72] Id. at 217.
[73] Id. at 214.
[74] Id. at 217.
[75] Id. at 216.
[76] Id.
[77] Id.

for recourse to philosophical argument—is that all criminal defendants (and indeed all humans) are like Mr. Puppet in the relevant respects. Although not designed by scientists, our beliefs, desires, and "rational" actions are all "rigged by external forces" beyond our control (some combination of genes, history, culture, and perhaps randomness). If Mr. Puppet is not morally responsible, then no one else is either.

Neuroscience will reveal the mechanical nature of our actions with examples such as the following:

Imagine, for example, watching a film of your brain choosing between soup and salad. The analysis software highlights the neurons pushing for soup in red and the neurons pushing for salad in blue. You zoom in and slow down the film, allowing yourself to trace the cause-and-effect relationships between individual neurons—the mind's clockwork revealed in arbitrary detail. You find the tipping-point moment at which the blue neurons in your prefrontal cortex out-fire the red neurons, seizing control of your pre-motor cortex and causing you to say, "I will have the salad, please."[78]

What goes for the soup-or-salad choice, also goes for the choice of whether to murder, rape, assault, or steal.

Greene and Cohen do not see these neuro-revelations as the end of criminal punishment, however. They note that the "law will continue to punish misdeeds, as it must for practical reasons,"[79] and that "if we are lucky" our retributivist reasons for punishment will give way to consequentialist reasons[80] because "consequentialist approaches to punishment remain viable in the absence of common-sense free will."[81] Under a consequentialist punishment regime, legal doctrine may, for deterrence purposes, make many of the same distinctions it does today (for example, regarding infancy and insanity) "but the idea of distinguishing the truly, deeply guilty from those who are merely

---

[78] Id. at 218.

[79] Id. Although Greene and Cohen conclude that retributivism will be undermined, they also conclude that we will still invoke folk psychological concepts for other practical purposes (including, for example, deciding who has committed a criminal act in the first place). It is only for the special case of determining criminal punishment that we will rely on the conclusion that retributive punishment is unjustified because no one is *really* responsible. But if folk psychology is founded on an illusion and is thus an illegitimate basis on which to ground and justify criminal punishment, it is not clear why Greene and Cohen think it would be an appropriate basis for singling out people to punish in the first place.

[80] Id. at 224.

[81] Id. at 209.

victims of neuronal circumstances will, we submit, seem pointless."[82] With rhetorical flourish, they conclude: "the law deals firmly but mercifully with individuals whose behavior is obviously beyond their control. Some day, the law may treat all convicted criminals this way. That is, humanely."[83]

There are a number of problems with this argument. Carefully examining each of these distinct problems will reveal how little the neuroscience of human action *tout court* bears on the normative project of justifying criminal punishment on the basis of moral blameworthiness or desert. Each problem by itself is sufficient to raise doubts about the conclusions Greene and Cohen draw regarding retributivism; collectively, the problems illustrate why the conclusions ought to be rejected.

The first problem with the argument is the assumption that the intuitions of most people necessarily address the normative questions of whether criminal punishment is justified or how it ought to be distributed. Although lay intuitions may be relevant to reform, and some agreement between punishment and lay intuitions may be *necessary* for the legitimacy of punishment, accord with the intuitions of most people is not *sufficient* to justify punishment decisions. It is possible for widely shared intuitions about just punishment to be mistaken. Thus, even if neuroscience were to cause a significant shift away from retributive intuitions (as Greene and Cohen predict),[84] it simply begs the question to assume that this shift would lead to more just (or more unjust) punishment decisions. The key issue is whether neuroscience will contribute evidence that provides epistemic support for arguments concerning determinism, compatibilism, moral blameworthiness, and just punishment.

The second problem with their argument is that the neuroscientific evidence that they envision would not provide this epistemic support.

---

[82] *Id.* at 218.

[83] *Id.* at 224.

[84] Although exposure to the basics of determinism may reduce punishment in certain circumstances, see Sandra D. Haynes, Don Rojas & Wayne Viney, *Free Will, Determinism, and Punishment*, 93 PSYCHOL. REV. 1013 (2003), in other circumstances accepting deterministic thinking may cause more, not less, punishment. For example, consider current practices of indefinite "civil commitment" of convicted sex offenders after they have completed their prison sentences because of fears of recidivism. The assumption that getting rid of retributivism will reduce punishment neglects the constraining or limiting effects retributivist thinking may provide. Moreover, exposure to determinism may cause other negative effects. *See* Kathleen D. Vohs & Jonathan W. Schooler, *The Value of Believing in Free Will: Encouraging a Belief in Determinism Increases Cheating*, 19 PSYCHOL. SCI. 49 (2008).

As Greene and Cohen appear to concede with their dismissal of "complicated [philosophical] arguments,"[85] neuroscience adds nothing new to existing arguments for or against compatibilism, incompatibilism, or hard determinism.[86] If this is so, and the presence of neuroscientific information causes people to form and hold new beliefs about these positions, then the neuroscience is persuading people for psychological reasons other than the epistemic support it provides. As may be the case in other contexts, the presence of neuroscientific information may cause people systematically to draw faulty or unsupported inferences rather than true or justified ones.[87] In other words, the very effects that Greene and Cohen predict may prove to be widespread cognitive errors. The neuroscientific information may cause people to draw problematic (or philosophically dubious) inferences regarding issues relating to free will, determinism, and criminal responsibility.[88] Perhaps Greene and Cohen would respond that this causal effect is at least pushing people toward the correct positions, albeit for the wrong reasons. But this presupposes that retributivism depends necessarily on libertarianism (for reasons unrelated to neuroscience). This takes us to a third problem with their argument.

That problem is that their presupposition is mistaken. It is not the case that retributivism depends necessarily on a metaphysically problematic version of libertarian incompatibilism. Greene and Cohen assume that retributivism—and indeed all moral blame and praise—must be built on a foundation of "uncaused causation." But

[85] See Greene & Cohen, supra note 11, at 217.

[86] Indeed, both the "Mr. Puppet" and "soup/salad" examples are consistent with a variety of different positions on these issues.

[87] The causal role played by neuroscientific evidence in drawing inferential conclusions may not be a justificatory role. See Jessica R. Gurley & David K. Marcus, The Effects of Neuroimaging and Brian Injury on Insanity Defenses, 26 BEHAV. SCI. & LAW 85 (2008); David P. McCabe & Alan D. Castel, Seeing Is Believing: The Effect of Brain Images on Judgments of Scientific Reasoning, 107 COGNITION 343 (2008); Deena Skolnick Weisberg et al., The Seductive Allure of Neuroscience Explanations, 20 J. COGNITIVE NEUROSCIENCE 470 (2008). Although some studies suggest that neuroimages may be playing a problematic role in inferences, the picture is complicated, and recent evidence challenges that claim. See N.J. Schweitzer et al., Neuroimages as Evidence in a Mens Rea Defense: No Impact, 17 PSYCHOL., PUB. POLICY & LAW 357 (2011). Whether the inferences are justified will depend on other criteria (including philosophical and conceptual arguments) beyond what caused them.

[88] For a recent argument exposing some of these problematic inferences, see Saul Smilansky, Hard Determinism and Punishment: A Practical Reductio, 30 LAW & PHIL. 353 (2011). See also Tom Buller, Rationality, Responsibility, and Brain Function, 19 CAMBRIDGE Q. HEALTHCARE ETHICS 196, 204 (2010) (discussing Greene and Cohen and arguing "there are equally good reasons for holding onto the law's compatibilist intuitions and its assumption of rational agency").

a retributivist can coherently reject the notion of uncaused causation and still allow for moral judgments. Even in a world of physical determinism, moral desert may be grounded in the control people have over their actions through the exercise of their practical rationality.[89] If people act for reasons—more generally, if they act on the basis of their beliefs, desires, and other mental states—then we can blame or praise their actions (in light of their mental states).[90] Indeed, in their appeal to consequentialist justifications for punishment based on deterrence, Greene and Cohen appear to concede this type of responsiveness to reason[91]: deterrence works precisely by affecting the practical rationality of potential offenders, by giving them a reason to refrain from criminal activity that (ideally) outweighs their reasons for criminal activity. Sufficient control over one's actions in light of one's practical rationality is sufficient to ground moral desert, regardless of whether the same actions may be explained in purely physical (i.e., nonmental) terms. In other words, one can coherently be a compatibilist and a retributivist, a combination that is consistent with current law.[92]

---

[89]   See JOHN MARTIN FISCHER & MARK RAVIZZA, RESPONSIBILITY AND CONTROL: A THEORY OF MORAL RESPONSIBILITY (1999). Rational control does not imply "uncaused causation." It implies that people have the ability and the opportunity to act in accord with their mental states. For a discussion that develops these points, see ANTHONY KENNY, FREEWILL AND RESPONSIBILITY 32 (1978).

[90]   This does not assume that actors are always conscious of their mental states or that mental states necessarily precede actions. In some cases, there may be no unique mental state that may be distinguished from the action that manifests the mental state (e.g., a want, knowledge, or intention).

[91]   Other aspects of their argument, however, may imply that this sort of reason-responsiveness is an illusion because mental states may not exist or may be epiphenomenal. We explore this tension in their argument below.

[92]   To suppose otherwise would be a mistake, regardless of how many people think so, and regardless of what neuroscience shows. Rather than causing people to abandon retributivism and a libertarian conception of free will, perhaps increased neuroscientific knowledge will instead cause people to abandon confused views about free will and its relationship with responsibility. Neuroscience may also help jurors, judges, and legislators to better appreciate the extent to which defendants in actual cases did or did not have control over their actions as well as the roles played by other social and biological factors. See Emad H. Atiq, How Folk Beliefs about Free Will Influence Sentencing: A New Target for the Neuro-Determinist Critics of Criminal Law, 16 NEW CRIMINAL L. REV. 449 (2013) (arguing that neuroscience may correct mistaken juror beliefs about libertarian free will and the extent to which social and biological factors affect behavior.) We concur with Atiq's general point that more accurate beliefs about human agency should lead to more morally justified punishment, and we see a role for both science and philosophy in improving understanding in this area. The role of philosophy in this endeavor will be to help integrate increased knowledge of the brain coherently into the conceptual schemes we use to explain human behavior and the world.

We first explicate this position in general terms and then illustrate it with Greene and Cohen's example of Mr. Puppet. Greene and Cohen assume that retributivism depends on "uncaused causation" because, if determinism is true, then agents could not have done otherwise and are thus not subject to moral evaluation.[93] Confusion arises because in discussions of whether an agent could have done otherwise, can act or refrain from acting, or has the power to act or not, the terms "could," "can," and "power" are ambiguous. As Anthony Kenny explains, these terms may be referring to one of four different notions: (1) *natural powers* (e.g., the ability of water to freeze) in which physical conditions may be sufficient for their instantiation; (2) *abilities* that depend for their exercise on an agent's wanting to exercise them; (3) *opportunities* to exercise one's abilities (e.g., one cannot ride a bicycle if there are no bicycles around); and (4) the presence of both an *ability* and an *opportunity* to exercise it. The fourth sense is the one that is relevant to moral blame and praise: agents who have the ability and the opportunity to act differently, but do not, are properly subject to moral evaluation.[94] A key issue is thus whether this conception is consistent with determinism. Greene and Cohen assume it is not and that neuroscience will illustrate this inconsistency. We disagree with both points.

The idea that people possess the ability and the opportunity to do otherwise is consistent with determinism.[95] How can ability and opportunity be consistent with determinism? First, consider ability. Possessing an ability (e.g., to ride a bicycle) depends on whether one satisfies the criteria for possessing the ability. These criteria include successfully exercising this ability when one wants to (and has the opportunity to) and refraining when one does not want to (and has the opportunity to refrain). Such criteria can be fulfilled even if one does not exercise the ability on the particular occasion in question. Second, consider opportunity. One has an opportunity to act (or not to act) if conditions external to the person are not forcing or preventing the exercise of the ability on a particular occasion. But are an agent's brain states forcing him to act in one way and preventing him from acting in another (are they an "external force rigging his behavior") and, thus,

---

[93] They could not have done otherwise because their actions are all "rigged by external forces" beyond their control. *See* Greene & Cohen, *supra* note 11, at 216.

[94] *See supra* note 89.

[95] *See* KENNY, *supra* note 89, at 34 ("it does not follow from determinism that agents always lack the opportunity and ability to do otherwise than they do. Consequently it does not follow from determinism that it is unfair to hold people responsible for their actions.").

depriving him of the opportunity to do otherwise? Not necessarily. We presume that if an agent had wanted to do something different (e.g., to ride a bicycle or not), then his brain states also would have been different. It would be a different story if his brain states caused him to ride a bicycle (or not) when he wanted to do the contrary. In such circumstances, there would be a breakdown of the type of rational control on which criminal responsibility depends.

The example of Mr. Puppet will help to illustrate these general points. Suppose Mr. Puppet has robbed a bank. Let us assume determinism is true and that we must decide whether to hold Mr. Puppet responsible for his actions. Assume further than Mr. Puppet is responsible only if he acted freely in robbing the bank, in the sense that he had the ability and the opportunity to not rob the bank. We ask him why he did so and he says, "I wanted the money." We might say the money (or his desire for the money) caused him to rob the bank, but surely this would not negate moral blame.[96] Presumably, Mr. Puppet had the ability to refrain from robbing the bank, in the sense that his mental states (his beliefs and desires) played some causal role in his conduct and he was responsive to reasons for and against his conduct at the time of his actions.[97] His ability to act or not in robbing the bank was thus distinct from someone sleepwalking or insane at the time. If, for example, Mr. Puppet were to learn that the police were waiting inside the bank, we presume that he would respond to this information and (given his beliefs and desires to have the money and not go to jail) abandon his plan to rob the bank—thus exercising this ability. By contrast, a sleepwalker or an insane person may not have the ability to respond to this information in a similar manner. Possessing an ability does not require exercising it whenever possible, so even though Mr. Puppet did not exercise it in the deterministic world in

---

[96] Causation, even abnormal causation, does not necessarily equal excuse. *See* Morse, *supra* note 12. Moreover, the wanting need not be a distinct event that precedes robbing the bank; it may be manifested in the robbing itself.

[97] This is based on the assumptions by Greene and Cohen that Mr. Puppet: "is as rational as other criminals and, yes, it was his desires and beliefs that produced his actions." Greene & Cohen, *supra* note 11, at 216. They also raise the possibility of defining "rationality" in neurocognitive rather than behavioral terms. *Id.* at 224 n.3. But this would either be changing the subject (i.e., we would no longer be talking about what we currently mean by rationality) or incoherent as an explanation of rationality as currently conceived. People, not brains, behave rationally (or not). It is an instance of the "mereological fallacy" (i.e., mistakenly ascribing attributes to parts that make sense only when ascribed to the whole) to assume rationality may refer to states of the brain. *See* Chapter One; M.R. BENNETT & P.M.S. HACKER, PHILOSOPHICAL FOUNDATIONS OF NEUROSCIENCE (2003).

which he robs the bank, this does not mean that he lacked the ability to do otherwise.[98]

But did Mr. Puppet have an opportunity to do otherwise? In an important sense, the answer is yes. No external forces were coercing Mr. Puppet when he acted.[99] We can also assume that if Mr. Puppet did not want the money, his brain states would be different from his brain states when he wanted the money and robbed the bank and, thus, he would have acted differently.[100] Therefore, whatever Mr. Puppet's neurological and other physical states are, it is not the case that if Mr. Puppet did not want to rob the bank, these physical states would cause him to do so anyway or deprive him of the opportunity to adhere to the law. Once again, compare Mr. Puppet with a person who cannot exercise this control. Suppose a person cannot bring her actions to conform to her desires, goals, plans, and intentions, or, for a variety of reasons, cannot control her bodily

---

[98] Mr. Puppet had the ability to refrain from robbing the bank if he could exercise that ability when he wanted to (and when there is an opportunity to do so).

[99] Although, under some formulations of the hypothetical, we might have grounds for inferring that the scientists who designed Mr. Puppet coerced his behavior. Some type of coercion by third parties is typically what people mean by the claim that one's action was not free. See Nahmias et al., *supra* note 58; van Inwagen, *supra* note 53, at 329 ("['Free will's'] non-philosophical uses are pretty much confined to the phrase 'of his/her own free will' which means 'uncoerced.'").

[100] Similarly, if one had wanted soup rather than salad in Greene and Cohen's previous example, we assume that one's neurons would have been different. To suppose otherwise, Greene and Cohen would have to defend much stronger claims than they do: namely, that (1) there is a one-to-one correspondence between brain states and particular mental states, and (2) the relationships between various mental states and between mental states and actions are governed by the same physical laws that govern brain states (or are reducible to those laws). They do not defend either claims, *cf.* Greene and Cohen, *supra* note 11, at 225 ("we do not wish to imply that neuroscience will inevitably put us in a position to predict any given action based on a neurological examination"), and neither claim necessarily follows from determinism. Plausible positions that reject either claim are consistent with physical determinism. See DONALD DAVIDSON, *Mental Events, in* ESSAYS ON ACTIONS AND EVENTS 207 (2d ed. 2001); Richard Rorty, *The Brain as Hardware, Culture as Software*, 47 INQUIRY 219, 231 (2004). Stronger claims may be implied by their claim that folk psychology is founded on an illusion, but these claims deny rather than explain the causal role of mental states. We turn to this aspect of the argument below. We also note that to explain someone's actions by citing their reasons, wants, beliefs, desires, intentions, and so on, may not be to offer a causal explanation at all, but rather a rational, teleological one. For an argument along these lines, see P.M.S. HACKER, HUMAN NATURE: THE CATEGORICAL FRAMEWORK 199–232 (2007). Whether one takes this path—or a Davidsonian one in which mental states may be characterized as causes—the type of normativity that we argue provides adequate grounds for judgments of blame (and praise) survives intact. In either instance, "uncaused causation" is not necessary.

movements.[101] It is precisely in such cases that we withhold judgments of moral blame—and indeed often do not even consider such movements to be "actions" at all—and the criminal law withholds punishment.

The consistency between moral judgment and determinism becomes even clearer when focusing on acts of moral praise. Suppose that, instead of a criminal act, Mr. Puppet commits an act of heroic bravery or kindness—for example, sacrificing himself in some way to save a stranger. Does his heroic or kind act cease to be morally praiseworthy if it takes place in a deterministic physical world and he is the product of his genes and upbringing? We think not. As with moral blame, what matters is whether Mr. Puppet can act for reasons and can exercise control over his actions on the basis of those reasons. Did he have the ability and opportunity to do otherwise and act voluntarily in performing this praiseworthy act? Contrast this with someone whose bodily movements were not within that person's rational control. For example, if someone in a state of epileptic seizure or while fainting engages in bodily movements that turn out to somehow save a third party, has the person acted heroically or bravely? Does the person deserve moral praise? Has the person acted at all? As with moral blame, we think the distinction here is plain as well.[102] Mr. Puppet deserves praise for his morally good acts, along with any other praiseworthy accomplishments, and blame for morally bad acts, when he had the ability and opportunity to do otherwise.

To suppose moral praise or blame require uncaused causation is to miss (or misconstrue) the normativity in human action. Our normative judgments about human actions are not inconsistent with explanations that involve physical action; they require, at a minimum, that our bodily movements be *human actions* and not mere bodily movements—that is, that they are explainable based on the actor's mental states[103]—and that these actions meet or fail to meet various moral standards or criteria,

---

[101] Examples of the latter might include some cases of "alien hand" syndrome or "utilization behavior." *See* Iftah Biran et al., *The Alien Hand Syndrome: What Makes the Alien Hand Alien?*, 23 COGNITIVE NEUROPSYCHOLOGY 563 (2006).

[102] We also doubt that most people would be persuaded by neuroscience to think otherwise, but this is an empirical question, perhaps one for "experimental philosophy." Similar to the "Knobe effect" with regard to ascriptions of intentions, see Joshua Knobe, *Intentional Actions and Side Effects in Ordinary Language*, 63 ANALYSIS 190 (2003), subjects might distinguish between good acts and bad acts for reasons other than the relationship between determinism and free will.

[103] *See* G.E.M. ANSCOMBE, INTENTION (1957).

not that they be the product "uncaused causation." Greene and Cohen deny normativity at this level, however, along with the distinctions we have been drawing with Mr. Puppet, by arguing that they are based on the "illusion" of the folk psychological system.

This leads to a fourth problem with their argument: it implies untenable claims about folk psychology. Neither determinism in general nor neuroscience in particular undermines folk psychology in the ways they presuppose. Recall that, for Greene and Cohen, (1) moral evaluation depends on folk psychological explanations of human behavior, (2) folk psychological explanations depend on the notions of mind and mental states (i.e., beliefs, desires, and intentions), and (3) mind and mental states depend on "uncaused causation." But the latter is an illusion. This implies that the notions of mind and mental states under this system are likewise illusory, which, for purposes of their argument, is what consequently leaves moral evaluation without a legitimate foundation. Although Greene and Cohen do not explicitly endorse the claim that mental states are nonexistent (or, alternatively, are epiphenomenal),[104] this implication appears to follow from their claim that the "crucial, if not the defining feature" of mind and mental states is "uncaused causation." Moreover, this implication is necessary to undermine moral evaluation. If moral evaluation depends on folk psychological explanations generally, and mental states exist and do causal work, then folk psychology is not illusory and provides a legitimate foundation for moral evaluation. In other words, to undermine moral evaluation in the ways they suppose, neuroscience would need to undermine the folk psychological system more generally.

If the argument by Greene and Cohen depends on this stronger implication about mental states, then it faces additional difficulties.[105] It is important to be clear about the aspect of their argument linking moral evaluation to folk psychology more generally. We can reconstruct this thread as follows: (1) retributivist punishment depends on moral evaluation; (2) moral evaluation requires that people punished had some control over their actions; (3) to have such control they must have been able to act or refrain from acting; (4) the ability to act or refrain from acting

[104] Indeed, they sometimes appear to endorse a causal role for mental states. *See, e.g., supra* note 77.
[105] We note that the other four problems that we explicate in our critique do not depend on this implication. Thus, readers who disagree that this implication follows are free to accept our other arguments.

requires that their mental states played a causal role in regulating their behavior; (5) but mental states do not exist or they do no causal work;[106] (6) thus people have no control over their actions; (7) thus retributive punishment is unjustified. Neuroscience enters the picture in support of premise (5) by illustrating that behavior is causally determined by physical states (including brain states). But this does not follow. Mental states may exist and play a causal role while also having underlying neurological correlates. Thus, the simple fact that mental states have accompanying brain states that are part of the physical universe and subject to its law does not render the former illusory or epiphenomenal. Moreover, as an empirical matter, some mental states (e.g., intentions) do appear to play a causal role in a manner that would be impossible if folk psychology generally were an "illusion."[107]

Moreover, reflect for a moment on what it would mean for folk psychology generally to be an illusion (i.e., that there are no such things as beliefs, desires, wants, fears, knowledge, intentions, or plans). One obvious implication is that there is no difference between us (and Mr. Puppet) and someone engaged in bodily movements caused by a seizure or conditions beyond his or her "rational" control. A second implication is that psychological explanations would be false, and there would be nothing real (or nothing that affects behavior) for psychology to explain. A third implication is that human action would indeed cease to be "human" or "action," at least as we currently conceive of these notions. Thus, if the argument by Greene and Cohen depends implicitly on these more radical claims about folk psychology, then this provides a reductio ad absurdum for their argument.[108]

---

[106] This aspect of the argument does not necessarily depend on a notion of "uncaused causation." Rather, we contend that premise (5) is implied by the fact that mind, mental states, and folk psychology (as conceived by Greene and Cohen) all depend on uncaused causation. If the latter does not exist, then neither does the former (at least as how they conceive of them). Notice also that if Greene and Cohen are not committed to premise (5), then, for the reasons given above, agents would have the requisite control over their actions and moral evaluation would follow.

[107] For an overview of some of the relevant literature, see Peter M. Gollwitzer & Paschal Sheeran, *Implementation Intentions and Goal Achievement: A Meta-Analysis of Effects and Processes*, 69 ADVANCES IN EXPERIMENTAL SOCIAL PSYCHOL. 69 (2006). For a discussion of the relevance of these studies to debates about free will, see ALFRED R. MELE, EFFECTIVE INTENTIONS: THE POWER OF CONSCIOUS WILL (2009). *See also* Mario Beauregard, *Mind Really Does Matter: Evidence from Neuroimaging Studies of Emotional Self-Regulation, Psychotherapy, and Placebo Effect*, 81 PROGRESS IN NEUROBIOLOGY 218 (2007).

[108] Notice also how self-defeating this is as a challenge to *retributivism* and as a defense of *consequentialist* criminal punishment. Recall, they argue that we will still punish for practical reasons, for example, to deter future crime. Well, why? Do we *want* to deter crime? Do

Finally, there is a fifth problem with their argument. Even if they are right in their predictions; even if people are persuaded by arguments based on neuroscience to believe in hard determinism; even if they therefore conclude that their folk psychological system for explaining human behavior is based on an illusion; and even if they therefore abandon retributivism as a basis for justifying punishment, Greene and Cohen are wrong to suppose that we would be "lucky" and punishment would necessarily be more "humane." Although Greene and Cohen predict that abandoning retributivist reasons for punishment will reduce punishment,[109] a brief history of actual criminal-sentencing practices in the United States during the past thirty years suggests the converse to be true. Indeed, when the U.S. Supreme Court upheld prison sentences of "25 years to life" and "50 years to life" for stealing golf clubs and shoplifting videotapes, respectively (both "three strikes" cases), it did not justify its decision based on notions of desert but rather on other penological purposes such as deterrence and incapacitation.[110] Moreover, abandoning retributivist rationales for punishment in favor of deterrence, incapacitation, and general crime control has also paved the way for harsh sentences for drug crimes, prosecuting juveniles as adults, strict liability crimes, proposals to abolish the insanity defense, and the felony-murder rule.[111] The absence of retributivist constraints also allows for the indefinite "civil commitment" of criminals after the completion of their prison sentences.[112] Indeed, more widespread acceptance of the idea that criminal offenders cannot stop and are "determined" to continue their criminal behavior does not appear to us to be a recipe for more compassionate and humane punishment. Moreover, psychologically persuasive but epistemically dubious neuroscience may only exacerbate rather than alleviate this

---

we *believe* or *know* punishment will deter crime? Will we therefore *choose* certain forms of punishment over others? Notice also that consequentialist justifications for punishment also involve folk psychological concepts; deterrence works by affecting the practical reasoning of potential criminals. Do potential criminals *believe* punishment will follow if they commit crime, do they not *want* to be punished, and therefore will they *choose* to not commit crimes? This aspect of Greene and Cohen's argument presupposes the existence of these entities. We concur with Anthony Kenny that "[a] legal system which took no account of states of mind would be as chimeric as it would be abhorrent." Kenny, *supra* note 89, at 93.

[109] *See* Greene & Cohen, *supra* note 11, at 224. *See also supra* note 84.

[110] Ewing v. California, 538 U.S. 11 (2003); Lockyer v. Andrade, 538 U.S. 63 (2003).

[111] *See* Paul H. Robinson, Owen D. Jones & Robert Kurzban, *Realism, Punishment, and Reform*, 77 U. Chi. L. Rev. 1611, 1630 (2010).

[112] *See* Kansas v. Hendricks, 521 U.S. 346 (1997).

problem.[113] We share what we believe to be the sentiment of Greene and Cohen that criminal punishment ought to be more humane, but we do not believe that the way to get there is by denying our shared humanity. A crucial part of that shared humanity is that our behavior may be explained and evaluated in the language of folk psychology.[114]

We close with a final point. Imagine a group of open-minded policy makers faced with the task of constructing a justified system of legal punishment. They decide to listen to and take seriously the arguments of Greene and Cohen regarding retributivism, hard determinism, and neuroscience. At the end of the day, they could evaluate the various claims and the reasons for them, deliberate about the various avenues open to them and the benefits and costs of each, and then choose a course of action that they think is justified or more justified than the alternatives. Or they could simply sit back and wait for their neurons to make the decision for them. Or they could flip a coin. For the normative project of justifying criminal punishment, these distinctions matter a great deal to the issue of whether the criminal punishment that followed would be justified and legitimate.[115] From the perspective of Greene and Cohen, however, these differences ultimately do not matter (just as they do not matter at the level of criminal responsibility). If no one is *really* blameworthy or praiseworthy, justified or unjustified, then the same goes for

[113] Richard Sherwin predicts that neuroimaging will contribute to more draconian punishment. *See* Richard K. Sherwin, *Law's Screen Life: Criminal Predators and What to Do about Them, in* IMAGINING LEGALITY: WHERE LAW MEETS POPULAR CULTURE (Austin Sarat ed., 2011). Notice this is the exact opposite of the prediction made by Greene and Cohen. For a critique of Sherwin, see Michael S. Pardo, *Upsides of the American Trial's "Anticonfluential" Nature: Notes on Richard K. Sherwin, David Foster Wallace, and James O. Incandenza, in* IMAGINING LEGALITY.

[114] Although we reject the global claim by Greene and Cohen, we endorse the idea that neuroscience may contribute to more humane punishment on a more local scale by correcting mistaken beliefs about excusing and mitigating conditions or by providing better evidence that these conditions obtain. *See* Atiq, *supra* note 92, at 481–82:

> The moral argument advanced here does *not* depend on the controversial incompatibilist assumption that to deserve punishment, it must be true that the criminal had a kind of control over his actions that he lacks in a deterministic world. On the view developed here, the fact that external factors causally influence human behavior does not *per se* mitigate or excuse criminal offenders. What the view relies on is merely the observation that the causal influence of *certain kinds* of external factors on an individual's propensity to act criminally, given the unique way in which those factors influence behavior, mitigates how much punishment the individual deserves.

We agree.

[115] And it appears to matter for Greene and Cohen, who apparently think that punishment should proceed for consequentialist reasons and not for retributivist reasons.

lawmakers who decide how and when to distribute punishment. If it is just causally determined neuronal activity all the way down, and if the folk psychological explanations of punishment behavior are founded on an illusion, then for purposes of moral evaluation *it does not matter why anyone chooses to engage in criminal punishment or how they do so.*[116] The same goes for theorists engaged in the normative project of critiquing and defending possible policies regarding the distribution of criminal punishment. If so, then one wonders why they bothered to make the argument.

[116] Notice also the deep irony between this argument by Greene and Cohen and the argument by Greene considered in Section II (the first challenge). For the first challenge, it matters a great deal which brain processes are correlated with a decision to punish ("emotional" or "cognitive"), as well as whether the punisher went through an explicit consequentialist/utilitarian/cost–benefit reasoning process. The irony is that this distinction between types of mental states, and the normative conclusions that follow from the distinction, presuppose the existence and significance of the very types of considerations that the second challenge asserts is an "illusion."

Conclusion

First and foremost, this book is a philosophical project. It is true that throughout this book we work through a variety of legal questions and propose arguments for how many controversial questions should be answered. But this emphasis on the law should not obscure the fact that our primary focus throughout this work has been on the philosophical problems that permeate discussions of the intersection between law and neuroscience. As we conclude, we would like to say a few things about the importance of philosophy for law and neuroscience and for the particular approach we take to the philosophical challenges.

If we have been successful, we have shown that no work on law and neuroscience can ignore fundamental philosophical issues. One of the most basic distinctions we draw is between empirical and conceptual questions. In the view of some, this distinction cannot be maintained because concepts, and the meanings of terms that express concepts, are always evolving in response to growth in scientific knowledge. We have shown that this way of approaching the issue is confused. Concepts can and do evolve, and the meanings of terms change: no one disputes this. Our point is that altering a concept or changing the meaning of a term alters the connection between meaning and the object of meaning. This is perhaps clearest in our discussion of brain-based lie detection. To say correctly that "X is lying" one first has to know the meaning of "lie." Judging the utterance of another to be a lie cannot be done correctly solely by reference to brain activity. The brain does not play a normative, regulative role: our concepts do that.

Similarly, the question of knowledge raises conceptual issues that cannot be reduced to facts about brain activity. Many scholars make the claim that knowledge is "embedded" in particular areas of the brain. We maintain that this way of approaching knowledge is devoid of sense. Knowledge is an ability, not a state of the brain. As philosophers like to say, "to know" is a success verb. Whether someone knows something typically can be determined only by what that person says and does.[1] Having a brain makes such behavior possible. But the brain is not the locus for the assessment of claims to knowledge.

If the conceptual and empirical issues were not sufficiently complicated and complicating, the addition of law moves the level of complexity higher still. The law takes complex and sometimes conflicting approaches toward the empirical and conceptual issues posed by neuroscience. Take just one example: rules of evidence. Although many scientists believe the results of fMRI technology provide insights into human capacities, the law is skeptical of such claims, and the rules of evidence limit the use of evidence for this purpose in several contexts. By contrast, the rules of evidence may in other instances allow for the admissibility of neuroscientific evidence for purposes that many neuroscientists would oppose. In short, the law lays down its own criteria of evidential admissibility and sufficiency—criteria that themselves depend in part on matters empirical but also on questions of fairness, the rights of parties, and other policy considerations. Thus, *even if* the conceptual and empirical issues underlying the relationship between mind and brain were adequately understood, there would still be significant conceptual and empirical issues connecting them to law.

As we said in the Introduction to this book, the intersection of law and neuroscience raises four types of questions: empirical, practical, ethical, and conceptual. We have touched on all of these categories, but our primary focus throughout has been on the conceptual. We have maintained that the conceptual issues are both the most ignored and, ironically, the most important. We close with a few words about our approach to philosophy and how that approach informs our work on these issues.

We conceive of philosophy as a therapeutic or corrective endeavor. We do not advance any philosophical "theses" as such. Of course, we have opinions and we have arguments. But what motivates our positions is the desire to remove obscurity and to achieve a clear view of

---

[1] There are exceptions—for example, someone with knowledge who does not or cannot manifest it in behavior—but these exceptions take place against the background of the various ways in which knowledge is usually expressed and ascribed to others.

the issues. In short, we think that clarity and perspicacity are the true products of philosophical reflection, not theorizing about embedded algorithms or modules. Our "conceptual analysis" (if one wants to call it that) is more method than doctrine. Throughout this book, we have employed this method in a wide variety of contexts and, we maintain, to useful effect. We believe that neuroscience has great promise for law. As the technological tools of the neuroscientist improve, the law will embrace some of the wonders of this rapidly evolving science. It is our hope that we have shown how philosophy can make a difference to the advancement of science and the improvement of law.[2]

[2] *See* ROBERT B. BRANDOM, *How Analytic Philosophy Has Failed Cognitive Science, in* REASON IN PHILOSOPHY 197 (2009) ("We analytic philosophers have signally failed our colleagues in cognitive science. We have done that by not sharing central lessons about the nature of concepts, concept use, and conceptual content that have been entrusted to our care and feeding for more than a century.").

Bibliography

Abe, Nobuhito et al., "Deceiving Others: Distinct Neural Responses of the Prefrontal Cortex and Amygdala in Simple Fabrication and Deception with Social Interactions," 19 *J. Cog. Neuroscience* 287 (2007).

Abend, Gabriel, "Thick Concepts and the Moral Brain," 52 *Euro. J. Sociology* 143 (2011).

Abend, Gabriel, "What the Science of Morality Doesn't Say about Morality," *Phil. Social Sci.* (forthcoming, published online July 20, 2012).

Adler, Jonathan, "Epistemological Problems of Testimony," in *Stanford Encyclopedia of Philosophy* (2012), available at: http://plato.stanford.edu/archives/fall2012/entries/testimony-episprob/.

Aharoni, Eyal et al., "Can Neurological Evidence Help Courts Assess Criminal Responsibility? Lessons from Law and Neuroscience," 1124 *Ann. N.Y. Acad. Sci.* 145 (2008).

Alder, Ken, *The Lie Detectors: The History of an American Obsession* (2007).

Allen, Ronald J., "*Miranda's* Hollow Core," 100 *Northwestern U. L. Rev.* 71 (2006).

Allen, Ronald J. & Kristen Mace, "The Self-Incrimination Clause Explained and Its Future Predicted," 94 *J. Crim. & Criminology* 243 (2004).

Allen, Ronald J. & Joseph S. Miller, "The Common Law Theory of Experts: Deference or Education?," 87 *Nw. U. L. Rev.* 1131 (1993).

Allen, Ronald J. & Michael S. Pardo, "The Problematic Value of Mathematical Models of Evidence," 36 *J. Legal Stud.* 107 (2007).

Alexander, Larry, "Criminal and Moral Responsibility and the Libet Experiments," in *Conscious Will and Responsibility* (Walter Sinnott-Armstrong & Lynn Nadel eds., 2011).

Alexander, Larry & Kimberly Kessler Ferzan (with Stephen Morse), *Crime and Culpability: A Theory of Criminal Law* (2009).

Alexander, Larry & Michael Moore, "Deontological Ethics," in *Stanford Encyclopedia of Philosophy* (2012), available at: http://plato.stanford.edu/entries/ethics-deontological/.

Amar, Akhil Reed, "Fourth Amendment First Principles," 107 *Harv. L. Rev.* 757 (1994).

Amar, Akhil Reed & Renee B. Lettow, "Fifth Amendment First Principles: The Self-Incrimination Clause," 93 *Mich. L. Rev.* 857 (1995).

Anscombe, G.E.M., *Intention* (1957).

Atiq, Emad H., "How Folk Beliefs about Free Will Influence Sentencing: A New Target for the Neuro-Determinist Critics of Criminal Law," 16 *New Criminal Law Review* 449 (2013).

Beccaria, Cesare, *On Crimes and Punishments* (1764).

Baker, G.P. & P.M.S. Hacker, *Wittgenstein: Understanding and Meaning, in An Analytical Commentary on the Philosophical Investigations.* Vol. 1. (1980).

Baker, G.P. & P.M.S. Hacker, *Wittgenstein: Rules, Grammar and Necessity, in An Analytical Commentary on the Philosophical Investigations.* Vol. 2. (1985).

Baker, G.P. & P.M.S. Hacker, *Wittgenstein: Understanding and Meaning, in An Analytical Commentary on the Philosophical Investigations.* Vol. 1. (2d ed., 2005).

Bartels, Andreas & Semir Zeki, "The Neural Basis of Romantic Love," 11 *Neuroreport* 3829 (2000).

Bartels, Andreas & Semir Zeki, "The Neural Correlates of Maternal and Romantic Love," 21 *NeuroImage* 1155 (2004).

Bauby, Jean-Dominique, *The Diving Bell and the Butterfly* (1997).

Beauregard, Robinson Mario, "Mind Really Does Matter: Evidence from Neuroimaging Studies of Emotional Self-Regulation, Psychotherapy, and Placebo Effect," 81 *Progress in Neurobiology* 218 (2007).

Bellin, Jeffrey, "The Significance (if any) for the Federal Criminal Justice System of Advances in Lie Detection Technology," 80 *Temp. L. Rev.* 711 (2007).

Bengson, John and Jeff A. Moffett eds., *Knowing How: Essay on Knowledge, Mind, and Action* (2012).

Bennett, Maxwell, "Epilogue" to *Neuroscience and Philosophy: Brain, Mind, and Language* (2007).

Bennett, M.R. & P.M.S. Hacker, *Philosophical Foundations of Neuroscience* (2003).

Bennett, M.R. & P.M.S. Hacker, "The Conceptual Presuppositions of Cognitive Neuroscience: A Reply to Critics," in *Neuroscience and Philosophy: Brain, Mind and Language* (2007).

Bennett, M.R. & P.M.S. Hacker, *History of Cognitive Neuroscience* (2008).

Bentham, Jeremy, *An Introduction to the Principles of Morals and Legislation* (1789).

Berker, Selim, "The Normative Insignificance of Neuroscience," 37 *Phil. & Pub. Affairs* 293 (2009).

Berman, Mitchell, "Two Kinds of Retributivism," in *Philosophical Foundations of the Criminal Law* (R.A. Duff & Stuart P. Green eds., 2011).

Bhatt, S. et al., "Lying about Facial Recognition: An fMRI Study," 69 *Brain & Cognition* 382 (2009).

Biran, I. & A. Chatterjee, "Alien Hand Syndrome," 61 *Archives Neurology* 292 (2004).

Biran, Iftah et al., "The Alien Hand Syndrome: What Makes the Alien Hand Alien?," 23 *Cognitive Neuropsychology* 563 (2006).

Birke, Richard, "Neuroscience and Settlement: An Examination of Scientific Innovations and Practical Applications," 25 *Ohio St. J. Dispute Res.* 477 (2011).

Blakemore, Colin, *The Mind Machine* (1988).

Boccardi, E., "Utilisation Behaviour Consequent to Bilateral SMA Softening," 38 *Cortex* 289 (2002).

Bockman, Collin R., Note, "Cybernetic-Enhancement Technology and the Future of Disability Law," 95 *Iowa L. Rev.* 1315 (2010).

Boire, Richard G., "Searching the Brain: The Fourth Amendment Implications of Brain-Based Deception Devices," 5 *Am. J. Bioethics* 62 (2005).

Braddon-Mitchell, David & Robert Nola eds., *Conceptual Analysis and Philosophical Naturalism* (2008).

Brain Waves Module 4: Neuroscience and the Law (Royal Statistical Society, 2011), available at: http://royalsociety.org/policy/projects/brain-waves/responsibility-law/.

Brandom, Robert B., *Making It Explicit: Reasoning, Representing, and Discursive Commitment* (1994).

Brandom, Robert B., "How Analytic Philosophy Has Failed Cognitive Science," in *Reason in Philosophy* (2009).

Bratman, Michael E., *Faces of Intention* (1999).

Brigandt, Ingo & Alan Love, "Reductionism in Biology," in *Stanford Encyclopedia of Philosophy* (2012), available at: http://plato.stanford.edu/entries/reduction-biology/.

Bronsteen, John, "Retribution's Role," 84 *Indiana L.J.* 1129 (2009).

Brown, Teneille & Emily Murphy, "Through a Scanner Darkly: Functional Neuroimaging as Evidence of a Criminal Defendant's Past Mental States," 62 *Stan. L. Rev.* 1119 (2012).

Buller, Tom, "Rationality, Responsibility, and Brain Function," 19 *Cambridge Q. Healthcare Ethics* 196 (2010).

Cahill, Michael T., "Punishment Pluralism," in *Retributivism: Essays on Theory and Policy* (Mark D. White ed., 2011).

Cappelen, Herman, *Philosophy without Intuitions* (2012).

Carlsmith, Kevin M., John M. Darley & Paul H. Robinson, "Why Do We Punish? Deterrence and Just Deserts as Motives for Punishment," 83 *J. Personality & Soc. Psych.* 284 (2002).

Chadwick, Martin J. et al., "Decoding Individual Episodic Memory Traces in the Human Hippocampus," 20 *Current Biology* 544 (2010).

Chomsky, Noam, *Aspects of the Theory of Syntax* (1965).

Chomsky, Noam, *New Horizons in the Study of Language and Mind* (2000).

Chorvat, Terrence & Kevin McCabe, "Neuroeconomics and Rationality," 80 *Chicago-Kent L. Rev.* 1235 (2005).

Chorvat, Terrence, Kevin McCabe & Vernon Smith, "Law and Neuroeconomics," 13 *Sup. Ct. Econ. Rev.* 35 (2005).

Christ, Shawn E., "The Contributions of Prefrontal Cortex and Executive Control to Deception: Evidence from Activation Likelihood Meta-Analyses," 19 *Cerebral Cortex* 1557 (2009).

Church, Dominique J., Note, "Neuroscience in the Courtroom: An International Concern," 53 *William & Mary L. Rev.* 1825 (2012).

Churchland, Patricia S., *Neurophilosophy: Toward a Unified Science of the Mind/Brain* (1986).

Churchland, Patricia S., "Moral Decision-Making and the Brain," in *Neuroethics: Defining the Issues in Theory, Practice, and Policy* (Judy Illes ed., 2006).

Churchland, Patricia S., *Braintrust: What Neuroscience Tells Us about Morality* (2011).

Churchland, Paul M., "Eliminative Materialism and the Propositional Attitudes," 78 *J. Phil.* 67 (1981).

Clark, Andy, *Supersizing the Mind: Embodiment, Action, and Cognitive Extension* (2008).

Clark, Andy & David J. Chalmers, "The Extended Mind," 58 *Analysis* 7 (1998).

Coleman, Jules L. & Ori Simchen, "'Law'," 9 *Legal Theory* 1 (2003).

Collier, Charles W., "Speech and Communication in Law and Philosophy," 12 *Legal Theory* 1 (2006).

Conway, Martin A., "Ten Things the Law and Others Should Know about Human Memory," in *Memory and Law* (Lynn Nadel & Walter Sinnott-Armstrong eds., 2012).

Corrado, Michael, "The Case for a Purely Volitional Insanity Defense," 42 *Tex. Tech. L. Rev.* 481 (2009).

Coulter, Jeff, "Is Contextualising Necessarily Interpretive?," 21 *J. Pragmatics* 689 (1994).

Coulter, Jeff & Wes Sharrock, *Brain, Mind, and Human Behaviour in Contemporary Cognitive Science* (2007).

Coulthard, E. et al. "Alien Limb Following Posterior Cerebral Artery Stroke: Failure to Recognize Internally Generated Movements," 22 *Movement Disord.* 1498 (2007).

Crick, Francis, *The Astonishing Hypothesis* (1994).

Darley, John M., "Citizens' Assignments of Punishments for Moral Transgressions: A Case Study in the Psychology of Punishment," 8 *Ohio St. J. Crim. L.* 101 (2010).

Damasio, Antonio R., *Descartes' Error: Emotion, Reason, and the Human Brain* (1996).

Dann, B. Michael, "The Fifth Amendment Privilege against Self-Incrimination: Extorting Physical Evidence from a Suspect," 43 *S. Cal. L. Rev.* 597 (1970).

Davidson, Donald, "Three Varieties of Knowledge," in *A.J. Ayer: Memorial Essays* (A. Phillips Griffiths ed., 1991), reprinted in Donald Davidson, *Subjective, Intersubjective, Objective* (2001).

Davidson, Donald, "Mental Events," in *Essays on Actions and Events* (2d ed. 2001).

Davachi, Lila, "Encoding: The Proof Is Still Required," in *Science of Memory: Concepts* (H.R. Roediger, Y. Dudai & S.M. Fitzpatrick eds., 2007).

Dean, Richard, "Does Neuroscience Undermine Deontological Theory?," 3 *Neuroethics* 43 (2010).

Denno, Deborah W., "Crime and Consciousness: Science and Involuntary Acts," 87 *Minn. L. Rev.* 269, 320 (2002).

DePaulo, P. et al., "Lying in Everyday Life," 70 *J. Personality & Soc. Psych.* 979 (1996).

Dery, George M., "Lying Eyes: Constitutional Implications of New Thermal Imaging Lie Detection Technology," 31 *Am. J. Crim. L.* 217 (2004).

Descartes, René, "Meditation VI," *Meditation on First Philosophy* (John Cottingham trans., 1996).

Dretske, Fred, *Explaining Behavior: Reasons in a World of Causes* (1988).

Duff, Anthony, "Legal Punishment," in *Stanford Encyclopedia of Philosophy* (2008), available at: http://plato.stanford.edu/entries/legal-punishment/.

Duff, R.A., *Intention, Agency, and Criminal Liability: Philosophy of Action and the Criminal Law* (1990).

Easton, Susan, *The Case for the Right to Silence* (2d ed. 1998).

Eggen, Jean Macchiaroli & Eric J. Laury, "Toward a Neuroscience Model of Tort Law: How Functional Neuroimaging Will Transform Tort Doctrine," 13 *Colum. Sci. & Tech. L. Rev.* 235 (2012).

Einesman, Floralynn, "Vampires among Us—Does a Grand Jury Subpoena for Blood Violate the Fourth Amendment?," 22 *Am. J. Crim. L.* 327 (1995).

Ellis, Jonathan1 & Daniel Guevara eds., *Wittgenstein and the Philosophy of Mind* (2012).

Faigman, David L. et al., *Modern Scientific Evidence: The Law and Science of Expert Testimony* § 40 (2011).

Fallis, Don, "What Is Lying?," 106 *J. Phil.* 29 (2009).

Farah, Martha J., & Cayce J. Hook, "The Seductive Allure of 'Seductive Allure,'" 8 *Perspectives Psych. Sci.* 88 (2013).

Farahany, Nita A., "Incriminating Thoughts," 64 *Stan. L. Rev.* 351 (2012).

Farahany, Nita A., "Searching Secrets," 160 *U. Pa. L. Rev.* 1239 (2012).

Farwell, Lawrence A. & Emanuel Donchin, "The Truth Will Out: Interrogative Polygraphy ('Lie Detection') with Event-Related Brain Potentials," 28 *Psychophysiology* 531 (1991).

Farwell, Lawrence A. & Sharon S, Smith, "Using Brain MERMER Testing to Detect Knowledge despite Efforts to Conceal," 46 *J. Forensic Sci.* 135 (2001).

Feldman, Richard, "Naturalized Epistemology," in *Stanford Encyclopedia of Philosophy* (2001), available at: http://plato.stanford.edu/entries/epistemology-naturalized/.

Ferzan, Kimberly Kessler, "Beyond Intention," 29 *Cardozo L. Rev.* 1147 (2008).

Fischer, John Martin & Mark Ravizza, *Responsibility and Control: A Theory of Moral Responsibility* (1999).

Foot, Philippa, "The Problem of Abortion and the Doctrine of Double Effect," in *Virtues and Vices* (2002).

Fox, Dov, "Brain Imaging and the Bill of Rights: Memory Detection Technologies and American Criminal Justice," 8 *Am. J. Bioethics* 34 (2008).

Fox, Dov, "The Right to Silence as Protecting Mental Control: Forensic Neuroscience and 'the Spirit and History of the Fifth Amendment,'" 42 *Akron L. Rev.* 763 (2009).

Frank, Lone, "The Quest to Build the Perfect Lie Detector," *Salon.com*, Jul. 23, 2011, available at: http://www.salon.com/2011/07/23/lie_detector_excerpt/.

Freidberg, Susanne, *Fresh: A Perishable History* (2009).

Fruehwald, Edwin S., "Reciprocal Altruism as the Basis for Contract," 47 *Louisville L. Rev.* 489 (2009).

Fullam, Rachel S. et al., "Psychopathic Traits and Deception: Functional Magnetic Resonance Imaging," 194 *British J. Psychiatry* 229 (2009).

Gamer, Matthias et al., "fMRI-Activation Patterns in the Detection of Concealed Information Rely on Memory-Related Effects," 7 *SCAN* 506 (2009).

Ganis, Giorgio et al., "Lying in the Scanner: Covert Countermeasures Disrupt Deception Detection by Functional Magnetic Resonance Imaging," 55 *Neuroimage* 312 (2011).

Ganis, Giorgio et al., "Neural Correlates of Different Types of Deception: An fMRI Investigation," 13 *Cerebral Cortex* 830 (2003).

Ganis, Giorgio & Julian Paul Keenan, "The Cognitive Neuroscience of Deception," 4 *Social Neuroscience* 465 (2008).

Garza, Gilbert & Amy Fisher Smith, "Beyond Neurobiological Reductionism: Recovering the Intentional and Expressive Body," 19 *Theory & Psychology* 519 (2009).

Gazzaniga, Michael S., *Nature's Mind: The Biological Roots of Thinking, Emotions, Sexuality, Language, and Intelligence* (1992).

Gazzaniga, Michael S., *Who's in Charge? Free Will and the Science of the Brain* (2012).

Gazzaniga, Michael S. & Jed S. Rakoff eds., *A Judge's Guide to Neuroscience: A Concise Introduction* (2010).

Gazzaniga, Michael S., Richard B. Ivry & George R. Mangun, *Cognitive Neuroscience: The Biology of the Mind* (3d ed. 2008).

Gettier, Edmund, "Is Justified True Belief Knowledge?," 23 *Analysis* 121 (1963).

Gibson, William G., Les Farnell & Max. R. Bennett, "A Computational Model Relating Changes in Cerebral Blood Volume to Synaptic Activity in Neurons," 70 *Neurocomputing* 1674 (2007).

Giridharadas, Anand, "India's Novel Use of Brain Scans in Courts Is Debated," *New York Times*, Sept. 14, 2008.

Glannon, Walter, "Our Brains Are Not Us," 23 *Bioethics* 321 (2009).

Godsey, Mark A., "Rethinking the Involuntary Confession Rule: Toward a Workable Test for Identifying Compelled Self-Incrimination," 93 *Cal L. Rev.* 465 (2005).

Goldberg, Sanford C., "Reductionism and the Distinctiveness of Testimonial Knowledge," in *The Epistemology of Testimony* (Jennifer Lackey & Ernest Sosa eds., 2006).

Goldberg, Steven, "Neuroscience and the Free Exercise of Religion," in *Law & Neuroscience: Current Legal Issues* (Michael Freeman ed., 2010).

Goldman, Alvin I., "Discrimination and Perceptual Knowledge," 73 *J. Phil.* 771 (1976).

Goldman, Alvin I., *Epistemology & Cognition* (1986).

Goldman, Alvin I., *Knowledge in a Social World* (1999).

Gollwitzer, Peter M. & Paschal Sheeran, "Implementation Intentions and Goal Achievement: A Meta-Analysis of Effects and Processes," 69 *Advances in Experimental Social Psychology* 69 (2006).

Goodenough, Oliver R., "Mapping Cortical Areas Associated with Legal Reasoning and Moral Intuition," 41 *Jurimetrics* 429 (2000–2001).

Goodenough, Oliver R. & Kristin Prehn, "A Neuroscientific Approach to Normative Judgment in Law and Justice," in *Law & the Brain* 77 (Semir Zeki & Oliver Goodenough eds., 2006).

Goodenough, Oliver R. & Micaela Tucker, "Law and Cognitive Neuroscience," 6 *Ann. Rev. L & Soc. Sci.* 28.1 (2010).

Greely, Henry T., "Prediction, Litigation, Privacy, and Property," in *Neuroscience and the Law: Brain, Mind, and the Scales of Justice* (Brent Garland ed., 2004).

Greely, Henry T. & Judy Illes, "Neuroscience-Based Lie Detection: The Urgent Need for Regulation," 33 *Am. J. L. & Med.* 377 (2007).

Greene, Joshua D., "From Neural 'Is' to Moral 'Ought': What Are the Moral Implications of Neuroscientific Moral Psychology?," 4 *Nature Rev. Neuroscience* 847 (2003).

Greene, Joshua D., "Reply to Mikhail and Timmons," in *Moral Psychology, Vol. 3: The Neuroscience of Morality: Emotion, Disease, and Development* (Walter Sinnott-Armstrong ed., 2007).

Greene, Joshua D., "The Secret Joke of Kant's Soul," in *Moral Psychology, Vol. 3: The Neuroscience of Morality: Emotion, Disease, and Development* (Walter Sinnott-Armstrong ed., 2007).

Greene, Joshua D. et al., "An fMRI Investigation of Emotional Engagement in Moral Judgment," 293 *Science* 2105 (2001).

Greene, Joshua D. et al., "The Neural Bases of Cognitive Conflict and Control in Moral Judgment," 44 *Neuron* 389 (2004).

Greene, Joshua D. et al., "Pushing Moral Buttons: The Interaction between Personal Force and Intention in Moral Judgment," 111 *Cognition* 364 (2009).

Greene, Joshua & Jonathan Cohen, "For Law, Neuroscience Changes Nothing and Everything," in *Law & the Brain* (Semir Zeki & Oliver Goodenough eds., 2006).

Greene, Joshua & Jonathan Haidt, "How (and Where) Does Moral Judgment Work?," 6 *Trends in Cog. Sci.* 517 (2002).

Greene, Joshua D. & Joseph M. Paxton, "Patterns of Neural Activity Associated with Honest and Dishonest Moral Decisions," 106 *Proc. Nat. Acad. Sci.* 12506 (2009).

Gurley, J.R. & D.K. Marcus, "The Effects of Neuroimaging and Brain Injury on Insanity Defenses," 26 *Behav. Sci. & Law* 85 (2008).

Hacker, P.M.S., "Language, Rules and Pseudo-Rules," 8 *Language & Comm.* 159 (1988).

Hacker, P.M.S., "Chomsky's Problems," 10 *Language & Comm.* 127 (1990).

Hacker, P.M.S., "Eliminative Materialism," in *Wittgenstein and Contemporary Philosophy of Mind* 83 (Severin Schroeder ed., 2001).

Hacker, P.M.S., *Human Nature: The Categorical Framework* (2007).

Hale, Bob & Crispin Wright eds., *A Companion to the Philosophy of Language* (1999).

Harman, Gilbert, Kelby Mason & Walter Sinnott-Armstrong, "Moral Reasoning," in *The Moral Psychology Handbook* (John M. Doris ed., 2010).

Hart, H.L.A., *Punishment and Responsibility* (2d ed., 2008).

Hawthorne, James, "Inductive Logic," in *Stanford Encyclopedia of Philosophy* (2012), available at: http://plato.stanford.edu/entries/logic-inductive/.

Hauser, Marc D., *Moral Minds* (2006).

Haynes, Sandra D., Don Rojas & Wayne Viney, "Free Will, Determinism, and Punishment," 93 *Psych. Rev.* 1013 (2003).

Henig, Marantz, "Looking for the Lie," *New York Times Magazine*, February 5, 2006.

Hetherington, Stephen, "How to Know (That Knowledge-That Is Knowledge-How)," in *Epistemology Futures* (Stephen Hetherington ed., 2006).

Hoffman, Morris B., "The Neuroeconomic Path of the Law," in *Law & the Brain* (Semir Zeki & Oliver Goodenough eds., 2006).

Hotz, Robert Lee, "The Brain, Your Honor, Will Take the Witness Stand," *Wall St. J.*, Jan. 16, 2009.

Ito, Ayahito et al., "The Dorsolateral Prefrontal Cortex in Deception When Remembering Neutral and Emotional Events," 69 *Neuroscience Research* 121 (2011).

Jackson, Frank, *From Metaphysics to Ethics: A Defence of Conceptual Analysis* (2000).

Jolls, Christine, Cass R. Sunstein & Richard Thaler, "A Behavioral Approach to Law and Economics," 50 *Stan. L. Rev.* 1471 (1998).

Jones, Owen D. et al., "Brain Imaging for Legal Thinkers: A Guide for the Perplexed," 5 *Stan. Tech. L. Rev.* (2009).

Kahane, Guy et al., "The Neural Basis of Intuitive and Counterintuitive Moral Judgment," 7 *Soc. Cognitive and Affective Neuroscience* 393 (2012).

Kamm, F.M., "Neuroscience and Moral Reasoning: A Note on Recent Research," 37 *Phil. & Pub. Affairs* 331 (2009).

Kant, Immanuel, *The Metaphysics of Morals* (Mary J. Gregor trans., 1996).

Katz, Leo, *Bad Acts and Guilty Minds* (1987).

Katz, Leo, *Why the Law Is so Perverse* (2011).

Kaylor-Hughes, Catherine J. et al., "The Functional Anatomical Distinction between Truth Telling and Deception Is Preserved among People with Schizophrenia," 21 *Crim. Behavior & Mental Health* 8 (2011).

Keckler, Charles N.W., "Cross-Examining the Brain: A Legal Analysis of Neural Imaging for Credibility Impeachment," 57 *Hastings L.J.* 509 (2006).

Kenny, Anthony, *Freewill and Responsibility* (1978).

Kenny, Anthony, *The Legacy of Wittgenstein* (1984).

Kitcher, Philip, *The Ethical Project* (2011).

Knobe, Joshua, "Intentional Actions and Side Effects in Ordinary Language," 63 *Analysis* 190 (2003).

Knobe, Joshua & Shaun Nichols eds., *Experimental Philosophy* (2008).

Kolber, Adam, "The Experiential Future of Law," 60 *Emory L.J.* 585 (2011).

Kolber, Adam, "Smooth and Bumpy Laws," 102 *Cal. L. Rev.* (forthcoming 2014), available at: http://ssrn.com/abstract=1992034.

Kong, J. et al., "Test-Retest Study of fMRI Signal Change Evoked by Electro-Acupuncture Stimulation," 34 *NeuroImage* 1171 (2007).

Kornblith, Hilary, "What Is Naturalistic Epistemology?," in *Naturalizing Epistemology* (Hilary Kornblith ed., 2d ed. 1997).

Kozel, F. Andrew et al., "A Pilot Study of Functional Magnetic Resonance Imaging Brain Correlates of Deception in Healthy Young Men," 16 *J. Neuropsychiatry Clin. Neurosci.* 295 (2004).

Kozel, F. Andrew et al., "Detecting Deception Using Functional Magnetic Resonance Imaging," *Biol. Psychiatry* 58 (2005).

Kozel, F. Andrew et al., "Functional MRI Detection of Deception after Committing a Mock Sabotage Crime," 54 *J. Forensic Sci.* 220 (2009).

Kozel, F. Andrew et al., "Replication of Functional MRI Detection of Deception," 2 *Open Forensic Sci. J.* 6 (2009).

Laird, Philip Johnson, *How We Reason* (2008).

Langleben, Daniel D. et al., "Brain Activity during Simulated Deception: An Event-Related Functional Magnetic Resonance Study," 15 *Neuroimage* 727 (2002).

Langleben, Daniel D. & Jane Campbell Moriarty, "Using Brain Imaging for Lie Detection: Where Science, Law and Policy Collide," 19 *Psych., Pub. Pol. & Law* 222 (2013).

Lee, Tatia M.C. et al., "Lie Detection by Functional Magnetic Resonance Imaging," 15 *Human Brain Mapping* 157 (2002).

Lee, Tatia M.C. et al., "Lying about the Valence of Affective Pictures: An fMRI Study," 5 *PLoS ONE* (2010).

LeDoux, Joseph, *The Emotional Brain: The Mysterious Underpinnings of Emotional Life* (1998).

Lehembre, Rémy et al., "Electrophysiological Investigations of Brain Function in Coma, Vegetative and Minimally Conscious Patients," 150 *Arch. Ital. Biol.* 122 (2012).

Lehrer, Keith, *Theory of Knowledge* (2d ed., 2000).

Leiter, Brian, *Nietzsche on Morality* (2002).

Leiter, Brian, "Legal Realism and Legal Positivism Reconsidered," in *Naturalizing Jurisprudence* (2007).

Leiter, Brian, "Postscript to Part II: Science and Methodology in Legal Theory," in *Naturalizing Jurisprudence* (2007).

Leiter, Brian, "Legal Formalism and Legal Realism: What Is the Issue?," 16 *Legal Theory* 111 (2010).

Levy, Neil, *Neuroethics: Challenges for the 21st Century* (2007).

Levy, Neil, "Introducing Neuroethics," 1 *Neuroethics* 1 (2008).

Lewis, David, "Are We Free to Break the Laws?," 47 *Theoria* 112 (1981).

Lhermitte, F., "Utilization Behaviour and Its Relation to Lesions of the Frontal Lobes," 106 *Brain* 237 (1983).

Libet, Benjamin, "Unconscious Cerebral Initiative and the Role of Conscious Will in Voluntary Action," 8 *Behav. & Brain Sci.* 529 (1985).

Libet, Benjamin, "Are the Mental Experiences of Will and Self-Control Significant for the Performance of a Voluntary Act?" 10 *Behav. & Brain Sci.* 783 (1997).

Libet, Benjamin, *Mind Time* (2004).

Luck, Steven J., *An Introduction to the Event-Related Potential Technique* (2005).

The MacArthur Foundation's "Research Network on Law and Neuroscience," available at: http://www.lawneuro.org/.

Marcus, Eric, *Rational Causation* (2012).

Margolis, Eric & Stephen Laurence, "Concepts," in *Stanford Encyclopedia of Philosophy* (2011), available at: http://plato.stanford.edu/entries/concepts/.

Markel, Dan, "What Might Retributive Justice Be? An Argument for the Confrontational Conception of Retributivism," in *Retributivism: Essays on Theory and Policy* (Mark D. White ed., 2011).

Maroney, Terry A., "The False Promise of Adolescent Brain Science in Juvenile Justice," 85 *Notre Dame L. Rev.* 89 (2009).

Maroney, Terry A., "Adolescent Brain Science after Graham v. Florida," 86 *Notre Dame L. Rev.* 765 (2011).

Maroney, Terry A., "The Persistent Cultural Script of Judicial Dispassion," 99 *Cal. L. Rev.* 629 (2011).

Matthews, Robert J., *The Measure of Mind: Propositional Attitudes and Their Attribution* (2010).

Mayberg, Helen, "Does Neuroscience Give Us New Insights into Criminal Responsibility?," in *A Judge's Guide to Neuroscience: A Concise Introduction* (Michael S. Gazzaniga & Jed S. Rakoff eds., 2010).

McCabe, David P. et al., "The Influence of fMRI Lie Detection Evidence on Juror Decision-Making," 29 *Behav. Sci. & Law* 566 (2011).

McCabe, David P. & Alan D. Castel, "Seeing Is Believing: The Effect of Brain Images on Judgments of Scientific Reasoning," 107 *Cognition* 343 (2008).

McCabe, Kevin & Laura Inglis, "Using Neuroeconomics Experiments to Study Tort Reform," *Mercatus Policy Series* (2007).

McKay, Thomas & Michael Nelson, "Propositional Attitude Reports," in *Stanford Encyclopedia of Philosophy* (2010), available at: http://plato.stanford.edu/entries/prop-attitude-reports/.

Meixner, John B., Comment, "Liar, Liar, Jury's the Trier? The Future of Neuroscience-Based Credibility Assessment in the Court," 106 *Nw. U. L. Rev.* 1451 (2012).

Meixner, John B. & J. Peter Rosenfeld, "A Mock Terrorism Application of the P300-Based Concealed Information Test," 48 *Psychophysiology* 149 (2011).

Mele, Alfred R., *Effective Intentions: The Power of Conscious Will* (2009).

Merrill, Thomas W. & Henry E. Smith, "The Morality of Property," 48 *Wm. & Mary L. Rev.* 1849 (2007).

Mertens, Ralf & John J.B. Allen, "The Role of Psychophysiology in Forensic Assessments: Deception Detection, ERPs, and Virtual Reality Mock Crime Scenarios," 45 *Psychophysiology* 286 (2008).

Mikhail, John, "Moral Cognition and Computational Theory," in *Moral Psychology, Vol. 3: The Neuroscience of Morality: Emotion, Disease, and Development* (Walter Sinnott-Armstrong ed., 2007).

Mikhail, John, "Universal Moral Grammar: Theory, Evidence, and the Future," 11 *Trends in Cognitive Sci.* 143 (2007).

Mikhail, John, "Moral Grammar and Intuitive Jurisprudence: A Formal Model of Unconscious Moral and Legal Knowledge," 50 *Psych. of Learning and Motivation* 5 (2009).

Mikhail, John, *Elements of Moral Cognition: Rawls' Linguistic Analogy and the Cognitive Science of Moral and Legal Judgments* (2011).

Mikhail, John, "Emotion, Neuroscience, and Law: A Comment on Darwin and Greene," 3 *Emotion Review* 293 (2011).

Mikhail, John, "Review of Patricia S. Churchland, *Braintrust: What Neuroscience Tells Us about Morality*," 123 *Ethics* 354 (2013).

Miller, Gregory A., "Mistreating Psychology in the Decades of the Brain," 5 *Perspectives Psych. Sci.* 716 (2010).

Milne, A.A., *Winnie-the-Pooh* (2009).

Moenssens, Andre A., "Brain Fingerprinting—Can It Be Used to Detect the Innocence of a Person Charged with a Crime?," 70 *UMKC L. Rev.* 891 (2002).

Mohamed, Feroze B. et al., "Brain Mapping of Deception and Truth Telling about an Ecologically Valid Situation: Functional MR Imaging and Polygraph Investigation—Initial Experience," 238 *Radiology* 697 (2006).

Monastersky, Richard, "Religion on the Brain," *Chron. Higher Ed.* A15 (May 26, 2006).

Monteleone, G.T. et al., "Detection of Deception Using fMRI: Better than Chance, but Well Below Perfection," 4 *Social Neuroscience* 528 (2009).

Moore, Michael, *Act and Crime: The Philosophy of Action and Its Implications for Criminal Law* (1993).

Moore, Michael, *Placing Blame: A General Theory of the Criminal Law* (1998).

Moore, Michael, "Libet's Challenge(s) to Responsible Agency," in *Conscious Will and Responsibility* (Walter Sinnott-Armstrong & Lynn Nadel eds., 2011).

Moore, Michael, "Responsible Choices, Desert-Based Legal Institutions, and the Challenges of Contemporary Neuroscience," 29 *Soc. Phil. & Policy* 233 (2012).

Moreno, Joëlle Anne, "The Future of Neuroimaged Lie Detection and the Law," 42 *Akron L. Rev.* 717 (2009).

Mnookin, Jennifer L., "The Image of Truth: Photographic Evidence and the Power of Analogy," 10 *Yale J.L. & Human.* 1 (1998).

Morse, Stephen J., "Diminished Rationality, Diminished Responsibility," 1 *Ohio St. Crim. L.* 289 (2003).

Morse, Stephen J., "New Neuroscience, Old Problems," in *Neuroscience and the Law: Brain, Mind, and the Scales of Justice* (Brent Garland ed., 2004).

Morse, Stephen J., "Criminal Responsibility and the Disappearing Person," 28 *Cardozo Law Review* 2545 (2007).

Morse, Stephen J., "The Non-Problem of Free Will in Forensic Psychiatry and Psychology," 25 *Behav. Sci. & Law* 203 (2007).

Morse, Stephen J., "Determinism and the Death of Folk Psychology: Two Challenges to Responsibility from Neuroscience," 9 *Minn. J.L Sci. & Tech.* 1 (2008).

Morse, Stephen J., "Mental Disorder and Criminal Law," 101 *J. Crim. & Criminology* 885 (2011).

Mueller, Pam, Lawrence M. Solan & John M. Darley, "When Does Knowledge Become Intent? Perceiving the Minds of Wrongdoers," 9 *J. Emp. Legal Stud.* 859 (2012).

Murphy, Erin, "DNA and the Fifth Amendment," in *The Political Heart of Criminal Procedure: Essays on Themes of William J. Stuntz* (Michael Klarman et al. eds., 2012).

Murphy, Erin, "The Politics of Privacy in the Criminal Justice System: Information Disclosure, The Fourth Amendment, and Statutory Law Enforcement Exemptions," 111 *Mich. L. Rev.* 485 (2013).

Murray, R. et al., "Cognitive and Motor Assessment in Autopsy-Proven Corticobasal Degeneration," 68 *Neurology* 1274 (2007).

Nadelhoffer, Thomas, "Neural Lie Detection, Criterial Change, and Ordinary Language," 4 *Neuroethics* 205 (2011).

Nadelhoffer, Thomas et al., "Neuroprediction, Violence, and the Law: Setting the Stage," 5 *Neuroethics* 67 (2012).

Nadler, Janice, "Blaming as a Social Process: The Influence of Character and Moral Emotion on Blame," 75 *Law & Contemp. Probs.* 1 (2012).

Nagareda, Richard A., "Compulsion 'to Be a Witness' and the Resurrection of Boyd," 74 *N.Y.U. L. Rev.* 1575 (1999).

Nahmias, Eddy et al., "Surveying Freedom: Folk Intuitions About Free Will and Moral Responsibility," 18 *Phil. Psych.* 561 (2005).

National Research Council, *The Polygraph and Lie Detection* (2003).

National Research Council, *Strengthening Forensic Science in the United States: A Path Forward* (2009).

Noë, Alva, *Out of Our Heads: Why You Are Not Your Brain, Other Lessons from the Biology of Consciousness* (2010).

Nunez, Jennifer Maria et al., "Intentional False Responding Shares Neural Substrates with Response Conflict and Cognitive Control," 267 *NeuroImage* 605 (2005).

Oakley, David A. & Peter W. Halligan, "Hypnotic Suggestion and Cognitive Neuroscience," 13 *Trends in Cog. Neuroscience* (2009).

O'Hara, Erin Ann, "How Neuroscience Might Advance the Law," in *Law & the Brain* (Semir Zeki & Oliver Goodenough eds., 2006).

Owen, Adrian M. & Martin R. Coleman, "Functional Neuroimaging of the Vegetative State," 9 *Nature Rev. Neuro.* 235 (2008).

Papineau, David, "Naturalism," in *Stanford Encyclopedia of Philosophy* (2007), available at: http://plato.stanford.edu/entries/naturalism/.

Pardo, Michael S., "Disentangling the Fourth Amendment and the Self-Incrimination Clause," 90 *Iowa L. Rev.* 1857 (2005).

Pardo, Michael S., "Neuroscience Evidence, Legal Culture, and Criminal Procedure," 33 *Am. J. Crim. L.* 301 (2006).

Pardo, Michael S., "Self-Incrimination and the Epistemology of Testimony," 30 *Cardozo L. Rev.* 1023 (2008).

Pardo, Michael S., "Testimony," 82 *Tulane L. Rev.* 119 (2007).

Pardo, Michael S., "Upsides of the American Trial's 'Anticonfluential' Nature: Notes on Richard K. Sherwin, David Foster Wallace, and James O. Incandenza," in *Imagining Legality: Where Law Meets Popular Culture* (Austin Sarat ed., 2011).

Pardo, Michael S., "Rationality," 64 *Ala. L. Rev.* 142 (2012).

Pardo, Michael S. & Dennis Patterson, "Philosophical Foundations of Law and Neuroscience," 2010 *Univ. Illinois L. Rev.* 1211 (2010).

Pardo, Michael S. & Dennis Patterson, "Minds, Brains, and Norms," 4 *Neuroethics* 179 (2011).

Pardo, Michael S. & Dennis Patterson, "More on the Conceptual and the Empirical: Misunderstandings, Clarifications, and Replies," 4 *Neuroethics* 215 (2011).

Pardo, Michael S. & Dennis Patterson, "Neuroscience, Normativity, and Retributivism," in *The Future of Punishment* (Thomas A. Nadelhoffer ed., 2013).

Patterson, Dennis, "The Poverty of Interpretive Universalism: Toward the Reconstruction of Legal Theory," 72 *Tex. L. Rev.* 1 (1993).

Patterson, Dennis, "Langdell's Legacy," 90 *Nw. U. L. Rev.* 196 (1995).

Patterson, Dennis, *Law and Truth* (1996).

Patterson, Dennis, "Fashionable Nonsense," 81 *Tex. L. Rev.* 841 (2003).

Patterson, Dennis, "Review of *Philosophical Foundations of Neuroscience*," *Notre Dame Philosophical Reviews* (2003), available at: http://ndpr.nd.edu/review.cfm?id=1335.

Patterson, Dennis, "Dworkin on the Semantics of Legal and Political Concepts," 26 *Oxford J. Legal Studies* 545 (2006).

Peter, Fabienne, "Political Legitimacy," in *Stanford Encyclopedia of Philosophy* (2010), available at: http://plato.stanford.edu/entries/legitimacy/.

Pettys, Todd E., "The Emotional Juror," 76 *Fordham L. Rev.* 1609 (2007).

Plato, *Theaetetus* (Robin H. Waterfield trans., 1987).

Poldrack, Russell A., "Can Cognitive Processes Be Inferred from Neuroimaging Data?," 10 *Trends in Cog. Sci.* 79 (2006).

Poldrack, Russell A., "The Role of fMRI in Cognitive Neuroscience: Where Do We Stand?," 18 *Curr. Opinion Neurobiology* 223 (2008).

Prinz, Jesse J. & Shaun Nichols, "Moral Emotions," in *The Moral Psychology Handbook* (John M. Doris ed., 2010).

Purdy, Jedediah, "The Promise (and Limits) of Neuroeconomics," 58 *Ala. L. Rev.* 1 (2006).

Pustilnik, Amanda C., "Violence on the Brain: A Critique of Neuroscience in Criminal Law," 44 *Wake Forest L. Rev.* 183 (2009).

Pustilnik, Amanda C., "Pain as Fact and Heuristic: How Pain Neuroimaging Illuminates Moral Dimensions of Law," 97 *Cornell L. Rev.* 801 (2012).

Pustilnik, Amanda C., "Neurotechnologies at the Intersection of Criminal Procedure and Constitutional Law," in *The Constitution and the Future of the Criminal Law* (John Parry & L. Song Richardson eds., forthcoming 2013), available at: http://ssrn.com/abstract=2143187.

Putnam, Hilary, "Aristotle's Mind and the Contemporary Mind," in *Philosophy in an Age of Science: Physics, Mathematics, and Skepticism* (Mario De Caro & David Macarthur eds., 2012).

Putnam, Hilary, "The Content and Appeal of 'Naturalism,'" in *Philosophy in an Age of Science: Physics, Mathematics, and Skepticism* (Mario De Caro & David Macarthur eds., 2012).

Putnam, Hilary & Martha Nussbaum, "Changing Aristotle's Mind," in *Essays on Aristotle's "De Anima"* (M.C. Nussbaum & A.O. Rorty eds., 1992).

Quine, W.V.O., "Epistemology Naturalized," in *Ontological Relativity and Other Essays* (1969).

Quine, W.V.O., "Two Dogmas of Empiricism," in *From a Logical Point of View* (1980).

Quine, W.V.O., *Pursuit of Truth* (2d ed. 1992).

Raichle, Marcus, "What Is an fMRI?," in *A Judge's Guide to Neuroscience: A Concise Introduction* (Michael S. Gazzaniga & Jed S. Rakoff eds., 2010).

Ramsey, William, "Eliminative Materialism," in *Stanford Encyclopedia of Philosophy* (2007), available at: http://plato.stanford.edu/entries/materialism-eliminative/.

Restack, Richard M., *The Modular Brain* (1994).

Risinger, D. Michael, "Navigating Expert Reliability: Are Criminal Standards of Certainty Being Left on the Dock?," 64 *Alb. L. Rev.* 99 (2000).

Rissman, Jesse, Henry T. Greely & Anthony D. Wagner, "Detecting Individual Memories through the Neural Decoding of Memory States and Past Experience," 107 *PNAS* 9849 (2012).

Ristroph, Alice, "Proportionality as a Principle of Limited Government," 55 *Duke L.J.* 263 (2005).

Robins, Sarah K. & Carl F. Craver, "No Nonsense Neuro-Law," 4 *Neuroethics* 195 (2011).

Robinson, Howard, "Dualism," in *Stanford Encyclopedia of Philosophy* (2011), available at: http://plato.stanford.edu/entries/dualism/.

Robinson, Paul H., "Empirical Desert," in *Criminal Law Conversations* (Paul Robinson, Stephen Garvey & Kimberly Ferzan eds., 2009).

Robinson, Paul H. & John M. Darley, "Intuitions of Justice: Implication for Criminal Law and Justice Policy," 81 *S. Cal. L. Rev.* 1 (2007).

Robinson, Paul H. & Jane A, Grall, "Element Analysis in Defining Criminal Liability: The Model Penal Code and Beyond," 35 *Stan. L. Rev.* 681 (1983).

Robinson, Paul H., Owen D. Jones & Robert Kurzban, "Realism, Punishment, and Reform," 77 *U. Chi. L. Rev.* 1611 (2010).

Rorty, Richard, "The Brain as Hardware, Culture as Software," 47 *Inquiry* 219 (2004).

Rorty, Richard, "Born to Be Good," *New York Times*, August 27, 2006.

Rosen, Jeffrey, "The Brain on the Stand," *New York Times Mag.*, March 11, 2007.

Rosenfeld, J. Peter et al., "A Modified, Event-Related Potential-Based Guilty Knowledge Test," 42 *Int'l J. Neuroscience* 157 (1988).

Roskies, Adina L., "Neuroimaging and Inferential Distance," 1 *Neuroethics* 19 (2008).

Rubinstein, Ariel, "Comment on Neuroeconomics," 24 *Econ. & Phil.* 485 (2008).

Ryle, Gilbert, *The Concept of Mind* (1949).

Sanfey, Alan G. et al., "The Neural Basis of Economic Decision-Making in the Ultimatum Game," 300 *Science* 1755 (2003).

Sanfey, Alan G. et al., "Neuroeconomics: Cross-Currents in Research on Decision-Making," 10 *Trends in Cog. Sci.* 108 (2006).

Sarkar, Shahotra, "Models of Reduction and Categories of Reductionism," 91 *Synthese* 167 (1991).

Shapira-Ettinger, Karen, "The Conundrum of Mental States: Substantive Rules and Evidence Combined," 28 *Cardozo L. Rev.* 2577 (2007).

Schauer, Frederick, "Can Bad Science Be Good Evidence? Neuroscience, Lie Detection, and Beyond," 95 *Cornell L. Rev.* 1191 (2010).

Schauer, Frederick, "Lie Detection, Neuroscience, and the Law of Evidence," available at: http://ssrn.com/abstract=2165391 (last visited 4-17-13).

Schmitz, Rémy, Hedwige Dehon & Philippe Peigneux, "Lateralized Processing of False Memories and Pseudoneglect in Aging," *Cortex* (forthcoming, published online June 29, 2012).

Schweitzer, N.J. et al., "Neuroimage Evidence and the Insanity Defense," 29 *Behav. Sci. & Law* 592 (2011).

Schweitzer, N.J. et al., "Neuroimages as Evidence in a *Mens Rea* Defense: No Impact," 17 *Psychol., Pub. Policy & Law* 357 (2011).

Schulte, Joachim, *Wittgenstein: An Introduction* (William H. Brenner & John F. Holley trans., 1992).

Searle, John, "End of the Revolution," *N.Y. Rev. Books*, Feb. 28, 2002.

Searle, John, "Putting Consciousness Back in the Brain: Reply to Bennett and Hacker, *Philosophical Foundations of Neuroscience*," in *Neuroscience and Philosophy: Brain, Mind and Language* (2007).

Segal, Jeffrey A. & Harold J. Spaeth, *The Supreme Court and the Attitudinal Model Revisited* (2002).

Seidmann, Daniel J. & Alex Stein, "The Right to Silence Helps the Innocent: A Game-Theoretic Approach to the Fifth Amendment Privilege," 114 *Harv. L. Rev.* 430 (2000).

Sharrock, Wes & Jeff Coulter, "ToM: A Critical Commentary," 14 *Theory & Psychol.* 579 (2004).

Shen, Francis X., "The Law and Neuroscience Bibliography: Navigating the Emerging Field of Neurolaw," 38 *Int. J. Legal. Information* 352 (2010).

Shen, Francis X. et al., "Sorting Guilty Minds," 86 *N.Y.U. L. Rev.* 1306 (2011).

Shen, Francis X. & Owen D. Jones, "Brain Scans as Legal Evidence: Truth, Proof, Lies, and Lessons," 62 *Mercer L. Rev.* 861 (2011).

Sherwin, Richard K., "Law's Screen Life: Criminal Predators and What to Do about Them," in *Imaging Legality: Where Law Meets Popular Culture* (Austin Sarat ed., 2011).

Simons, Daniel J. & Christopher F. Chabris, "What People Believe about How Memory Works: A Representative Survey of the U.S. Population," 6 *PLoS ONE* 5 (2011).

Simons, Kenneth W., "Rethinking Mental States," 72 *B.U. L. Rev.* 463 (1992).

Simons, Kenneth W., "Retributivism Refined—or Run Amok?," 77 *U. Chi. L. Rev.* 551 (2010).

Simons, Kenneth W., "Statistical Knowledge Deconstructed," 92 *B.U. L. Rev.* 1 (2012).

Sinnott-Armstrong, Walter et al., "Brain Scans as Legal Evidence," 5 *Episteme* 359 (2008).

Sinnott-Armstrong, Walter & Ken Levy, "Insanity Defenses," in *The Oxford Handbook of Philosophy of Criminal Law* (John Deigh & David Dolinko eds., 2011).

Sip, Kamila E. et al., "The Production and Detection of Deception in an Interactive Game," 48 *Neuropsychologia* 3619 (2010).

Slobogin, Christopher, *Proving the Unprovable: The Role of Law, Science, and Speculation in Adjudicating Culpability and Dangerousness* (2007).

Smilansky, Saul, "Hard Determinism and Punishment: A Practical *Reductio*," 30 *Law & Phil.* 353 (2011).

Snead, O. Carter, "Neuroimaging and the 'Complexity' of Capital Punishment," 82 *N.Y.U. L. Rev.* 1265 (2007).

Sorensen, Roy, "Epistemic Paradoxes," in *Stanford Encyclopedia of Philosophy* (2011), http://plato.stanford.edu/entries/epistemic-paradoxes/#MooPro.

Spence, Sean A. et al., "Behavioural and Functional Anatomical Correlates of Deception in Humans," 12 *NeuroReport* 2849 (2001).

Spence, Sean A. et al., "A Cognitive Neurobiological Account of Deception: Evidence from Functional Neuroimaging," 359 *Phil. Trans. R. Soc. Lond.* 1755 (2004).

Spence, Sean A. et al., "Speaking of Secrets and Lies: The Contribution of Ventrolateral Prefrontal Cortex to Vocal Deception," 40 *NeuroImage* 1411 (2008).

Spranger ed., *International Neurolaw: A Comparative Analysis* (2012).

Stake, Jeffrey Evans, "The Property 'Instinct,'" in *Law & the Brain* (Semir Zeki & Oliver Goodenough eds., 2006).

Stanley, Jason, *Know How* (2011).

Strawson, P.F., *Analysis and Metaphysics* (1992).

Stuntz, William J., "Self-Incrimination and Excuse," 88 *Colum. L. Rev.* 1227 (1988).

Stuntz, William J., *The Collapse of American Criminal Justice* (2011).

Sumner, Petroc & Masud Husain, "At the Edge of Consciousness: Automatic Motor Activation and Voluntary Control," 14 *Neuroscientist* 476 (2008).

Sutton, Samuel et al., "Evoked-Potential Correlates of Stimulus Uncertainty," 150 *Science* 1187 (1965).

Tallis, Raymond, "License My Roving Hands," *Times Literary Supplement* 13 (Apr. 11, 2008).

Tallis, Raymond, *Aping Mankind: Neuromania, Darwinitis, and the Misrepresentation of Humanity* (2011).

Tancredi, Laurence R., "Neuroscience Developments and the Law," in *Neuroscience & the Law: Brain, Mind, and the Scales of Justice* (Brent Garland ed., 2004).

Taylor, Charles, "Interpretation and the Sciences of Man," in *Philosophy and the Human Sciences: Philosophical Papers* 2 (1985).

Thagard, Paul, *The Brain and the Meaning of Life* (2012).

Thomson, Judith Jarvis, "The Trolley Problem," 94 *Yale L.J.* 1395 (1985).

Thomson, Judith Jarvis, "Turning the Trolley," 36 *Phil. & Pub. Affairs* 359 (2008).

Thompson, Sean Kevin, Note, "The Legality of the Use of Psychiatric Neuroimaging in Intelligence Gathering," 90 *Cornell L. Rev.* 1601 (2005).

Tversky, Amos & Daniel Kahneman, "Extensional Versus Intuitive Reasoning: The Conjunction Fallacy in Probability Judgment," in *Heuristics and Biases: The Psychology of Intuitive Judgment* (Thomas Gilovich et al. eds., 2002).

Uttal, William R., *The New Phrenology: The Limits of Localizing Cognitive Processes in the Brain* (2003).

Uviller, H. Richard, "Foreword: Fisher Goes on Quintessential Fishing Expedition and Hubbell Is Off the Hook," 91 *J. Crim. & Criminology* 311 (2001).

van Inwagen, Peter, "How to Think about the Problem of Free Will," 12 *Ethics* (2008): 327, 330.

Varzi, Achille, "Mereology," in *Stanford Encyclopedia of Philosophy* (2009) http://plato.stanford.edu/entries/mereology/

Vidmar, Neil & Valerie P. Hans, *American Juries: The Verdict* (2007).

Vohs, Kathleen D. & Jonathan W. Schooler, "The Value of Believing in Free Will: Encouraging a Belief in Determinism Increases Cheating," 19 *Psych. Sci.* 49 (2008).

Wagner, Anthony, "Can Neuroscience Identify Lies?," in *A Judge's Guide to Neuroscience: A Concise Introduction* (Michael S. Gazzaniga & Jed S. Rakoff eds., 2010).

Wegner, Daniel M., *The Illusion of Conscious Will* (2003).

Weisberg, Deena Skolnick et al., "The Seductive Allure of Neuroscience Explanations," 20 *J. Cog. Neuroscience* 470 (2008).

Westen, Peter, "Getting the Fly Out of the Bottle: The False Problem of Free Will and Determinism," 8 *Buffalo Crim. L. Rev.* 599 (2005).

White, Amy E., "The Lie of fMRI: An Examination of the Ethics of a Market in Lie Detection Using Functional Magnetic Resonance Imaging," *HEC Forum* (2012).

Williams, Meredith, *Wittgenstein, Mind and Meaning: Toward a Social Conception of Mind* (1999).

Williamson, Timothy, "Past the Linguistic Turn?," in *The Future for Philosophy* (Brian Leiter ed., 2004).

Williamson, Timothy, *The Philosophy of Philosophy* (2007).

Wilson, Mark, *Wandering Significance: An Essay on Conceptual Behavior* (2006).

Wittgenstein, Ludwig, *Philosophical Investigations* (G.E.M. Anscombe trans., 1953).

Wittgenstein, Ludwig, *The Blue and Brown Books* (1958).

Wolpe, Paul Root, Kenneth Foster & Daniel D. Langleben, "Emerging Neurotechnologies for Lie Detection: Promises and Perils," 5 *Am. J. Bioethics* 39 (2005).

Wood, David, "Punishment: Nonconsequentialism," 5 *Philosophy Compass* 470 (2010).

Woods, Andrew K., "Moral Judgments & International Crimes: The Disutility of Desert," 52 *Va. J. Int. L.* 633 (2012).

Wright, R. George, "Electoral Lies and the Broader Problems of Strict Scrutiny," 64 *Fla. L. Rev.* 759 (2012).

Yaffe, Gideon, "Libet and the Criminal Law's Voluntary Act Requirement," in *Conscious Will and Responsibility* (Walter Sinnott-Armstrong & Lynn Nadel eds., 2011).

Zak, Paul, "Neuroeconomics," in *Law & the Brain* (Semir Zeki & Oliver Goodenough eds., 2006).

Table of Cases

Other Legal Materials

Index

CPSIA information can be obtained
at www.ICGtesting.com
Printed in the USA
BVOW06s1248150317
478326BV00009B/6/P